Definitions for the Law of the Sea

Report of the International Law Association American Branch Law of the Sea Committee

Martin H. Belsky,
William Burns,
John King Gamble,
Gunther F. Handl,
Andrew J. Jacovides,
Coalter G. Lathrop,
Margaret M. Mahoney,
Dennis L. Mandsager,
John Morgan,
Allison Morris,
John E. Noyes,
Michael W. Reed,
J. Ashley Roach,
Davis Robinson,
Howard S. Schiffman,
Kelly Swanston,
John Temple Swing,
Richard M. J. Thurston,
Elaine Vullmahn,
Reid E. Whitlock,
Members

George K. Walker, Chair

Definitions for the Law of the Sea

Terms Not Defined by the 1982 Convention

General Editor
George K. Walker

MARTINUS
NIJHOFF
PUBLISHERS

LEIDEN • BOSTON
2012

This book is printed on acid-free paper.

Library of Congress Cataloging-in-Publication Data

Definitions for the law of the sea : terms not defined by the 1982 Convention / general editor, George K. Walker.
p. cm.
ISBN 978-90-04-21160-5 (hardback : alk. paper) 1. Law of the sea--Dictionaries. I. Walker, George K., 1938-
KZA1125.D44 2012
341.4'503--dc23

2011034842

ISBN 978-90-04-21160-5

Printed by Printforce, United Kingdom

CONTENTS

FOREWORD

John Norton Moore[1]

The United Nations Convention on the Law of the Sea (UNCLOS) is one of the most important multilateral conventions in history. Adopted in 1982, and effectively completed in 1994 with a revision of Part XI on Deep Seabed Mining, the Convention is today in force for 160 nations plus the European Union. In its 17 parts encompassing 320 articles with nine annexes (and Final Act with six annexes) the Convention is the authoritative contemporary basis for the law of the sea. Over a quarter century in the making, the Convention has achieved a remarkable breakthrough in oceans law ending the struggle lasting more than four centuries between coastal nations seeking expanded control over coastal resources and maritime powers seeking to protect navigational freedom so essential for global trade and commerce. The answer embodied in the Convention is a simple functional division of ocean space, with coastal nations given jurisdiction over an extended 200 nautical mile exclusive economic zone for fisheries and other economic interests while navigation remains a high seas freedom beyond the territorial sea. In so doing the Convention has implemented the community common interest on both issues and has achieved a true win/win situation. Further, the Convention strengthens navigational rights through modernization of the regime of innocent passage as embodied in the 1958 Geneva Conventions and adopts an important new regime of transit passage for international straits. In addition, the

[1] John Norton Moore is the Walter L. Brown Professor of Law at the University of Virginia and Director of the Center for Oceans Law and Policy and the Center for National Security Law. Formerly he served as a United States Ambassador for the Law of the Sea Negotiations, Deputy Special Representative of the President for the Law of the Sea Negotiations, and Chairman of the National Security Council Interagency Task Force on Law of the Sea and head of D/LOS, the Department of State/National Security Council Office coordinating law of the sea policy for the United States Government. Subsequently he served as a member of the National Advisory Committee on Oceans and Atmosphere, was awarded the 1994 Compass Award of the Marine Technology Society, and was a founding director of the Rhodes Academy of Oceans Law and Policy. He has also served as the Counselor on International Law to the Department of State and as the first Chairman of the Board of the United States Institute of Peace.

Convention embodies an impressive framework environmental regime for the oceans, modernizes the regimes for the continental margin (still termed "continental shelf") and marine scientific research. Following the 1994 revision, it sets out a workable regime for deep seabed mining in areas beyond national jurisdiction. The Convention also creates an effective dispute resolution mechanism, offering a choice between the International Court of Justice, a new Law of the Sea Tribunal and arbitration. Certainly UNCLOS is in the category of the United Nations Charter, the Vienna Convention on the Law of Treaties, and the 1949 Geneva Conventions on the Law of War, as among the most important and successful multilateral international agreements in history.

A starting point for analyzing UNCLOS is the multivolume *Commentary*[2] prepared with broad international participation under the auspices of the University of Virginia's Center for Oceans Law and Policy. Virginia also maintains one of the largest collections of oceans law materials in the world, as well as what is believed to be the only oceans law archive in the world.

Definitions for the Law of the Sea, reflecting the work of the International Law Association (American Branch) Law of the Sea Committee in providing definitions for over 200 terms not defined in UNCLOS, is an indispensable additional source for governmental officials, academics and practitioners of oceans law as a supplement to the Virginia *Commentary*. It has been prepared with the participation of many top experts in oceans law, including important oceans law scholars from around the world and submission for comment to the United Nations Division for Oceans Affairs in the United Nations Office of Legal Affairs.

Particular thanks for this outstanding book are due J. Ashley Roach who, as the then top expert in oceans law of the United States Department of State, initially suggested the project, and the Chair of the International Law Association (American Branch) Law of the Sea Committee, Professor George K. Walker, who as Committee Chair undertook the work of compiling the volume, an enormously time consuming task normally undertaken by a committee reporter. Professor Walker, as a former Stockton Professor of International Law,

---

[2] United Nations Convention on the Law of the Sea 1982: A Commentary, vols. 1–7 (Myron H. Nordquist editor-in-chief).

is widely regarded as one of the top experts in the law of the sea. This work certainly confirms that reputation. The law of the sea community owes him a debt of gratitude for this important work.

There is yet another reason why it is a special pleasure for me to recognize this important new contribution to law of the sea scholarship and the outstanding work of Professor Walker. For Professor Walker, the force behind this splendid addition to the law of the sea, was one of the outstanding Master of Laws[3] graduates of the University of Virginia School of Law. It was my pleasure to admit Professor Walker to the program and to have him as a student during my tenure as Director of the Graduate Program at Virginia. As such, I have long admired Professor Walker's scholarship and appreciated his friendship.

---

[3] The Master of Laws program at the University of Virginia School of Law, as at all American law schools, is effectively a post-doctoral program in law, as today the first degree in law, the Juris Doctor degree, is itself a doctorate. Retention of the degrees Master of Laws (LL.M.) and Doctor of Jurisprudence (J.S.D. or S.J.D.) for the post-doctoral programs in American law is an artifact of the time when the first degree in law was called a Bachelor of Laws (LL.B.).

CHAPTER I

INTRODUCTION TO THE REPORT[4]

In 2001 the International Law Association, American Branch, Law of the Sea Committee began its project of defining terms in the 1982 UN Convention on the Law of the Sea[5] or in UNCLOS analysis for which this treaty does not supply definitions. J. Ashley Roach, a longstanding Committee member, suggested the project to the Committee chair and submitted some of the first terms for analysis.

As an experiment, the Committee chair decided to undertake the project without a reporter. Committee membership has been small in number, from 10 to 22; the thought was that the chair could communicate directly with members and prepare drafts for direct consideration by them.

After preparing Tentative Drafts and a Revised Tentative Draft on one occasion, the chair submitted them to Committee members for comment. The chair particularly recognizes the strong support, detailed comments and suggestions of Committee members John E. Noyes and Howard S. Schiffman. Alex G. Oude Elferink of the Netherlands Institute for the Law of the Sea and the University of Utrecht was also most helpful in providing comments and suggestions for definitions. Dr. Ibne Hassan made detailed comments on many terms.

The chair also sent copies of Committee research drafts to others in the United States and around the world, including the Division for

[4] Part I begins the Report as published in 2009–10 ABILA Proc., where it was published as Part I. Part I is identical with its Proceedings counterpart except for the General Editor's adding the name of his current secretary, Brenda Sargent, in Part I.3, and renumbered footnotes. The rest of the book is identical with the 2009–10 ABILA Proc. version except Parts III.A and Part III.D. Part III.A was edited to remove duplicate material discussed in Part I.1 at the request of the publisher, to add updated material, and to publish the ABILA LOS Committee's unanimous resolution, *2009 Resolution Supporting U.S. Accession to the Law of the Sea Convention*, 2009–10 ABILA Proc. 541, voted after Committee approval of the Report. John Noyes submitted a revised Part III.D to combine Parts III.D and III.E of the Report and to conserve pages. Part III.E is the Report's Part III.F with no amendments other than renumbered footnotes.

[5] Abbreviated as UNCLOS in this Report. *See* Part II, *Table of Abbreviated (Short) Citations and Terms; Conventions for Citations.*

Ocean Affairs and the Law of the Sea of the UN Office of Legal Affairs for comment and expresses appreciation for comments received from these sources. Drafts also appeared in the *Proceedings* of the American Branch and in articles published in the *California Western International Law Journal* available in print and on line format.[6] Other reviews, *e.g.*, the *Journal of Maritime Law & Commerce*, noted the *California Western Journal* articles. The work of the Committee also went to the American Branch Directors of Research and Presidents of the American Branch. The Committee chair mailed *California Western Journal* offprints to colleagues in the United States and around the world, inviting comment.

The Committee sponsored panel discussions at American Branch annual fall meetings. Besides communications from Committee members, these discussions produced useful suggestions for revisions and additional terms for research and analysis.

The Committee has reviewed and commented on this draft, which was published in the 2009–10 ABILA *Proceedings*.

A. Format of the Report; Rationale for and Uses of the Report

Part II lists abbreviated citation forms and terms commonly used throughout this *Report*. Part III reprints previously-published articles, in whole or in part, on the project with updated citations.[7] Part IV recites definitions for terms the Convention does not define and terms for use with UNCLOS analysis with *Comments* for each definition; it is the heart of this *Report*. Part V offers general conclusions.

There are several reasons for and uses of the *Report*. As its title suggests, it attempts to provide meanings for words and phrases in UNCLOS for which the Convention does not give definitions, and definitions for terms used in Convention analysis. The *Report* attempts to consolidate and publish definitions for these terms after research in

[6] The Journal gave reprint publication for extracts from or republication of these copyrighted articles, whose full titles are given in Part II: Walker & Noyes, *Definitions*; Walker & Noyes, *Definitions II*; Walker, *Defining*; Walker, *Last Round*. Parts III and IV republish them, in whole or in part, sometimes in amended format, *e.g.*, for more current citations. The chair also published *Filling Some of the Gaps: The International Law Association (American Branch) Law of the Sea Definitions Project*, 32 Fordham Int'l L.J. 1336 (2009), describing the project, in an issue honoring Professor Joseph C. Sweeney, his longtime friend and colleague.

[7] *See* note 5 and accompanying text.

several sources, some of which are on line and some are in print, perhaps in less than accessible books. Some sources may be out of date although in print or on line.[8] As Part III.A emphasizes, the Committee has not sought to rewrite UNCLOS by redefining terms for which the Convention supplies meanings. Some glossaries have done so.[9] The result for a less than careful user of the latter sources is that they can lead a researcher to apply UNCLOS-defined words or phrases in a way that is incompatible with the Convention. For all definitions in this *Report*, the Committee has endeavored to publish a definition that is oriented toward UNCLOS and not a geographic or geological definition; these may be similar but not identical.

As Parts III.B and III.C emphasize, this *Report*'s product is at best a secondary source, or perhaps a source that aids in determining and giving content to primary sources like custom, treaties (including interpretive statements appended to UNCLOS) and general principles of law.[10] The definitions can be a counterweight or support to the research from other, similar secondary sources. Where there is no other source, the *Report* may be the only source; it is hoped that the wide distribution of the work of the Committee, through publication in the ABILA *Proceedings* and the *California Western International Law Journal*, offprint distribution and discussion and correspondence has broadened the Committee's resources beyond its membership.

The published discussion of the context of the project, reprinted in Parts III.C-III.E, cautions UNCLOS researchers; this *Report* is not the end of the story. For example, the UNCLOS Commission on the Limits of the Continental Shelf and the ILA Committee on the Outer Limits of the Continental Shelf have supplied and will supply context in the future for UNCLOS terms. A new ILA Committee on baselines may also supply future context.

The *Report* has served, and hopefully will continue to serve, as a platform for discussion among those who research UNCLOS and those, including governments, who as oceans users are governed or guided by UNCLOS. Part III.A emphasizes that this *Report* does not represent the views of any government or government department,

---

[8] *E.g.*, the Former Glossary, partly published in Annex A1-5 to NWP 1-14M Annotated, which is itself under revision. The fourth edition of the Consolidated Glossary is thus far available only on line. *See* Part II for full citations to these sources.

[9] *E.g.*, some terms in the Consolidated Glossary.

[10] ICJ Statute arts. 38, 59; Restatement (Third) §§ 102-03; Churchill & Lowe 5-27; Jennings & Watts §§ 8-16.

the ILA or the ABILA. Committee members who are or have been in government service spoke, corresponded or wrote did so in their private capacities. Their views are their personal opinions and are not to be considered as the views of the governments they serve or have served.

Part IV, the definitions portion of the *Report*, follows this general format:

1. Statement of a term preceded by a section number for ease of citation and perhaps followed by appositive or similar terms;
2. A *Comment* with these parts:
   a. A statement that the law of armed conflict (LOAC); law developed under the UN Charter through, *e.g.*, UN Security Council decisions under UN Charter Articles 25, 48 or 94; or jus cogens norms may result in a different definition;
   b. The source(s) for the term;
   c. Discussion of the term as it appears in UNCLOS and the 1958 LOS Conventions;
   d. Cross-references to other related terms in the *Report*;
   e. Citation to general primary and secondary authorities, including previously-published research.

Where a term has appositive words or abbreviations, those appear in separate sections, with reference to the section with discussion and analysis. A researcher seeking meaning of a word or phrase may consult the Table of Contents and proceed directly to analysis, whether that researcher has an abbreviation or appositive term or the analyzed term. There is no index for the *Report*.

Part IV also attempts to place definitions in broader contexts of international law.

First, it is axiomatic that Security Council decisions (a term of art distinguishing them from Council recommendations and the like) trump treaties through a combination of UN Charter Articles 25, 48, 94 and 103. To be sure, thus far the Council has usually spoken in general terms in its resolutions, but applying Charter-based law might come in implementing actions, *e.g.*, peacemaking or peacekeeping operations or agreements under a general Council mandate. Parts III.B and III.C should also be consulted.

Second, applying the LOAC may result in a different definition where the LOAC applies. Parts III.B-III.C and Section 132 of Part IV, analyzing "other rules of international law" and similar phrases that appear throughout UNCLOS and the 1958 LOS Conventions, discuss this issue. Section 56 of Part IV, analyzing the phrase "due regard" primarily in the UNCLOS context, notes a trend toward requiring belligerents to have regard for certain UNCLOS principles during armed conflict and should also be consulted.

Third, it is also axiomatic in today's international law that jus cogens-girded rules trump traditional sources like treaties and custom; there is, of course, the problem of finding jus cogens for a situation. Part III.B offers analysis on this point.

The result is that researchers seeking a definition for an UNCLOS term or a term used in UNCLOS analysis must consider the factors of Charter-based law, the LOAC for situations involving armed conflict, and jus cogens in their research.

The *Report*'s citations under the definitions are not a research mine of every journal on the subject. Researchers should continue beyond these general, frequently-cited sources, *e.g.*, the *Restatement (Third)*, into secondary and newer primary sources, *e.g.*, LOS treaties subordinate to UNCLOS. Part III.B discusses the UNCLOS primacy principles for these treaties.

Cross-references to other definitions at the end of every Comment should help with terms related to defined terms and words within each definition for a more complete understanding of what a word or phrase means. Common abbreviations, *e.g.* "NOTMAR" for "notice to mariners," are also included for cross-reference.

B. Projections for the Future

This aspect of the Committee's work is at an end, at least for now. Will there be a second edition or supplement to the *Report*? The International Hydrographic Organization *Consolidated Glossary* appeared in its fourth edition in early 2006. This suggests that meanings, like Justice Oliver Wendell Holmes's definition of a word as the skin of a living thought,[11] have evolved and will evolve through time. State practice under UNCLOS, new international agreements, judicial and other tribunal decisions, researchers' conclusions, and intergovernmental and nongovernmental organizations' work, all assure that the process of definition, like the process of decision for use of UNCLOS terms, will

[11] Tower v. Eisner, 245 U.S. 418, 425 (1918).

not be static. More terms in UNCLOS, or used in UNCLOS analysis and suggesting the need for a definition, may be uncovered. What role the Committee, the ABILA or the ILA will play is for the future to determine.

C. Notes of Thanks

The Committee expresses thanks to those who are no longer current Committee members for the contributions they made to this project: Sherri Burr, Hungdah Chiu, Joseph Dellapenna, Bahman Aghai Diba, Valerie Epps, Malvina Halberstam, Todd M. Jack, James Kraska, Charlotte Ku, Cynthia C. Lichtenstein, Joel E. Marsh, Samuel Pyeatt Menefee, Peter Oppenheimer, Walter E. Stewart, Jon A. Van Dyke, Jorge A. Vargas, Ruth Wedgwood, Edwin Williamson, and Norman Gregory Young. The Committee is also grateful for the strong support of three ABILA presidents, James A.R. Nafziger, Charles Siegal and John Noyes; the ABILA research directors; and annual meeting program planners who allocated time for panel discussions related to this project.

The Committee membership received support from institutions with which they have been affiliated, *e.g.*, for travel to annual meetings during times when budgets have been tight, for which thanks to those institutions are in order.

Thanks also go to the editors and staff of the *California Western International Law Journal* who worked with the chair to publish four articles on the work of the Committee, and to Professors Noyes and Jefferey Cyril Atik, ABILA *Proceedings* editors, who also worked with the chair to publish the LOS Committee *Reports* that parallel the *Journal* articles.

The chair takes this opportunity to express appreciation for support given this project by the Wake Forest University School of Law. In particular, he is grateful for help given by the late Thomas M. Steele and Marian Parker, law library Directors; Howard D. Sinclair, former Research Librarian; Shannon D. Gilreath, former Research Librarian and now Assistant Director of the Master of Laws LL.M. in American Law Program and Associated Professor in the Wake Forest University Divinity School; Michael V. Greene, library technical services; Ellen Makaravage, library reference. He also expresses thanks for the secretarial assistance of Peggy W. Brookshire, now retired; Mickie

Burrow, now retired; and Brenda Sargent; who ably assisted with preparing correspondence, draft material, earlier ABILA Committee *Reports*, law journal articles and this and previous versions of this *Report*.

Without all of this support and help, the work of the Committee and its chair would have foundered long ago. The scope and quality of this project, which began with less than 10 definitions to consider a decade ago and today publishes over 200 definitions, including cross-references and abbreviations for terms UNCLOS does not define or which are useful in UNCLOS analysis, bespeaks the excellent work of many.

Respectfully submitted,

International Law Association, American Branch
Law of the Sea Committee

Members:

Martin H. Belsky,
William Burns,
John King Gamble,
Gunther F. Handl,
Andrew J. Jacovides,
Coalter G. Lathrop,
Margaret M. Mahoney,
Dennis L. Mandsager,
John Morgan,
Allison Morris,
John E. Noyes,
Michael W. Reed,
J. Ashley Roach,
Davis Robinson,
Howard S. Schiffman,
Kelly Swanston,
John Temple Swing,
Richard M. J. Thurston,
Elaine Vullmahn,
Reid E. Whitlock;
George K. Walker, Chair.

CHAPTER II

TABLE OF ABBREVIATED (SHORT) CITATIONS AND TERMS; CONVENTIONS FOR CITATIONS

This *Report* cites certain treaties and other international agreements, commentaries and law review articles, and some terms or phrases, repeatedly. Part II lists abbreviated, or short, citations for these sources, terms or phrases. The *Report* also deviates from citation style in a few cases. In some instances a longer version, perhaps the full, formal title, may be used to make the context clearer.

Rather than employing "supra," "infra" or "hereinafter" as some journals and books do, the *Report* notes these frequently-cited sources in abbreviated format. If a note in the *Report* cites a source or material from a previous note, the initial noted source may be abbreviated in parentheses, *e.g.*, by an author's name, "(Brown)," after the initial full citation, without, *e.g.*, "hereinafter." A later citation would refer, *e.g.*, to "Brown, note 3, 457," without the "supra" or "at" before the page or section number that a style manual might mandate. Reference to earlier material might be cited, *e.g.*, as "*See* note 2 and accompanying text," as was done in Part I, if noted material is in the same Part. *Comments* for definitions avoid footnote citations if, *e.g.*, a treaty Article is cited in the *Comment* text. There is no need for citation redundancy in a footnote.

Unless there is a specific reason for it, short citations do not refer to published sources; *e.g.*, a High Seas Convention reference does not cite its publication in United States Treaties and Other International Agreements (UST) or the United Nations Treaty Series (UNTS), or page citations to particular provisions.

In all cases the *Report* refers to English language versions of treaties or other international agreements and judicial and similar decisions unless otherwise noted.[12]

---

[12] Because Part II is part of the Report the ABILA LOS Committee approved September 1, 2009, Part II's citations have not been updated to reflect current editions, *e.g.*, the 2010 and later TIF editions. The General Editor has reviewed these citations in their current version, and there is little, if any, change except page numbers. As they would with any book, researchers should consult the current version. The only addition, cited occasionally in this version, is Proceedings of the American Branch of the International Law Association 2009–2010 (Jefferey Atik ed. 2010), abbreviated as 2009–10 ABILA Proc. in this book.

Short Citation/ Term	Full Citation
ABILA	International Law Association (American Branch), as distinguished from the ILA, the central organization
2001–02 ABILA Proc.	Proceedings of the American Branch of the International Law Association 2001–2002 (John E. Noyes ed. 2002)
2003–04 ABILA Proc.	Proceedings of the American Branch of the International Law Association 2003–2004 (John E. Noyes ed. 2004)
2005–06 ABILA Proc.	Proceedings of the American Branch of the International Law Association 2005–2006 (Jefferey Atik ed. 2006)
2007–08 ABILA Proc.	Proceedings of the American Branch of the International Law Association 2007–2008 (Jefferey Atik ed. 2008)
1994 Agreement	Agreement Relating to the Implementation of Part XI of the United Nations Convention on the Law of the Sea of 10 December 1982, July 28, 1994, 1836 UNTS 3, 42
Annex 1	Annex 1: Glossary of Technical Terms, in Peter J. Cook & Chris M. Carleton eds., Continental Shelf Limits: The Scientific and Legal Interface 321–30 (2000). Besides the Consolidated Glossary, Annex 1 sources are American Geological Institute, Dictionary of Geological Terms (Robert L. Bates & Julia A. Jackson, eds., 3d ed. 1984); id., Glossary of Geology (Julia A. Jackson, ed., 4th ed. 1997); Association for Geographic Information & Edinburgh University, Online Dictionary (1996, rev. 2003), available at www.agi.org.uk/public/gis.resources/index.htm (visited Feb. 10, 2003; server failure noted June 1, 2008). Since Annex 1 represents consolidated thinking on definitions, this Report does not cite the latter publications separately. The Committee thanks Professor Noyes for suggesting Annex 1.

Aust	Anthony Aust, Modern Treaty Law and Practice (2d ed. 2007)
Brownlie	Ian Brownlie, Principles of Public International Law (7th ed. 2008)
Churchill & Hedley	Robin R. Churchill with Christopher Hedley, The Meaning of the "Genuine Link" Requirement in Relation to the Nationality of Ships (Oct. 2000), republished, http://oceanlaw.net/projects/consultancy/pdf/ITF-Oct2000.pdf (visited Aug. 6, 2009) (copy in ABILA Committee chair's file)
Churchill & Lowe	R.R. Churchill & A.V. Lowe, The Law of the Sea (3d ed. 1999)
COCS Second Report	International Law Association Committee on Legal Issues of the Outer Continental Shelf, Legal Issues of the Outer Continental Shelf: Second Report, Report of the Seventy-Second Conference: Held in Toronto: 4–8 June 2006, pp. 215–49 (2006)
1 Commentary	1 United Nations Convention on the Law of the Sea 1982: A Commentary (Myron H. Nordquist ed.-in-chief 1985)
2 Commentary	2 Satya N. Nandan & Shabtai Rosenne, United Nations Convention on the Law of the Sea 1982: A Commentary (Myron H. Nordquist ed.-in-chief, Neal R. Grandy ass't ed. 1993)
3 Commentary	3 United Nations Convention on the Law of the Sea 1982: A Commentary (Satya N. Nandan & Shabtai Rosenne eds., Myron H. Nordquist ed.-in-chief, 1995)
4 Commentary	4 Shabtai Rosenne & Alexander Yankov, United Nations Convention on the Law of the Sea 1983: A Commentary (Myron H. Nordquist ed.-in-chief, Neal R. Grandy ass't. ed. 1991)
5 Commentary	5 United Nations Convention on the Law of the Sea 1982: A Commentary (Shabtai Rosenne & Louis B. Sohn eds., Myron H. Nordquist ed.-in-chief, 1989)

Consolidated Glossary	International Hydrographic Organization International Hydrographic Bureau, Manual on Technical Aspects of the United Nations Convention on the Law of the Sea - 1982, Appendix 1: Glossary (Special Pub. No. 51, 4th ed. Mar. 2006), available at http://ohi.schom.fr/publicat/free/files/S-51_Ed4-EN.pdf (visited Aug. 6, 2009), superseding Former Glossary
Crawford	James Crawford, The International Law Commission's Articles on State Responsibility: Introduction, Text and Commentaries (2002)
DOD Dictionary	United States Department of Defense, DOD Dictionary of Military and Associated Terms: Joint Publication 1-02 (Apr. 12, 2001, amended through Mar. 17, 2009), available at http://www.dtic.mil/doctrine/jel/new_pubs/jpl_02.pdf (visited Aug. 6, 2009)
ECDIS Glossary	1 International Hydrographic Organization, Hydrographic Dictionary: Glossary of ECDIS-Related Terms; Special Publication No. 32, Appendix 1 (Sept. 2007), available at http://ohi.schom.fr/publicat/free/files/S-32_App1_English.pdf (visited Aug. 6, 2009); page numbers in this Report are to those on line
EEZ	Exclusive economic zone; sometimes the acronym is spelled out
Fishing Convention	Convention on Fishing and Conservation of the Living Resources of the High Seas, Apr. 29, 1958, 17 UST 138, 559 UNTS 285
Former ECDIS Glossary	International Hydrographic Organization International Hydrographic Bureau, Glossary of ECDIS-Related Terms, Appendix 3, Special Publication No. 52 (3d ed. Dec. 1997), formerly available at http://ohi.schom.fr/publicat/free/files/S-52 (visited July 3, 2006); page numbers in this Report are to those formerly on line. There is no known publication in hard copy or on line to Former ECDIS Glossary

Former Glossary	International Hydrographic Organization Technical Aspects of the Law of the Sea Working Group, Consolidated Glossary of Technical Terms Used in the United Nations Convention on the Law of the Sea, in International Hydrographic Bureau Special Publication No. 51 (1989) and United Nations Office for Ocean Affairs and the Law of the Sea, Baselines 46–62 (1989) (hereinafter Consolidated Glossary), and reprinted in part as Annex A1-5 in NWP 1-14M Annotated; superseded by Consolidated Glossary
Goodrich	Leland F. Goodrich et al., Charter of the United Nations (3d & rev. ed. 1969)
High Seas Convention	Convention on the High Seas, Apr. 29, 1958, 13 UST 2312, 450 UNTS 82
ICJ	International Court of Justice, sometimes referred to as the World Court
ICJ Statute	Statute of the International Court of Justice, June 26, 1945, 59 Stat. 1055, annexed to the UN Charter
ILA	International Law Association, as distinguished from the ABILA, one of the national or regional organizations under the ILA
ILC	International Law Commission
ILC Responsibility Articles	International Law Commission, Responsibility of States for Internationally Wrongful Acts, in Report of the International Law Commission to the General Assembly: Report on the Work of Its Fifty-Third Session (23 April - 1 June and 2 July - 10 August 2001), UN GAOR, 56th Sess., Supp. No. 10, UN Doc. A/56/10 & Corr. 1, p. 59 and ff. (Oct. 24, 2001), reprinted in Crawford, p. 77 and ff.
ILM	International Legal Materials

IMO	International Maritime Organization, formerly Intergovernmental Maritime Consultative Organization (IMCO), constituted by Convention on the Intergovernmental Maritime Consultative organization, Mar. 6, 1948, 9 UST 621, 289 UNTS 48, amended, Sept. 15, 1964, 18 UST 1299, 607 UNTS 276; Sept. 28, 1965, 19 UST 4855, 649 UNTS 334; Oct. 17, 1974, 28 UST 4607, 1080 UNTS 375; Nov. 14, 1975, 34 UST 497, 1276 UNTS 478, 1285 UNTS 318; Nov. 17, 1977, TIAS 11094, 1380 UNTS 268; Nov. 15, 1979, TIAS 11094, 1380 UNTS 288; Nov. 7, 1991, — UNTS — ; Nov. 4, 1993, — UNTS —
Jennings & Watts	Robert Jennings & Arthur Watts, Oppenheim's International Law (9th ed. 1996)
LNTS	League of Nations Treaty Series
LOAC	Law of armed conflict; sometimes the acronym is spelled out
LOS	Law of the sea; sometimes the acronym is spelled out
LOS Committee	ABILA Law of the Sea Committee; sometimes referred to as the Committee or the ABILA LOS Committee
LOS Convention	Alternative short citation form for UNCLOS
LOS Conventions	The plural form of LOS Convention; refers to UNCLOS and the 1958 LOS Conventions collectively
1958 LOS Conventions	Collective reference to Fishing Convention, High Seas Convention, Shelf Convention and Territorial Sea Convention
McNair	Lord McNair, The Law of Treaties (1961)
MSR	Marine scientific research; sometimes the acronym is spelled out; see also Part IV.B, § 100
Multilateral Treaties	United Nations, Office of Legal Affairs, Multilateral Treaties Deposited with the Secretary-General: Status As at 1 April 2009, U.N. Doc. ST/LEG/SER.E/26 (3 v. 2009), available at http://treaties.un.org./Pages/Publications.aspx?pathpub=Publication/MTSDG/page1_en.xml (visited Aug. 7, 2009),

	http://treaties.un.org/Pages/DB.aspx?path=DB/MTDSG/page1_en.xmlPrint versions, e.g., United Nations, Office of Legal Affairs, Multilateral Treaties Deposited with the Secretary-General: Status As at 31 December 2006, UN Doc. ST/LEG/SER.E/25 (2 v. 2007) are no longer current
Noyes, Definitions	John E. Noyes, Definitions for the 1982 Law of the Sea Convention and the Importance of Context: "Ships" and Other Matters, 33 Cal. W. Int'l L.J. 310 (2003), pub. as part of Walker & Noyes, Definitions II
Noyes, Treaty	John E. Noyes, Treaty Interpretation and Definitions in the Law of the Sea Convention: Comments on Defining Terms in the 1982 Law of the Sea Convention, 32 Cal. W. Int'l L.J. 367 (2002), 2001–02 ABILA Proc. 175, pub. as part of Walker & Noyes, Definitions
NWP 1-14M Annotated	A.R. Thomas & James C. Duncan, eds., Annotated Supplement to The Commander's Handbook on the Law of Naval Operations (Nav. War C. Int'l L. Stud., v. 73, 1999), currently under revision for a new edition
O'Connell	D.P. O'Connell, International Law of the Sea (2 v., I.A. Shearer ed. 1982, 1984)
R.C.A.D.I.	Recueil des cours Academie de droit international
Roach & Smith	J. Ashley Roach & Robert W. Smith, United States Responses to Excessive Maritime Claims (2d ed. 1996)
Restatement (Third)	Restatement (Third) of Foreign Relations Law of the United States (1987)
San Remo Manual	International Lawyers & Naval Experts Convened by the International Institute of Humanitarian Law, San Remo Manual on International Law Applicable to Armed Conflicts at Sea (Louise Doswald-Beck ed. 1995)
Schindler & Toman	Dietrich Schindler & Jiri Toman, The Laws of Armed Conflicts (rev. ed. 2004)
Shelf Convention	Convention on the Continental Shelf, Apr. 29, 1958, 15 UST 471, 499 UNTS 311

Ship Registration Convention	UN Convention on Conditions for Registration of Ships, Feb. 7, 1986, 26 ILM 1229 (1987)
Simma	Bruno Simma, ed., The Charter of the United Nations: A Commentary (2 v., 2d ed. 2002)
Sinclair	Ian Sinclair, The Vienna Convention on the Law of Treaties (2d ed. 1984)
Territorial Sea Convention	Convention on the Territorial Sea and Contiguous Zone, Apr. 29, 1958, 15 UST 1606, 516 UNTS 205
TIAS	Treaties and International Agreements Series, followed by a number
TIF	United States Department of State, Treaties in Force: A List of Treaties and Other International Agreements of the United States in Force on January1, 2009 (2009), available at http://state.gov/documents/organization/89668.pdfhttp://www.state.gov/s/l/treaty/treaties/2009/index.htm (visited Aug. 7, 2009); http://state.gov/documents/organization/89668. The 2009 print version has limited availability; the electronic version may be updated periodically; id. § 1 lists bilateral agreements; id. § 2 lists multilateral agreements
UN	United Nations
UN Charter	Charter of the United Nations, June 26, 1945, 59 Stat. 1031, amended Dec. 17, 1963, 16 UST 1134, 557 UNTS 143; Dec. 20, 1965, 19 UST 5450, 638 UNTS 308; Dec. 20, 1971, 24 UST 2225, 892 UNTS 119
UNCLOS	United Nations Convention on the Law of the Sea, Dec.10, 1982, 1833 UNTS 3, 397
UNTS	United Nations Treaty Series
UST	United States Treaties and Other International Agreements
Vienna Convention	Vienna Convention on the Law of Treaties, May 23, 1969, 1155 UNTS 331
Walker, Consolidated Glossary	George K. Walker, Definitions for the 1982 Law of the Sea Convention — Part II; Analysis of the IHO Consolidated Glossary, 33 Cal. W. Int'l L.J. 219 (2003), pub. as part of Walker & Noyes, Definitions II

Walker, Defining	George K. Walker, Defining Terms in the 1982 Law of the Sea Convention (Sept. 4, 2001 Initial Draft, Rev. 1, Jan. 22, 2002), 32 Cal. W. Int'l L.J. 347 (2002), 2001–02 ABILA Proc. 195, pub. as part of Walker & Noyes, Definitions
Walker, Definitions	George K. Walker, Definitions for the 1982 Law of the Sea Convention (Revised Tentative Draft No. 1, Feb. 10, 2003), 33 Cal. W. Int'l L.J. 196 (2003), 2003–04 ABILA Proc. 196, pub. as part of Walker & Noyes, Definitions II
Walker, ECDIS Glossary	George K. Walker, Defining Terms in the 1982 Law of the Sea Convention III: The International Hydrographic Organization ECDIS Glossary, 34 Cal. W. Int'l L.J. 211 (2004), also pub. as Report of the Law of the Sea Committee: Defining Terms in the 1982 Law of the Sea Convention III: Analysis of Selected IHO ECDIS Glossary and Other Terms (Dec. 12, 2003 Initial Draft, Revision I), 2003–04 ABILA Proc. 187
Walker, Introduction	George K. Walker, General Introduction, 33 Cal. W. Int'l L.J. 191 (2003), pub. as part of Walker & Noyes, Definitions II
Walker, Last Round	George K. Walker, Defining Terms in the 1982 Law of the Sea Convention IV: The Last Round of Definitions Proposed by the International Law Association (American Branch) Law of the Sea Committee, 36 Cal. W. Int'l L.J. 133 (2005), 2005–06 ABILA Proc. 23
Walker, The Tanker	George K. Walker, The Tanker War, 1980–88: Law and Policy (U.S. Nav. War C. Int'l L. Stud. v. 74, 2000)
Walker, Words	George K. Walker, "Words, Words, Words": Definitions for the 1982 Law of the Sea Convention, 32 Cal. W. Int'l L.J. 345 (2002), pub. as part of Walker & Noyes, Definitions
Walker & Noyes, Definitions	George K. Walker& John E. Noyes, Definitions for the 1982 Law of the Sea Convention, 32 Cal. W. Int'l L.J. 343 (2002), 2001–02 ABILA Proc. 154

Walker & Noyes, Definitions II	George K. Walker & John E. Noyes, Definitions for the 1982 Law of the Sea Convention — Part II, 33 Cal. W. Int'l L.J. 191 (2003)
Wiktor	Christian L. Wiktor, Multilateral Treaty Calendar 1648–1995 (1998)

CHAPTER III

COMMENTARIES ON FORMULATING DEFINITIONS FOR THE 1982 LAW OF THE SEA CONVENTION

Part III has five subparts: III.A, Plan and Progression of the Project; III.B, Sources of Law, the 1982 Law of the Sea Convention, and the ABILA LOS Committee Definitions Project; III.C, The Role and Relationship of Understandings, Declarations and Statements, Also Collectively Known as Interpretative or Interpretive Statements, Appended to the 1982 Law of the Sea Convention and the ABILA LOS Committee Definitions Project; III.D, Treaty Interpretation and Definitions in the 1982 Law of the Sea Convention; III.E, "Words, Words, Words": Dilemmas in Definitions.

Parts III.A-III.E, commentaries by two participants in the ABILA LOS Committee project, attempt to place the Committee's work in the larger context of public international law affecting the oceans. Part IV, which publishes over 200 definitions of terms, abbreviations for terms and cross-references to them, refers to this research. To attain a better understanding of the definitions, it is necessary to refer to this material, perhaps initially before using Part IV and maybe after researching the definition of a particular term.

A. PLAN AND PROGRESSION OF THE PROJECT

George K. Walker[13]

As Part I.A notes, this project has consumed the better part of a decade to proceed to a *Final Report.*[14] What follows are a few caveats and a comment on events since the Committee approved the September 1, 2009 *Final Report.*

The general format of the definitions differs from early drafts as published in early draft *Reports* and law journals republishing them. What were proposed definitions are now Committee-approved definitions. A *Comment,* noting a possibility of other meanings under UN Charter law or the LOAC, and updated material from the drafts' Discussions and Analyses, follows each definition, with cross-references to other, related definitions. Drafts and this *Final Report* have followed an English alphabetical order, *e.g.*, "mile" ahead of "ocean space."

This method of analysis was similar to that which the ILA employed in drafting the *Helsinki Principles of Maritime Neutrality,*[15] the American Law Institute in developing its *Restatements* and similar publications, and the International Institute of Humanitarian Law in preparing the *San Remo Manual.*[16]

The project has not revisited or tried to redefine terms UNCLOS defines. These include:

"archipelagic sea lane;"[17]
"archipelagic state;"[18]

---

[13] Part III.A has been extracted, with amendments and updated material, *e.g.*, the new fourth edition of the Consolidated Glossary, from Walker, *Consolidated Glossary* 217–25. It has also been edited to delete material in Part I and to comment on events related to the Report since its Sept. 1, 2009 limited publication in 2009–10 ABILA Proc.162.

[14] For a more detailed history, *see also* ABILA LOS Committee, *Final Report on Definitions of Terms in the 1982 LOS Convention*, 2009–10 ABILA Proc. 162, 190–92.

[15] ILA Committee on Maritime Neutrality, *Final Report: Helsinki Principles on Maritime Neutrality*, in ILA, Report of the Sixty-Eighth Conference Held at Taipei, Taiwan, Republic of China 24–30 May 1998, at 496 (1998) (*Helsinki Principles*).

[16] Cited in this Report as the San Remo Manual. *See* Part II.

[17] UNCLOS art. 53.

[18] *Id.* art. 46.

"Area;"[19]
"continental margin;"[20]
"continental shelf;"[21]
"enclosed sea;"[22]
"exclusive economic zone" (EEZ);[23]
"internal waters;"[24]
"island;"[25]
"low-tide elevation;"[26]
"semi-enclosed sea;"[27]
"territorial sea."[28]

This *Final Report* cites and discusses these definitions in *Comments* to definitions for UNCLOS terms not otherwise defined in the Convention, or for terms useful in UNCLOS analysis, however. In a few cases where there are parallel UNCLOS and geographical definitions, *e.g.*, for straits,[29] the *Report* includes entries for these but attempts to explain the difference. Similarly, although it cites and discusses definitions in the 1958 LOS Conventions, which UNCLOS supersedes for States that have ratified or acceded to UNCLOS,[30] *e.g.*, for the continental shelf,[31] the *Report* does not attempt to redefine those terms.

The *Report* does not debate what are the customary norms requiring no definition of terms[32] or the wisdom of ratifying UNCLOS.[33]

---

19 *Id.* art. 1(1)(1); *but see* Part IV.B § 9, "area and Area," analyzing the difference between "Area" capitalized, which has a specific meaning in UNCLOS art. 1(1)(1), and "area" in lower case, a word often used in *id.* but which the treaty does not define.

20 UNCLOS art. 76(3); *see also* Victor Prescott, *Resources of the Continental Margin and International Law*, in Peter J. Cook & Chris M. Carleton eds., Continental Shelf Limits: The Scientific and Legal Interface ch. 5 (2000); Philip A. Symonds et al., *Characteristics of Continental Margins*, in *id.* ch. 4.

21 UNCLOS art. 76(1); *see also* Robert W. Smith & George Taft, *Legal Aspects of the Continental Shelf*, in Cook & Carleton, note 20, ch. 3.

22 UNCLOS art. 122.

23 *Id.* art. 55; *compare* DOD Dictionary 193.

24 UNCLOS art. 8(1).

25 *Id.* art. 121(1). This Report defines "rock," Part IV.B § 147, demonstrating why rocks are not islands under UNCLOS and discussing other meanings of the word.

26 UNCLOS art. 13(1).

27 *Id.* art. 122.

28 *Id.* arts. 2–16; *compare* DOD Dictionary 552.

29 *See* Part IV.B, § 177.

30 UNCLOS art. 311(1); *see also* Part III.B.

31 *Compare* UNCLOS art. 76 *with* Shelf Convention art. 1.

32 *E.g.*, the now largely resolved debate on the customary maximum width of the territorial sea. *See generally* Walker, The Tanker 260–68.

33 *See id.* 305–06; Walker, *Last Round* 135–39, 2005–06 ABILA Proc. 29–32; Part III.C.

As in all ILA and ABILA projects, the *Final Report* does not necessarily represent any State's or international organization's practice, position, view or policy, unless that State or international organization chooses to adopt it in whole or part.[34] Government officials of the United States and other States or international organizations who participated in this project spoke or wrote in their personal capacities. These officials' views, opinions or positions do not necessarily represent the practice, positions, views or policies of their governments or any agency of their governments or of their international organizations or any agency of their international organizations. The same is true for participants who were officials or members of nongovernmental organizations or private organizations.

Nor does the *Final Report* represent the official position of the ILA or the ABILA. ABILA committees, *e.g.*, the LOS Committee, may advocate views; thus the *Final Report*, although its research and drafting process remained nonpartisan, is, technically speaking, an advocate's brief for the definitions proposed.

The *2009 Resolution Supporting U.S. Accession to the 1982 Law of the Sea Convention* is an example of advocacy by an ABILA committee:

> RESOLVED, that the International Law Association (American Branch) Law of the Sea Committee, its Members speaking in private capacity and not for any government, governmental organization, nongovernmental organization or private organization with which they may be affiliated, no Members dissenting, supports United States Senate advice and consent, and United States accession, to the 1982 United Nations Convention on the Law of the Sea, along with [the] 1994 Agreement Relating to the Implementation of Part XI of the United Nations Convention on the Law of the Sea of 10 December 1982, which is to be interpreted and applied together with the 1982 Convention as a single instrument, with such advice and consent, accession and ratification accompanied by appropriate understandings and declarations.[35]

The Committee approved this resolution by mail vote after approving the *Final Report*. The Resolution is not part of the *Report* as approved by the Committee but is included here as part of the history of the work of the Committee after completing the *Report* and for analysis and citation by researchers.

---

[34] *See also* Parts III.B and III.C for this Report's possible influence on the future law of the sea.

[35] ABILA LOS Committee, *2009 Resolution Supporting U.S. Accession to the 1982 Law of the Sea Convention*, 2009–10 ABILA Proc. 541, 542.

B. SOURCES OF LAW, THE 1982 LAW OF THE SEA CONVENTION, AND THE ABILA LOS COMMITTEE DEFINITIONS PROJECT

George K. Walker[36]

Part III.B comments on the role and relationship of general sources of international law on UNCLOS and the 1994 Agreement when they are considered with sources like the ABILA LOS Committee definitions project. There are important considerations on the place of commentator definitions.

Definitions that commentators research and publish as their work are a secondary source of law. They can provide content to primary sources, *e.g.*, treaty or customary rules or general principles of law or other secondary sources like court or arbitral decisions.[37] They may be considered by analogy to subsequent practice under a treaty.[38] If LOS Committee definitions vary from other secondary sources, decision makers should weigh the ABILA LOS Committee definitions with

[36] Part III.B was extracted and enlarged from Walker, *Last Round* 143–51, 2005–06 ABILA Proc. 32–40.

[37] ICJ Statute arts. 38, 59; Restatement (Third) §§ 102–03; *see also* Brownlie, ch. 1; Churchill & Lowe 5–13; Jennings & Watts §§ 8–17.

[38] Vienna Convention art. 31(3)(b) declares subsequent practice is an interpretation principle along with other factors. *See also* Aust 238–41; Brownlie 633–34; Jennings & Watts, § 632, pp. 1274–75; McNair 424 (parties' relevant conduct after conclusion of treaty has "high probative value" of parties' intention when treaty concluded); Gerald Fitzmaurice, *The Law and Procedure of the International Court of Justice 1951–4: Treaty Interpretation and Other Treaty Points*, 33 Brit. Y.B. Int'l L. 203, 223–25 (1957); *id.*, *The Law and Procedure of the International Court of Justice: Treaty Interpretation and Certain Other Treaty Points*, 28 Brit. Y.B. Int'l L. 1, 20–21 (1951) (subsequent practice "superior" source to determine meaning); Jimenez de Arechaga, *International Law in the Last Third of a Century*, 159 R.C.A.D.I. 9, 42–43 (1978). International Law Commission, Report on the Work of Its Eighteenth Session, U.N. Doc. A/6309/Rev. 1 (1966), *reprinted in* 2 (1966) Y.B. Int'l L. Comm'n, U.N. Doc. A/CN.4/Ser.A/1966/Add. 1, p. 236 (1966) (1966 ILC Rep.) notes that Vienna Convention Conference negotiators rejected a proposed provision: "A treaty may be modified by subsequent practice in the application of the treaty establishing the agreement of the parties to modify its provisions." *See also* Restatement (Third) § 325(2) & cmt. c (rule that subsequent practice can modify treaty conforms to U.S. practice); Sinclair 135–38 (subsequent practice can modify treaty terms); Richard D. Kearney & Robert E. Dalton, *The Treaty on Treaties*, 64 AJIL 495, 523–25 (1970).

other commentary to derive rules of law.[39] If a primary source, *e.g.*, a treaty definition in custom or practice under a treaty, or in the treaty itself, recites a different definition, the latter source(s) should have priority.[40] This is a reason why the LOS Committee did not attempt to define terms for which UNCLOS supplies a definition.[41]

UNCLOS, as a "constitution for the oceans,"[42] establishes priorities for other international agreements related to the law of the sea. First, to clarify any ambiguity that might arise under law of treaties analysis,[43]

---

[39] Sosa v. Alvarez-Machain, 542 U.S. 692, 734 (2004) (Souter, J., joined by Stevens, O'Conner, Kennedy, Ginsburg, Breyer, JJ.), cites The Pacquete Habana, 175 U.S. 677, 700 (1900) for cautionary use of scholars' opinions, as evidence of the law where there is no treaty or custom:

> [W]here there is no treaty, and no controlling executive or legislative act or judicial decision, resort must be had to the customs and usages of civilized nations; and as evidence of these, to the works of jurists and commentators, who by years of labor, research and experience, have made themselves peculiarly well acquainted with the subjects of which they treat. Such works are resorted to by judicial tribunals, not for the speculations of what their authors concerning what the law ought to be, but for trustworthy evidence of what the law really is.

This is the U.S. view of the matter. The Restatement (Third) does not mention this aspect of the *Habana* case.

[40] ICJ Statute art. 38(1); Restatement (Third) §§ 102–03.

[41] *See* Part III.A.

[42] Tommy T.B. Koh, *Statement: A Constitution for the Oceans*, 1 Commentary 11.

[43] Vienna Convention art. 59(1)(a) declares that a treaty shall be considered terminated if all parties to it conclude a later treaty relating to the same subject-matter and it appears from the later treaty or is otherwise established that the parties intended that the matter should be governed by that treaty. Not all 1958 LOS Convention parties are UNCLOS parties; notably, the United States remains party to the 1958 treaties. TIF 364, 395–96. Vienna Convention art. 59(1)(b) provides that a treaty shall be considered terminated if all parties to it conclude a later treaty relating to the same subject-matter, and the later treaty's terms are so far incompatible with those of the earlier one that the two treaties are not capable of being applied at the same time. *See also* Aust 215–18, 221–23, 292–93; Sinclair 184. Vienna Convention art. 54(a) says that treaty termination may take place in conformity with that treaty's provisions. *See also* Aust 278; McNair 515; Restatement (Third) § 322(1)(a); Sinclair 164–65, 182–85. Vienna Convention art. 30(4) provides that when parties to a later treaty do not include all parties to the earlier one, as between States parties to both, the earlier treaty applies only to the extent that its provisions are compatible with those of the later treaty. As between a State party to both and a State party to one, the treaty to which both States are party governs mutual rights and obligations. *See also* Aust 223–24, 228, 274; Restatement (Third) § 323(3); Sinclair 94–98, 108, 184–85. A.V. Lowe, *The Commander's Handbook on the Law of Naval Operations and the Contemporary Law of the* Sea, in The Law of Naval Operations 109, 120–21 (Nav. War C. Int'l L. Stud., v. 64, Horace B. Robertson, Jr. ed. 1991) (Robertson) argues that because the 1958 Conventions have no denunciation clauses, they cannot be denounced. However, Vienna Convention art. 56 governs denunciations, inter alia providing for a one-year notice. *See also* Aust 289–92; Restatement (Third) § 332; Sinclair 186–88. UNCLOS art. 311(1) scotches any

UNCLOS supersedes the 1958 LOS Conventions for parties to UNCLOS and one or more of the 1958 Conventions.[44] Second, UNCLOS declares that the Convention does not alter existing rights "which arise from other agreements compatible with" UNCLOS and which do not affect enjoyment of other parties' UNCLOS rights or performance of their UNCLOS obligations.[45] Third, UNCLOS-bound States may also conclude agreements modifying or suspending operations of UNCLOS, provided that the suspension or modification is not incompatible with effective execution of UNCLOS's object and purpose or UNCLOS's principles, and provided that such agreements do not affect enjoyment of other States' rights or performance of other States' obligations under UNCLOS. States intending to conclude such an agreement must notify other UNCLOS parties of their intentions and the modification or suspension for which the agreement provides.[46]

Besides these general rules, UNCLOS includes special rules for Part XII, which recites principles of maritime environmental law:

> 1. The provisions of this Part are without prejudice to the specific obligation assumed by States under special conventions and agreements concluded previously which relate to the protection and preservation of the marine environment and to agreements which may be concluded in furtherance of the general principles … in this Convention.
> 2. Specific obligations assumed by States under special conventions, with respect to the protection and preservation of the marine environment, should be carried out in a manner consistent with the general principles and objectives of this Convention.[47]

---

argument that the 1958 treaties remain effective for UNCLOS parties inter se alongside UNCLOS. That does not foreclose analyzing an earlier treaty's terms for their impact on a later one, analysis this Report employs for the 1958 Conventions. UNCLOS art. 317 allows denunciations, subject to a one-year notice. *See also* 5 Commentary ¶¶ 317.1–317.9.

[44] UNCLOS art. 311(1); *see also* 5 Commentary ¶¶ 311.1–311.5, 311.11.

[45] UNCLOS art. 311(2); *see also* Vienna Convention arts. 30(3), 30(4); Aust 216, 218, 224–29, 274–76; 5 Commentary ¶¶ 311.1–311.8, 311.11; Jennings & Watts §§ 590–91, 648; Restatement (Third) § 323; Sinclair 94–98, 108, 184–85.

[46] UNCLOS arts. 311(3)–311(4); *see also* Vienna Convention art. 41; Aust 216–18, 228–29, 272–75, 288–89; Brownlie 633–34; 5 Commentary ¶¶ 311.1–311.8, 311.11; Restatement § 334(3) & cmts. b, c, r.n. 2, 3; Sinclair 14, 106–09, 160, 185. Vienna Convention art. 54 allows withdrawal from an agreement but only if all parties agree to it or the agreement so provides. *See also* Aust 278, 288; Brownlie 621–22; Restatement (Third) § 332(1)(a); Sinclair 164–65, 182–85. Vienna Convention art. 58 allows suspending a treaty by some but not all parties to it. *See also* Aust 216, 289; Restatement (Third) § 333; Sinclair 185.

[47] UNCLOS art. 237.

This lex specialis for Part XII[48] is consistent with UNCLOS's allowing particular rules varying its general rules, so long as a special environmental protection rule is not incompatible with effective execution of UNCLOS's object and purpose or UNCLOS's principles, and provided that such agreements do not affect enjoyment of other States' rights or performance of other States' obligations under UNCLOS. States intending to conclude such an agreement must notify other UNCLOS parties of their intentions and the modification or suspension for which the agreement provides.[49]

There is also the possibility that a parallel but contradictory custom[50] or other source of law, *e.g.*, a general principle,[51] may develop alongside UNCLOS norms. The developing custom might be the same as, and thereby strengthen, the treaty norm.[52] If in opposition, custom may weaken or dislodge a treaty norm.[53] UNCLOS seeks to deflect this possibility through its preamble, which inter alia "*Affirm*[*s*] that matters not regulated by [UNCLOS] continue to be governed by the rules and principles of general international law."[54] The standard view on a treaty preamble's worth in interpreting the law of the agreement relates to its object and purpose, the second pillar behind a treaty's "ordinary meaning" for its terms,[55] is that the preamble must be considered along with a treaty's terms.[56] There is always a possibility, however, that a

---

[48] 4 Commentary ¶ 237.7(a); *see also* Jonathan I. Charney, *The Marine Environment and the 1982 United Nations Convention on the Law of the Sea*, 28 Int'l Law. 879, 884 (1994).

[49] UNCLOS art. 311(5); *see also* Vienna Convention art. 30(2); 5 Commentary ¶ 311.11; Jennings & Watts § 590, p. 1213; Sinclair 97–98; note 46 and accompanying text.

[50] Vienna Convention, pmbl., arts. 38, 43; Aust 260–61, 303; Brownlie 6–15; Jennings & Watts §§ 10–11; Sinclair 6, 9–10, 103–04.

[51] *Cf.* ICJ Statute, art. 38(1); Restatement (Third) §§ 102–03.

[52] Nicaragua Case, 1986 ICJ 31–38, 91–135; Corfu Channel, 1949 ICJ 4, 22; Brownlie 6–15; Jennings & Watts §§ 10–11; Restatement (Third) § 102 cmt. j.

[53] Michael Akehurst, *Custom as a Source of International Law*, 47 Brit. Y.B. Int'l L. 49–52 (1974).

[54] By contrast, High Seas Convention, pmbl, "*Recogniz*[*ed*] that the United Nations Conference on the Law of the Sea … adopted the following provisions as generally declaratory of established principles of international law[.]" For States still parties to this treaty, the result is a confluence of custom and treaty rules as recited in the High Seas Convention. Vienna Convention arts. 31(a)–31(b); *see also* notes 60–62 and accompanying text. Once these countries ratify UNCLOS, under UNCLOS art. 311(1) this support for customary rules will be lost. *See also* notes 50–53 and accompanying text. The other 1958 LOS Conventions do not have such preamble language.

[55] Vienna Convention arts. 31(1)–31(2).

[56] Aust 236, 424–27; Brownlie 631–33; Jennings & Watts § 632, p. 1273; McNair 365; Restatement (Third) § 325(1) & cmt. b; Sinclair 128.

custom or general principles-based norm might be held to totally outweigh an UNCLOS rule under traditional source-balancing principles.[57] For countries that are not UNCLOS parties, a new customary norm might be held to outweigh an UNCLOS-based customary rule.[58] This might be contrasted with a situation where UNCLOS as a treaty and UNCLOS-based custom face a claim of a new customary norm that contradicts UNCLOS and the UNCLOS-based norm.[59]

These UNCLOS treaty-trumping provisions raise issues for the place of LOS Committee definitions if a treaty subordinate to UNCLOS does supply a definition. Assuming subordinate treaty compatibility, etc. with UNCLOS, a definition ancillary to a subordinate treaty cannot operate to destroy that compatibility. If, *e.g.*, an authoritative decision maker (*e.g.*, a court or perhaps an UNCLOS institution like the Area Authority) accepts a Committee definition, that definition applies to the subordinate treaty to insure compatibility with UNCLOS.

For countries like the United States that are not yet UNCLOS parties but which have accepted some or all UNCLOS provisions as customary law,[60] a Committee definition might be cited to give content to custom. If a custom or other source contrary to UNCLOS develops, the Committee definition might be cited to support the contrary custom or other source, to be thrown into the analysis, or the definition on an UNCLOS term might be employed on the other side of the analysis to support UNCLOS.[61] If a treaty subordinate to UNCLOS faces a general, UNCLOS-based but contrary custom and the proponent of a Committee definition for that subordinate treaty's term is faced with the general UNCLOS custom, the UNCLOS general custom should prevail. If a treaty subordinate to UNCLOS faces a general, UNCLOS-based but contrary custom and a definition related to that custom,

---

[57] *See* note 50 and accompanying text.

[58] *E.g.*, the United States. *See* Part III.C.

[59] This has been one argument advanced for U.S. Senate advice and consent for UNCLOS and the 1994 Agreement. *See* Part III.C, note 96 and accompanying text.

[60] *Cf.* President Ronald Reagan, *United States Ocean Policy*, 19 Wkly. Comp. Presid. Docts. 383 (Mar. 14, 1983). Commentators have agreed with the U.S. view. Restatement (Third) Part V, *Introductory Note*, pp. 3–5; NWP 1-14M Annotated ¶ 1.1; John Norton Moore, *Introduction*, in 1 Commentary, p. xxvii; Bernard H. Oxman, *International Law and Naval and Air Operations at Sea*, in Robertson, note 43, 19, 29; *but see* Churchill & Lowe 24; 1 O'Connell 48–49. The latter, researched through 1978, may reflect thinking during UNCLOS' early drafting years. Walker, The Tanker 306 n.3. *See also* note 101 and accompanying text.

[61] ICJ Statute arts. 38, 59; Restatement (Third) §§ 102–03.

the UNCLOS general custom should also prevail. However, given the relative weight that might be accorded to sources under international law analysis,[62] the opposite result is possible.

Overarching UNCLOS and its internal trumping provisions are UN Charter Article 103 and the principle of jus cogens. Where there is a conflict between a definition in the Charter (admittedly a rare possibility), a definition in a UN Security Council decision or a jus cogens-supported definition and a commentator definition, the Charter,[63] a definition in a Council decision[64] or a jus cogens[65]-supported definition has priority. To be sure, commentators say that today jus cogens "has little relevance to the law of the sea,"[66] but that may change in the future. At least two Charter provisions, Articles 2(4) and 51, have been

---

[62] *See* note 40 and accompanying text.

[63] Although UN Charter art. 103 declares Charter primacy over treaties and not custom or other sources, Charter definitions should prime secondary-source definitions like those the LOS Committee proposes. *See also* Goodrich 614–17; Jennings & Watts § 592; 2 Simma 1292–1302.

[64] U.N. Charter arts. 25, 48, 94(2), 103; *see also* Goodrich 207–11, 334–37, 555–59, 614–17; 1 & 2 Simma 454–62, 776–80, 1174–79, 1292–1302; W. Michael Reisman, *The Constitutional Crisis in the United Nations*, 87 AJIL 83, 87 (1993) (principles flowing from Council decisions pursuant to U.N. Charter arts. 25, 48, 103 are treaty law binding UN Members and override other treaty obligations). Article 103 does not apply to custom or jus cogens derived independently of a treaty, however, unless Article 103 might be considered a jus cogens norm itself, and a jus cogens norm superior to other jus cogens norms, or its principles might be considered a norm that is superior to conflicting custom. *See also* ICJ Statute art. 38(1); Restatement (Third) §§ 102–03.

[65] *See* Vienna Convention, pmbl., arts. 53, 64, 71. Jus cogens has uncertain contours. *See generally* Brownlie 510–12, 626 (jus cogens' content uncertain); T.O. Elias, The Modern Law of Treaties 177–87 (1974) (same); Jennings & Watts §§ 2, 642, 653 (same); McNair 214–15 (same); Restatement (Third) §§ 102 r.n. 6, 323 cmt. b, 331(2), 338(2) (same); Shabtai Rosenne, Developments in the Law of Treaties 1945–1986, at 281–88 (1989); 1 Simma 62 (dispute over self-determination as jus cogens); Sinclair 17–18, 218–26 (Vienna Convention principles considered progressive development in 1984); Grigorii I. Tunkin, Theory of International Law 98 (William E. Butler trans. 1974); Levan Alexidze, *Legal Nature of Jus Cogens in Contemporary Law*, 172 R.C.A.D.I. 219, 262–63 (1981); John N. Hazard, *Soviet Tactics in International Lawmaking*, 7 Denv. J. Int'l L. & Pol. 9, 25–29 (1977); Jimenez de Arechaga, note 38, pp. 64–67; Dinah Shelton, *Normative Heirarchy in International Law*, 100 Am. J. Int'l L. 291 (2006); Mark Weisburd, *The Emptiness of the Concept of* Jus Cogens, *As Illustrated by the War in Bosnia-Herzegovina*, 17 Mich. J. Int'l L. 1 (1995). An International Law Commission study acknowledged primacy of UN Charter art. 103-based law and jus cogens but declined to catalogue what are jus cogens norms. International Law Commission, Report on Its Fifty-Seventh Session (May 2-June 3 and July 11-August 5, 2005), UN GAOR, 60th Sess., Supp. No. 10, pp. 221–25, UN Doc. A/60/10 (2005) (2005 ILC Rep.); *see also* Michael J. Matheson, *The Fifty-Seventh Session of the International Law Commission*, 100 AJIL 416, 422 (2006).

[66] Churchill & Lowe 6.

said to approach, or to have attained, jus cogens status.[67] Disputes continue as to these provisions' content, *e.g.*, the longstanding argument on whether individual and collective self-defense includes anticipatory self-defense,[68] or whether self-defense can be invoked only after an

---

[67] Legality of Threat or Use of Nuclear Weapons, 1996 ICJ 226, 245 (Nuclear Weapons); Military & Paramilitary Activities in & Against Nicaragua (Nicar. v. U.S.), 1986 ICJ 14, 100–01 (UN Charter art. 2[4] approaches jus cogens status) (Nicaragua Case). Armed Activities on Terr. of Congo (Dem. Rep. of Congo v. Rwanda), 2006 ICJ 3, 29–30, 49–50 (jurisdiction, admissibility of application) held a jus cogens violation allegation was not enough to deprive the Court of jurisdiction, preliminarily stating that Convention on Prevention & Punishment of Crime of Genocide, Dec. 9, 1948, TIAS —, 78 UNTS 277 represented erga omnes obligations. Vienna Convention art. 53 was among other treaties cited; *see supra* note 65 and accompanying text. While also citing the Nicaragua and Nuclear Weapons Cases, Shelton, note 65 pp. 305–06 says Armed Activities is the first ICJ case to recognize jus cogens, but its holding seems not quite the same as ruling on an issue and applying jus cogens. The case compromis included the Vienna Convention, which raises jus cogens issues that the Court could have decided under that law as well as traditional sources. ICJ Statute arts. 36, 38, 59. *See also* ILC State Responsibility Articles, art. 50 & Commentary ¶¶ 1–5, p. 247–49, *reprinted in* Crawford 288–89 ("fundamental substantive obligations"); Jennings & Watts § 2 (Art. 2[4] a fundamental norm); Restatement (Third) §§ 102, cmts. h, k; 905(2) & cmt. g (same); Carin Kaghan, *Jus Cogens and the Inherent Right Self-Defense*, 3 ILSA J. Int'l & Comp. L. 767, 823–27 (1997) (UN Charter art. 51 represents jus cogens norm). 2001 ILC Rep., pp. 177–80, art. 21 & Commentary, *reprinted in* Crawford 166, resolving the issue of conflict between UN Charter arts. 2(4) and 51 through saying that no art. 2(4) issues arise if there is a lawful self-defense claim, appears to give art. 51 the same status as art. 2(4). UNCLOS art. 88 declares that States shall use the high seas for peaceful purposes. *Id.* art. 301 requires that when States exercise rights or perform duties under the Convention, they must refrain from any threat or use of force against the territorial integrity or political independence of any State, "or in any other manner inconsistent with" international law principles embodied in the UN Charter. These provisions are consonant with the Charter, *see* UN Charter art. 103; they do not forbid legitimate military activities, *e.g.*, naval exercises, which are among high seas freedoms UNCLOS Art. 87(1) ("*inter alia*") preserves. Charter rights and duties to which art. 301 refers includes a right of self-defense. *See* 3 Commentary ¶¶ 87.9(i)–87.9(j), 88.1–88.7(d); 5 *id.* ¶¶ 301.1–301.5. UNCLOS could not purport to curtail the right of individual and collective self-defense. UN Charter arts. 51, 103.

[68] United Nations, A More Secure World: Our Shared Responsibility: Report of the Secretary-General's High-Level Panel on Threats, Challenges and Change ¶¶ 188–92 (2004), citing Wolfgang Friedmann, The Changing Structure of International Law 259–60 (1964); Louis Henkin, How Nations Behave 143–45 (2d ed. 1979); Oscar Schachter, The Right of States to Use Armed Force, 82 Mich. L. Rev. 1620, 1633–34 (1984), says UN Charter art. 51 allows a threatened State, "according to long-established international law," to take military action "as long as the threatened attack is imminent, no other means would deflect it and the action is proportionate." However, a State cannot purport to act in anticipatory self-defense, not just preventive but also "preemptively." The latter cases should be brought to the U.N. Security Council for possible action. Article 51 should not be rewritten or reinterpreted.

This approach is in line with advocates of a right of anticipatory individual and collective self-defense based on the Charter and customary law. ILC State Responsibility Articles, art. 25 & Commentary ¶ 5, *reprinted in* Crawford 178–79, recognize anticipatory self-defense under the necessity doctrine. *See also* Nuclear Weapons, note 67, 1996 ICJ 245; Nicaragua Case, note 52, 1986 ICJ 94, 347 (Schwebel, J., dissenting); Stanimar A. Alexandrov, Self-Defense Against the Use of Force in International Law 296 (1996); D.W. Bowett, Self-Defence in International Law 187–93 (1958); Hans Kelsen, Collective Security Under International Law 27 (Nav. War C. Int'l L. Stud., v. 49, 1957); Timothy L.H. McCormack, Self-Defense in International Law: The Israeli Raid on the Iraqi Nuclear Reactor 122–24, 238–39, 253–84, 302 (1996); Myres S. McDougal & Florentino Feliciano, Law and Minimum World Public Order 232–41 (1961); Walter Gary Sharp, Sr., Cyberspace and the Use of Force 33–48 (1999) (real debate is scope of anticipatory self-defense right; responses must be proportional); Jennings & Watts § 127; Oscar Schachter, International Law in Theory and Practice 152–55 (1991); Julius Stone, Of Law and Nations: Between Power Politics and Human Hopes 3 (1974); Ann Van Wynen Thomas & A.J. Thomas, The Concept of Aggression in International Law 127 (1972); Richard W. Aldrich, *How Do You Know You Are At War in the Information Age?*, 35 Hous. J. Int'l L. 223, 231, 248 (2000); Louis Rene Beres, *After the Scud Attacks: Israel, "Palestine," and Anticipatory Self-Defense,* 6 Emory Int'l L. Rev. 71, 75–77 (1992); George Bunn, *International Law and the Use of Force in Peacetime: Do U.S. Ships Have to Take the First Hit?*, 39 Nav. War C. Rev. 69–70 (May-June 1986); James H. Doyle, Jr., *Computer Networks, Proportionality, and Military Operations*, in Michael N. Schmitt & Brian T. O'Donnell, Computer Network and International Law 147, 151–54 (Nav. War C. Int'l L. Stud., v. 76, 2002); Thomas M. Franck, *When, If Ever, May States Deploy Military Force Without Prior Security Council Authorization?*, 5 Wash. U.J.L. & Pol'y 51, 68 (2001); Christopher Greenwood, *Remarks,* in Panel, *Neutrality, The Rights of Shipping and the Use of Force in the Persian Gulf War (Part I)*, 1988 Proc. Am. Soc'y Int'l L. 158, 160–61; David K. Linnan, *Self-Defense, Necessity and U.N. Collective Security: United States and Other Views,* 1991 Duke J. Comp. & Int'l L. 57, 65–84, 122; Lowe, *The Commander's*, note 43, pp. 127–30; James McHugh, *Forcible Self-Help in International Law,* 25 Nav. War C. Rev. 61 (No. 2, 1972); Rein Mullerson & David J. Scheffer, *Legal Regulation of the Use of Force,* in Beyond Confrontation: International Law for the Post-Cold War Era 93, 109–14 (Lori Fisler Damrosch et al. ed. 1995); John F. Murphy, *Commentary on Intervention to Combat Terrorism and Drug Trafficking,* in Lori Fisler Damrosch & David J. Scheffer, Law and Force in the New International Order 241 (1991) (Law and Force); W. Michael Reisman, *Allocating Competences to Use Coercion in the Post-Cold War World: Practices, Conditions, and Prospects,* in *id.* 25, 45; Horace B. Robertson, Jr., *Self-Defense Against Computer Network Attack under International Law,* in Schmitt & O'Donnell 121, 140; Michael N. Schmitt, Bellum Americanum: *The U.S. View of Twenty-First Century War and Its Possible Implications for the Law of Armed Conflict,* 19 Mich. J. Int'l L. 1051, 1071, 1080–83 (1998); Abraham D. Sofaer, *Sixth Annual Waldemar A. Solf Lecture: International Terrorism, the Law, and the National Defense,* 126 Mil. L. Rev. 89, 95 (1989); Robert F. Turner, *State Sovereignty, International Law, and the Use of Force in Countering Low-Intensity Aggression in the Modern World,* in Legal and Moral Constraints on Low-Intensity Conflict 43, 62–80 (Alberto R. Coll et al. eds., Nav. War C. Int'l L. Stud., v. 67, 1995); Claude Humphrey Meredith Waldock, *The Regulation of Force by Individual States in International Law,* 81 R.C.A.D.I. 451, 496–99 (1952) (anticipatory self-defense permissible, as long as principles of necessity, proportionality observed); George K. Walker, *Information Warfare and Neutrality,* 33 Vand. J. Transnat'l L. 1079, 1122–24 (2000); Ruth Wedgwood, *Responding to Terrorism: The Strikes Against bin Laden,* 24 Yale J. Int'l L. 559, 566 (1999). My article, *The Lawfulness of Operation Enduring Freedom's Self-Defense Responses*, 37 Valparaiso L. Rev. 489, 536 (2003), says preemption "seems" equivalent to anticipatory self-defense, armed attack.[69] Articles 2(4)and 51 are as relevant for LOS issues as for confrontations entirely on States' land territory.

Because of Charter requirements that UN Members agree to carry out their Charter obligations,[70] a recommendatory Council or General

---

citing contradicting views of the day. "Seems" is not the same as saying preemption and prevention are interchangeable, as William C. Bradford, *"The Duty to Defend Them": A Natural Law Justification for the Bush Doctrine of Preemption*, 79 Notre Dame L. Rev. 1365, 1368 n.13 (2004), wrote that I said. Anticipatory self-defense and preemption may be the same, as Abraham D. Sofaer, *Iraq and International Law*, Wall St. J., Jan. 31, 2003, cited in Walker, *The Lawfulness*, p. 536 n. 198, thought, and for which my page proofs cited him. I also cited Richard Falk, *Pre-Emptive War Flagrantly Contradicts the UN's Legal Framework: Why International Law Matters*, The Nation 19, 20 (Mar. 10, 2003) to illustrate an opposing view. The *Valparaiso Law Review* editors did not insert my qualifying phrase for Sofaer, "thought so," as I indicated in final page proofs. Letter of the author to *Valparaiso Law Review* Editor-in-Chief, Mar. 31, 2003 (copy in author file). In any event I did not say that preemption and prevention are the same. Walker, *The Lawfulness*, p. 536 & n.198 tried to present differing sides of a developing issue not directly relevant to allied and coalition operations in Afghanistan. The preemption issue will be resolved after a time of interactive claim and counterclaim, *cf.* Myres S. McDougal, *The Hydrogen Bomb Tests*, 49 AJIL 357–58 (1955), much as the dispute over the territorial sea's breadth has been resolved. *See* Part III.A. Jane Gilliland Dalton, *The United States National Security Strategy: Yesterday, Today and Tomorrow*, 52 Nav. L. Rev. 60, 68–75 (2005), takes the view that preemption and anticipatory self-defense are not necessarily different, but national strategy should adhere to the anticipatory self-defense doctrine.

[69] Those arguing that anticipatory self-defense is unlawful in the Charter era include Ian Brownlie, International Law and the Use of Force by States 257–61, 275–78, 366–67 (1963); Anthony D'Amato, International Law: Process and Prospect 32 (1987); Yoram Dinstein, War, Aggression and Self-Defence 159–85 (3d ed. 2001); Louis Henkin, International Law: Politics and Values 121–22 (1995), a change in view from Henkin, note 68, pp. 143–45, in 1979; Philip C. Jessup, A Modern Law of Nations 166–67 (1948); D.P. O'Connell, The Influence of Law on Sea Power 83, 171 (1979); 2 Lassa Oppenheim, International Law § 52aa, at 156 (Hersch Lauterpacht ed., 7th ed. 1952); Ahmed M. Rifaat, International Aggression 126 (1974); Natalino Ronzitti, Rescuing Nationals Abroad Through Military Coercion and Intervention on Grounds of Humanity 4 (1985); 1 Simma 803–04; Tom Farer, *Law and War*, in 3 Cyril E. Black & Richard A. Falk, The Future of the International Legal Order 30, 36–37 (1971); Yuri M. Kolosov, *Limiting the Use of Force: Self-Defense, Terrorism, and Drug Trafficking*, in Law and Force, note 68, 232, 234; Josef L. Kunz, *Individual and Collective Self-Defense in Article 51 of the Charter of the United Nations*, 41 AJIL 872, 878 (1947); Rainer Lagoni, *Remarks*, in Panel, note 68, 161, 162; Jules Lobel, *The Use of Force to Terrorist Attacks*, 24 Yale J. Int'l L. 537, 541 (1999); Robert W. Tucker, *The Interpretation of War Under Present International Law*, 4 Int'l L.Q. 11, 29–30 (1951); *see also id.*, *Reprisals and Self-Defense*, 66 AJIL 586 (1972) (states may respond only after being attacked). Recent commentary supports an expanded view of reactive self-defense to include acting in self-defense against preparations for attack. *See, e.g.*, Christine Gray, International Law and the Use of Force 130, 133 (2d ed. 2004); Mary Ellen O'Connell, *Lawful Self-Defense to Terrorism*, 63 U. Pitt. L. Rev. 889, 894 (2002).

[70] UN Charter arts. 2(2), 2(5); *see also* Goodrich 40–41, 56–58; 1 Simma 91–101, 136–39.

Assembly resolution[71] would almost always have primacy over a Committee definition, and certainly so if a resolution recites a jus cogens or customary norm.[72] On the other hand, if a resolution does not restate positive law, it should be seriously considered along with secondary sources like the ABILA LOS Committee research. The Committee's reported research underscores its recognition of superior norms in the Charter,[73] as does UNCLOS:

> In exercising their rights and performing their duties under this Convention, States Parties shall refrain from any threat or use of force against the territorial integrity or political independence of any State, or in any other manner inconsistent with the principles of international law embodied in the Charter …[74]

The foregoing principles for UN resolutions should also apply to pronouncements of other intergovernmental organizations whose resolutions apply to the law of the sea, e.g., the International Maritime Organization (IMO).[75] If a resolution is mandatory, like Security Council decisions, such a resolution defining a term trumps a

---

[71] UN Charter arts. 10–11, 13–14, 33, 36–37, 39–41; *see also* Sydney D. Bailey & Sam Daws, The Procedure of the UN Security Council 18–21, 236–37 (3d ed. 1998); Brownlie 15; Jorge Castenada, Legal Effects of United Nations Resolutions 78–79 (Alba Amoia trans. 1969); Goodrich 111–29, 133–44, 257–65, 277–87, 290–314; Jennings & Watts § 16; Restatement (Third) § 103(2)(d) & r.n.2; 1 Simma 257–87, 298–326, 583–94, 616–43, 717–49.

[72] *See* notes 65–67 and accompanying text.

[73] *See, e.g.*, Walker, *Defining* 234.

[74] UNCLOS art. 301; *see also id.* art. 88; Restatement (Third) § 521, cmt. b, citing UN Charter art. 2(4), UNCLOS, arts. 88, 301 and referring to Restatement (Third) § 905, cmt. g; *accord* Nuclear Weapons, note 67, 1996 ICJ 244; 3 Commentary ¶¶ 87.9(I), 88.1–88.7(d); 5 *id.* ¶¶ 301.1–301.6; *see also, e.g.*, Boleslaw Boczek, *Peaceful Purposes Provisions of the United Nations Convention on the Law of the Sea*, 20 Ocean Devel. & Int'l L. 359 (1989); *Helsinki Principles*, note 15, Principle 1.2, p. 499; Bernard H. Oxman, *The Regime of Warships Under the United Nations Convention on the Law of the Sea*, 24 Va. J. Int'l L. 809, 814 (1984); John E. Parkerson, Jr., *International Legal Implications of the Strategic Defense Initiative*, 116 Mil. L. Rev. 67, 79–85 (1987); Frank Russo, Jr., *Targeting Theory in the Law of Naval Warfare*, 30 Nav. L. Rev. 1, 8 (1992); *see also* Part IV.B § 132, "other rules of international law."

[75] Originally the Intergovernmental Maritime Consultative Organization (IMCO), IMCO is now IMO, with a different constitutive treaty, organization and procedures, etc. *Compare* Convention on the Intergovernmental Maritime Consultative Organization, Mar. 6, 1948, pmbl., 9 UST 621, 623, 289 UNTS 48, *with* Amendments to Convention on the Intergovernmental Maritime Consultative Organization of March 6, 1948, Nov. 14, 1975, Title of the Convention & Preamble, 34 UST 497, 499, 1276 UNTS 468, 470. There were amendments to the Convention before and after the 1975 amendments. *See* 3 Multilateral Treaties ch. 12, pts. 1-1.h; 379–80; Wiktor 481.

commentary definition. If the resolution is nonmandatory but restates a customary, treaty or general principles norm, it will also have primacy. If the resolution does not do so, it should be considered along with other secondary sources like the ABILA LOS Committee research. If a definition emerges from a nongovernmental organization (NGO), an NGO definition should be given weight according to principles for competing claims of scholars.[76]

As noted earlier, in terms of UNCLOS itself, the Committee chose to minimize these kinds of conflicts by declining to redefine terms the Convention defines.[77]

The Committee has also been sensitive to the possibility of another definition for a term in law of armed conflict (LOAC) situations, *e.g.*, when UNCLOS and the 1958 LOS Conventions declare a separate standard of international law through their "other rules" clauses,[78] which traditionally have meant that the 1958 and 1982 law of the sea treaties are subject to the LOAC in armed conflict situations.[79] Since the LOAC, and the law of naval warfare and the law of neutrality in particular, rely in large part on primary sources, *i.e.*, treaties, custom and general principles,[80] a LOAC-based definition will have primacy over a Committee definition for the UNCLOS, although circumstances

---

[76] *See* notes 60, 64 and accompanying text.

[77] *See* notes 17–31 and accompanying text.

[78] This clause, sometimes stated slightly differently, appears throughout UNCLOS, *i.e.*, in *id.*, pmbl.; arts. 2(3) (territorial sea); 19, 21, 31 (territorial sea innocent passage); 34(2) (straits transit passage); 52(1) (archipelagic sea lanes passage; incorporation by reference of Arts. 19, 21, 31); 58(1), 58(3) (exclusive economic zone); 78 (continental shelf; coastal State rights do not affect superjacent waters, *i.e.*, territorial or high seas; coastal State cannot infringe or unjustifiably interfere with "navigation and other rights and freedoms of other States as provided in this Convention"); 87(1) (high seas); 138 (the Area); 293(1) (court or tribunal having jurisdiction for settling disputes must apply UNCLOS and "other rules of international law" not incompatible with UNCLOS); 303(4) (archeological, historical objects found at sea, "other international agreements and rules of international law regarding the protection of objects of an archeological and historical nature"); *id.*, Annex III art. 21(1) prospecting, exploration, exploitation contracts for Area governed by contract terms; Area Authority rules, regulations, procedures; of UNCLOS, Part XI; "other rules of international law not incompatible with" UNCLOS); Annex VI arts. 23, 38(1) (incorporating UNCLOS art. 293).

[79] The Committee settled on a definition for "other rules of international law" that includes a possibility that the phrase may mean law other than the LOAC, including the law of neutrality, in some situations. *See* Part IV.B § 132, "other rules of international law."

[80] Schindler & Toman remains the indispensable collection for reprints of these sources; *see also* NWP 1-14M Annotated, pp. xxxvii–xxxviii.

might call for borrowing an LOS definition.[81] Similarly, self-defense situations might also call for a different definition that will have primacy because of the status of the right of individual and collective self-defense as a customary, Charter, and perhaps jus cogens norm.[82] As in the case of LOAC-governed situations,[83] however, an LOS-based definition might be borrowed. The Committee did, however, note the possibility of another meaning in LOAC situations in Part IV.B § 132, which defines "other rules of international law."

---

[81] *See, e.g.*, applying UNCLOS "due regard" principle in law of naval warfare situations, San Remo Manual ¶¶ 12, 34, 44, 88, 106(c) & cmts.; *see also* NWP 1-14M Annotated ¶ 8.1.3; Walker, The Tanker 536–46; Horace B. Robertson, Jr., *The "New" Law of the Sea and the Law of Naval Warfare*, in Readings on International Law from the Naval War College Review ch. 19 (Nav. War C. Int'l L. Stud., v. 68, John Norton Moore & Robert F. Turner eds. 1995). For analysis of and definitions for "due regard" in UNCLOS for LOS issues, *see* Part IV.B § 56, "due regard."

[82] U.N. Charter arts. 51, 103; *see also* notes 63–71 and accompanying text.

[83] *See* notes 78–79 and accompanying text.

C. THE ROLE AND RELATIONSHIP OF UNDERSTANDINGS, DECLARATIONS AND STATEMENTS, ALSO COLLECTIVELY KNOWN AS INTERPRETATIVE OR INTERPRETIVE STATEMENTS, APPENDED TO THE 1982 LAW OF THE SEA CONVENTION AND THE ABILA LOS COMMITTEE DEFINITIONS PROJECT

George K. Walker[84]

Although 158 States and the European Union had ratified or acceded to UNCLOS as of August 6, 2009, and 137 were parties to the 1994 Agreement[85] amending and implementing UNCLOS, a handful of countries, including the United States, have not done so.

The United States had UNCLOS and the 1994 Agreement on the U.S. Senate floor in 2004 for advice and consent[86] after the Senate Foreign Relations Committee favorably endorsed the agreements during the 108th Congress.[87] Pursuant to Senate rules, UNCLOS and the Agreement returned to the Foreign Relations Committee at the end of the session.[88] On May 15, 2007 the President urged the Senate to act favorably on the Convention during the current Congressional session.[89] On December 19, 2007 the Foreign Relations Committee reported UNCLOS

---

[84] Part III.C was extracted and enlarged from Walker, *Last Round* 134–39, 149–51, 2005–06 ABILA Proc. 24–29, 39–40.

[85] Multilateral Treaties ch. 21, pts. 6, 6.a. *See generally* 1 Commentary ch. 5 (discussing UNCLOS negotiations); Churchill & Lowe 18–22 (same; also discussing negotiation of 1994 Agreement, Agreement for Implementation of UN Convention on the Law of the Sea of 10 December Relating to Straddling Fish Stocks & Highly Migratory Fish Stocks, Aug. 4, 1995, 2167 UNTS 3 [Straddling Stocks Agreement], which complete the UN LOS "package" to date); S. Treaty Doc. No. 104–24, at v–xvi (1998) (discussion of 1994 Agreement). As of August 6, 2009, 75 States were Straddling Stocks Agreement parties. Multilateral Treaties ch. 21, pt. 7.

[86] *Cf.* U.S. Const. art. II, § 2, cl. 2.

[87] S. Exec. Rep. No. 108–10, *United Nations Convention on the Law of the Sea,* 108th Cong., 2d Sess. (2004); *see also* Standing Rules of the Senate, S. Doc. No. 106–15, R. 30(1) (2000).

[88] S. Doc. No. 106–15, note 87, R. 30(2).

[89] President George W. Bush, President's Statement on Advancing U.S. Interests in the World Oceans, May 15, 2007, *available at* http://www.whitehouse.gov/news/releases/2007/05/20070515-2.html (visited May 29, 2007).

and the Agreement out again, favorably.[90] There was no action in 2008, and under Senate rules the agreements again returned to the Committee at the end of the session. Despite similar statements from President Barack Obama and his administration, the agreements remained in the Committee as of mid-2011.

In recommending Senate advice and consent in 2004, the Foreign Relations Committee report appended over 25 understandings,[91] declarations and conditions for the treaty and the 1994 Agreement

---

[90] S. Exec. Rep. No. 110-9, *Convention on the Law of the Sea,* 110th Cong., lst Sess. (2007).

[91] Restatement (Third) § 313, cmt. g defines an understanding:

> ... When signing or adhering to an international agreement, a state may make a unilateral declaration that does not purport to be a reservation. Whatever it is called, it constitutes a reservation in fact if it purports to exclude, limit, or modify [a] state's legal obligation. Sometimes ... a declaration purports to be an "understanding," an interpretation of the agreement in a particular respect. Such an interpretive declaration is not a reservation if it reflects the accepted view of the agreement. But another contracting party may challenge the expressed understanding, treating it as a reservation which it is not prepared to accept.

Whiteman's *Digest* defines understandings, declarations and statements:

> ... "[U]nderstanding" is often used to designate a statement when it is not intended to modify or limit any of the provisions of the treaty in its international operation but is intended merely to clarify or explain or to deal with some other matter incidental to the operation of the treaty in a manner other than as a substantive reservation. Sometimes an understanding is no more than a statement of policies or principles or perhaps an indication of internal procedures for carrying out provisions of the treaty.
>
> ... "[D]eclaration" and "statement" are used most often when it is considered essential or desirable to give notice of certain matters of policy or principle, without an intention of derogating from the substantive rights or obligations stipulated in a treaty.

Treaties and Other International Agreements: Reservations, 14 Whiteman, Digest § 17; *see also id.* § 21; Aust 126–28; Treaties: Reservations, 5 Hackworth, Digest § 479, quoting Research in International Law of the Harvard Law School, *Law of Treaties: Draft Convention with Comment,* art. 13, 29 AJIL 4, 663, 843 (1935 Supp.) (Harvard Draft Convention); 2 Charles Cheney Hyde, International Law: Chiefly As Interpreted and Applied by the United States § 519, at 1436 (2d rev. ed. 1947); Frank Horn, Reservations and Interpretative Declarations to Multilateral Treaties 237–42 (1988); Jennings & Watts § 614; Sinclair 52-54. Before the Vienna Convention, an "impressive number" of writers said interpretative declarations, *i.e.*, understandings, or interpretive declarations in Restatement § 313 cmt. g parlance, must be assimilated to reservations. Horn 230. McNair 32 did not examine understandings, declarations or statements, except in contexts of their amounting to international agreements or as options to a treaty. *See generally id.* 7–15. Horn Part 2 refers to unilateral declarations, statements or understandings as "interpretative declarations." The International Law Commission multilateral treaties project defines interpretative declarations:

in recommending Senate advice and consent.[92] The 2007 list is identical.[93]

The treaty is a "package deal," *i.e.*, it does not allow reservations unless the Convention permits them.[94] UNCLOS does allow understandings, however. It

---

> "Interpretative declaration" means a unilateral statement, however phrased or named, made by a State or by an international organization whereby that State or that organization purports to specify or clarify the meaning or scope attributed by the declarant to a treaty or to certain of its provisions. ... The character of a unilateral statement as a reservation or an interpretative declaration is determined by the legal effect it purports to produce.

Text of Draft Guidelines on Reservations to Treaties Provisionally Adopted So Far by the Commission, in Report of the International Law Commission on the Work of its Fifty-fifth Session, 58 U.N. GAOR Supp. (No. 10), U.N. Doc. A/58/10, at 165, 168 (1996) (2003 ILC Rep.). The ILC is researching the law of treaties related to multilateral reservations after receiving UN General Assembly endorsement for the project. *Id.* 148, citing G.A. Res. 48/31, U.N. GAOR, 48th Sess., Supp. No. 49, at 328, U.N. Doc. A/48/49 (1993); G.A. Res. 49/51, U.N. GAOR, 49th Sess., Supp. No. 49, at 292, U.N. Doc. A/49/51 (1994); *see also* Matheson, *The Fifty-Seventh*, note 65, pp. 418–19; Alain Pellet, Tenth Report on Reservations to Treaties, UN Doc. A/CN.4/558 (2005).

Restatement (Third) § 314 cmt. d discusses understandings in the U.S. practice context:

> ... A treaty that is ratified or acceded to by the United States with a statement of understanding becomes effective in domestic law (Restatement § 111) subject to that understanding. If no such statement is made, indication that the President or the Senate ascribed a particular meaning to the treaty is relevant to the interpretation of the treaty by a United States court in much the same way that the legislative history of a statute is relevant to its interpretation. See [*id.*] § 325, Reporters' Note 5; § 326, Reporters' Note 2. Although the Senate's resolution of consent may contain no statement of understanding, there may be such statements in the report of the Senate Foreign Relations Committee or in the Senate debates. In that event, the President must decide whether they represent a general understanding by the Senate and, if he finds that they do, must respect them in good faith.

See also id. § 303 cmt. d.

[92] *Text of Resolution of Advice and Consent to Resolution*, in S. Exec. Rep. No. 108-10, note 87, pp. 17–22 (*Text*). S. Exec. Rep. No. 108-10 Part III publishes *Summary of Key Provisions of the Convention and Implementing Agreement*; for another analysis from the U.S. Executive perspective, *see Commentary — The 1982 United Nations Convention on the Law of the Sea and the Agreement on Implementation of Part XI*, in S. Treaty Doc. 103–39, Message from the President of the United States, United Nations Convention on the Law of the Sea, with Annexes, and the Agreement Relating to the Implementation of Part XI of the United Nations Convention on the Law of the Sea, with Annex, 103d Cong., 2d Sess. 1-97 (1994).

[93] *Compare Text,* in S. Exec. Rep. No. 110-9, note 90, *with Text of Resolution of Advice and Consent to Resolution*, note 92, pp. 19–24.

[94] UNCLOS art. 309. Vienna Convention art. 1(d) defines a reservation as "a unilateral statement, however phrased or named, made by a State, when signing, ratifying,

> ... does not preclude a State when signing, ratifying or acceding to this Convention, from making declarations or statements, however phrased or named, with a view, inter alia, to the harmonization of its laws and regulations with the provisions of this Convention, provided that such declarations or statements do not purport to exclude or to modify the legal effect of the provisions of this Convention in their application to that State.[95]

The 2004 Senate Foreign Relations Committee proposals for understandings, declarations and conditions were subject to Senate floor action, including amendments, and perhaps recommittal to the Committee. The Senate could, of course, have refused advice and consent to UNCLOS and or the 1994 Agreement with or without understandings, conditions and declarations. UNCLOS and the Agreement emerged from the Committee in 2007 with the same understandings, conditions and declarations.[96]

Although the U.S. Departments of State and Defense and Foreign Relations Committee witnesses strongly endorsed UNCLOS,[97] debate over whether the United States should accede erupted in 2004 and again in 2007–08.[98] Final Senate action may come in the future. If the

---

accepting, approving or acceding to a treaty, whereby it purports to exclude or to modify the legal effect of certain provisions of the treaty in their application to that State[.]" *See also* Brownlie 612–15; McNair ch. 9; Jennings & Watts §§ 614–19; Restatement (Third) § 313, cmt. a (repeating Vienna Convention definition); Sinclair ch. 3. Restatement § 314 & cmts. a-c define and discuss U.S. international reservations practice.

[95] UNCLOS art. 310 (emphasis in original), referring to *id.* art. 309.

[96] *See* notes 91–93 and accompanying text.

[97] John F. Turner, Ass't Sec'y of State for Oceans & Int'l Envt'l & Sci. Affs., *Accession to the 1982 Law of the Sea Convention and Ratification of the 1994 Agreement Amending Part XI of the Law of the Sea Convention*, Testimony Before U.S. Senate Envt'l. & Pub. Works Comm., Mar. 23, 2004, *available at* http://www.state.gov/g/oes/rls/rm/2004/30723.htm (visited Aug. 22, 2004), recites the Department's reasons for advocating advice and consent and responds to arguments against ratification; *see also* testimony in S. Exec. Rep. No. 108–10, note 92; S. Treaty Doc. 103–39, note 92.

[98] *E.g.*, *Bottom-of-the-Sea Treaty*, Wall St. J., Mar. 29, 2004, p. A18 (opposing advice and consent); Sen. Richard G. Lugar, Chair, U.S. Senate Foreign Relations Comm., letter to the Editor, *Don't Cut the Hawsers on Law of Sea Treaty*, *id.*, Apr. 1, 2004, p. A15 (failure of U.S. interests if no ratification); Rhonda McMillion, *Troubled Waters*, 90 A.B.A.J. 62 (June 2004) (Am. B. Ass'n UNCLOS support); *Rescuing the Law of the Sea*, N.Y. Times, Aug. 22, 2004, p. WK8 (advocating advice and consent). In 2007 the same debate arose, although opposition may have weakened. *E.g.*, Vern Clark & Thomas R. Pickering, *A Treaty that Lifts All Boats*, N.Y. Times, July 14, 2007, p. A25; George V. Galdorisi, *Treaty at a Crossroads*, Nav. Instit. Proc. 51 (July 2007); Neil King, Jr., *U.S. Resistance to Sea Treaty Thaws*, Wall St. J., Aug. 22, 2007, p. A6; *Lost at Sea*, Wall St. J., June 2, 2007, p. A10; *Minority Views*, in S. Exec. Rep. 110–9, note 90, p. 24; Horace B. Robertson, Jr., *Law of the Sea Guarantees U.S. Rights*, *id.*, June 16,;

Senate approves the treaty and its protocol, the President had been expected to exchange ratifications, after which it would be in force for the United States. The President may choose not to exchange ratifications.[99] If the President exchanges ratifications, UNCLOS will supersede the four 1958 LOS Conventions[100] upon which the United States has relied for nearly a half century along with customary rules,[101] for the United States and its UNCLOS treaty partners.[102]

2007, p. A7 Howard S. Schiffman, *Letter to the Editor*, N.Y. Times, July 17, 2007, p. A20; F.L. Wiswall, *UNCLOS — It's Time for Uncle to Get Onboard,* 5 Benedict's Marit. Bull. 82 (No. 2, 2007).

[99] Nothing requires a President to exchange ratifications after Senate advice and consent.

[100] UNCLOS art. 311(1). Unlike *id.*, the 1958 LOS Conventions allow reservations to some or all of their terms. Fishing Convention art. 19 (states may make reservations at signature, ratification or accession; reservations to *id.* arts. 6–7, 9–12 barred); High Seas Convention (no reservation exclusions); Shelf Convention art. 12 (states may make reservations at signature, ratification or accession; reservations to *id.* arts. 1–3 barred); Territorial Sea Convention (no reservation exclusions). They are still in force for states not UNCLOS parties and are subject to reservations, declarations and statements in accordance with their terms. *See generally* Multilateral Treaties ch. 21, pts. 1–4 (reservations, understandings, objections to reservations for 1958 LOS Conventions); TIF 364, 395–96. Although some States and commentators argue that reservations to these Conventions are impermissible, International Law Commission Draft Guideline 3.1 declares that States may reserve to a treaty unless the agreement prohibits them, the treaty provides for only specified reservations, or the reservation is incompatible with the treaty's object and purpose. 2005 ILC Rep., note 65, 145–46; Lowe, *The Commander's*, note 43, 121; Pellet, note 91, 5–9; *see also* Vienna Convention art. 56; note 43.

[101] Since 1983 the United States has recognized UNCLOS's navigational articles as reflecting customary law. President Reagan, *United States Oceans Policy*, note 60. Commentators have agreed with the U.S. view. Restatement (Third) Part V, *Introductory Note* pp. 3–5; NWP 1-14M Annotated ¶ 1.1; John Norton Moore, *Introduction*, 1 Commentary xxvii; Oxman, *International Law*, note 60, p. 29; *but see* Churchill & Lowe 24; 1 O'Connell 48–49, researched through 1978, which may reflect thinking during UNCLOS's early drafting years. Walker, The Tanker 306 n.3.

[102] UNCLOS art. 311(1). This is consonant with Vienna Convention art. 59(1)(a). *See also* Aust 173–74, 181–83, 235–36; Brownlie 621; 1966 ILC Rep., note 38, 252–53; Jennings & Watts § 648; McNair ch. 31; Restatement (Third) § 332; Sinclair 184; 5 Commentary ¶¶ 311.1–311.5, 311.11. Although Aust 290; Multilateral Treaties ch. 21, pt. 1 n.8 (Statement of United Kingdom regarding Senegal's denunciation of Territorial Sea Convention) and Lowe, *The Commander's,* note 43, 121 report some States' views that the 1958 LOS Conventions cannot be terminated because they lack denunciation clauses, this is largely moot. Most 1958 treaty parties are UNCLOS and 1994 Agreement parties; the United States is a major exception. Many, including the United States, are provisional parties under the 1994 Agreement. *Compare* Multilateral Treaties ch. 21, pts. 1–4, 6 (Afghanistan, Cambodia, Central African Republic, Dominican Republic, Israel, Malawi, Swaziland, Switzerland, Thailand, United States parties to one or more 1958 LOS Conventions but not UNCLOS parties). Commentators differ on the effect of lack of a denunciation clause. Vienna Convention art. 56 does not allow denunciation unless it is established the parties intended that possibility, or

Debates over U.S. ratification and the law of treaties related to understandings and the like apart, a separate issue that the LOS Committee project raises is the relationship between commentator-developed definitions and States' declarations, understandings or statements, commonly referred to as interpretative (or interpretive) statements to UNCLOS. In practice understandings and declarations, allowed by UNCLOS Article 309, are frequently very difficult to distinguish from reservations or any declaration purporting to modify or exclude the legal effect of provisions of the Convention. UNCLOS Article 310 forbids the latter.[103]

The same principles governing definitions for terms in UNCLOS should apply for definitions in reservations to UNCLOS; these will not be repeated in Part III.C.[104]

UNCLOS does not allow reservations, statements or declarations to change Convention rules, unless UNCLOS permits them.[105] (For treaties allowing them, reservations become part of the law of the treaty as much as the primary document, subject to law of treaty rules on multilateral conventions.[106]) The same rules relating to treaty primacy,

---

denunciation may be implied by a treaty's nature, with 12 months notice required in either case. *See also* Aust 289–92; Brownlie 621; Jennings & Watts § 647; McNair ch. 32; Restatement (Third) § 332; Sinclair 186–88. UNCLOS art. 317 allows denunciation with a year's notice; an international organization cannot denounce it if an organization member is a party. *Id.*, Annex 9, art. 8(c); *see also* 5 Commentary ¶¶ 317.1-317.9, A.IX.11. The 1958 LOS Conventions remain in force for States parties to them that are not UNCLOS parties.

[103] *E.g.*, in the March-April 2001 China-U.S. aerial incident, China used its declaration, reciting the right to exclude other States from its EEZ, to support its case. UNCLOS art. 58(1) preserves all States' right to overflight as a freedom of the high seas under *id.* art. 87. Under *id.* art. 310 States' parties to the Convention cannot employ a declaration, however phrased or named, to exclude or modify UNCLOS provisions' legal effect. Howard S. Schiffman, Marine Conservation Agreements: The Law and Policy of Reservations and Vetoes 38–39 (2007); *see also* 5 Commentary ¶¶ 310.1-310.6. In 2001 the United States was not party to UNCLOS; China was as of 1996 but had filed a declaration asserting sovereign rights over its 200-mile EEZ. Multilateral Treaties ch. 21, pt. 6. A similar controversy erupted in 2009; China tried to exclude USNS Impeccable, a U.S. Military Sealift Command ocean survey vessel, a U.S. noncombatant, civilian-crewed ship in noncommercial service, from its EEZ. Both States filed protests. Cam Simpson, *U.S. Says China Harassed Naval Ship*, Wall St. J., Mar. 10, 2009, p. A9; Ian Johnson, *China Says U.S. Violated Maritime Law in Incident*, *id.*, Mar. 11, 2009, p. A8. The U.S. President told China's Foreign Minister that the countries needed to raise "the level and frequency" of military dialogue "to avoid future incidents" like the confrontation. Peter Baker, *China: Obama Urges Military Dialogue*, N.Y. Times, Mar. 13, 2009, p. 9.

[104] *See* Part III.B.

[105] UNCLOS arts. 309–10; *see also* notes 94–95 and accompanying text.

[106] Vienna Convention arts. 1(d), 19–23; *see also* notes 94–99 and accompanying text.

practice under treaties and developing custom should apply to reservations, statements or declarations, collectively known as interpretative or interpretive statements, to treaties;[107] definitions related to them can rise no higher than definitions related to treaty language.

Understandings, statements or declarations not amounting to reservations, collectively known as interpretative or interpretive statements, should be on similar footing. For treaties permitting them, they become part of the law of the treaty as much as the primary document and should be subject to analogous rules to those for reservations.[108] Therefore, the same rules relating to treaty primacy, practice under treaties, and custom and general principles should apply to properly appended understandings, statements or declarations.[109] Definitions so related to the latter can rise no higher than definitions related to treaty language. An example might be the definition of "serious" act of pollution in the U.S. understandings and the ABILA LOS Committee definition in this project.[110]

A problem that may arise is that no source — a Security Council decision, other UN or other international organizations' resolutions, a jus cogens norm, a primary source, a reservation if permitted by a treaty, an understanding, declaration or statement if permitted by a treaty, or secondary sources — may offer guidance. It is here that the quality of the Committee analysis is critical. Hopefully, the Committee research and comment process has produced definitions to fill these kinds of voids[111] as well as adding context to situations where there are definitions available in other, perhaps senior, sources.

---

[107] *See* notes 94–95 and accompanying text.

[108] George K. Walker, *Professionals' Definitions and States' Interpretive Declarations (Understandings, Statements or Declarations) for the 1982 Law of the Sea Convention*, 21 Emory Int'l L. Rev. 461 (2007), analyzes these issues in greater depth; *see also* notes 94–95 and accompanying text.

[109] *See* notes 94–95 and accompanying text.

[110] *Compare Text*, note 94 § 3, ¶ (11), *with* Part IV.B § 161, "serious act of pollution."

[111] *See* Part III.A.

D. INTERPRETING THE 1982 LAW OF THE SEA CONVENTION AND DEFINING ITS TERMS

John E. Noyes[112]

Professor George Walker and the ABILA Law of the Sea Committee deserve many thanks for tackling the important and difficult project of defining terms in UNCLOS. The project has generated considerable discussion, even in its draft stages, and should become a standard reference.

My comments first reflect on what it means to interpret treaties and define treaty terms. These general observations set the scene for an analysis of several particular definitions of law of the sea terms, some concerning physical objects and some concerning juridical concepts.

1. Treaty Interpretation and Definitions of Treaty Terms

Why define terms in UNCLOS? The goal of the ABILA law of the sea definitions project was not to propose amendments or formal modifications to the Convention.[113] The proposed definitions were not put forward in connection with an effort to negotiate a new law of the sea treaty. Any effort to reopen issues in UNCLOS could not realistically be limited to "definitions" or "clarifications," and there appears to be no enthusiasm for a Fourth UN Conference on the Law of the Sea. This project most profitably can *interpret* some of the undefined terms in the Convention, seek to ascertain commonly held understandings concerning those terms, and then propose definitions that reflect those shared understandings. The definitions and their accompanying commentary may well be useful to decision makers or scholars who use UNCLOS. At the core of the endeavor is the question of how to interpret (or read) treaty texts.[114]

[112] Part III.D is a consolidated and revised version of Noyes, *Treaty* 367, 2001–02 ABILA Proc. 175, and Noyes, *Definitions* 310–23; *compare* 2009–10 ABILA Proc. 219–56.

[113] *See* UNCLOS arts. 312–14; Part III.A.

[114] The literature about interpretation is vast. For discussion of interpretation in general, *see*, e.g., Guora Binder & Robert Weisberg, Literary Criticisms of Law (2000). For discussion of standard approaches to treaty interpretation, *see*, e.g., Sinclair 114–59.

It is appropriate to consider what a text "means," or what underlying reality words describe, from the perspectives of both a present-day interpreter and the drafter of the text. The meaning of a text cannot be determined exclusively by appeal to the intended meaning of its author. Any interpreter of a treaty (or any other text) brings his or her own world view — his or her own sense of the relative importance of competing values, his or her own sense of the background framework of law and legal process — to the task of interpretation. Any treaty interpreter will also usually have in mind concrete legal problems, because he or she must either argue or decide that certain behavior is or is not legal. These problems are not always within the purview of the author, and they therefore "color" what the text means beyond what the author intended. Even when definitions are discussed in the abstract, today's readers inevitably have in mind certain current or potential applications and disputes. The definitions are significant because of the situations in which they may be applied.

Saying that someone who is interpreting a treaty today necessarily brings his or her own understandings and views to the task of interpretation does not mean, however, that the views of the drafters of a treaty are entitled to no weight. Indeed, a reader/interpreter typically finds it desirable to try to determine the understandings of the drafters *as expressed in the treaty text*. Many treaty interpreters find this rather conservative interpretive focus to be valuable. Someone interpreting a treaty today usually values respecting a past political bargain that can provide a relatively stable framework for the future. The reader therefore chooses to give considerable weight to the drafters' carefully negotiated compromises as expressed in the treaty text. These compromises were designed to resolve — or at least frame — certain controversies and to provide guidance for the future. In general, the act of treaty interpretation is a search for a common understanding between the treaty interpreter and the treaty drafters. If the treaty text is being applied to some unanticipated problem or to some problem about which the drafters had no precise intention, attention to the text may at least help insure a reading that is not inconsistent with the drafters' general goals. The focal point of this search for a common understanding is therefore the treaty text. "Fidelity to the text" signals that the compromises and views of the authors will not be disregarded.

But the words in a treaty text alone can never solve all interpretive disputes. The "ordinary meaning" of words is at some level inevitably (if not usefully) vague. There will be disputes about "what words mean" in concrete situations — disputes about whether the words refer to one thing or conception, or another. The disputes may be particularly sharp when words or phrases are not defined. It is important to emphasize the word "may" in the preceding sentence, for definitions cannot completely cure indeterminacy. Furthermore, the meaning of some undefined terms may be relatively more determinate than some defined terms. Concerns about the indeterminacy of words may also be particularly prominent when the treaty negotiators, because of their inability to agree on more determinate formulations, purposefully chose ambiguous phrases.

Treaty interpreters, faced with words whose meanings are in dispute, typically seek other evidence of what the words mean. They may seek direct evidence of drafters' intent. For four reasons, however, it is particularly difficult to determine drafters' intent in the case of UNCLOS, which was negotiated at the Third UN Conference on the Law of the Sea (UNCLOS III).[115] First, we have the familiar difficulty — some would say impossibility — of trying to determine the "intent" of a collegium.[116]

Second, particular words or phrases in UNCLOS had different origins. The same word or phrase may have emerged from more than one of the three main Committees at UNCLOS III, or may have emerged from the Drafting Committee as a result of its efforts to reconcile slightly different verbal formulations.[117] It is not always clear that each Committee had in mind the same meaning of a term or phrase. Furthermore, some phrases, such as "genuine link," had their origins in the work of the International Law Commission leading up to the 1958 LOS Conventions.[118] In short, more than one collective entity may have contributed words or phrases to UNCLOS.

---

[115] For discussion of the negotiating process at UNCLOS III, see Edward L. Miles, Global Ocean Politics: The Decision Process at the Third United Nations Conference on the Law of the Sea, 1973–1982 (1986). For thoughtful analysis of interpretive issues involving UNCLOS, *see* James Harrison, *Judicial Law-Making and the Developing Order of the Oceans*, 22 Int'l J. Marine & Coastal L. 283(2007).

[116] *See, e.g.*, Max Radin, *Statutory Interpretation*, 43 Harv. L. Rev. 863, 870–71 (1930).

[117] *E.g.*, the phrase "other rules of international law," defined in Part IV.B § 132, is used in UNCLOS articles that emerged from different Committees at UNCLOS III.

[118] *See, e.g.*, *Report of the International Law Commission to the General Assembly*, UN Doc. A/3159, *reprinted in* [1956] 2 Y.B. Int'l L. Comm'n 253, 278–79, UN Doc. A/CN.4/SER.A/1956/Add. 1. Part IV.B § 72 defines "genuine link."

Third, some of the sources we traditionally use to try to determine the intent of treaty drafters are lacking. There are no detailed written records of the proceedings or collective views of the three main Committees at UNCLOS III. Many UNCLOS III negotiations were informal, including intersessional meetings, and the details of most informal negotiations were not preserved in writing. In addition, the formal statements of delegates from many different countries often reflected general political stances and did not purport to define words or phrases.[119]

Fourth, some words and phrases in UNCLOS were in fact intentionally left ambiguous.[120] They were formulated to paper over differences in views, in order not to have the whole complex negotiating process founder. UNCLOS III delegates doubtless thought that some of the papered-over differences would be resolved later, through subsequent international agreements, state practice or judicial decisions. With respect to these purposefully vague phrases, it would be particularly hard to find the drafters' intended substantive meaning. In sum, although some valuable resources provide insights into the drafters' intent at UNCLOS III,[121] there are problems in pinning down this intent. These problems include the difficulty in ascertaining the intent of a collective, the origins of words or phrases with different Committees or groups, the lack of a detailed written negotiating record, and the fact that some formulations in UNCLOS were purposefully left ambiguous.

What should we do, then, in our search for some common understanding among authors and readers, among treaty drafters and treaty interpreters? When the text is ambiguous, interpreters traditionally consider a treaty's "context," an approach that is deferential to treaty makers. Article 31 of the Vienna Convention, which embodies the most commonly invoked approach to treaty interpretation, says that a treaty should be construed "in accordance with the ordinary meaning to be given to the terms of the treaty in their context and in the light of its object and purpose."[122] The reference to "object and

---

[119] 1–6 Commentary contain much of the relevant background that was preserved.

[120] *See, e.g.*, Erik Franckx, *Coastal State Jurisdiction with Respect to Marine Pollution — Some Recent Developments and Future Challenges*, 10 Int'l J. Marine & Coastal L. 253, 254 (1995) (discussing the requirement in UNCLOS arts. 74[1] and 83[1] that maritime boundaries be delimited "to achieve an equitable solution").

[121] *See, e.g.*, 1–6 Commentary.

[122] International courts and tribunals consider Vienna Convention Articles 31–33 on treaty interpretation to reflect customary international law. *See* Responsibilities &

purpose" here is linked to the treaty text and preamble,[123] and does not invite the sort of teleological interpretation, the resort to fundamental values, that could lead an interpreter to disregard the terms of a treaty.[124] Overall, the context includes: the text of the treaty; the treaty preamble and annexes; any agreement relating to the treaty "made between all the parties in connexion with the conclusion of the treaty;"[125] and any instrument made by parties "in connexion with the conclusion of the treaty and accepted by the other parties as an instrument related to the treaty."[126]

The Vienna Convention also authorizes recourse to other sources that we might colloquially label "context," although the Convention confines its definition of "context" to the sources just noted. In particular, the Convention provides in Article 31(3):

> There shall be taken into account, together with the context:
> (a) any subsequent agreement between the parties regarding the interpretation of the treaty or the application of its provisions;
> (b) any subsequent practice in the application of the treaty which establishes the agreement of the parties regarding its interpretation;
> (c) any relevant rules of international law applicable in the relations between the parties.

We thus have, in our search for common understanding, a list of materials to consult: treaty text; treaty preamble; treaty annexes; agreements relating to the treaty that are made in connection with its conclusion; instruments accepted by other parties that are made in connection with the conclusion of a treaty and that are related to it; subsequent agreements regarding interpretation or application of the treaty; subsequent practice, at least if it "establishes the agreement of the parties regarding" interpretation of the treaty; and other relevant rules of international law. In addition, Vienna Convention Article 32 authorizes recourse to "supplementary means of

---

Obligations of States Sponsoring Persons & Entities with Respect to Activities in the Area (adv. op.) ¶¶ 57–58 (ITLOS Seabed Disputes Chamber, 2011), *available at* http://www.itlos.org/start2_en.html.

123 Sinclair 118, 130–38.

124 *See* Myres S. McDougal et al., The Interpretation of Agreements and World Public Order: Principles of Content and Procedure 42 (1967); Gerald Fitzmaurice, Vae Victis *or Woe to the Negotiators! Your Treaty or Our Interpretation of It?*, 65 AJIL 358 (1971).

125 Vienna Convention art. 31(2)(a).

126 *Id.* art. 31(2)(b).

interpretation, including the preparatory work of the treaty and the circumstances of its conclusion."[127]

An interpreter, a decision maker faced with a particular dispute, must exercise judgment. Deciding what method of treaty interpretation to use is a threshold matter of discretion or judgment. If a treaty interpreter follows the approach of the Vienna Convention, judgment is still needed, in order to apply the words of a treaty in their context (as defined in the Convention) and in light of the other items that the Convention suggests should be taken into account. Judgment is required to apply these materials in light of a current set of facts or a current dispute. Particularly when treaty terms are applied to novel historical circumstances, treaty interpretation necessarily becomes a somewhat fluid process. When the words of a legal text are brought to bear on some new problem, the scope of application of those words and thus their "meaning" expand in compass. Meaning is historically contextual, influenced not just by the past, but by the present as well.

These reflections on treaty interpretation suggest four points about the project of defining treaty terms. First, to define, by definition, means to limit or set boundaries.[128] A definition of a word limits its possible meanings. The core issue is whether and when it is appropriate to try to narrow the range of possible meanings.

Second, a definition should conform to the term being defined. A definition's degree of conformity depends on how closely it reflects a generally shared interpretation of the defined term. If a definition does reflect a widely shared interpretation, it will gain wide acceptance. When various treaty interpreters follow the same interpretive methodology, they increase the chances that they will reach a common understanding of the "meaning" of terms and phrases in a text. A commonly used method of treaty interpretation, such as that in the Vienna Convention, may reveal an understanding of a term common to drafters and present interpreters. And if the definition truly conforms to and reflects that shared understanding, it will be generally well-regarded and perhaps can help clarify and stabilize meaning for future interpreters. If, however, a definition of a treaty term does not reflect a

[127] Recourse to *travaux préparatoires* is limited, however, to confirming "the meaning resulting from the application of article 31," or to "determining the meaning when interpretation according to article 31: (a) leaves the meaning ambiguous or obscure, or (b) leads to a result which is manifestly absurd or unreasonable." *Id.* art. 32.

[128] 1 The Compact Edition of the Oxford English Dictionary 672 (1971).

shared, common understanding, then it may appear to be a politicized effort to confine, limit or distort the treaty text.

Third, no definition can "pin down" meaning perfectly or exactly. As noted above, meaning is, inevitably, historically contextual. Our understanding of the meaning of words, defined or not, will continue to be shaped by new problems and new events. That fact suggests that we should have a healthy skepticism about the prospects for clarifying and stabilizing the meaning of treaty terms through definitions.

Fourth, a discussion about what particular words mean can lead to important knowledge about a situation to which the words apply and about our reactions to that situation. Considering the question, "What should we say here?," may tell us a lot about the complexities of a situation, revealing points of agreement and disagreement concerning the concept or thing to which the words refer. When we consider that question, we are not just, or perhaps not at all, concerned to know about words themselves. We are concerned about the phenomena at issue, about the broader political and legal realities and controversies to which the words relate. Disagreements about the "meaning of words" may in essence be disagreements over substance that will not disappear just by collecting data concerning drafters' intent or the context of a treaty. The discussion about definitions may lead to valuable ideas about why various observers disagree and about what, if anything, should be done about the disagreements. Indeed, one significant value of the ABILA law of the sea definitions project is that it can sharpen our perception of some fundamental controversies.

2. Definitions in the Law of the Sea Convention

Let me comment specifically about some of the words and phrases defined in the ABILA LOS Committee definitions. Each of these words and phrases — "mile," various words used in connection with UNCLOS Article 76 and the continental shelf, "ship" or "vessel," "other rules of international law," and "genuine link" — deserves comment because they raise different conceptual problems.[129] The discussion of these

[129] Professor Noyes's analysis and criticism of "genuine link," "mile" or "nautical mile" and "other rules of international law," Noyes, *Treaty* 372–83, 2001–02 ABILA Proc. 181–93, resulted in modified definitions for "genuine link" and "other rules of international law," after further critique in Noyes, *Definitions* 310–24. For the result for

terms reveals in specific contexts some of the challenges associated with any definitions project.

a. *"Mile"*

The term "mile" refers to some physical reality, rather than to a purely juristic or political reality. The need for a precise definition is important, because so many of UNCLOS's rules relate to different zones, which are determined according to their distance in miles from the baseline. The ABILA project does define "mile" precisely, as "the international nautical mile, *i.e.,* 1852 meters or 6076.115 feet, corresponding to 60 nautical miles per degree of latitude."[130]

Is this definition of "mile" appropriate? That a "mile" should be conceived of as a nautical mile rather than a geographic mile creates no controversy. The community of maritime and international lawyers, oceans policy makers, and users of the seas have long shared the view that a mile on the ocean is a nautical mile. The number of suggested possible meanings of "nautical" mile is relatively small, and it makes no political difference, *ex ante*, which definition is chosen. It is not important whether we agree on 1850 meters or 1852 meters or 1853.248 meters.[131] It is important, however, given what Professor Walker calls "Murphy's Law of Measurements,"[132] that we agree on one definition. It is also important that the definition be set in terms of a fixed distance, rather than in terms of an arc of one minute of latitude, a measurement that will vary depending on the particular latitude.[133]

There is considerable support for the use of 1852 meters as the relevant distance. The negotiators at UNCLOS III apparently understood that 1852 meters was the length of the nautical mile,[134] and subsequent practice has reinforced the use of 1852 meters.[135] The ABILA definition

---

these three terms, *see* Part IV.B § 72, "genuine link;" § 105, "mile" or "nautical mile;" § 132, "other rules of international law."

[130] *See* Part IV.B, § 90, "latitude;" § 105, "mile" or "nautical mile."

[131] *See also* Bruce E. Alexander, *The Territorial Sea of the United States: Is It Twelve Miles or Not?*, 20 J. Mar. L. & Com. 449, 450 n. 10 (1989) (noting definitions of "nautical mile") besides those discussed in Part IV.B § 105, "mile" or "nautical mile."

[132] *See* Part IV.B § 105, "mile" or "nautical mile."

[133] *See* Commission on the Limits of the Continental Shelf, *Scientific and Technical Guidelines of the Commission on the Limits of the Continental Shelf*, CLCS/11, ¶ 3.2.2 and Fig. 1 (1999), *available at* http://www.un.org/Depts/lostemplclcs/docs/clcs/CLCS_11.htm (*CLCS Guidelines*).

[134] 2 Commentary ¶ 1.27.

[135] *E.g., CLCS Guidelines*, note 133, ¶ 3.2.1.

of "mile" is appropriate, although the last phrase ("corresponding to 60 nautical miles per degree of latitude") may be unnecessary. Even with this precise formulation, however, disputes may still arise in applying the 1852-meter definition, because the Earth is an ellipsoid rather than a perfect sphere and because it is possible to use different coordinate systems in marking locations.[136]

b. *Definitions Relating to the Continental Shelf*

The ABILA LOS Committee definitions include 26 terms appearing in UNCLOS Article 76, which defines the continental shelf. These are: adjacent coasts, bank, basepoint or point, cap, chart, continental rise, continental slope, deep ocean floor, due publicity, foot of the continental slope, geodetic data, isobath, latitude, line of delimitation, longitude, oceanic ridge, opposite coasts, outer limit, rock, seabed, sedimentary rock, shelf, spur, straight line, submarine ridge and subsoil.[137] Many of these terms refer to physical phenomena, but the meaning of some of them appears less "solid" than the meaning of "mile," discussed above. Indeed, the meaning of some of these terms could change with evolving scientific knowledge.

Determining the outer limits of the continental shelf beyond 200 miles from baselines presents particularly difficult challenges. This issue has been the subject of work in the Commission on Legal Issues of the Limits of the Continental Shelf (CLCS)[138] and in the ILA Committee on the Outer Limits of the Continental Shelf.[139] The work of these organizations and other expert bodies — the International Hydrographic Organization, on whose studies Professor Walker has relied, and other expert organizations (the Association for Geographic Information and the American Geological Institute)[140] — could lead to a consistent understanding of the concepts being defined.

---

[136] *See* Part IV.B § 105, "mile" or "nautical mile;" Alan Dodson & Terry Moore, *Geodetic Techniques*, in Cook & Carleton, note 20, 87.

[137] Walker, *Consolidated Glossary* 295; *see also* Part IV.B §§ 2, 15, 16, 22, 23, 37, 38, 47, 54, 67, 74, 87, 90, 94, 97, 128, 130, 133, 147, 156, 160, 162, 173, 176, 182, 184.

[138] *See* UNCLOS art. 76(8) & *id.* Annex II.

[139] *See* Committee on Legal Issues of the Outer Continental Shelf, *Second Report*, in International Law Association, Report of the Seventy-Second Conference, Toronto 215 (2006) (*Second Report*); *id.*, *Report*, in International Law Association, Report of the Seventy-First Conference, Berlin 773 (2004).

[140] *Annex I* of Cook & Carleton, note 20, consolidates the Association and Institute definitions.

However, the meaning of some terms, such as "oceanic ridge" and "submarine elevation," could change in light of changing scientific knowledge. Judge Dolliver Nelson, who chaired the ILA Committee on the Outer Limits of the Continental Shelf, has argued that the CLCS should "take the evolution of these scientific and technical terms into account," and that the concepts "were *not intended* to be static but by their very nature evolutionary."[141] While the concept of "mile" discussed in Part III.D.2.a appears quite settled, the same may not be true of other terms describing some geographic realities. A broadly worded definition, such as that of "oceanic ridge," which the ABILA LOS Committee defines as "a long elevation of the ocean floor ...,"[142] might encompass a range of new scientific understandings.

Determining the meaning some terms related to the continental shelf may well be politically sensitive. For example, there are likely to be disputes over just what does and does not constitute an "oceanic ridge." The term is important, since under UNCLOS Article 76(3) "the deep ocean floor with its oceanic ridges" cannot be considered part of the continental margin. The CLCS has compiled a nonexhaustive list of eight different kinds of ridges derived from different geologic processes.[143] Instead of defining just which of these ridges were "oceanic ridges," the CLCS concluded that "the issue of ridges" should be "examined on a case-by-case basis."[144] In some areas, geologic formations that may literally conform to the ABILA LOS Committee definition of an oceanic ridge could include rocks intruding into a continental margin along a fault line. Should these intrusive rocks still be considered part of the oceanic ridge and thus excluded from the continental margin? In other areas, formations that may satisfy the LOS Committee's proposed definition have islands on them. Concluding that an island is located on an "oceanic ridge," rather than on some other type of submarine elevation, could have important implications. UNCLOS Article 121(3) provides that islands capable of sustaining human habitation or economic life shall have their own continental shelf. If an island is located on an "oceanic ridge," however, Article 76(3), read in conjunction with Article 76(1), appears to limit the island's continental shelf to

---

[141] L.D.M. Nelson, *The Continental Shelf: Interplay of Law and Science*, in 2 Liber Amicorum Judge Shigeru Oda 1235, 1243 (Nisuke Ando et al. eds. 2002).

[142] *See* Part IV.B § 128, "oceanic ridge."

[143] *CLCS Guidelines*, note 133, ¶ 7.2.1.

[144] *Id.* ¶ 7.2.11.

200 nautical miles.[145] Should the geologic formation on which islands sit be deemed an "oceanic ridge"? Would that conclusion sufficiently acknowledge Article 76(1)'s emphasis on the continental shelf as the "natural prolongation" of land territory? It is not clear that the ABILA LOS Committee definition of "oceanic ridge" will help resolve the questions noted above. Adopting geologic or geomorphologic definitions as legal definitions can be a sensitive matter, particularly with respect to definitions relating to the continental shelf.

c. *"Ship" or "Vessel"*

A "ship" or "vessel" is a concrete physical object, but that does not mean we can satisfactorily define it. Here, the difficulty is that the legal contexts in which the word "ship" is used vary so significantly that it may be inappropriate to specify one definition.

Drafters and decision makers have struggled with the problem of defining "ship" in national and international law. In a British case involving insurance policy coverage, the lower court had found that a crane floating on pontoons was not a "ship" or "vessel." On appeal Lord Justice Scrutton was troubled by the lack of a definition of those terms:

> One might possibly take the position of the gentleman who dealt with the elephant by saying he could not define an elephant, but he knew what it was when he saw one, and it may be that is the foundation of the learned Judge's judgment [in the court below], that he cannot define "ship or vessel" but he knows this thing is not a ship or vessel. I should have liked to be able to give a definition here, because ... it is rather a pity that the Courts are not able to give a definition of the words which are constantly turning up in a mercantile transaction. But the discussion today ... of the various incidents and various kinds of things to which the words "ships or vessels" [have] been applied, has convinced me that it is of no use at present to try to define it, and the only thing I can do in this case is to treat it as a question of fact and to say that I am not satisfied that the learned Judge was wrong.[146]

---

[145] Philip A. Symonds et al., *Ridge Issues*, in Cook & Carleton, note 20, p. 285 analyzes many difficult issues relating to ridges. *See also* Harald Brekke & Philip A. Symonds, *The Ridge Provisions of Article 76 of the UN Convention on the Law of the Sea*, in Legal and Scientific Aspects of Continental Shelf Limits 169 (Myron H. Nordquist et al. eds. 2004); Ron Macnab, *Submarine Elevations and Ridges: Wild Cards in the Poker Game of UNCLOS Article 76*, 39 Ocean Dev. & Int'l L. 223 (2008); Robert W. Smith & George Taft, *Legal Aspects of the Continental Shelf*, in Cook & Carleton, p. 17.

[146] Merchants Marine Ins. Co. v. North of England Protecting & Indem. Ass'n, 26 Lloyd's List L. Rep. 201, 203 (Ct. App. 1926) (Scrutton, J.).

We assuredly can say more about the concept of "ship" or "vessel" than "I know one when I see one," but it does not necessarily follow that an all-encompassing definition is essential to that end. The ABILA LOS Committee initially proposed the following definition for UNCLOS:

> "Ship" [and] "vessel" have the same, interchangeable meaning in the English language version of the 1982 LOS Convention. "Ship" is defined as a vessel of any type whatsoever operating in the marine environment, including hydrofoil boats, air-cushion vehicles, submersibles, floating craft and floating platforms. Where, *e.g.*, "ship" or "vessel" is modified by other words, or prefixes or suffixes, as in the Article 29 definition of a warship, those particular definitions apply.[147]

I fear that this definition, or any one definition proposed for use in UNCLOS, may be either too broad or too narrow, depending on the context in which it is used. Interpretation of "ship" may well vary from issue to issue, and when we seek a definition that applies to as wide a range of situations and issues as does UNCLOS, it becomes particularly difficult to agree on an acceptable definition.

Before I explore my concerns with the proposed definition, let me note that there is much in the definition with which I agree. First, I agree that particular subcategories of ships may need to be addressed separately. This is certainly true of warships, the subject of UNCLOS Article 29. My comments do not address warships.

Second, I agree that "ship" is a general term, referring to a variety of different craft. There was a time in the age of sail when "ship" may have had a relatively specific and determinant meaning. A "ship" was "a vessel with three or more masts and fully square-rigged throughout."[148] A "ship" was thus distinguishable from smaller craft; a "ship" was not a brig, a schooner, or a cutter. Today, however, the connotation of "ship" is not so specific.

Third, I agree that the terms "ship" and "vessel" should be equated. As has been noted,[149] the terms were viewed as identical at UNCLOS III. Use of different terms in the UNCLOS English language version came about because two different committees at the Conference worked on different articles; one committee used "ship" in its articles, and the other used "vessel."[150] This point suggests the need for a technical

---

147 Walker, *Defining* 366, 2001–02 ABILA Proc. 174; Walker, *Definitions* 218.

148 David Cordingly, Under the Black Flag 277 (1995) (also noting, however, that "ship" sometimes was used to refer to broader categories of craft).

149 Walker, *Defining* 366, 2001–02 ABILA Proc. 174; Walker, *Definitions* 217.

150 2 Commentary ¶ 1.28.

change in the proposed definition. The word "vessel" in the second sentence should be changed, because if "ship" and "vessel" are synonyms, then the sentence in effect reads, "Vessel is defined as a vessel ..." It would be better to substitute a phrase like " 'Ship' or 'vessel' is defined as a device capable of traversing the sea ...."

The critical issue, though, is whether we can arrive at any sensible definition capturing all the various types of craft and all the different purposes for which we have international legal rules related to ships. With respect to types of craft, the concern with whether a definition is suitable is likely to occur at the margins. All will agree that an oil tanker, navigating the high seas under its own power and exposed to maritime risks, is a "ship" or "vessel." But, with respect to various issues, should we include as ships: floating platforms or drilling rigs (with or without engines), temporarily fixed platforms, hydrofoils, seaplanes on the water, amphibious craft, submersibles, very small boats, houseboats or docked hotels like *Queen Elizabeth I*, boats towed for repairs, abandoned craft, wrecks (capable of being raised or not), craft in drydock for repair or safekeeping, craft under construction (launched or yet to be launched)? If we all could agree on what to include or exclude as a ship or vessel in all cases, drafting challenges arise. For example, the initial proposed definition indicated a preference to exclude fixed platforms from the category of "ship."[151] Yet the proposed definition, which encompasses "a vessel of any type whatsoever operating in the maritime environment," may be ambiguous in this regard, unless the word "including" is read as a term of limitation rather than a term of illustration, *i.e.*, is read to mean "including the specified examples and excluding other examples not listed."

Although we can massage the drafting if need be, the difficult question remains: In a general convention, is it appropriate to use the same conception of "ship" for all purposes? Consider the issue of whether to exclude temporarily fixed platforms to illustrate the possibility that the definition should vary depending on the purposes for construing the term. It may be nonsense to consider fixed platforms as vessels if there is a concern with a rule like UNCLOS Article 111 on the right of hot pursuit, which contemplates a vehicle capable of self-propulsion. Yet with respect to other legal rules, *e.g.*, rules related to the duty to rescue or to serious marine pollution, the case for a restrictive definition is

---

[151] Walker, *Defining* 365–66, 2001–02 ABILA Proc. 174; Walker, *Definitions* 217.

not compelling.[152] For example, the MARPOL Convention definition of "ship" is indeed broad, including fixed platforms.[153] That seems appropriate: if important objectives could be damaged by pollution from fixed platforms, or by failing to rescue from fixed platforms, our conception of "ship" should encompass fixed platforms. One might, I suppose, leave the broader definition, which includes fixed platforms, to MARPOL and not construe the meaning of "ship" in UNCLOS so broadly. But is there any good reason to do that? I question whether the fact that UNCLOS contains articles referring to "platforms or other man-made structures at sea" and to "artificial islands, installations, and structures"[154] means that temporary fixed platforms should be excluded from the category of ships when considering the application of rules concerning the protection of life.

Even if we focus on UNCLOS and set aside concerns over the compatibility of a definition for UNCLOS with definitions in other oceans treaties, we still should conclude that different definitions of "ship" make sense in different settings. For example, UNCLOS Article 91(2) provides: "Every State shall issue to ships to which it has granted the right to fly its flag documents to that effect." The problem is that not every State — including States part of the unanimous support in 1956 in the International Law Commission (ILC) for the identically worded predecessor to Article 91(2), High Seas Convention Article 5(2)[155] — issues documents to small boats entitled to fly its flag. Rather than presume such states violate Article 91(2), it seems more sensible, as has been suggested, to construe the term "ship" in this context as not including "small yacht."[156] Compare, however, Article 91(1), providing that "every State shall fix the conditions for the grant of its nationality to ships," and that there must be "a genuine link between the State and

---

[152] *See* Laurent Lucchini, *Le Navire et Les Navires*, in Le Navire en Droit International ¶ 34 (Societe Francaise pour le Droit International ed. 1992).

[153] MARPOL 73/78 defines "ship" as "a vessel of any type whatsoever operating in the marine environment … includ[ing] hydrofoil boats, air-cushion vehicles, submersibles, floating craft and fixed or floating platforms." Protocol of 1978 Relating to International Convention for Prevention of Pollution from Ships, 1973, Feb. 17, 1978, art. 1 & Annex: Modifications & Additions to the International Convention for Prevention of Pollution from Ships, 1973, Annex I, TIAS —, 1340 UNTS 61, 63, 66 (MARPOL 78), incorporating by reference International Convention for Prevention of Pollution from Ships, Nov. 2, 1973, art. 2(4), 1340 UNTS 184, 185 (MARPOL 73).

[154] *See* references in Walker, *Defining* 366 n. 85, 2001–02 ABILA Proc. 174 n. 81; Walker, *Definitions* 217 n. 97.

[155] Herman Meyers, The Nationality of Ships 17 (1967).

[156] *Id.*

the ship." There is no reason to exclude small yachts from those Article 91(1) rules.[157] The dilemma posed by these examples is obvious; one definition cannot at the same time include and exclude small yachts.

One could even read "ship" in UNCLOS to refer, at times, to individuals. Article 94(1), setting out every State's general obligation to "effectively exercise its jurisdiction and control in administrative, technical and social matters over ships flying its flag," seemingly refers both to the craft and to its master, officers and crew. Subsequent Article 94 paragraphs reinforce this notion; they specify particular obligations that flesh out the general Article 94(1) obligation. Those particular obligations certainly apply both to the craft (*e.g.*, the flag State must maintain ship registers[158]) and to the master, officers and crew (*e.g.*, the flag State must set crew labor conditions[159]). A flag State's general Article 94(1) obligation to exercise jurisdiction "over ships flying its flag" thus appears to encompass an obligation to exercise jurisdiction with respect to those ships' masters, officers and crew.[160]

An attempt to draft a generally applicable definition of "ship" at the International Law Commission in the 1950s was not successful. The special rapporteur for the ILC in its work leading up to the 1958 LOS Conventions proposed this definition: "A ship is a device capable of traversing the sea but not the air space, with the equipment and crew appropriate to the purpose for which it is used."[161] When the definition came up for discussion, the special rapporteur said he "had doubts as to the necessity of the definition of a ship," and the ILC unanimously voted to delete the definition from its articles on the high seas in 1955.[162] An observer has suggested that the ILC discussion may have indicated that the definition was not suitable for all purposes.[163] The ILC decided it was preferable not to have a fixed definition.

---

157 *See id.* 17–18.

158 UNCLOS art. 94(2)(a).

159 *Id.* art. 94(3)(b).

160 *See* Meyers, note 155, pp. 12–13. UNCLOS art. 92(1), providing that "[s]hips ... shall be subject to" flag State exclusive jurisdiction on the high seas, is to the same effect. That rule seemingly applies to the physical ship and to the master, officers and crew. *See* Meyers, p. 11. *See also* George Lazaratos, *The Definition of Ship in National and International Law*, 1969 Revue Hellenique de Droit International et Etranger 57, 66.

161 [1955] 1 Y.B. Int'l L. Comm'n 10 n. 5, UN Doc. A/CN.4/SER.A/1955.

162 *Id.* 10. For the special rapporteur's discussion of the issue, see [1950] 2 Y.B. Int'l L. Comm'n 38, UN Doc. A/CN.4/SER.A/1950/Add.1.

163 Meyers, note 155, p. 16.

Others have studied in great detail the conception of "ship" in national and international law. They have concluded that international law lacks one general conception of "ship." Some have also concluded that one definition is undesirable, in light of various situations and rules applying to "ships." Lazaratos argued that a general definition of "ship" was desirable but noted the "unbridgeable" variety in national law definitions and found no customary international law definition.[164] He also did not specify a text for a proposed definition, although he suggested some features, such as a limitation to ocean-going vessels,[165] that he thought should characterize a "ship" in international law. Lucchini noted the impossibility of using particular treaties to discern characteristics of any common definition of "ship."[166] He suggested that academic discussion of ships, which recognized the ability to navigate, ability to float, and regular exposure to maritime risks, could help decision makers — not by providing a fixed definition, but by suggesting factors that could be examined case by case in determining what is and what is not a ship.[167] The judge in each case should also assess the purposes for which it is important to determine whether a device is a ship.[168] He concluded that the diversity of vessels and applicable rules made any effort to find one unified conception extraordinarily complex, and that a general definition of "ship" could not be inferred from practice and doctrine.[169] Meyers stressed that an object that cannot float and is not capable of traversing the sea could not be considered a ship[170] but concluded that a uniform definition suitable for all purposes was impossible:

> There may be good grounds in favour of either very broad or very narrow definitions. It all depends upon what subject-matter is at issue. It would seem quite undesirable to adopt one and the same definition as

---

[164] Lazaratos, note 160, p. 92.

[165] *Id.* In addition, in examining national laws, Lazaratos expressed concern with exposure to maritime risks, which he thought should preclude devices from being considered ships before they were launched. He also suggested that sunken wrecks should not be considered ships because they lacked ability to navigate. *See id.* 77–78.

[166] Lucchini, note 152, ¶ 35.

[167] *Id.* ¶ 42.

[168] *Id.* ¶ 43(1).

[169] "On est frappé par l'extraordinaire complexité de toute tentative visant a faire rentrer dans l'unité des navires. … Une définition générale et commune du navire n'a pa pu être dégagée, la variabilité de sa notion dans le temps and dans l'espace en étand la cause principale." *Id.* ¶ 57.

[170] Meyers, note 155, p. 23.

> obtaining for the whole of the law of the sea. ... One detailed, all-embracing concept: ship, obtaining under all circumstances, does not and cannot exist for all the purposes of international law.[171]

In short, "water-tight definitions do not exist."[172]

Because so many different rules apply to ships, because those rules may fulfill so many different purposes, and because those rules might apply to so many different types of objects, I doubt that one all-encompassing definition for UNCLOS would be satisfactory. The definitions of "ship" in national laws and in treaties addressing specific LOS issues certainly vary considerably.[173] This illustrates the difficulty in fashioning a "one size fits all" definition. It is unremarkable in the law that the same term may mean somewhat different things in different contexts. As the International Court of Justice has stated, a word "obtains its meaning from the context in which it is used. If the context requires a meaning which connotes a wide choice, it must be construed accordingly, just as it must be given a restrictive meaning if the context in which it is used so requires."[174] The ILC decision not to include a definition of "ship" in a general LOS convention was wise.

The final ABILA LOS Committee definition of "ship" or "vessel" reads:

> "Ship" or "vessel" have the same, interchangeable meaning in the UNCLOS English language version. "Ship" is defined as a human-made device, including a submersible vessel, capable of traversing the sea. Where "ship" or "vessel" is modified by other words, prefixes or suffixes in UNCLOS as in its Article 29 definition of "warship," those particular definitions apply. A narrower definition of "ship" or "vessel," otherwise unmodified, should be used if a particular rule's context or purposes indicate a narrower definition is appropriate.[175]

This revised definition is an improvement on the initial proposed definition, because it acknowledges the importance of context in construing the meaning of "ship" or "vessel."

---

[171] *Id.* 22–23. *Accord id.* 17. *See also* Tullio Treves, *Navigation*, in 2 A Handbook, note 148, pp. 835, 842 (concept of "ship" depends on a link to a State, and that concept "may take on a different hue according to the zone of the sea concerned").

[172] Meyers, note 155, p. 15.

[173] *See* the surveys in Lazaratos, note 160; Lucchini, note 152; and Meyers, note 155.

[174] Constitution of the Maritime Safety Comm. of the Inter-Governmental Maritime Consultative Org., 1960 ICJ 150, 158 (adv. op., June 8) (construing meaning of "elected").

[175] Part IV.B § 163, defining "ship" or "vessel."

d. *"Other Rules of International Law"*

The phrase "other rules of international law" of course does not concern any physical object, but refers to a purely juridical concept. The *Initial Draft* defined the phrase in terms of the law of armed conflict (LOAC): "'Other rules of international law' ... means the law of armed conflict, including the law of naval warfare and the law of maritime neutrality as components of the law of armed conflict."[176] Implicitly (and properly), the focus of the *Initial Draft* was on the word "other;" the meaning of "rules of international law" is the subject of much jurisprudential debate.

Use of the phrase "other rules of international law" in UNCLOS raises several important questions, but it is doubtful whether a definition of that phrase can or should answer all of them. Some of the questions have to do with hierarchy of sources, should UNCLOS's Articles conflict with other rules. The priority of UNCLOS rules and various other rules must be ascertained in light of UNCLOS Articles 293 and 311, UNCLOS Annex III's Article 21, and international law concepts affecting hierarchy (*e.g.*, jus cogens). The *Initial Draft* definition did not address those hierarchy questions.

The *Initial Draft* definition of "other rules of international law" did, however, implicitly respond to other important questions, having to do with *which* "other rules" might apply and whether the "other rules" formulation provides a way to take into account new, post-UNCLOS legal developments. In specifying that "other rules" means the LOAC, the *Initial Draft* definition narrowed the apparent ordinary meaning of "other." According to the ordinary meaning of "other," "other rules of international law" could simply mean "rules of international law not found in UNCLOS."

The context of a treaty may help us determine whether the apparent plain meaning of a treaty term is in fact its appropriate or intended meaning.[177] Professor Walker, examining the history of the "other

---

[176] Walker, *Defining* 363, 2001–02 ABILA Proc. 167.

[177] Sinclair 116.

> Every text, however clear on its face, requires to be scrutinised in its context and in the light of the object and purpose which it is designed to serve. The *conclusion* which may be reached after such a scrutiny is, in most instances, that the clear meaning which originally presented itself is the correct one, but this should not be used to disguise the fact that what is involved is a process of interpretation.

Id. (emphasis in original). *Accord* Aust 235.

rules" clauses in several of UNCLOS's Articles, marshaled evidence to support the argument that the "other rules clauses in the [1958 and 1982] LOS Conventions refer to the LOAC, which includes the law of naval warfare and the law of maritime neutrality."[178] It seems clear that the LOAC rules may sometimes apply. The critical question is whether "refer to the LOAC" should mean "refer *exclusively* to the LOAC." If it should not, then defining "other rules of international law" solely in terms of the LOAC would exclude other appropriate rules of international law from consideration.

The plain meaning of "other" — a meaning not defined in the LOAC — should apply when construing the phrase "other rules of international law" as used in Article 293, which is found in UNCLOS's Part XV concerning dispute settlement. Article 293(1) provides: "A court or tribunal having jurisdiction under [Part XV, § 2] shall apply this Convention and other rules of international law not incompatible with this Convention."[179] The *Initial Draft*'s restrictive definition of "other rules of international law" is inappropriate when this Article is construed in the context of Part XV. The words "not incompatible with this Convention" in Article 293 suggest that the reference to "other rules" is not to the LOAC, which might be incompatible with the Convention.[180] Article 293(1)'s negotiating history does not suggest that its "other rules" clause is limited to the LOAC.[181]

---

[178] Walker, *Defining* 363, 2001–02 ABILA Proc. 242.

[179] *Accord* UNCLOS Annex VI art. 23 (providing that the International Tribunal for the Law of the Sea (ITLOS) "shall decide all disputes and applications in accordance with article 293"). The Article 293(1) phrase "having jurisdiction under [Part XV, §2]" suggests that Article 293 does not expand the jurisdiction of a court or tribunal. That is, Article 293 should not allow a party to pursue non-LOS claims falling outside the scope of the Article 288 jurisdictional provision. *See also* UNCLOS art. 293(2) (authorizing decisions *ex aequo et bono*, "if the parties so agree"); *id.* Annex III art. 21 (referring to "other rules of international law not incompatible with this Convention").

[180] *Compare, e.g.*, UNCLOS art. 19(1).

[181] According to one reference, the phrase "other rules of international law not incompatible with this Convention" in Article 293(1) served several purposes. First, the phrase was chosen over "any other rules of law," a formulation that might have led to controversies concerning the relevance of national legal instruments in LOS disputes. Second, the phrase "other rules of international law" was chosen for its conciseness, to avoid possible theoretical debates spelling out the sources of public international law. Third, the "not incompatible with" portion emphasized "[t]he primacy of [UNCLOS] as the main rule of law applicable to disputes." Raymond Ranjeva, *Settlement of Disputes*, in 2 A Handbook on the New Law of the Sea 1333, 1376 (Rene-Jean Dupuy & Daniel Vignes eds. 1991) (A Handbook). *See id.* 1377. Ranjeva does not mention the LOAC as a consideration relevant in the development of Article 293(1). *Accord* 5 Commentary ¶¶ 293.1, 293.3.

Decisions of international tribunals and the arguments of States in several cases confirm that the "other rules" clause in Article 293(1) is not limited to the LOAC. First, an international court or tribunal must use rules of treaty interpretation in construing UNCLOS, and rules of treaty interpretation — one example of "rules of international law" — are not themselves stated in UNCLOS. In its 2011 advisory opinion in *Responsibilities and Obligations of States Sponsoring Persons and Entities with Respect to Activities in the Area*, the Seabed Disputes Chamber of ITLOS noted that Article 293(1) "set[s] out the law to be applied by the Chamber"[182] and then determined:

> Among the rules of international law that the Chamber is bound to apply, those concerning the interpretation of treaties play a particularly important role. The applicable rules are set out in ... articles 31 to 33 of the 1969 Vienna Convention on the Law of Treaties (hereinafter "the Vienna Convention"). These rules are to be considered as reflecting customary international law.
>
> ... [T]he rules of the Vienna Convention on the interpretation of treaties apply to the interpretation of provisions of the Convention and the 1994 Agreement.[183]

Second, even if we restrict our inquiry to rules of decision (*i.e.*, not rules of treaty interpretation), a nonrestrictive interpretation of the "other rules" clause in Article 293(1) appears appropriate. The 1999 ITLOS decision in the *M/V Saiga (No. 2) Case* provides an example of how the phrase "other rules of international law" has been construed. In that case the ITLOS considered, along with several issues to which UNCLOS articles expressly refer, the legality of Guinea's use of force in a peacetime seizure of a foreign flag vessel. Guinea allegedly fired on the *Saiga*, an unarmed tanker plodding along at ten knots, with automatic weapons. St. Vincent and the Grenadines, *Saiga*'s flag State, claimed this behavior constituted an excessive and unreasonable use of force during peacetime (*i.e.*, outside the LOAC context) in stopping and arresting the vessel. The Tribunal referred to "other rules of law" in addressing this claim:

> In considering the force used by Guinea in the arrest of the *Saiga*, the tribunal must take into account the circumstances of the arrest in the context of the applicable rules of international law. Although the

[182] Responsibilities & Obligations of States Sponsoring Persons & Entities with Respect to Activities in the Area (adv. op.) ¶ 51 (ITLOS Seabed Disputes Chamber 2011), *available at* http://www.itlos.org/start2_en.html.

[183] *Id.* ¶¶ 57–58.

> Convention does not contain express provisions on the use of force in the arrest of ships, *international law, which is applicable by virtue of article 293 of the Convention*, requires that the use of force must be avoided as far as possible and, where force is unavoidable, it must not go beyond what is reasonable and necessary in the circumstances.[184]

The ITLOS went on to cite international law materials, including two arbitral decisions, to support its statement of the law concerning limits on permissible use of force.[185] The Tribunal's recourse in the *Saiga Case* to rules of international law outside UNCLOS allowed one forum to decide all the relevant, law of the sea-related issues in the case. The *Saiga Case* supports the view that "other rules of international law" in Article 293(1) should be given its plain meaning and not defined — confined — just in terms of the LOAC.

Recourse to non-LOAC "other rules" has occurred and could occur in other litigation contexts. Arbitral tribunals constituted pursuant to UNCLOS Annex VII have indicated that Article 293(1) allows use of a variety of rules not found in UNCLOS.[186] The ITLOS has regularly invoked its obligation to apply non-LOAC "other rules of international law" in considering what constitutes a "reasonable bond" in applications seeking the prompt release of a vessel or its crew,[187] perhaps to emphasize that it is not reviewing the legality under municipal law of national court decisions concerning detention of vessels and crews.[188]

---

[184] *Id.* p. 196 (emphasis added).

[185] *Id.* (citing I'm Alone (Can./U.S. 1935), 3 R.I.A.A. 1609; The Red Crusader (Comm'n of Enquiry, Den-U.K. 1965), 35 I.L.R. 485. In a similar vein the ITLOS discussed the necessity defense in *Saiga*, citing International Law Commission, Draft Articles of State Responsibility, Aug. 9, 2001 and Gabcikovo-Nagymaros Project (Hun. v. Slov.), 1997 ICJ 7, 40–41 (Project Case). This discussion also illustrates the ITLOS's reliance on non-LOAC rules of law under the "other rules of international law" clause of UNCLOS art. 293. *See* 120 I.L.R. 190–92. For an argument that ITLOS's use of Article 293 to incorporate rules on use of force in *Saiga* impermissibly expanded the ITLOS's jurisdiction, *see* Harrison, note 121, pp. 300–01.

[186] *See* In re Arbitration between Barbados & Republic of Trinidad & Tobago, 139 I.L.R. 449, 493–94 (2006) (noting Barbados's invocation of the principle of intertemporality under the Article 293[1] "other rules" clause); In re Arbitration between Guyana & Suriname, *id.* 566, 682–83 (2007) (rules on use of force).

[187] *See* UNCLOS art. 192. For discussion of the "reasonable bond" requirement, *see* Erik Franckx, *"Reasonable Bond" in the Practice of the International Tribunal for the Law of the Sea*, 32 Cal. W. Int'l L.J. 303 (2002). For the definition of "ship" or "vessel," *see* Part IV.B § 163.

[188] *See* The "Monte Confurco" (Sey. v. Fr., Prompt Release, 2000), 125 I.L.R. 220, 244–45; The "Volga" (Russ. v. Austr., Prompt Release, 2002), 126 *id.* 433, 453; The "Juno Trader" (St. Vincent v. Guinea-Bissau, Prompt Release, 2004), 128 *id.* 267, 291; The "Hoshinmaru" (Japan v. Russ., Prompt Release, 2007) ¶ 95, *available at* http://www.itlos.org/start2_en.html. UNCLOS does not define "reasonable bond," thus

Courts or tribunals exercising jurisdiction pursuant to UNCLOS Article 288(2) "over any dispute concerning the interpretation or application of an international agreement related to the purposes of this Convention, which is submitted to it in accordance with the agreement,"[189] may apply non-LOAC "other rules of international law." Such international agreements incorporate by reference UNCLOS's dispute settlement provisions, including Article 293.[190]

Other UNCLOS articles also use the phrase "other rules of international law" in contexts where the phrase does not appear to refer to the LOAC. For example, Article 303(4) provides that Article 303, on underwater cultural heritage, "is without prejudice to other … rules of international law." A leading commentator found that "Article 303(4) should be interpreted … to refer to *future international agreements and rules of international law regarding the protection of archaeological objects*."[191] Another authority concluded that "[p]resumably … this incipient new branch of law will be completed by the competent international organization, above all UNESCO, and by State practice."[192] Article 303's reference to "other rules" thus seems to encompass rules not related to the LOAC — in this case, rules concerning underwater cultural heritage. Furthermore, this reference to "other rules" contemplates use of rules of international law developed after UNCLOS III.[193]

The ABILA LOS Committee and Professor Walker took account of Articles 293(1) and 303 in a revised definition of "other rules of

---

requiring ITLOS judges to give specific content under international law to the general concept of reasonableness. *See* Franckx, note 187, p. 309.

[189] UNCLOS art. 288(2). *See also id.* Annex VI art. 21 (referring to "any other agreement which confers jurisdiction" on the ITLOS. Article 288(1) provides for jurisdiction for disputes "concerning the interpretation or application of UNCLOS itself. The courts and tribunals to which Article 288 refers are those listed in Article 287, *i.e.*, the ITLOS, the ICJ, an arbitral tribunal established under UNCLOS Annex VII, and a special arbitral tribunal established under UNCLOS Annex VIII.

[190] *E.g.*, Straddling Stocks Agreement, note 85, arts. 7(4)-7(6). For further discussion, *see* Noyes, *Treaty* 375–77, 2001–02 ABILA Proc. 184–86.

[191] Anastasia Strati, The Protection of Underwater Cultural Heritage: An Emerging Objective of the Contemporary Law of the Sea 176 (1995) (emphasis added).

[192] 5 Commentary ¶ 303.10, p. 162. UNESCO has adopted Convention on Protection of the Underwater Cultural Heritage, Nov. 2, 2001, 41 ILM 40 (2002). *See also* Part IV.B § 35, defining "competent international organization" or "competent international organizations."

[193] *Cf.* Sinclair 140 (arguing that in construing Vienna Convention art. 31[3], "there is scope for the narrow and limited proposition that the evolution and development of the law can be taken into account in interpreting certain terms in a treaty which are by their very nature expressed in such general terms as to lend themselves to an evolutionary approach"). "Other rules" clauses might refer to other new, non-LOAC rules of customary international law.

international law."[194] As slightly modified in its final version, the definition reads:

> The traditional understanding is that "other rules of international law" and similar phrases in UNCLOS restate a customary rule, *i.e.*, that the phrase means the law of armed conflict (LOAC), including its components of the law of naval warfare and the law of maritime neutrality. In some instances, however, *e.g.*, UNCLOS Articles 293(1) and 303, the phrase may include international law other than the LOAC in situations where the LOAC does not apply.

It is not clear that it was necessary to include the last phrase ("where the LOAC does not apply") as part of the definition.

The final ABILA LOS Committee definition lists Articles 293(1) and 303 as "examples" of instances in which it may make sense to give "other rules of international law" its ordinary meaning. There may indeed be other instances. For example, Satya Nandan, Rapporteur of the UNCLOS III Second Committee, and David Anderson, a member of the U.K. delegation to UNCLOS III and a former ITLOS judge, commented on the phrase "other rules of international law" in UNCLOS Article 34(2).[195] Article 34(2), part of the provisions on straits fashioned at UNCLOS III, provides: "The sovereignty or jurisdiction of the States bordering on the straits is exercised subject to this Part [III of UNCLOS] and to other rules of international law." First, Nandan and Anderson commented that the "precise meaning of the reference to 'other rules of international law' may not always be clear in practice."[196] Second, they noted that Article 34(2) referred to "other rules of international law, *e.g.*, those on the non-use of force or delimitation. In other words, in so far as non-navigational questions may arise, other rules of international law, including other Parts of the Convention, apply."[197] Article 34(2) — unlike, *e.g.*, Articles 19(1) and 21(1) — does not refer to the "*Convention* and other rules of international law," but instead to "*this Part* and to other rules of international law." Article 34(2) implicitly places UNCLOS rules not found in UNCLOS Part III

---

194 Walker, *Definitions* 215, 2001–02 ABILA Proc. 172.

195 S.N. Nandan & D.H. Anderson, *Straits Used for International Navigation: A Commentary on Part III of the United Nations Convention on the Law of the Sea*, 60 Brit. Y.B. Int'l L. 159 (1989).

196 *Id.* 172 n. 39 (also referring to use of the phrase in UNCLOS arts. 2[3], 49[3]).

197 *Id.* 172 (footnote omitted).

within the "other rules" category.[198] Third, Nandan and Anderson suggested that "other rules of international law," as used in certain Spanish and Moroccan proposals concerning straits,[199] referred to rules of general international law relating to civil aviation.[200] Although these proposals were not accepted at UNCLOS III, they suggest that at least some States participating in the Conference did not regard the phrase "other rules of international law" as limited to the LOAC. If that is true, it becomes harder to support the notion that the Article 34(2) reference to "other rules of international law" has a customary meaning based exclusively on the LOAC.

The ABILA LOS Committee definition in its final form moves us toward the position that "other rules of international law" may, depending on the context, mean either the LOAC or non-LOAC rules. The above discussion suggests it is appropriate to interpret the phrase non-restrictively, as it is used in UNCLOS Article 293(1), Article 303, and some other UNCLOS articles as well.[201]

My fundamental concern is that UNCLOS not be narrowly construed to preclude recourse to other UNCLOS-consistent norms.[202] UNCLOS serves, at least in part, as a constitution,[203] establishing institutions and broad principles to stabilize and govern a wide range of oceans issues. Use of other rules of international law that are consistent with UNCLOS's principles may be necessary to flesh out those principles, and to allow them to be applied in conjunction with other bodies of international law.

Different routes may be available towards this end. The conclusion that tribunals operating within their jurisdiction under UNCLOS may apply non-Convention rules is fortified by several considerations. UNCLOS itself explicitly refers to some non-Convention rules of

---

198 *Id.* 172 n. 39 (citing UNCLOS art. 233 concerning safeguards for straits used for international navigation as an example of such an "other rule.")

199 *Informal Suggestion by Spain*, C.2/Informal Meeting/4 (1978) (Spain), *reprinted in* 5 Third United Nations Conference on the Law of the Sea: Documents 6 (Renate Platzolder ed. 1984); *Informal Suggestion by Morocco — Straits Used for International Navigation*, C.2/Informal Meeting/22 (1978) (Morocco), *reprinted in id.* 30.

200 Nandan & Anderson, note 195, p. 182.

201 For discussion of another situation — in addition to UNCLOS arts. 34(2), 293(1) and 303 — in which the phrase might be interpreted nonrestrictively, *see* Noyes, *Treaty* 378, 2001–02 ABILA Proc. 188.

202 For an excellent article addressing when courts and tribunals applying UNCLOS may have recourse to general international law, *see* Michael Wood, *The International Tribunal for the Law of the Sea and General International Law*, 22 Int'l J. Marine & Coastal L. 351 (2001).

203 *Cf.* Koh, note 42.

international law. For example, UNCLOS Article 304 states: "The provisions of this Convention regarding responsibility and liability for damage are without prejudice to the application of existing rules and the development of further rules regarding responsibility and liability under international law." Reference to principles of international law is made in Articles 295 (exhaustion of local remedies) and 300 (good faith and abuse of rights), and Articles 74 and 83 (on marine boundary delimitation) invoke "international law, as referred to in Article 38 of the Statute of the International Court of Justice." Article 311 recognizes the applicability of certain other international agreements that are consistent with UNCLOS. UNCLOS also obliquely may bring into play operation of non-Convention rules of international law through its "applicable" and "generally accepted" clauses.[204] The UNCLOS Preamble affirms "that matters not regulated by this Convention continue to be governed by the rules and principles of general international law."[205] In addition, certain "trumping" rules not stated in UNCLOS may apply. These include UN Charter Article 103, Security Council decisions, and jus cogens.[206]

Some "other rules of international law" clauses also, however, authorize the use of UNCLOS-consistent, non-LOAC rules of international law to clarify or complement Convention provisions. Reliance on the ordinary meaning of "other" is one appropriate way to accomplish these ends. The plain meaning of "other" would not, of course, preclude reference to the LOAC in matters relating to armed conflict.

e. *"Genuine Link"*

The phrase "genuine link," like the words "other rules of international law," reflects a juristic concept. Unlike the word "other" in the latter phrase, however, the words "genuine link" lack a determinate ordinary meaning. "Genuine" is a term of evaluation. The *Initial Draft* defined "genuine link" in functional terms to mean "that a flag State under whose laws a ship is registered must effectively exercise its jurisdiction and control in administrative, technical and social matters over ships flying its flag."[207] This was a bold (*i.e.*, restrictive) definition of a concept about which there is little agreement.

---

[204] *See* Part IV.B § 5, defining "applicable" and "generally accepted."

[205] *See generally* Part III.C.

[206] *See generally* Part III.B.

[207] *See* Walker, *Defining* 357, 2001–02 ABILA Proc. 162–65; *see also* Part IV.B § 66, defining "flag State;" § 163, "ship" or "vessel."

The *goal* of the genuine link requirement is to promote the ability of flag States to effectively exercise adequate jurisdiction and control over the ships they register. But is *actual* "effective exercise of jurisdiction and control" required to establish a genuine link? That obligation is of course specified in UNCLOS Article 94 and in other treaties. The genuine link requirement appears in UNCLOS Article 91 concerning the nationality of vessels, suggesting to some that "genuine link" may be a *condition* of establishing nationality.[208] Just what criteria might satisfy such a condition is the subject of considerable debate. Requiring "effective exercise of control" as a condition of nationality raises the specter of a ship losing its nationality should a flag State not exercise such control. More fundamentally, it is not certain that a "genuine link" is a condition of nationality. Some instead view the genuine link requirement as an aspiration, linked to the purpose of facilitating effective jurisdiction and control by a flag State over its vessels.[209] This confusion over whether "genuine link" is a condition of nationality or a relationship intended to facilitate effective jurisdiction and control complicates any effort to define the concept.

Lack of agreement concerning the meaning of "genuine link" is not surprising, given the political controversies surrounding nationality of vessels and the growth of open registers. States and commentators disputed whether the genuine link concept, taken from the *Nottebohm Case* with respect to links between an individual and his or her State of nationality, should be transposed to vessels at all. Some observers thought it should not.[210] They stressed the need to assure there was one certain, clearly identifiable State of nationality of a vessel, whose laws would apply to it. One clearly identifiable flag State was necessary to preserve order on the oceans, to guard against interference with the freedom of navigation, and to prevent vessels arguably lacking a genuine link from being treated as stateless. Critics of the genuine link requirement thought such a requirement could undercut those values, if it was viewed as a condition of nationality. And once the International Law Commission decided to use "genuine link" in its drafts[211] (which led to incorporation of the words into High Seas Convention

---

[208] *See* Vincent P. Cogliati-Bantz, *Disentangling the "Genuine Link": Enquiries in Sea, Air and Space Law*, 79 Nordic J. Int'l L. 383, 398–400 (2010) (discussing this view).

[209] *See id.* 407, 412.

[210] *See, e.g.*, Myres S. McDougal & William T. Burke, The Public Order of the Oceans 1013–35 (1962).

[211] *See* note 118 and accompanying text.

Article 5[1]), proposals to give the words specific content revealed a huge political rift. On the one hand, flag of convenience States feared that detailed requirements might cut into an important source of revenue, and ship owners desired the lower taxes, cheaper crewing costs, and, sometimes, lax inspections that came with registering in a flag of convenience State. On the other hand, those concerned with safe working conditions for mariners or with the environmental risks of oil spills favored giving some teeth to the genuine link requirement. (So did some developing States that were not prepared themselves to develop open registers.) In terms of values, the conflict was often phrased in terms of economic sovereignty versus concerns for safety and the environment.

The end product of the debate was a lack of agreement, and an extremely indeterminate treaty term. Although the words "genuine link" signaled a concern with the adequate exercise of flag State jurisdiction and control, no precise meaning of "genuine link" was specified or agreed for the 1958 High Seas Convention. Nor did UNCLOS clarify the concept. UNCLOS III really did not focus on the issue; the Conference gave little consideration to most provisions carried over from the High Seas Convention.[212] Although UNCLOS Article 94 was new, containing extensive provisions about flag State responsibilities, many other high seas articles — including Article 91 on nationality of vessels, which contains the "genuine link" requirement — simply repeated language from the High Seas Convention. The UNCLOS III negotiators, facing a slew of new and controversial matters relating to the EEZ, the continental shelf, straits transit passage, innocent passage, archipelagoes, the seabed beyond the limits of national jurisdiction, landlocked and geographically disadvantaged State, MSR and dispute settlement, chose not to open another controversial issue by debating the meaning of "genuine link."[213]

[212] UNCLOS art. 91 tracks High Seas Convention art. 5(1). Article 5(1)'s clause referring to a State's obligation to "effectively exercise its jurisdiction and control in administrative, technical and social matters over ships flying its flag," *id.*, was omitted from UNCLOS art. 91. That clause became the basis for Article 94(1).

[213] According to David Anderson, a U.K. UNCLOS III delegation member and a former ITLOS judge, the intention in splitting the two parts of the last sentence of High Seas Convention art. 5(1) between UNCLOS arts. 91 and 94 "was not to weaken the argument that 'a failure by a flag State to perform its duties under article 94 would provide evidence of the absence of a genuine link between it and the ship concerned.'" David Anderson, *Freedoms of the High Seas in the Modern Law of the Sea*, in The Law of the Sea: Progress and Prospects 327, 333 (David Freestone et al. eds. 2006), *quoting*

Post-1982 efforts to agree on even general formulations of "genuine link" have also foundered. Witness what happened with the 1986 Ship Registration Convention.[214] That Convention, containing a broadly worded attempt to specify the meaning of "genuine link," has received little support and is not in force. State practice regarding conditions necessary for granting nationality to ships is also extraordinarily diverse,[215] suggesting lack of consensus on the meaning of "genuine link." More recently, experts from international organizations, including IMO and the Food and Agriculture Organization (FAO), have studied the subject of "genuine link," without arriving at any concrete definitions.[216] The resulting reports did reemphasize the *purpose* behind the genuine link requirement, *i.e.*, to facilitate more effective exercise of flag State responsibilities.[217]

The "genuine link" norm is also indeterminate from a process perspective. Considerable authority suggests that a vessel's lack of a genuine link with a flag State does not entitle another State to refuse to recognize that vessel's nationality.[218] Proposals to that effect were not

---

E.D. Brown, The International Law of the Sea 289 (1994). I do not dispute that the goal of the genuine link language has been to promote more effective flag State control, nor do I deny that a flag State's failure to perform its Article 94 duties might have evidential value with respect to the absence of a genuine link. However, accepting these points leaves us, I submit, short of being able to say that there is a consensus that "genuine link" is defined to mean that, in the words of the *Initial Draft*, a flag State "must effectively exercise its jurisdiction and control." It is conceivable, for example, that a State failing to meet its basic Article 94 obligation to exercise effective jurisdiction and control with respect to a vessel registered in that State, but which has significant connections with the crew, owner, and master of the vessel, would be considered to have a "genuine link" with the vessel, even when violating Article 94.

[214] *See* Moira L. McConnell, *Business as Usual: An Evaluation of the 1986 UN Convention on Conditions for Registration of Ships*, 18 J. Mar. L. & Com. 435 (1987).

[215] Churchill & Hedley § 4.2, p. 43.

[216] *See* Report of the Ad Hoc Consultative Meeting of Senior Representatives of International Organizations on the "Genuine Link," in U.N. Doc. A/61/160, p. 4 (2006); Examination and Clarification of the Role of the "Genuine Link" in Relation to the Duty of Flag States to Exercise Effective Control Over Ships Flying their Flags, Including Fishing Vessels, Submitted by the International Labour Office, in *id.* 16; Ariella D'Andrea, *The "Genuine Link" Concept in Responsible Fisheries: Legal Aspects and Recent Developments*, FAO Legal Papers Online no. 61 (Nov. 2006).

[217] Participants in the IMO-convened Ad Hoc Consultative Meeting noted "the objective and purpose of the 'genuine link' requirement, that is, assuring the *ability* of the flag State to effectively exercise its jurisdiction over ships flying its flag." Report of the Ad Hoc Consultative Meeting, note 219, p. 9 (emphasis added). *See also* D'Andrea, note 216, p. 7.

[218] M/V Saiga No. 2 Case (St. Vincent v. Guinea), 1999 ITLOS No. 2, ¶¶ 79–86, 38 ILM 1323, 1342–43 (1999) (Judgment, July 1).

accepted at UNCLOS I.[219] If a flag State fails to establish a genuine link, other States could protest to the flag State.

The genuine link requirement appears unlikely to contribute significantly to the important goals of improving safety on vessels, combating illegal fishing and other illegal activities, and reducing environmental risk. Indeed, efforts to promote these goals have taken other tacks. International law has specified flag State obligations[220] and expanded the authority of coastal States and port States (*e.g.*, coastal State authority to prescribe and enforce environmental laws;[221] port State inspections coordinated through Memoranda of Understanding[222]). Such detailed requirements, often coupled with mechanisms to promote compliance, appear better tailored to promote improved safety standards, fishing practices and environmental protection than does a restrictive "genuine link" definition.

The *Initial Draft* definition, which stressed that the "genuine link" means "that a flag State ... must effectively exercise its control," does not,

---

[219] *See* Cogliati-Bantz, note 208, pp. 391–97 (reviewing consideration by the International Law Commission and at UNCLOS I of the possibility of non-recognition in the absence of a genuine link).

[220] *E.g.*, UNCLOS arts. 94, 211(2), 217.

[221] *See generally, e.g.*, Erik Jaap Molenaar, Coastal State Jurisdiction Over Vessel-Source Pollution (1998); Vessel-Source Pollution and Coastal State Jurisdiction (Erik Franckx ed. 2001); *see also* Part IV.B § 137, defining "port."

[222] *E.g.*, Memorandum of Understanding on Port State Control in the Caribbean Region, 36 ILM 231 (1987). *See* Tatjana Keselj, *Port State Jurisdiction in Respect of Pollution from Ships: The 1982 United Nations Convention on the Law of the Sea and the Memoranda of Understanding*, 30 Ocean Dev. & Int'l L. 127 (1999). Port state control "memorandums of understanding" or "memoranda of understanding" (MOUs) provide that participating maritime authorities are to consult, cooperate and exchange information regarding substandard vessels. In general, there has been debate whether MOUs are legally binding, although nothing would seem to preclude parties from intending that an instrument entitled "Memorandum of Understanding" be considered as a binding treaty. Some authorities, noting that MOUs may be known as gentlemen's agreements, non-binding agreements, de facto agreements or non-legal agreements, Aust 21, do not consider MOUs as legally binding like treaties. *Id.* ch. 3 (MOUs not binding but might be applied as "soft law"); 1966 ILC Rep., note 38, p. 188 (MOUs binding); Jennings & Watts §§ 582, pp. 1201–03; 586, p. 1209 & n. 8 (MOUs not binding; ILC Rep., erred); Jan Klabbers, The Concept of Treaty in International Law chs. 1–3 (1996) (doubtful if distinction between treaties, MOUs valid); McNair 15 (MOU a legal agreement); Restatement (Third) § 301, cmt. e & r.n. 1 (MOUs not binding); Jimenez de Arechaga, note 38, p. 37 (same). Charles I. Bevans, Assistant Legal Adviser for Treaty Affairs, Memorandum of Law, Aug. 5, 1973, The Law of Treaties and Other International Agreements: 1974 Digest § 1, p. 198, citing 1966 ILC Rep., opined that whether an MOU is binding depends on the parties' intent. Some documents considered binding international agreements have been titled MOUs. Aust 25–27, citing examples.

in my opinion, reflect a consensus view. Churchill & Hedley's careful study of the meaning of "genuine link" in its context (as the Vienna Convention uses "context"), in a work prepared for the International Transport Workers' Federation,[223] pointed out the lack of consensus on the meaning of "genuine link."[224] The underlying political controversies make their conclusion all the more understandable. They found:

> There is no single or obligatory criterion by which the genuineness of a link is to be established. A State has a discretion as to how it ensures that the link between a ship having its nationality and itself is genuine, be it through requirements relating to the nationality of the beneficial owner or crew, its ability to exercise its jurisdiction over such a ship, or in some other way.[225]

A flag State's effective exercise of jurisdiction and control over its ships, they continued, "is not an obligatory criterion for establishing the genuineness of a link."[226] Furthermore, "effective exercise of flag State jurisdiction" really connotes only that a flag State "must be *in a position* to exercise effective jurisdiction and control over a ship *at the time it grants its nationality to that ship*."[227] This conception is not as bold as the one set out in the *Initial Draft* definition, according to which "genuine link" means the actual effective exercise of jurisdiction and control. The *Initial Draft* definition would be difficult to apply because it would mandate "constant examination of how the flag State is exercising its jurisdiction in practice" and would focus on continuing behavior rather than on links that exist when nationality is obtained.[228] For these reasons, it would be preferable to conceptualize "genuine link" in terms of the *ability* of flag States to exercise jurisdiction and control rather than in terms of *actual* "effective exercise of jurisdiction and control."

In short, "genuine link" should mean something more than "link." But we lack consensus about what that "something more" is, and many States are reluctant to qualify their grants of nationality to ships by adding definite content to the genuine link concept. In contrast to the phrase "other rules of international law," the words "genuine link" carry

---

223 Churchill & Hedley, cover.
224 *Id.* §§ 3.5, p. 37; 6, p. 68.
225 *Id.* § 6, p. 70 (footnotes omitted).
226 *Id.*
227 Churchill & Hedley § 6, p. 17 (emphasis added).
228 *Id.*

no evident plain meaning. Consensus on the meaning of "genuine link" might in theory develop in the future and be reflected in State practice. At present, however, it may only be appropriate to suggest a nonexclusive range of options, such as in the formulation I proposed to replace the *Initial Draft* definition:

> "Genuine link" means more than a mere link, requiring, *e.g.*, connections between the flag State and the vessel such that the flag State has the ability to exercise effective control over the vessel when nationality is granted, or connections between the flag State and the vessel's crew, or connections between the flag State and the vessel's officers, or connections between the flag State and the vessel's beneficial owners.[229]

Such options would be consistent with the purpose beyond the "genuine link": promoting a flag State's ability to effectively exercise jurisdiction and control over vessels it registers.

Following my comments about the *Initial Draft* definition,[230] Professor Walker and the ABILA LOS Committee proposed a revised definition of "genuine link," which read:

> "Genuine link," in the LOS Convention, Article 91, means that a flag State under whose laws a ship is registered must be able to effectively exercise its jurisdiction and control in administrative, technical and social matters over ships flying its flag.[231]

This definition differed from the one originally proposed in the *Initial Draft* by inserting "be able to" between "must" and "effectively exercise its jurisdiction and control." It is better to conceptualize "genuine link" in terms of "ability to exercise jurisdiction and control" rather than in terms of actual "effective exercise of jurisdiction and control." Yet, concerns remain. When must the flag State be able to exercise its jurisdiction and control? If the definition is read to require *continuing* ability to exercise control, and if the genuine link requirement is read as a condition of nationality, the destabilizing prospect of vessels losing their nationality presents itself. Suppose a flag State were able to exercise control when a vessel was registered but later lost that ability. If "genuine link" is a component of nationality, would the vessel thus become stateless? If the vessel were stateless, it might be difficult to find

---

[229] Noyes, *Treaty* 383, 2001 ABILA Proc. 193.

[230] *See id.* 380–83, 2001–02 ABILA Proc. 189–93.

[231] Walker, *Definitions* 208; *see also* Part IV.B § 66, defining "flag State;" § 163, defining "ship" or "vessel;" Part III.E.2.

any State responsible under State responsibility doctrines for, say, serious pollution by the vessel.[232] At the least, debates about whether a putative flag State was in fact able to exercise jurisdiction and control could create uncertainties as to the nationality of vessels.

That concern is less prominent if the genuine link requirement is not a condition of nationality. Authorities disagree about this fundamental question. Respected commentators have taken the position that a genuine link is required for nationality,[233] and Article 91 and High Seas Convention Article 5(1), which contain the genuine link requirement, expressly concern the nationality of vessels. Yet some States and commentators dispute that position, viewing the genuine link requirement as essentially aspirational.[234] In the face of such controversy, it is difficult to arrive at a definition of "genuine link" that will not be regarded as political, favoring one position over the other. Even for those maintaining that "genuine link" is a condition of vessel nationality, giving specific content to the concept remains elusive.

Some things are clear. We should not equate the genuine link requirement with the actual duties of the flag State to exercise effective jurisdiction and control over vessels. UNCLOS Articles 94 and 217 specify in detail each flag State's obligations to exercise jurisdiction and control over its vessels. These duties are separate from the Article 91 requirement that "[t]here must exist a genuine link between the State and its ship." There also does appear to be general agreement that the overall purpose of the genuine link requirement is to encourage flag States to find effective ways to exercise jurisdiction and control over their registered vessels. According to Alex Oude Elferink, "the requirement of a genuine link in Article 91, while not defined, does imply that the link must be such so as to enable the flag State to exercise effective control over the ship and meet its obligations under UNCLOS and other instruments."[235] Noting a range of possible ways to further this goal may facilitate this end.

The final definition of "genuine link" adopted by the ABILA LOS Committee suggests that any of a range of factors could establish the requisite connection between the flag State and the vessel:

---

[232] *See generally* Brian D. Smith, State Responsibility and the Marine Environment (1988); *see also* Part IV.B § 161, defining "serious act of pollution."

[233] *See* Churchill & Hedley § 6, p. 69; note 208.

[234] *See* Cogliati-Bantz, note 208, pp. 407, 412; D'Andrea, note 216, p. 16.

[235] Alex G. Oude Elferink, *The Genuine Link Concept: Time for a* Post Mortem?, in On the Foundations and Sources of International Law 41, 47–48 (Ige F. Dekker & Harry H.G. Post eds. 2003).

> "Genuine link" in UNCLOS Article 91 means more than mere registration of a ship with a State; "genuine link" requires, *e.g.*, connections between a flag State under whose laws a ship is registered such that the flag State has the ability to exercise effective jurisdiction and control over the ship when registration is granted; connections between the flag, *i.e.*, registry, State and the ship's crew; connections between the flag, *i.e.*, registry, State and the ship's officers; or connections between the flag, *i.e.*, registry, State and the ship's beneficial owners.[236]

This definition, in my view appropriately, stipulates that the formal or mechanical act of registration does not by itself establish a genuine link, a point some might dispute.[237] For those holding the view that the genuine link requirement involves setting conditions for nationality, the definition's focus on a flag State's ability to exercise jurisdiction and control "when registration is granted" is sensible. That focus avoids mandating a continuing relationship between a flag State and its registered vessels, which could result in a ship's being "denationalized" if the ability to exercise such jurisdiction and control disappeared. The definition implicitly recognizes that economic connections may not be the only way a flag State could develop the ability to exercise effective jurisdiction and control. It appropriately provides examples of connecting factors, without maintaining these are the only route to establishing a "genuine link." If we keep in mind the ultimate goal of the genuine link requirement, *i.e.*, to promote a flag State's ability to effectively exercise jurisdiction and control over the vessels it registers, the Committee definition may help further understanding of this difficult concept.

Problems associated with lax flag State control are not likely to be ameliorated by a definition of "genuine link." Indeed, one may ask whether continued emphasis on the genuine link requirement "diverts attention from the real problem, which is the need for greater flag State control of vessels, regardless of whether the registry is open or closed."[238] We should instead directly ask what abuses relating to flag State control deserve attention and identify and implement the measures that can best correct those problems. Is the concern with vessels prone to

---

[236] Part IV.B § 72.

[237] "[I]t seems unclear whether the mere act of registration suffices to establish a 'genuine link' with the flag State." Maria Gavouneli, *From Uniformity to Fragmentation: The Ability of the UN Convention on the Law of the Sea to Accommodate New Uses and Challenges,* in Unresolved Issues and New Challenges to the Law of the Sea 205, 208 (Anastasia Strati et al. eds. 2006).

[238] Expert Workshop on Flag State Responsibilities: Assessing Performance and Taking Action 15 (25–28 March 2008, Vancouver, Canada). *See also* D'Andrea, note 216, pp. 16–17.

oil spills? With vessels posing other safety hazards? With the use or potential use of vessels for terrorist activities? These are critical issues. Agreements supplementing flag State duties in UNCLOS Articles 94 and 217, technical support to enable flag States to carry out their obligations, port State controls, and coordination among port States strike me as the routes that must be pursued.

3. Conclusion

A common theme running through this essay is that it may sometimes be valuable to leave terms undefined or to define them very broadly. Sometimes the concept for which a word stands is a matter of great political controversy. In that case a limiting definition is unlikely to solve the controversy and will not reflect any generally shared understanding among past treaty negotiators and present treaty interpreters. Other times, it may be sensible for the meaning of a word to vary in various legal contexts. In that case, defining the word — confining its meaning — could lead to a decision maker's refusing to apply a treaty provision containing the word when it is sensible not to.

The ABILA LOS Committee definitions project has sought to understand and define concepts in UNCLOS that will be used in many situations. The project requires us to think about the appropriateness of defining words and phrases that seem to reflect a generally shared understanding (such as "mile"), as well as words and phrases that do not. Interpreting a treaty in accordance with a standard interpretive methodology may reveal shared, common understandings and may lead to definitions that conform to those shared understandings. Even if the process of debating proposed definitions reveals points of significant disagreement, however, the process in itself is valuable. That process can sharpen our perceptions of legal consequences and the contexts in which they arise.

E. "WORDS! WORDS! WORDS!": DILEMMAS IN DEFINITIONS

George K. Walker[239]

Professor Noyes has illustrated problems in defining words or phrases in UNCLOS.[240] He notes the problem of controversial terms, *e.g.*, "genuine link;"[241] the issue of new usages for established principles, *e.g.*, "other rules of international law;"[242] and concern about seemingly less controversial words, *e.g.*, "mile."[243] A few words in mild rebuttal may be in order.

First, defining even the most noncontroversial terms may expose differences of view on their meaning; "mile" is a case in point. Relations among States being what they are in a multipolar world and Murphy's Law of Measurements reflecting the possible future reality of conflicting claims, even defining these terms may raise differences. If a dispute over sovereignty or jurisdiction under the law of the sea as reflected in UNCLOS will arise, it is likely that it will involve claims over areas within the minimum and maximum meanings of "mile."[244] One risk, even here, is that a decision maker may apply a definition "outside the box," to the chagrin of many.

Justice Oliver Wendell Holmes once wrote that a word is the skin of a living thought.[245] The line from *My Fair Lady*, "Words! Words! Words!,"[246] used in the title above,[247] is a commonplace illustration of

[239] Part III.F originally appeared as Walker, *Words* 384, 2001–02 ABILA Proc. 195 and has been changed in a few places.

[240] *See* Part III.D.

[241] *See* Part III.D.2.e.

[242] *See* Part III.D.2.d.

[243] *See* Part III.D.2.a.

[244] *See* Part IV.B § 105, defining "mile" or "nautical mile."

[245] Towne v. Eisner, 245 U.S. 418, 425 (1918).

[246] Alan Jay Lerner, *Show Me*, in the musical play, My Fair Lady (1956) and movie: "Words, words, words. I'm so sick of words. I get words all day through, first from him, now from you! Is that all you blighters can do?"

[247] International law is not the only field with the problem; *see, e.g.*, Stephen B. Cohen, *Words! Words! Words!: Teaching the Language of Tax*, 55 J. Legal Educ. 600 (No. 4, 2005).

the point. Although Audrey Hepburn was pictured on the screen in the movie version of the song, her voice was dubbed in. What was the reality, Ms. Hepburn on the screen, the dubbed song, the lyrics as they appeared in print, the memory of a film with a happy ending, or some combination of the foregoing? What is the "thought," or idea or concept, that the *Report* should convey?

There are opposing policies in the law of the sea as in all systems of jurisprudence. Advocates of original intent would counsel static content to the Constitution of the United States. Others say it is a living document, designed to meet issues not dreamed of when the Framers met in Philadelphia, when the first Congress and the states approved the Bill of Rights a few years later, or when later Congresses and the states approved other amendments, notably the Thirteenth, Fourteenth and Fifteenth Amendments. In 1789 Thomas Jefferson wrote James Madison that "*the earth belongs in usufruct to the living*,"[248] a philosophical support for the latter view. Or, as James Russell Lowell wrote a century later, new occasions teach new duties; new truth makes ancient good uncouth.[249] On the other hand, the Constitution and the Bill of Rights are fairly precise about some matters, *e.g.*, that federal criminal trials by jury may be heard only in the state and district where the crime shall have been committed.[250] But how precise is "state" or "district"? The Constitution and its amendments leave these matters to statute,[251] and, in the case of judicial districts, boundaries can be and have been amended from time to time. The original docket of the Supreme Court of the United States continues to have cases involving boundaries of the states. Some Constitutional provisions, *e.g.*, two Senators for each state, fixed at two despite states' size or population, are immutable; but even here the method of election has changed.[252] If UNCLOS is a "constitution" for the law of the sea[253] because of its trumping provisions,[254] it has the same kind of problems inherent in its

---

[248] Letter of Thomas Jefferson to James Madison, Sept. 6, 1789, mailed Jan. 9, 1790, 15 The Papers of Thomas Jefferson 392 (Julian P. Boyd ed. 1958) (emphasis in original); *see also id.* p. 396; 2 Dumas Malone, Jefferson and His Time: Jefferson and the Rights of Man 179 (1951).

[249] James Russell Lowell, *The Present Crisis*, in 1 James Russell Lowell, Poetical Works 185, 190 (1890).

[250] U.S. Const. art. III, § 2, cl. 3; *id.* amend. VI.

[251] *Id.* arts. I, § 8, cl. 9; § 8, cl. 18; III, §§ 1–2; IV, § 3, cl. 1.

[252] *Id.* art. I, § 3, cl. 1–3; *id.* amend. XVII.

[253] Koh, note 42.

[254] *See* Part III.B for further analysis.

interpretation.[255] The rules for interpreting a constitution and a treaty are of course different, but the general parallels in philosophy of interpretation would seem to be analogous.

There is also the problem, inherent in new occasions that may teach new duties, of a balance between these new duties through new meanings for UNCLOS terms, and meanings for treaty terms established in custom, general principles, decisions of tribunals and what may be the weight of scholarly opinion.[256] The phrase "other rules of international law" is an example; the term had a fairly uniform definition, however obscure to some, as meaning the law of armed conflict.[257] Justice Holmes also counseled that a page of history, including perhaps legal history, is worth a volume of logic.[258] How should the history of a phrase like "other rules of international law," historically relatively established in custom, principles or commentators' views, be weighed in the balance? The Committee's decision for the phrase, "other rules of international law," was to go forward with a definition.[259] The issue will surely arise in other contexts for definitions of other terms in the *Report* and perhaps other terms not defined in UNCLOS for which the *Report* does not publish a definition.

Professor Noyes has urged caution where opinion on a term has divided sharply, *e.g.*, on "genuine link," to leave resolution to the future.[260] He would have support from constitutional law commentators who say that "fuzziness" in judicial decision making is in the nature of human language, and that fuzzy logic can help judges do their work more intelligently.[261] Madison, recipient of Jefferson's letter,[262] called language a "cloudy medium"[263] at about the same time that

---

[255] *Cf.* George K. Walker, *Oceans Law, the Maritime Environment, and the Law of Naval Warfare*, in Protection of the Environment During Armed Conflict 185, 189, 203 (Nav. War C. Int'l L. Stud., v. 69, Richard J. Grunawalt et al. ed. 1996). Part III.B analyzes the UN Charter 103 trumping provision, which might come into play in UN Security Council decision situations under UN Charter arts. 25, 48, 94, or in circumstances of individual or collective self-defense. *See id.* art. 51.

[256] *See, e.g.*, ICJ Stat. arts. 38, 59; Restatement (Third) §§ 102–03; Part III.B.

[257] *See* Parts III.B-III.C and Part IV § 132, defining "other rules of international law," for further analysis.

[258] New York Trust Co. v. Eisner, 256 U.S. 345, 349 (1921).

[259] *See* Parts III.B-III.C and Part IV § 132, defining "other rules of international law."

[260] *See* Part III.D.2.e.

[261] Beverly Blair Cook, *Fuzzy Logic and Judicial Decision Making*, 85 Judicature 70, 99 (2001).

[262] *See* note 248 and accompanying text.

[263] The Federalist No. 37 (James Madison).

Jefferson wrote him. The problem for LOS issues is that disputes involving the oceans can be frequent, extraordinarily expensive and dangerous, and perhaps leading to armed conflict. These, including claims and counterclaims over ocean boundaries and baselines, overflight rights, fishing rights, EEZ issues, the continental shelf, high seas confrontations, straits passage, territorial sea delimitations and passage, rocks, islands and archipelagoes, are many and need no lengthy citation.[264] If workable definitions emerge from this *Report* and forestall or contribute to just and fair resolution of a few of these disputes, the *Report* should be deemed a success.[265] To the extent the *Report* may stray from demands of new occasions, its definitions are but secondary sources and can be superseded by other, primary sources and perhaps secondary sources.[266]

The Committee's continued study and collective decision making has been to go forward, attempting to achieve as much consensus on definitions as possible. It has seemed to the Committee to be better to see a glass as half full rather than half empty. The *Report* recites majority-minority or differing views where research has uncovered them, so that those using the Report will have the benefit of Committee research and the basis of its decisions.

Moreover, as Justice Benjamin Cardozo wrote in another definitional context,

> What is needed is something of that common-sense accommodation of judgment to kaleidoscopic situations which characterizes the law in its treatment of causation. … To set bounds to the pursuit, the courts have formulated the distinction between controversies that are basic and

---

[264] For a survey of such disputes, *see, e.g.*, Roach & Smith.

[265] On a world scale, ILA reports have influenced treaty language and customary or general principles norms. *E.g.*, ILA, *Budapest Articles of Interpretation: Final Text*, in Report of the 38th Conference 66–67 (1934), *reprinted in Rights and Duties of States in Case of Aggression*, 33 AJIL 819, 825–26 n.1 (1939), interpreting the Pact of Paris, also known as the Kellogg-Briand or Briand-Kellogg Pact, Treaty Providing for the Renunciation of War as an Instrument of National Policy, Aug. 28, 1923, 46 Stat. 2343, 94 LNTS 57, still in force. TIF 437–38. The *Budapest Articles* and Harvard Draft Convention on Rights & Duties of States in Case of Aggression, 33 AJIL 819 (Supp. 1939) were partial justification for Lend-Lease aid, through U.S. legislation and treaties, to the Allies opposing the Axis before the United States entered World War II. Walker, The Tanker 182–84.

[266] ICJ Stat. arts. 38, 59; Restatement (Third) §§ 102–03; *see also* Part III.B. Professor Noyes's comments and the work of the ILA Committee on the Outer Limits of the Continental Shelf are examples of commentator counterclaims that may, in the end, carry the day for a definition.

> those that are collateral, between disputes that are necessary and those that are merely possible. We shall be lost in a maze if we put that compass by.[267]

It is hoped and believed that the Committee and its *Report* have followed that compass, too.

[267] Gully v. First Nat'l Bank, 299 U.S. 109, 117–18 (1936) (citations omitted).

CHAPTER IV

DEFINITIONS FOR THE LAW OF THE SEA: TERMS NOT DEFINED BY THE 1982 CONVENTION

Chapter IV reflects the collective work of the ABILA LOS Committee and is the heart of this *Report*. A separate section number, followed by the title of the term, begins each definition. Analysis of the definition of a term, *i.e.*, its source(s), the term's location in UNCLOS and other treaties or international agreements, and other relevant material follow the definition in *Comments*. If two or more terms share the same meaning, or if a term is frequently known by its abbreviation or acronym, *e.g.*, "notice to mariners" and "Ntm" or "NOTMAR," defined in Part IV.B § 122, cross-references to the two terms or the term and its abbreviation or acronym are given.

As noted in Chapters I and III.A, the *Report* does not republish definitions that UNCLOS supplies, except perhaps to explain an otherwise undefined term, *e.g.*, "area," defined in Part IV.B § 9, as distinguished from "Area," defined in UNCLOS Art. 1(1)(1).[268]

A. Preliminary Observations

The definitions that follow in Chapter IV.B refer to terms as understood in UNCLOS. Charter law, *e.g.* UN Security Council decisions under UN Charter Arts. 25, 48 and 94(2), may involve different meanings or may use a term as defined under the Convention.[269] The definitions that follow in Chapter IV.B may or may not involve different meanings under the LOAC; UNCLOS and the 1958 LOS Conventions declare their terms are subject to the LOAC in situations governed by the LOAC.[270] Sometimes the LOAC applicable to armed conflict at sea may borrow a term from the peacetime law of the sea, notably, *e.g.*, "due regard."[271] In those cases the LOS term assumes the meaning the

---

[268] Part IV, the heart of this book, is identical with Part IV of *Final Report*, 2009-10 ABILA Proc. 261–537, except renumbered footnotes and similar amendments.

[269] UN Charter Art. 103; *see also* Part III.B.2.

[270] *Cf., e.g.,* UNCLOS Art. 87(1); *see also* § 132, defining "other rules of international law;" Part III.B.2.

[271] *See* § 56, defining "due regard;" *see also* Part III.B.2.

LOAC ascribes to it. Jus cogens principles also may require a different definition.[272]

B. Definitions for the 1982 Law of the Sea Convention

§ 1. *Accuracy*

In UNCLOS analysis, "accuracy" means the extent to which a measured or enumerated value, such as "mile" or "nautical mile," agrees with an assumed or accepted value.

Comment

In LOAC-governed situations under the "other rules of international law" clauses in UNCLOS, a different definition may apply. The same may be the situation if the UN Charter supersedes UNCLOS or if jus cogens norms apply.[273]

Former ECDIS Glossary, page 1, defined "accuracy" as "[t]he extent to which a measured or enumerated value agrees with the assumed or accepted value." The current ECDIS Glossary does not define "accuracy." Section 105 defines "mile" or "nautical mile," noting the problem of measurement accuracy; § 138 defines "precision."[274]

§ 2. *Adjacent coasts*

As used in UNCLOS Articles 15, 74(1) and 83, "adjacent coasts" means coasts lying on either side of the land boundary between two adjoining States. States may have adjacent coasts under UNCLOS even if they do not share a common land boundary.

Comment

In LOAC-governed situations under the "other rules of international law" clauses in UNCLOS, a different definition may apply. The same may be the situation if the UN Charter supersedes UNCLOS or if jus cogens norms apply.[275]

---

[272] *See* Part III.B.2.

[273] *See* Parts III.B-III.D and § 132, defining "other rules of international law."

[274] *See also* DOD Dictionary 192 ("evaluation"); Walker, *ECDIS Glossary* 240–41, 2003–04 ABILA Proc. 211–12.

[275] *See* Parts III.B-III.D and § 132, defining "other rules of international law."

Consolidated Glossary ¶ 1 defines "adjacent coasts" as "[t]he coasts lying either side of the land boundary between two adjoining States."

UNCLOS Article 15, echoing Territorial Sea Convention Article 12(1), provides that

> Where the coasts of two States are opposite or adjacent to each other, neither of the two States is entitled, failing agreement between them to the contrary, to extend its territorial sea beyond the median line every point of which is equidistant from the nearest points on the baselines from which the breadth of the territorial seas of each of the two States is measured. The above provision does not apply, however, where it is necessary by reason of historic title or other special circumstances to delimit the territorial seas of the two States in a way which is at variance therewith.[276]

Territorial Sea Convention Article 14(1) also provides that

> The boundary of the territorial sea between two adjacent States shall be determined by agreement between them. In the absence of such agreement, and unless another boundary line is justified by special circumstances, the boundary is drawn by application of the principle of equidistance from the nearest points on the baseline from which the breadth of the territorial sea of each country is measured.

With respect to the continental shelf, UNCLOS Article 76(10) provides that Article 76's other terms "are without prejudice to the question of delimitation of the continental Shelf between States with opposite or adjacent coasts."[277] The Shelf Convention does not have an equivalent provision, but its Article 6 provides:

> 1. Where the same continental shelf is adjacent to the territories of two or more States whose coasts are opposite each other, the boundary of the … shelf appertaining to such States shall be determined by

[276] *See also* 2 Commentary ¶¶ 15.1–15.12(d).

[277] *See also id.* 76.18(m). COCS *Second Report*, Conclusion 14, p. 18 says Article 76(10)

> … implies that the provisions of Article[s] 76(8) and 76(9) concerning the final and binding nature of outer limits of the continental shelf may not be invoked against another State where the delimitation of the … shelf between neighboring States is concerned.
>
> Other States have to consider whether or not to accept the consideration of a submission of a coastal State involving a land or maritime dispute by the Commission [on the Continental Shelf] taking into account article 76(10) …

See also § 162, "shelf."

agreement between them. In the absence of agreement, and unless another boundary line is justified by special circumstances, the boundary is the median line, every point of which is equidistant from the nearest points of the baselines from which the breadth of the territorial sea of each State is measured.

2. Where the same continental shelf is adjacent to the territories of two adjacent States, the boundary of the … shelf shall be determined by agreement between them. In the absence of agreement, and unless another boundary line is justified by special circumstances, the boundary shall be determined by application of the principle of equidistance from the nearest points of the baselines from which the breadth of the territorial sea of each State is measured.
3. In delimiting the boundaries of the continental shelf, any lines which are drawn in accordance with the principles set out in paragraphs 1 and 2 … should be defined with reference to charts and geographical features as they exist at a particular date, and reference should be made to fixed permanent identifiable points on the land.[278]

UNCLOS Article 83 is different:

1. The delimitation of the continental shelf between States with opposite or adjacent coasts shall be effected by agreement on the basis of international law, as referred to in Art[.] 38 of the Statute of the International Court of Justice, … to achieve an equitable solution.
2. If no agreement can be reached within a reasonable period of time, the States concerned shall resort to the procedures provided for in Part XV[, UNCLOS dispute resolution procedures, Articles 279–99].
3. Pending agreement as provided for in paragraph 1, the States concerned, in a spirit of understanding and cooperation, shall make every effort to enter into provisional arrangements of a practical nature and, during this transitional period, not to jeopardize or hamper the reaching of the final agreement. Such arrangements shall be without prejudice to the final delimitation.
4. Where there is an agreement in force between the States concerned, questions relating to the delimitation of the … shelf shall be determined in accordance with the provisions of that agreement.[279]

UNCLOS Article 74(1) recites principles for the EEZ between States with opposite or adjacent coasts analogous to those for the continental shelf in Article 83.[280]

[278] Continental Shelf Cases (F.R.G. v. Den., F.R.G. v. Neth.), 1969 ICJ 3, 41–45 held Shelf Convention art. 6 did not then restate or otherwise constitute customary international law.

[279] *See also* UNCLOS art. 134(4); *id.*, Annex II, art. 9; 2 Commentary 952–85.

[280] *Compare* UNCLOS art. 74 *with id.* art. 83.

Under UNCLOS Article 47(6), if part of an archipelagic State's archipelagic waters lies between two parts of "an immediately adjacent neighboring State," existing rights and all other legitimate interests the latter State has traditionally exercised in such waters and all rights in agreements between those States must continue and be respected.

Although "adjacent States" usually is thought of where States have a common land boundary, it is possible that two States may have adjacent coasts even though they do not share a common land boundary. The definition includes this possibility.

Section 23 defines "chart" or "nautical chart;" § 28, "coast;" § 31, "coastal State;" § 130, "opposite coasts;" § 176, "straight line, straight baseline; straight archipelagic baseline."[281]

§ 3. *Aid(s) to Navigation; Navigational Aid(s); Facility (Navigational)*

(a) "Aid to navigation" means the same as "navigational aid" or "facility (navigational)" as used in UNCLOS Articles 21(1)(b) and 43(a), and means a device, external to a vessel, charted or otherwise published, serving the interests of safe navigation. "Aid to navigation" may also include "warning signals" as used in Articles 60(3), 147(2)(a) and 262.

(b) Depending on the context, "navigational aid" may also mean a shipboard instrument or similar device used to assist in navigating a vessel.

Comment

This is the definition the 2006 Consolidated Glossary recommends, expanded to cover some "warning signals" and adding "or similar" before "device." Nowhere does UNCLOS define "aids to navigation," "navigational aids" or "warning signals" as the latter phrase is used in UNCLOS Articles 60(3), 147(2)(a) and 262. Mariners and publications related to ocean navigation refer to "aid(s) to navigation" and "navigational aid(s)" interchangeably.

---

[281] The Glossary definition is the same as the *Annex 1* definition; *see Annex 1*, p. 321. *See also* 2007–08 ABILA Proc. 135–38; Churchill & Lowe 183, 191–92, 194–96; 2 Commentary ¶¶ 15.1–15.12(c), 47.1–47.9(m), 83.1–83.19(f); NWP 1-14M Annotated ¶¶ 1.4.3, particularly n.42; 1.6, particularly n.57 & Fig. A1-2; 2 O'Connell 681, 684–90, 699–732; Restatement (Third) §§ 511–12, 516–17; *Annex 1*, p. 321; Noyes, *Definitions* 322–23 & Part III.D; Walker, *Consolidated Glossary* 223–25.

Some warning signals may aid navigation; some may not, *e.g.*, a warning signal, like a light, aboard an MSR vessel, whether underway or at anchor, would not be an aid to navigation, although it would warn of the vessel's presence. In the latter case lawfulness of the signal would be subject to other rules, *e.g.*, Rules of the Road in the Collision Regulations, acronymed COLREGS.[282] On the other hand, warning signals on artificial islands would almost certainly be aids to navigation in most cases. The phrase "or similar" has been added before "device" in 3(b) to project into the future, when navigational aids based on computer or similar technology may come into common use.

In LOAC-governed situations under the "other rules of international law" clauses in UNCLOS, a different definition may apply. The same may be the situation if the UN Charter supersedes UNCLOS or if jus cogens norms apply.[283]

Consolidated Glossary ¶ 2 defines "aid to navigation" as a "device, external to a vessel, charted or otherwise published, serving the interests of safe navigation." Former Glossary ¶ 2 defined "aid to navigation" as a "[v]isual, acoustical or radio device external to a craft designed to assist in the determination of a safe course or of a vessel's position, or to warn of dangers and obstructions." "Navigational aid" has the same meaning, as does "facility (navigational)." Consolidated Glossary ¶ 65 defines "navigational aid" as "a shipboard instrument or device used to assist in the navigation of a vessel." There is no equivalent in the Former Glossary.

UNCLOS Article 21(1)(b) includes, among laws and regulations a coastal State may adopt relating to innocent passage, in conformity with UNCLOS and other rules of international law, laws and regulations for "protection of navigational aids and facilities...." Article 43(a) provides that "User States and States bordering a strait should by agreement cooperate ... in the establishment and maintenance in a strait of

[282] Convention on International Regulations for Preventing Collisions at Sea, Oct. 20, 1972, 28 UST 3459, 1050 UNTS 16, replacing International Convention for Preventing Collisions at Sea, with Attached Regulations, June 17, 1960, 16 UST 794, 536 UNTS 27, for most States. *See* TIF 399–400. Many mariners know these treaties as the Collision Regulations or COLREGS. UNCLOS arts. 21(1)(a), 22(1), 39(2)(a), 41, 42(1)(a), 60(3), 94(3), 98(2), 147(2)(c), 194(3)(b), 194(3)(c), 194(3)(d), 225, 242(2), 262 authorize promulgation of safety at sea rules, sometimes by international agreement and sometimes by coastal States, an example of the latter being innocent passage rules. *See also* Roach & Smith 382–86. Agreements like COLREGS cannot be inconsistent with the Convention. UNCLOS, art. 311.

[283] *See* Parts III.B-III.D and § 132, defining "other rules of international law."

necessary navigational and safety aids or other improvements in aid of international navigation...." Territorial Sea Convention Article 16(2), requires "a coastal State ... to give due publicity to any dangers to navigation of which it has knowledge."

UNCLOS also provides for signals "warning" of various dangers. Article 60(3) inter alia requires coastal States declaring an EEZ to give "Due notice ... of the construction of such artificial islands, installations or structures, and permanent means for giving warning of their presence must be maintained." Articles 208(1) (standards for regulating pollution from seabed activities subject to national jurisdiction) and 246(5)(c) (standards for withholding consent for other States' MSR) incorporate its standards by reference.

Article 147(2)(a) requires that installations used for carrying out activities in the Area must be subject to, inter alia, this condition: "[S]uch installations shall be erected, emplaced and removed solely in accordance with this Part [XI, law governing the Area] and subject to the rules, regulations and procedures of the Authority. Due notice must be given of the erection, emplacement and removal of such installations, and permanent means for giving warning of their presence must be maintained...." UNCLOS Article 1(1)(1) defines the Area.[284]

With respect to MSR, UNCLOS Article 262 requires for identification markings and warning signals:

> Installations or equipment referred to in this section [XIII.4] shall bear identification markings indicating the State of registry or the international organization to which they belong and shall have adequate internationally agreed warning signals to ensure safety at sea and the safety of air navigation, taking into account rules and standards established by competent international organizations.

Shelf Convention Article 5(5) requires permanent means of warning of presence of artificial islands or other installations a coastal State installs on its continental shelf.

Section 10 defines "artificial island, offshore installation, installation (offshore);" § 28, "coast;" § 31, "coastal State;" § 152, "Rules of the Road;" § 157, "sea-bed," "seabed" or "bed;" § 163, "ship" or "vessel;" § 199, "warning."[285]

---

[284] *See also* § 9, defining "area."

[285] *Annex 1*, p. 321, provides a more general definition: "A device, external to a vessel, charted or otherwise published, serving the interests of safe navigation, *e.g.*, buoys, lights, radio beacons." *See also* Churchill & Lowe 155, 270–71, 414; 2 Commentary ¶¶ 1.16–1.19, 21.1–21.11(a), 43.1–43.8(a), 60.15(f), 60.15(*l*)-60.15(m); 4 *id.*

§ 4. *Alarm*

In UNCLOS analysis, "alarm" means a device or system that announces by audible means, or audible and visual means, a condition requiring attention.

Comment

In LOAC-governed situations under the "other rules of international law" clauses in UNCLOS, a different definition may apply. The same may be the situation if the UN Charter supersedes UNCLOS or if jus cogens norms apply.[286]

The ECDIS Glossary, page 1, defines "alarm" as "[a] device or system which alerts by audible means, or audible and visual means, a condition requiring attention." Former ECDIS Glossary, page 1, defined "alarm" as "[a]n alarm or alarm system which announces by audible means, or audible and visual means, a condition requiring attention." The Committee definition reflects the later ECDIS Glossary definition.

Section 84 defines "indicator;" § 199, "warning."[287]

§ 5. *Applicable and Generally Accepted*

Owing to different usages in different UNCLOS provisions, there are four definitions of "applicable" and "generally accepted":

(a) The meaning of "applicable" when modifying "law" in UNCLOS is governed by the particular Article in which the phrase "applicable law" appears.
(b) "Applicable regulations" in UNCLOS Article 42(1)(b) means the same as "generally accepted regulations," but no such regulations may have the effect of interfering with straits passage as provided in UNCLOS.
(c) "Applicable" means the same as "generally accepted" where the word "applicable" modifies "international rules and standards" in UNCLOS Articles 94(3)(b), 213, 217(1), 218(1), 219, 220(1), 220(2), 220(3), 222, 226(1)(b), 226(1)(c), 228(1), 230(1), 230(2) and

¶¶ 208.1–208.10(d), 246.1–246.17(f), 262.1–262.5; DOD Dictionary 18 ("air facility" is "An installation from which air operations may be or are being conducted"), 199 ("facility" is "real property entity consisting of one or more of the following: a building, a structure, a utility system, pavement, and underlying land"); NWP 1-14M Annotated ¶ 2.4.2.1.4; Restatement (Third) §§ 513–15; Walker, *Consolidated Glossary* 226.

[286] *See* Parts III.B-III.D and § 132, defining "other rules of international law."

[287] *See also* Walker, *ECDIS Glossary* 241, 2003–04 ABILA Proc. 212.

297(1)(c), and where "applicable" modifies "international regulations" in UNCLOS Article 94(4)(c).

(d) "Generally accepted," as employed in UNCLOS Articles 21(2), 21(4), 39(2), 41(3), 53(8), 60(3), 60(5), 60(6), 94(2)(a), 94(5), 211(2), 211(5), 211(6)(c) and 226(1)(a), means those international rules, standards or regulations that bind States parties to UNCLOS through international agreements, or bind States through customary law, or reflect State practice that has not necessarily matured into custom that reflects UNCLOS standards. In many cases these will be those international rules, standards or regulations IMO establishes.

Comment

UNCLOS declares few if any specific international rules and standards or international regulations. However, since UNCLOS Articles 311(2)-311(4) do not allow agreements contrary to UNCLOS, the result should be that generally accepted standards cannot differ from UNCLOS or implementing treaties, *e.g.*, regional conventions establishing pollution standards. The § 5(d) formulation would not limit generally accepted customary standards to those declared as treaty-based standards under UNCLOS but would also encompass widespread State practice in the absence of a treaty or customary norm, as the ILA Committee on Coastal State Jurisdiction Relating to Marine Pollution (ILA Pollution Committee) advocated.[288]

In law of armed conflict (LOAC)-governed situations under the "other rules of international law" clauses in UNCLOS, a different definition may apply. The same may be the situation if the UN Charter supersedes UNCLOS or if jus cogens norms apply.[289]

The terms "applicable" and "generally accepted" are related, for reasons that follow. "Applicable" appears in UNCLOS Articles 42(1)(b), 94(4)(c), 211(6)(c), 213, 217(1), 218(1), 219, 220(1), 220(2), 220(3), 222, 226(1)(b), 226(1)(c), 228(1), 230(1), 230(2), 293 and 297(1)(c). The term also appears in UNCLOS Annex III, Basic Conditions of Prospecting, Exploration and Exploitation, Article 21; Annex VI,

---

[288] This analysis partly relies on ILA Committee on Coastal State Jurisdiction Relating to Marine Pollution, *Second Report*, in ILA, Report of the Sixty-Eighth Conference Held at Taipei, Taiwan, Republic of China 24–30 May 1998, p. 372 (*Second Report*); *id.*, *First Report*, in ILA, Report of the Sixty-Seventh Conference Held at Helsinki, Finland, 12–17 August 1996, p. 148 (1996) (*First Report*).

[289] *See* Parts III.B-III.D and § 132, defining "other rules of international law."

Statute of the International Tribunal for the Law of the Sea, Articles 23 and 38.

"Generally accepted" appears in UNCLOS Articles 21(2), 21(4), 39(2), 41(3), 53(8), 60(3), 60(5), 60(6), 94(2)(a), 94(5), 211(2), 211(5), 211(6)(c) and 226(1)(a). In all instances "generally accepted" modifies words or phrases like "international rules or standards" (Article 21[2]), "international rules and standards" (Articles 211[2], 211[5], 211[6][c], 226[1][a]), "international regulations" (Articles 21[4], 41[3], 53[8], 94[2][a], 94[5]), "international regulations, procedures and practices" (Articles 39[2][a], adding "for safety at sea, including the International Regulations for Preventing Collisions at Sea;" 39[2][b], adding "for the prevention, reduction and control of pollution from ships"), "international standards" (Articles 60[3]; 60[5]; 60[6], adding "regarding navigation in the vicinity of artificial islands, installations, structures and safety zones").

In titles to UNCLOS Article 293; Annex III, Article 21; and Annex VI, Articles 23 and 28, "applicable" modifies "law." Annex VI, Articles 23 and 28 refer to UNCLOS Article 293. Article 293(1) says that "A court or tribunal having jurisdiction under this section [UNCLOS Articles 286–96] shall apply this Convention and other rules of international law not incompatible with this Convention."[290] Annex III, Article 21, referring to contracts for prospecting, exploring and exploiting the Area, says such contracts "shall be governed by the terms of the contract, the rules, regulations and procedures of the Authority, Part XI [UNCLOS Articles 133–91] and other rules of international law not incompatible with this Convention." The negotiating history record is sparse[291] on what "applicable law" means other than the supremacy of UNCLOS, at least where UN Charter decision issues are not at stake.[292] The principle of UNCLOS's supremacy over other agreements appears in, *e.g.*, UNCLOS Articles 311(2)-311(4). There is no point in recommending a further definition for "applicable" where it modifies "law."[293]

In vessel-source rules of reference, UNCLOS Articles 94(3)(b), 213, 217(1), 218(1), 219, 220(1), 220(2), 220(3), 222, 226(1)(b),

---

[290] UNCLOS art. 293(2) allows the tribunal or court to decide a case ex aequo et bono if the parties so agree; *see also* ICJ Statute art. 38(2).

[291] *See generally* 5 Commentary ¶¶ 293.1–293.5, A.VI.131–32, A.VI.198–200.

[292] UN Charter arts. 25, 48, 94(2), 103; *see also* Parts III.B, III.C.

[293] *See* § 132's analysis of "other rules of international law" and how it relates to UNCLOS.

226(1)(c), 228(1), 230(1), 230(2) and 297(1)(c), "applicable" qualifies "international rules and standards" with respect to ocean environment matters. UNCLOS Article 94(4)(c) requires:

> 4. Such measures [for ships flying its (a registry State's) flag] shall include those necessary to ensure: ...
>   (c) that the master, officers and, to the extent appropriate, the crew are fully conversant with and required to observe the applicable international regulations concerning the safety of life at sea, the prevention of collisions, the prevention, reduction and control of marine pollution, and the maintenance of communications by radio.

In UNCLOS Article 42(1)(b), however, the word "applicable" is employed in a different context:

> 1. Subject to the provisions of this section [relating to straits transit passage], States bordering straits may adopt laws and regulations relating to transit passage through straits, in respect of all or any of the following:
> ... (b) the prevention, reduction and control of pollution, by giving effect to applicable international regulations regarding the discharge of oil, oily wastes and other noxious substances in the strait; ...

In its declaration upon signature of UNCLOS, Spain insisted that "applicable" in Article 42(1)(b) should have been replaced by "generally accepted." Spain's declaration upon ratification submitted that strait States can "enact and enforce in straits used for international navigation its own regulations, provided that such regulations do not interfere with the right of transit passage."[294] The ILA Pollution Committee "suggests that flag States should not have to submit to the enforcement of rules and standards that they have not somehow accepted[, but that] it would not be correct to transpose conclusions arrived at there to a more general enforcement perspective."[295]

There is no record in the UNCLOS negotiating history on the origin or intention of "applicable." The UNCLOS Drafting Committee English language group had recommended that the words "generally accepted" be substituted for "applicable" in Articles 42(1)(b), 94(4)(c), 218(1) and 219. There is no formal attitude of States toward the concept of "generally accepted."[296] For Article 21(4), the "generally accepted" international regulations, practices and

[294] *Second Report,* note 288, p. 373 n.6.
[295] *Id.* 373–74.
[296] *Id.* 373, 378.

procedures mean those adopted within the International Maritime Organization (IMO) framework.[297] The same is true for Articles 39(2), 41(3), and 53(8),[298] and perhaps Articles 94(2)(a) and 94(5),[299] for the "generally accepted international rules or standards" of Articles 21(2), 211(2), 211(5) and 211(6)(c),[300] and for "international standards" requirements of Articles 60(3), 60(5) and 60(6).[301] On the other hand, analysts cite other international agreements, but also the possibility of IMO action, for the "generally accepted rules and standards" to which Article 226(1)(a) refers.[302] In view of Articles 311(2)-311(4), prohibiting any treaties with standards incompatible with UNCLOS, "generally accepted" must mean that any international law, rule, regulation or other standard UNCLOS allows or requires cannot be incompatible with it.[303] This would appear to take into account differing views of commentators: (1) "generally accepted" means whatever customary international law is on the point; (2) "generally accepted" means whatever norms a State has accepted through ratification of treaties, a position taken by States during the Ship Registration Convention negotiations; (3) "generally accepted" refers to standards of IMO conventions in force, whether or not a State is a party to the conventions; or (4) for States party to UNCLOS, ratification means they have agreed to be bound by a less strict standard than those postulated by advocates of options (1), (2) or (3).[304] The ILA Pollution Committee rejected options (1), (2) and (3), advocating adoption of widespread State practice, as distinguished from customary international law with a possibility of the persistent objector and the time over which custom must mature, for "generally accepted."[305] The Pollution Committee adopted this definition in the context of UNCLOS maritime pollution

[297] 2 Commentary ¶¶ 21.11(g)-21.11(I); *see also* 4 *id.* ¶¶ 211.15(c)-211.15(d); *First Report,* note 288, p. 169.

[298] 2 Commentary ¶¶ 39.10(I), 41.9(c), 53.9(*l*); *see also First Report,* note 288, p. 169.

[299] 2 Commentary ¶¶ 94.8(b), 94.8(I); *see also First Report,* note 288, p. 169.

[300] 2 Commentary ¶¶ 21.11(g)-21.11(I); 4 *id.* ¶¶ 211.15(c)-211.15(d); *see also First Report,* note 288, p. 169.

[301] 2 Commentary ¶ 60.15(f); *see also First Report,* note 288, p. 169.

[302] *See generally* 4 Commentary ¶ 226.11(b) & n.6; *see also First Report,* note 288, p. 169.

[303] *See also* 5 Commentary ¶¶ 311.1–311.8, 311.11.

[304] *First Report,* note 288, pp. 170–71, inter alia referring to the Ship Registration Convention. As of April 1, 2009 14 States were parties. 3 Multilateral Treaties ch. 12, pt. 7.

[305] *First Report,* note 288, pp. 174–77.

issues, where many (but not all) uses of "generally accepted" appear. There is risk of inapposite results if the ocean pollution definition is applied to other uses of the term, particularly if "applicable" is equated to "generally accepted." This requires careful consideration.

Under the circumstances it seemed appropriate to the ABILA LOS Committee to formulate a special definition for "applicable law" wherever appearing in UNCLOS, a special definition for "applicable" in UNCLOS Article 42(1)(b), and another, more general definition for other provisions using "applicable." It is appropriate to adopt the ILA Committee approach for "generally accepted" wherever the phrase appears in UNCLOS.[306]

§ 6. *Appropriate; appropriation*

As used in UNCLOS Article 137(1), "appropriate" means taking any action through national judicial proceedings, self-help measures or other action by a State, a natural person or a juridical person, that takes, or attempts to take, title or possession, exercise of sovereignty or exercise of sovereign rights, or exercise of jurisdiction. As used in UNCLOS Article 137(1), "appropriation" is the noun form of "appropriate."

Comment

In LOAC-governed situations under the "other rules of international law" clauses in UNCLOS, a different definition may apply. The same may be the situation if the UN Charter supersedes UNCLOS or if jus cogens norms apply.[307]

UNCLOS Article 137(1), which follows Article 136's proclamation that "The Area and its resources are the common heritage of mankind," declares:

> No State shall claim or exercise sovereignty or sovereign rights over any part of the Area or its resources, nor shall any State or natural or juridical person appropriate any part thereof. No such claim or exercise of sovereignty or sovereign rights nor such appropriation shall be recognized.

---

[306] *See also* Roach & Smith ¶ 13.2.4, noting commentators' differing views on whether "generally accepted" and "applicable" have the same meaning; Walker, *Defining* 349–53.

[307] *See* Parts III.B-III.D and § 132, defining "other rules of international law." An example of a different LOAC standard is the rule that title to warships sunk during war remains in the flag State until title is formally relinquished or abandoned. NWP 1-14M Annotated ¶ 2.1.2.2.

The remainder of UNCLOS Article 137 provides:

> 2. All rights in the resources of the Area are vested in mankind as a whole, on whose behalf the [International Sea-Bed] Authority shall act. These resources are not subject to alienation. The minerals recovered in the Area, however, may only be alienated in accordance with this Part and the rules, regulations and procedures of the Authority.
> 3. No state or natural or juridical claim, acquire or exercise rights with respect to the minerals recovered from the Area except in accordance with this Part [XI, governing the Area]. Otherwise, no such claim, acquisition or exercise of such rights shall be recognized.[308]

Reading Article 137 as a whole, it seems clear that the Article 137 drafters intended a comprehensive prohibition on State or private claims to Area resources, defined in Article 133(a) as "all solid, liquid or gaseous mineral resources *in situ* in the Area or beneath the sea-bed, including polymetallic nodules," and to "minerals," defined in Article 133(b) as "resources, when recovered from the Area." Although the meaning of "appropriate" and "appropriation" is less than clear, it would seem that those words refer to attempts by States, natural persons or juridical persons (*e.g.*, corporations) to attempt to take, or to take, title or possession to Area resources or minerals, as defined in Article 133, by legal process (*e.g.*, admiralty in rem procedures, proceedings under the law of finds, or the like[309]) or action without benefit of private law processes, *e.g.*, private party seizure of Area resources or minerals under a claim of the law of finds. The comprehensive rules in Articles 137(2) and 137(3) tend to bear this out. Article 149 lends further support to this view:

> [O]bjects of an archeological and historical nature found in the Area shall be preserved or disposed of for the benefit of mankind as a whole, particular regard being paid to the preferential rights of the State or country of origin, or the State of cultural origin, or the State of historical and archeological origin.[310]

If this is the rule for historical or archeological objects at the bottom of the sea in the Area, *i.e.*, that they are not subject to admiralty in rem,

[308] UNCLOS art. 1(2) defines the Authority.

[309] *See generally* Thomas M. Schoenbaum, Admiralty and Maritime Law § 14-7 (4th ed. 2004) for a general analysis of the U.S. law of treasure salvage and the law of finds.

[310] *See also* UNESCO Convention on the Protection of the Underwater Cultural Heritage, Nov. 2, 2001, 41 ILM 40.

law of finds proceedings, self-help claims or the like, it is also true for Area resources that can be exploited commercially.

Section 9 defines "area" as contrasted with "Area;" § 34, "common heritage of mankind" or "common heritage of humankind."

§ 7. *Appropriate international organization or appropriate international organizations*

"Appropriate international organization" or "appropriate international organizations," as used in UNCLOS, means that international organization or those international organizations typically associated by principles, purposes and functions with action required by a particular article of UNCLOS or its Annexes. The appropriate organization may be global, regional or sub-regional, depending on the circumstances of the particular issue, and may be an intergovernmental organization (IGO) organized under the UN Charter, an independent IGO or a nongovernmental organization.

Comment

In LOAC-governed situations under the "other rules of international law" clauses in UNCLOS, a different definition may apply. The same may be the situation if the UN Charter supersedes UNCLOS or if *jus cogens* norms apply.[311]

These general definitions, which may rightly be characterized as almost no definitions at all, follow from UNCLOS' relatively scanty preparatory works and from practical necessity.

For example, FAO, cited in commentary for UNCLOS Article 64, is organized under the Charter;[312] UNCLOS Article 64 commentary adds that IGOs subordinate to FAO or independent IGOs were also considered. The FAO Committee on Fisheries has been

> the only intergovernmental forum in which fishery problems are examined periodically on a worldwide basis, and could, in some respects, be considered a global organization to which [A]rticle 61 refers. Alongside this Commission [sic], there are a number of regional fishery bodies

[311] *See* Parts III.B-III.D and § 132, defining "other rules of international law."

[312] Constitution of the United Nations Food and Agriculture Organization, Oct. 16, 1945, 60 Stat. 1886. There have been many amendments to *id.* since 1945. *See id.*, 12 UST 980 (composite text as amended to 1957); TIF 366–67; Wiktor 440–41.

> both inside and outside FAO, the activities of which are of more direct relevance to the actual management of fishery resources.[313]

UNCLOS Article 65 commentary, mentioning the International Whaling Commission,[314] is generic in its discussion ("in particular," "other conventions"), leading to the conclusion that its drafters did not intend a specific international organization. The same can be said for the UNCLOS Article 297 preparatory works. As an introductory commentary puts it, "It will usually appear from the context of the issue involved which international organization is competent for that particular purpose."[315]

The practicality aspect of the definition is that international organizations, whether organized and operating under the Charter or organized and operating independently outside the UN Charter umbrella as an IGO or an NGO, can change in function or organization or disappear, perhaps to be replaced by another organization or organizations. The IMO is a case in point. Originally organized as the Intergovernmental Maritime Consultative Organization (IMCO), IMCO is now IMO, with a different constitutive treaty, organization and procedures, etc.[316] If a definition would have named IMCO as the "appropriate international organization" in 1948 when the IMCO Convention was signed, *i.e.*, well before 1982, when the 1975 name change became effective,[317] the result might have been confusion thereafter, since IMCO remained in existence for some States during the transition, and IMO was the IGO for other situations. This is a simplistic example; more fundamental issues can arise if, *e.g.*, an international organization "appropriate" at one time under UNCLOS changes its functions, etc., while perhaps retaining its name, so that it is in reality no longer "appropriate." To choose a name or name today for organizations thought "appropriate" invites almost instant obsolescence of the definition. Moreover, as the

---

313 2 Commentary ¶ 61.12(e).

314 *See* International Convention for Regulation of Whaling, Dec. 2, 1946, art. 3, 62 Stat. 1716, 1717, 161 UNTS 72, 76, establishing the International Whaling Commission. The Convention has been amended often by protocol or has been modified. *See* TIF 467; Wiktor 461.

315 2 Commentary ¶ INTRO.27.

316 *Compare* Convention Establishing Intergovernmental Maritime Consultative Organization, note 75, pmbl. *with* Amendments to Convention on the Intergovernmental Maritime Consultative Organization of March 6, 1948, note 75, Title of the Convention & Preamble. There were Convention amendments before and after the 1975 amendments. *See* 3 Multilateral Treaties ch. 12, pts. 1.a-1.h; TIF 379–80.

317 TIF 379–80 note *.

UNCLOS Article 64 and 65 commentaries suggest, UNCLOS negotiators obviously had different international organizations in mind for different purposes of different UNCLOS provisions.

UNCLOS Article 64(1) refers to "appropriate international organizations" in the plural and to "appropriate international organization" in the singular:

> 1. The coastal State and other States whose nationals fish in the region for the highly migratory species listed in Annex I [of the Convention] shall cooperate directly or through appropriate international organizations with a view to ensuring conservation and promoting the objective of optimum utilization of such species throughout the region, both within and beyond the exclusive economic zone. In regions for which no appropriate international organization exists, the coastal State and other States whose nationals harvest these species in the region shall cooperate to establish such an organization and participate in its work.

UNCLOS Article 65 refers to "appropriate international organization" in the singular:

> Nothing in this Part [V of the Convention] restricts the right of a coastal State or the competence of an international organization, as appropriate, to prohibit, limit or regulate the exploitation of marine mammals more strictly than provided in this Part. States shall cooperate with a view to the conservation of marine mammals and in the case of cetaceans shall in particular work through the appropriate international organizations for their conservation, management and study.

UNCLOS Article 143(3)(b) refers to "other international organization as appropriate:"

> 3. States parties may carry out marine scientific research in the Area. States Parties shall promote international cooperation in marine scientific research in the area by:
>
> … (b) ensuring that programs are developed through the Authority or other international organizations as appropriate for the benefit of developing States and technologically less developed states with a view to:
>
> (i) strengthening their research capabilities;
>
> (ii) training their personnel and the personnel of the Authority in the techniques and applications of research;
>
> (iii) fostering the employment of their qualified personnel in research in the Area …

UNCLOS Article 297(3)(d), referring to disputes referred to compulsory procedures entailing binding decisions and limitations and exceptions to these procedures, provides: "The report of the conciliation commission shall be communicated to appropriate international organizations."

UNCLOS Annex VIII, Article 3(e), referring to special arbitration procedures for fisheries, environmental protection, marine scientific research or navigation issues, refers to "appropriate international organization" in providing:

> For the purposes of proceedings under this Annex, the special arbitral tribunal shall, unless the parties otherwise agree, be constituted as follows: ...
>
> (e) Unless the parties agree that the appointment be made by a person or a third State chosen by the parties, the Secretary-General of the United Nations shall make the necessary appointments within 30 days of receipt of a request under subparagraphs (c) and (d) [of Article 3]. The appointment referred to in this subparagraph shall be made from the appropriate list or lists of experts referred to in Article 2 of this Annex and in consultation with the parties to the dispute and the appropriate international organization. The members so appointed shall be of different nationalities and may not be in the service of, ordinarily resident in the territory of, or nationals of, any of the parties to the dispute.

Commentary for UNCLOS Article 64 says that "appropriate international organization" means the U.N. Food and Agriculture Organization, perhaps one of its regional fishery bodies, or fishery organizations like the International Commission for Conservation of Atlantic Tunas (ICCAT), not affiliated with FAO.[318]

Commentary for UNCLOS Article 65 says:

> There is no indication of what constitutes a competent international organization in these matters. Special arrangements regarding the conservation and utilization of whales in particular have been established under the International Whaling Commission. Failure to conserve stocks has also led to the application of other conventions to cetaceans.[319]

Article 297 preparatory works show this formula in a compromise draft for what became Article 297(d)(e): "The report of the conciliation commission shall be communicated to the appropriate global, regional or sub-regional intergovernmental organizations."[320]

---

318 2 Commentary ¶ 64.9(c).

319 *Id.* ¶ 65.11(b).

320 5 *id.* ¶ 297.15, p. 103.

UNCLOS Article 63 refers to "appropriate subregional or regional organizations;" *see also* §§ 7, defining "appropriate international organization or appropriate international organizations;" 141, defining "regional organization or subregional organization."

Fishing Convention Article 9 establishes a procedure for a special commission, involving the UN Secretary-General, the ICJ President and the FAO Director-General, for resolving fishing disputes arising under Fishing Convention Articles 7–8.

Section 35 defines "competent international organization" or "competent international organizations;" § 141, "regional" or "sub-regional" organization.[321]

§ 8. *Appropriate notice*

See Due notice, § 54.

§ 9. *Area and area*

(a) As used in UNCLOS, "Area" is defined in Article 1(1)(1) of that Convention.
(b) The word "area" is defined as the two-dimensional or three-dimensional representation of a geographic space, specifying its location in ocean space covered by UNCLOS.

Comment

In LOAC-governed situations under the "other rules of international law" clauses in UNCLOS, a different definition may apply. The same may be the situation if the UN Charter supersedes UNCLOS or if jus cogens norms apply.[322]

Former ECDIS Glossary, page 1, defines "area" as "the 2-dimensional *geometric primitive* of an *object* that specifies location," referring to Figure 4, ECDIS Former Glossary, page 27. The newer ECDIS Glossary definition is the same, minus the cross-reference. The Former Glossary, page 11 defined "geometric primitive" as "[o]ne of the three basic

---

[321] *See also* Churchill & Lowe 311–14; Walker, *Last Round* 151–55, 2005–06 ABILA Proc. 40–45; *"Competent or Relevant International Organizations" Under the United Nations Convention on the Law of the Sea,* Law of the Sea Bull. 79 (No. 31, 1995) (*Competent*).

[322] *See* Parts III.B-III.D and § 132, defining "other rules of international law."

geometric units of representation: *point, line* and *area*." The newer Glossary definition, page 5, is the same. The Former Glossary, page 16 defined "object" as "[a]n identifiable set of information. An object may have *attributes* and may be related to other objects." The newer Glossary definition, page 9, is the same. Although representations on charts, diagrams or, *e.g.*, computer-generated models, are two-dimensional in the sense that they are flat, these representations can convey a pictorial description that is two- or three-dimensional. A traditional chart is a two-dimensional representation. On the other hand, a diagram or a computer-generated model might be a three-dimensional representation portraying water surface dimensions and depth in an ocean space. The "area" definition covers both situations.

UNCLOS Article 1(1)(1) defines "Area" as "the sea-bed and ocean floor and subsoil thereof, beyond the limits of national jurisdiction."

Section 16 defines "basepoint" or "point;" § 28, "coast;" § 31, "coastal State;" § 47, "deep ocean floor;" § 66, "flag state," § 67, "foot of the continental shelf;" § 78, "geometric primitive;" § 93, "line;" § 94, "line of delimitation;" § 125, "object;" § 126, "ocean space" or "sea;" § 133, "outer limit;" § 157, "sea-bed," "seabed" or "bed;" § 176, "straight line," "straight baseline" and "straight archipelagic baseline;" § 184, "subsoil;" § 185, "superjacent waters" or "water column."[323]

§ 10. *Artificial island, offshore installation, installation (offshore)*

An "artificial island" or "offshore installation," or "installation (offshore)," as used in UNCLOS means a human-made edifice in the territorial sea, in the EEZ, on the continental shelf, in archipelagic waters, or in ocean space governed by UNCLOS, which is usually employed to explore for or exploit marine resources. Artificial islands, offshore installations or installations (off-shore) may also be built for other purposes, such as marine scientific research, tide observations, resorts or residences, air terminals, transportation centers, traffic control, etc. Artificial islands or other offshore installations as here defined are subject to all other jurisdictional and other limitations and requirements in UNCLOS, *e.g.*, that artificial islands or offshore installations can possess neither territorial sea nor be considered as permanent harbor works and that coastal States are responsible under UNCLOS for environmental protections required for artificial islands.

[323] *See also* Churchill & Lowe ch. 12; Walker, *ECDIS Glossary* 241–42, 2003–04 ABILA Proc. 212–13.

Comment

In LOAC-governed situations under the "other rules of international law" clauses in UNCLOS, a different definition may apply. The same may be the situation if the UN Charter supersedes UNCLOS or if jus cogens norms apply.[324]

The Consolidated Glossary does not offer a separate definition for "artificial island;" in ¶ 47, following Former Glossary ¶ 41, it defines "installation (off-shore):" "Man-made structure in the territorial sea, the exclusive economic zone or on the continental shelf usually for the exploration or exploitation of marine resources. They may also be built for other purposes such as marine scientific research, tide observations, etc." The Committee definition substitutes "human-made" for "man-made" for gender neutralization, and "edifice" for "structure," which is used in UNCLOS Articles 1(1)(5), 56(1)(b)(1), 60(4)-60(8), 180, 208(1), 209(2), 214 and 246(5)(c).

UNCLOS Article 11 says that offshore installations or artificial islands are not considered permanent harbor works and may not be used as part of the baseline to measure the territorial sea's breadth. Articles 7(4) and 47(4) say that low-tide elevations having lighthouses or similar installations may be used as basepoints for otherwise straight baselines or archipelagic baselines. A coastal State has jurisdiction over artificial islands, installations and structures it erects within its EEZ under Article 56(1)(b)(i). However, artificial islands, installations and structures do not have the status of islands. They have no territorial sea; their presence does not affect the territorial sea, the EEZ or the continental shelf, according to Article 60(8). Article 60 also lays down rules for notice of construction or removal of artificial islands; permanent means of warning of their presence must be maintained. Safety zones, not over 500 meters, may be established. Abandoned or disused installations must be removed under generally accepted international standards. UNCLOS Articles 208(1) (standards for regulating pollution from seabed activities subject to national jurisdiction) and 246(5)(c) (standards for withholding consent for other States' MSR) incorporate Article 60 standards by reference. Article 60 rules apply to artificial islands erected on the continental shelf, according to Article

---

[324] *See* Parts III.B-III.D and § 132, defining "other rules of international law." An example of the interface of the LOAC might be erection of coastal defenses on artificial islands in, *e.g.*, a State's territorial sea during armed conflict. If a coastal State erects artificial islands in, *e.g.*, its territorial sea for self-defense purposes, a third set of principles would come into play.

80; under Article 79(4), a State declaring a continental shelf may lay pipelines or cables to be used in connecting artificial islands, installations or structures under its jurisdiction. Subject to rules governing the continental shelf, UNCLOS Part VI, UNCLOS Article 87(1)(d) lists as a high seas freedom the right to construct artificial islands and other installations. Coastal States may withhold consent to another State's or a competent international organization's conducting a MSR project if it involves constructing, operating or using artificial islands, installations or structures in a coastal State's EEZ or on its continental shelf, according to UNCLOS Article 246(5)(d). A coastal State must adopt laws and regulations to prevent, reduce and control pollution of the marine environment arising from or in connection with artificial islands, installations and structures in its EEZ or on its continental shelf, according to Article 208(1). UNCLOS Article 214 requires enforcing these laws and adopting laws and regulations, and taking other measures to implement applicable international rules and standards established through competent international organizations or diplomatic conferences to prevent, reduce and control marine environmental pollution from artificial islands, installations and structures under coastal States' EEZ and continental shelf jurisdiction.

The 1958 LOS Conventions do not provide for artificial islands or similar installations except in connection with continental shelf activity. Territorial Sea Convention Article 10, anticipating UNCLOS Article 121(1), defines an island as "an area of land, surrounded by water, which in normal circumstances is permanently above [the] high-water mark." By implication these definitions exclude artificial islands. Shelf Convention Article 5 anticipated many UNCLOS principles:

1. The exploration of the continental shelf and the exploitation of its natural resources must not result in any unjustifiable interference with navigation, fishing or the conservation of the living resources of the sea, nor result in any interference with fundamental oceanographic or other scientific research carried out with the intent of open publication.
2. Subject to ... paragraphs 1 and 6 ..., the coastal State is entitled to construct and maintain or operate on the ... shelf installations and other devices necessary for its exploration and the exploitation of its natural resources, and to establish safety zones around such installations and devices and to take in those zones measures necessary for their protection.

3. The safety zones ... may extend to ... 500 meters around the installations and other devices which have been erected.... Ships of all nationalities must respect these ... zones.
4. Such installations and devices, though under the jurisdiction of the coastal State, do not possess the status of islands. They have no territorial sea ..., and their presence does not affect the delimitation of the territorial sea of the coastal State.
5. Due notice must be given of the construction of any such installations, and permanent means for giving warning of their presence must be maintained. Any installations which are abandoned or disused must be entirely removed.
6. Neither the installations or devices, nor ...zones around them, may be established where interference may be caused to the use of recognized sea lanes essential to international navigation.
7. The coastal State is obliged to undertake, in the ... zones, all appropriate measures for the protection of the living resources of the sea from harmful agents.
8. The consent of the coastal State shall be obtained [for] ... any research concerning the ... shelf and conducted there. Nevertheless, the ... State shall not normally withhold its consent if the request is submitted by a qualified institution with a view to purely scientific research into the physical or biological characteristics of the ... shelf, subject to ... the coastal State['s] ... [having] the right ... to participate or to be represented in the research, and that in any event the results shall be published.

Section 28 defines "coast;" § 31, "coastal State;" § 79, "harbor works" or "facility (port);" § 81, "high seas;" § 100, "marine scientific research;" § 157, "sea-bed," "seabed" or "bed;" § 176, "straight line, straight baseline; straight archipelagic baseline."[325]

§ 11. *Associated species or dependent species*

"Associated" or "dependent" species, as used in UNCLOS Articles 61, 63 and 119, means species interdependent with fish stocks, including marine mammals interdependent with fish and other stocks,

[325] *See also* 2007–08 ABILA Proc. 154–56; Churchill & Lowe 50–51, 153–55, 167–68, 207, 220, 412–14; 2 Commentary ¶¶ 7.1-7.9(a), 7.9(f), 11.1-11.5(d), 47.1–47.8, 47.9(f), 56.1-56.11(e), 60.1-60.15(c), 60.15(k)-60.15(m), 79.1-79.7, 79.8(d), 79.8(f); 3 *id.* ¶¶ 87.1-87.9(b), 87.9(f), 87.9(I) (1995); 4 *id.* ¶¶ 208.1-208.10(d), 214.1-214.7(c); DOD Dictionary 267 ("installation"), 395 ("offshore assets"); NWP 1-14M Annotated ¶ 1.4.2.2; 1 O'Connell 196–97, 562–63; 2 *id.* 798, 843, 846–47, 890, 905–07; Restatement (Third) §§ 511–12, 514–15; Roach & Smith ¶ 4.5.5; Walker, *Consolidated Glossary* 228–30.

e.g., species that interlock among and between fish and other stocks to be conserved, such as the food chain among stocks and other species.

Comment

In LOAC-governed situations under the "other rules of international law" clauses in UNCLOS, a different definition may apply. The same may be the situation if the UN Charter supersedes UNCLOS or if *jus cogens* norms apply.[326]

The phrases "associated species" and "associated or dependent species" are in UNCLOS Article 61(4), dealing with EEZ living resources conservation:

> 4. In taking such [coastal State-ensured proper conservation and management[327]] measures the coastal State shall take into consideration the effects on species associated with or dependent upon harvested species with a view to maintaining or restoring populations of such associated or dependent species above levels at which their reproduction may become seriously threatened.

The phrase "associated species" is in UNCLOS Article 63, also dealing with the EEZ:

> 1. Where the same stock or stocks of associated species occur within the exclusive economic zones of two or more coastal States, these states shall seek, either directly or through appropriate subregional or regional organizations, to agree upon the measures necessary to coordinate and ensure the conservation and development of such stocks without prejudice to the other provisions of this Part [V, provisions for the EEZ].
> 2. Where the same stock or stocks of associated species occur both within the exclusive economic zone and in an area beyond and adjacent to the zone, the coastal State and the States fishing for such stocks in the adjacent area shall seek, either directly or through appropriate subregional or regional organizations, to agree upon the measures necessary for the conservation of these stocks in the adjacent area.

The phrase "associated or dependent species" is also in UNCLOS Article 119, dealing with high seas living resources conservation:

> 1. In determining the allowable catch and establishing other conservation measures for the living resources in the high seas, States shall: …
>   (b) take into consideration the effects on species associated with or dependent upon harvested species with a view to maintaining or

[326] *See* Parts III.B-III.D and § 132, defining "other rules of international law."
[327] *See* UNCLOS art. 61(2).

> restoring populations of such associated or dependent species above levels at which their reproduction may become seriously threatened.

UNCLOS Article 61, tracing its origin from Fishing Convention Articles 1(2) and 2, formulates coastal States' rights and duties with respect to the EEZ; UNCLOS Article 63 sets out part of the scope of these rights and duties.[328] UNCLOS Article 119 parallels Article 61's function for the high seas and should be read with UNCLOS Article 118, requiring States to cooperate in conserving and maintaining high seas living resources.[329] Preparatory works and commentary on UNCLOS Articles 61, 63 and 119 say little about the definition of "associated" or "dependent" species. The phrases are related to interdependence of species, however:

> [UNCLOS Article 61(4)] deals with one aspect of the interdependence of fish stocks in relation to the conservation of the living resources. It obligates the coastal State to take into consideration the effects mentioned. It is not, however, limited to that; there is interdependence with other species, especially marine mammals. Identical language is used in [UNCLOS A]rticle 119, paragraph 1(b).[330]

UNCLOS Article 119 commentary has the same theme.[331] The general proposed definition for Articles 61, 63 and 119, focuses on general interdependence of species. For example, the definition contemplates known food chains among and between fish stocks to be conserved and other species of living resources of the seas.[332] These terms, associated or dependent species, are understood to be underpinnings of the ecosystem approach to conservation and management.

Section 28 defines "coast;" 31, "coastal State;" § 65, "fishing;" § 81, "high seas."

§ 12. *Atoll*

As used in UNCLOS Articles 6 and 47, "atoll" means a reef with or without an island situated on it surrounded by the open sea, that encloses or nearly encloses a lagoon.

---

328 2 Commentary ¶¶ 61.1–61.2.

329 3 *id.* ¶ 119.7(a).

330 2 *id.* ¶ 61.12(i).

331 *Compare id. with* 3 *id.* ¶¶ 119.7(b), 119.7(d).

332 *See also* Churchill & Lowe 294, 296–97; Walker, *Last Round* 156–58, 2005–06 ABILA Proc. 45–47.

Comment

In LOAC-governed situations under the "other rules of international law" clauses in UNCLOS, a different definition may apply. The same may be the situation if the UN Charter supersedes UNCLOS or if jus cogens norms apply.[333]

Consolidated Glossary ¶ 9 defines "atoll" as "[a] ring-shaped reef with or without an island situated on it surrounded by the open sea, that encloses or nearly encloses a lagoon."[334]

UNCLOS Article 121 defines "island" as:

> 1. … a naturally formed area of land, surrounded by water, which is above water at high tide.
> 2. Except as provided for in paragraph 3, the territorial sea, the contiguous zone, the exclusive economic zone and the continental shelf of an island are determined in accordance with the provisions of this Convention applicable to other land territory.
> 3. Rocks which cannot sustain human habitation or economic life of their own shall have no exclusive economic zone or continental shelf.

Territorial Sea Convention Article 10 is similar to UNCLOS Articles 121(1) and 121(2) and refers to other provisions of that Convention.[335]

UNCLOS Article 6 declares that for islands situated on an atoll or an island having a fringing reef, the baseline for measuring the territorial sea is the seaward low water line of the reef as shown by the appropriate symbol on charts the coastal State officially recognizes. Article 47(7) similarly says that for computing the ratio of water to land when establishing archipelagic waters of an archipelagic State as UNCLOS defines that State in Article 46(a), atolls and waters within them may be included as part of the land area of an archipelagic State. Under Article 47(1), an archipelagic State may draw straight archipelagic baselines joining outermost points of the outermost islands and drying reefs of the archipelago, defined in Article 46(b), provided that within such baselines are included the main islands and an area in which the ratio of the area of the water to the area of the land, including atolls, is between 1 to 1 and 9 to 1.

---

333 *See* Parts III.B-III.D and § 132, defining "other rules of international law."

334 *Accord*, 2 Commentary ¶ 6.7(a); *Annex 1* 322 has a similar definition: "A ring-shaped reef with or without an island situated on it surrounded by the open sea, which encloses or nearly encloses a lagoon. An atoll is usually formed on the top of a submerged volcano by coral growth."

335 *See also* 3 *id.* ¶¶ 121.12(a)-121.12(c).

UNCLOS and the Glossary do not define "lagoon." While defining "basepoint" and "point," § 16 discusses baselines. Section 9 defines "Area" and "area;" 23, "chart" or "nautical chart;" § 28, "coast;" § 31, "coastal State;" § 126, "ocean space" or "sea;" § 140, "reef;" § 147, "rock;" § 160, "sedimentary rock;" § 176, "straight line, straight baseline; straight archipelagic baseline."[336]

§ 13. *Attributes*

In UNCLOS analysis, "attributes" means a characteristic of an object.

Comment

In LOAC-governed situations under the "other rules of international law" clauses in UNCLOS, a different definition may apply. The same may be the situation if the UN Charter supersedes UNCLOS or if jus cogens norms apply.[337]

The ECDIS Glossary, page 1, defines "attributes" as "[a] characteristic of an *object*." This is identical with the Former ECDIS Glossary, page 1, definition.

Section 125 defines "object."[338]

§ 14. *Azimuth*

In UNCLOS analysis, "azimuth" means the bearing of a geographical position, measured clockwise from true or magnetic north through 360 degrees.

Comment

In LOAC-governed situations under the "other rules of international law" clauses in UNCLOS, a different definition may apply. The same may be the situation if the UN Charter supersedes UNCLOS or if jus cogens norms apply.[339]

---

[336] *See also* Churchill & Lowe 51–52, 120–26; 2 Commentary ¶¶ 6.1-6.7(e) (also offering no definition of "lagoon"), 47.1–47.8, 47.9(*l*); NWP 1-14M Annotated ¶ 1.3.5 n.25; 1 O'Connell 185, 195–96; Restatement (Third) §§ 511–12; Walker, *Consolidated Glossary* 231–32.

[337] *See* Parts III.B-III.D and § 132, defining "other rules of international law."

[338] *See also* Walker, *ECDIS Glossary* 256, 2003–04 ABILA Proc. 229.

[339] *See* Parts III.B-III.D and § 132, defining "other rules of international law."

The ECDIS Former Glossary, page 2, defined "azimuth" as "[t]he *bearing* of a geographical position, measured clockwise from north through 360 degrees." The ECDIS Glossary does not define "azimuth." The DOD Dictionary suggested amending the ECDIS definition to include either true or magnetic north. Depending on the situation, mariners and other oceans users may use true north, *i.e.*, as charts would publish bearings from the actual pole, or magnetic north, as might be observed from a magnetic compass.

Section 17 defines "bearing;" § 76, "geographic coordinates" or "geographical coordinates" or "coordinates;" § 90, "latitude;" § 97, "longitude."[340]

§ 15. *Bank; bank(s)*

There are two definitions for "bank," depending on its use in UNCLOS:

(a) The word "banks" in UNCLOS Article 9, when referring to river banks, means those portions of land that confine a river.
(b) The word "bank" in UNCLOS Article 76(6) means a submarine elevation located on the seabed of a continental margin over which the depth of water is relatively shallow; this includes the seabed of an island's continental shelf as permitted by Article 121, over which the depth of water is relatively shallow.

Comment

In LOAC-governed situations under the "other rules of international law" clauses in UNCLOS, a different definition may apply. The same may be the situation if the UN Charter supersedes UNCLOS or if jus cogens norms apply.[341]

Consolidated Glossary ¶ 10 has two definitions related for "bank." The first relates to the continental shelf: "[a] submarine elevation located on a continental margin over which the depth of water is relatively shallow." Former Glossary ¶ 10 phrased this definition differently: "an elevation of the sea floor located on a continental (or an island) shelf, over which the depth of water is relatively shallow."

[340] *See also* DOD Dictionary 55 (noting possibility of reference to true or magnetic north; Committee definition does not differentiate); Walker, *ECDIS Glossary* 242, 2003–04 ABILA Proc. 213–14.

[341] *See* Parts III.B-III.D and § 132, defining "other rules of international law."

The second relates to the term as used in connection with a river: "that portion of land that confines a river." Former Glossary ¶ 10 phrased this definition differently: "a shallow area of shifting sand, gravel, mud, etc., as a sand bank, mud bank, etc., usually constituting a danger to navigation and occurring in relatively shallow waters."[342] Because of the term's use as related to river banks and banks beneath the ocean's surface, a two-part definition is necessary.

UNCLOS Article 9 says that if a river flows directly into the sea, the baseline shall be a straight line across its mouth between points on the low water line of its banks. Territorial Sea Convention Article 13 applies the same rule for the low tide line. UNCLOS Article 76(6), as part of the continental shelf definition, says that notwithstanding its Article 76(5) submarine ridge provisions, the shelf's outer limit shall not exceed 350 nautical miles from baselines from which the territorial sea's breadth is measured. The Article 76(6) proviso does not apply to submarine elevations that are natural components of the continental margin, *e.g.*, its plateaus, rises, caps, banks and spurs. Under UNCLOS Article 121(2), an island's sovereign may claim a continental shelf for the island.

Section 16, in discussing baselines, defines "basepoint" or "point;" § 93, "line;" § 126, "ocean space" or "sea;" § 143, "river;" § 156, "seabed, seabed or bed;" § 176, "straight line, straight baseline; straight archipelagic baseline."[343]

§ 16. *Basepoint or point*

A "basepoint" when employed in UNCLOS analysis means any point on the baseline. In the method of straight baselines, where one straight baseline meets another at a common point, one line may be said to "turn" at that point to form another baseline. Such a point may be termed a "baseline turning point" or simply "basepoint." In either case "point" means a location that can be fixed by geographic coordinates and geodetic datums meeting UNCLOS standards.

---

[342] *Accord*, 2 Commentary ¶ 76.18(I), p. 880. *Annex 1* 322, concerned with continental shelf issues, agrees with the first definition of "bank": "A submarine elevation located on a continental margin over which the depth of water is relatively shallow."

[343] *See also* 2007–08 ABILA Proc. 161–62; Churchill & Lowe 46–47; 2 Commentary ¶¶ 9.1–9.5(e); 76.1–76.18(a), 76.18(I); NWP 1-14M Annotated ¶¶ 1.3.4, 1.6, Fig. A1-2; 1 O'Connell 221–30; Restatement (Third) §§ 511–12, 515; Noyes, *Definitions* 322–23 & Part III.D.3; Walker, *Consolidated Glossary* 232–33.

Comment

In LOAC-governed situations under the "other rules of international law" clauses in UNCLOS, a different definition may apply. The same may be the situation if the UN Charter supersedes UNCLOS or if jus cogens norms apply.[344]

Consolidated Glossary ¶ 11 generally describes "baseline" as a "line from which the outer limits of a State's territorial sea and certain other outer limits of coastal State jurisdiction are measured." Former Glossary ¶ 11 defined "baseline" as a "line from which the seaward limits of a State's territorial sea and certain other maritime zones of jurisdiction are measured." However, under either definition baselines must be determined from particular UNCLOS articles regulating each situation.[345] Although these are workable general definitions, "baseline" has not been included as a term to be defined; UNCLOS supplies different definitions for "baseline," depending on a particular ocean area.[346]

Consolidated Glossary ¶ 12 defines "basepoint" as "any point on the baseline. In the method of straight baselines, where one straight baseline meets another at a common point, one line may be said to 'turn' at that point to form another baseline. Such a point may be termed a 'baseline turning point' or simply 'basepoint.'"

UNCLOS Article 5 provides that except as otherwise provided in UNCLOS, "the normal baseline for measuring the breadth of the territorial sea is the low-water line along the coast as marked on large-scale charts officially recognized by the coastal State." Territorial Sea Convention Article 3 applies the same rule. UNCLOS Article 121(2) applies the same rule for islands, as does Territorial Sea Convention Article 10(2).

UNCLOS Article 33(2) says that a contiguous zone may not be declared beyond 24 nautical miles "from the baselines from which the breadth of the territorial sea is measured." Article 57 declares the same

---

[344] *See* Parts III.B-III.D and § 132, defining "other rules of international law."

[345] *Annex 1* 322 defines "basepoint" as "any point on the baseline." Commentaries reflect continued debate on measuring or determining baselines; *see, e.g.*, Churchill & Lowe ch. 2; 2 Commentary chs. 5–16, 33, 35, 47–48, 76, 82; NWP 1-14M Annotated ¶¶ 1.3–1.3.6; Fig. A1-2; Tables A1-3, A1-7; 1 O'Connell 171–85, 199–218, 345, 352–53, 390–99; Restatement (Third) §§ 511–12; Roach & Smith ch. 2. This analysis has no view on the issue; its purpose is to define point(s) from which measurements are made. For further analysis of delimitation issues, *see* Roach & Smith ch. 2; Chris M. Carleton, *Delimitation Issues*, in Cook & Carleton, note 20, ch. 20.

[346] No term already defined in UNCLOS will be defined anew. *See* Part III.A.

principle for an EEZ, which cannot extend "beyond 200 nautical miles from the baselines from which the breadth of the territorial sea is measured."

UNCLOS Article 76(1) measures the continental shelf "beyond [a coastal State's] territorial sea throughout the natural prolongation of its land territory, or to a distance of 200 nautical miles from the baselines from which the breadth of the territorial sea is measured where the outer edge of the continental margin does not extend up to that distance."[347] However, the shelf may not extend beyond limits Articles 76(4) and 76(6) declare. UNCLOS Article 76(4) declares that

> (a) For the purposes of this Convention, the coastal State shall establish the outer edge of the continental margin wherever the margin extends beyond 200 nautical miles from the baselines from which the territorial sea is measured, by either:
>   (i) a line delineated in accordance with [Article 76(7)] by reference to the outermost fixed points at each of which the thickness of sedimentary rocks is at least 1 percent of the shortest distance from such point to the foot of the continental slope; or
>   (ii) a line delineated in accordance with [Article 76(7)] by reference to fixed points not more than 60 nautical miles from the foot of the continental slope.
>
> (b) In the absence of evidence to the contrary, the foot of the continental slope shall be determined as the point of maximum change in the gradient at its base.

UNCLOS Article 76(5) says that the fixed points comprising the line of the shelf's outer limits on the seabed, drawn in accordance with Articles 76(4)(a)(i) and 76(4)(a)(ii) either may not exceed 350 nautical miles "from the baseline from which the breadth of the territorial sea is measured" or may not exceed 100 nautical miles from the 2500-meter isobath, a line connecting the depth of 2500 meters.[348] However,

---

[347] COCS *Second Report*, Conclusion 2, p. 217 defines "natural prolongation" of the continental shelf in UNCLOS Article 76(1):

> Article 76(1) … refers to the natural prolongation of the land territory to define the continental shelf. To establish which areas are comprised by the reference to natural prolongation, the starting point is the land territory. The connection between the land territory and the natural prolongation can be geomorphological and/or geological. One of the implications of the definition of the continental shelf by reference to natural prolongation is that the continental shelf may consist of areas that are either continental and/or oceanic in origin.

[348] Article 76(5) imposes two constraints on fixed points resulting from applying Article 76(4). For the 2500-meter isobath a coastal State may have a choice between

Article 76(6) sets a 350 nautical mile limit, again measured "from the baselines from which the breadth of the territorial sea is measured." Under Article 76(7) a coastal State must delineate its shelf's outer limits "where that shelf extends 200 nautical miles from the baselines from which the breadth of the territorial sea is measured, by straight lines not exceeding 60 nautical miles in length, connecting fixed points," defined by latitude and longitude coordinates.[349]

The ILA Committee on Legal Issues of the Outer Limits of the Continental Shelf comments on the interplay of Articles 76(4), 76(6) and 76(7):

> There are cases in which the outer limit of the continental shelf beyond 200 nautical miles has to be connected with the outer limit of the continental shelf at 200 nautical miles. This situation raises the question whether a coastal State is required to select a fixed point that meets the requirements ... in article[s] 76(4) to 76(6) and is either located at the 200 nautical mile limit or within that distance from the baseline (in the latter case, the outer limit of the continental shelf beyond 200 nautical miles may be connected to the outer limit line at 200 nautical miles at the point at which both lines intersect). A second view would be that a coastal State can use any point at the 200 nautical mile outer limit that can be connected to a fixed point beyond 200 nautical miles that meets the requirements of article 76(4) to article 76(6). In the above cases a choice between these two positions depends on the interpretation of articles 76(4) and 76(7).[350]

Article 76(8) requires a coastal State establishing a shelf more than 200 nautical miles "from the baselines from which the breadth of the territorial sea is measured" to submit data on that shelf to the Commission on the Limits of the Continental Shelf; its recommendations on limits for this kind of shelf are binding.[351] Articles 82(1) and 82(4)

---

two or more isobath lines. The only requirement such a line must meet is that it be located inside the natural prolongation of that coastal State's land territory on features that are continental margin components. COCS *Second Report,* Conclusion 7, p. 225.

349 A coastal State is entitled to a continental shelf even if that State has no established the outer limits of its continental shelf; "[t]he absence of outer limits does not entitle the coastal State to exercise sovereign rights beyond the outer limits of the continental shelf provided for in article 76 ..." COCS *Second Report,* Conclusion 1, p. 216.

350 *Id.* Conclusion 5, p. 223.

351 *Id.* Conclusion 8, p. 226 would also require a coastal State to submit information to the Commission on an area beyond 200 nautical miles that is wholly surrounded by 200 nautical mile zones if its continental margin extends into such an area. This duty also applies where all of the area is part of the continental shelf and there are no outer limits delineated under Article 76(7). *See also id.* Conclusion 9, p. 227 on the Commission's competence; *id.* Conclusion 10, p. 231, on the meaning of "on the basis of" in

require States exploiting the shelf beyond 200 nautical miles from the baselines from which the territorial sea is measured to make payments or contributions in kind through the Authority, which must distribute them to UNCLOS parties on the basis of equitable sharing.

UNCLOS Article 246(5) recites certain situations, including projects of direct significance for exploring and exploiting natural resources as stated in Article 246(5)(a), when coastal States may withhold EEZ and continental shelf MSR consent, which normally must be given other States or competent international organizations under Articles 246(3) and 246(4). However, coastal States may not withhold consent under Articles 246(5)(a) on the shelf beyond 200 nautical miles from baselines from which the breadth of the territorial sea is measured, outside specific areas coastal States may publicly designate for exploitation or detailed exploration operations focused on those areas.

The Shelf Convention uses only depth of waters or exploitability as criteria:

> "[C]ontinental shelf" ... refer[s] ... (a) to the seabed and subsoil of the submarine areas adjacent to the coast but outside the area of the territorial sea, to a depth of 200 meters or, beyond that limit, to where the depth of the superjacent waters admits of the exploitation of the natural resources of the said areas; (b) to the seabed and subsoil of similar submarine areas adjacent to the coasts of islands.

UNCLOS Article 83, providing for delimiting a shelf between opposite or adjacent States, has no provision involving baselines, but Shelf Convention Article 6(1) says that if there is no agreement between opposite States, and unless "special circumstances" justify another line, the boundary is "the median line, every point of which is equidistant from the nearest points of the baselines" from which the States' territorial sea are measured. Article 6(2) recites the same rule for adjacent States. Article 6(3) says that lines drawn in accordance with Articles 6(1) or 6(2) must refer to "fixed permanent identifiable points on the land."

The territorial sea baseline is therefore the standard benchmark for determining most seaward boundaries. UNCLOS Article 5 declares that except as otherwise provided in the Convention, "the normal baseline for measuring the territorial sea is the low-water line along the coast as marked on large-scale charts officially recognized by the

---

UNCLOS Article 78(8); *id.* Conclusion 11, p. 232, on the meaning and consequences of "final and binding" in Article 78(8).

coastal State." Territorial Sea Convention Article 3 applies the same standard.

For islands on atolls or islands with fringing reefs, UNCLOS Article 6 provides that the baseline for the territorial sea is the seaward low-water line of the reef, as shown by the same kind of charts.

Where the coastline is deeply indented and cut into, or if there is a fringe of islands along the coast "in its immediate vicinity," UNCLOS Article 7(1) provides that "the method of straight baselines joining appropriate points may be employed in drawing the baseline from which the breadth of the territorial sea is measured." If Article 7(1) applies, Article 7(5) allows account to be taken to determine particular baselines of "economic interests peculiar to the region concerned, the reality and importance of which are clearly evidenced by long usage." Territorial Sea Convention Articles 4(1) and 4(4) are to the same effect.

UNCLOS Article 7(2) says that where a delta and other natural conditions produce a "highly unstable" coastline, "the appropriate points may be selected along the furthest seaward extent of the low-water line, and notwithstanding subsequent regression" of this line, the straight baselines remain effective until the coastal State changes them in accordance with UNCLOS.

UNCLOS Article 7(3) provides: "The drawing of straight baselines must not depart to any appreciable extent from the general direction of the coast, and the sea areas lying within the lines must be sufficiently linked to the land domain to be subject to the regime of internal waters." Territorial Sea Convention Article 4(2) is to the same effect.

UNCLOS Article 7(4) adds that straight baselines must not be drawn to and from low-tide elevations unless lighthouses or similar installations permanently above sea level have been built on them, except where drawing baselines to and from such elevations "has received general international recognition." Apart from the last exception, Territorial Sea Convention Article 4(3) uses the same language.

UNCLOS Article 7(6) says that a State cannot apply a straight baseline system to cut off another State's territorial sea from the high seas or EEZ. Territorial Sea Convention Article 4(5) applies the same rule to another State's territorial sea.

UNCLOS Article 8 says that except for archipelagic waters situations under UNCLOS Part IV, internal waters are those on the landward side of territorial sea baselines. If an Article 7-determined straight baseline has the effect of enclosing as internal waters an ocean area not previously considered as such, a right of innocent passage under UNCLOS exists. Territorial Sea Convention Article 5 is to the same effect, except that there is no reference to archipelagic States.

For river mouths, UNCLOS Article 9 provides that if it flows directly into the sea, the baseline is a straight line across its mouth between points on the low-water line of its banks. Territorial Sea Convention Article 13 recites the same language.

UNCLOS Article 10 declares rules for bays where their coasts belong to one State. Article 10(5) says that where the distance between low-water marks of the natural entrance points of a bay exceeds 24 nautical miles, a straight baseline of 24 nautical miles must be drawn within the bay so as to enclose the maximum area of water possible with a line of that length. Territorial Sea Convention Article 7(4) has the same language. UNCLOS Article 10(6) excludes "historic bays" and cases where Article 7's straight baseline system applies, as does Territorial Sea Convention Article 7(6).

For ports under UNCLOS Article 11, the outermost permanent harbor works forming an integral part of the harbor system are part of the coast. Offshore installations and artificial islands are not. Except for the proviso for offshore installations and artificial islands, Territorial Sea Convention Article 8 is the same. Under UNCLOS Article 12, roadsteads normally used for loading, unloading and anchoring ships and which would otherwise be wholly or partly outside the territorial sea are included in the territorial sea. Territorial Sea Convention Article 10 is to the same effect.

Under UNCLOS Article 13, a low-tide elevation, a naturally formed area of land surrounded by and above water at low tide but below water at high tide, is wholly or partly at a distance not exceeding the territorial sea's breadth from the mainland or an island, the low-water line on that elevation may be used as a baseline for measuring the territorial sea. If wholly situated at a distance exceeding the breadth of the territorial sea from the mainland or an island, an elevation has no territorial sea. Territorial Sea Convention Article 11 uses the same language.

UNCLOS Article 14 allows a coastal State to "determine baselines in turn by any ... method ... in the foregoing articles [Articles 1-13?] to suit different conditions."

UNCLOS Article 15 recites rules for States with opposite or adjacent coasts. The rules are the same as in Territorial Sea Convention Article 12.[352]

---

[352] For text, *see* § 2, "adjacent coasts."

UNCLOS Article 16 requires that baselines for measuring the territorial sea's breadth determined under Articles 7, 9 and 10, or limits derived from these Articles, and delimitation lines drawn in accordance with Articles 12 and 15, must be shown on charts of a scale or scales adequate for ascertaining their position. Alternatively, a list of geographical coordinates of points, specifying the geodetic datum, may be submitted. The coastal State must give due publicity to these charts or lists and must deposit a copy of each chart or list with the UN Secretary-General.

UNCLOS Article 35(a) declares that nothing in the UNCLOS rules for straits used for international navigation affects areas of internal waters within a strait, except where establishing a straight baseline by Article 7 has the effect of enclosing as internal waters areas not previously considered as such.

There are separate rules for archipelagic baselines applying to archipelagic States and archipelagoes as defined in UNCLOS Article 46. Under Article 47(1), an archipelagic State may draw straight archipelagic baselines joining outermost points of the outermost islands and drying reefs of the archipelago, provided that within such baselines are included the main islands and an area in which the ratio of the area of the water to the area of the land, including atolls, is between 1 to 1 and 9 to 1. Article 47(2) says these baselines' length must not exceed 100 nautical miles; up to 3 percent of the total number of baselines enclosing an archipelago may exceed that length, to an 125 nautical mile maximum. Drawing these baselines may not depart "to any appreciable extent" from an archipelago's general configuration, according to Article 47(3). Article 47(4) says these baselines may not be drawn to and from low-tide elevations, unless lighthouses or similar installations have been built on them or where an elevation is situated wholly or partly at a distance not exceeding the breadth of the territorial sea from the nearest island. Article 47(5) declares that an archipelagic State cannot apply this baseline system cannot be applied to cut off another State's territorial sea from its EEZ or the high seas. Under Article 47(6), if part of an archipelagic State's archipelagic waters lies between two parts of an immediately neighboring adjacent State, existing rights and all other legitimate interests the latter State has traditionally exercised in such waters and all rights in agreements between those States must continue and be respected. Under Article 47(7), in computing ratio of water to land when establishing archipelagic waters of an archipelagic State as UNCLOS defines that State, atolls and waters within them may be included as part of the land area of that State. Article 47(8) says that baselines drawn in accordance with Article 47 must be shown on charts of a scale or scales adequate for determining their position. Lists of geographical coordinates of points, specifying the geodetic datum may be substituted for these. Article 47(9) requires archipelagic States to give due publicity to these charts or lists and to deposit a copy of each with the UN Secretary-General.

UNCLOS Article 48 provides that an archipelagic State's breadth of territorial sea, contiguous zone, EEZ and continental shelf are measured from Article 47 archipelagic baselines. Under Article 49(1), archipelagic State sovereignty extends to waters archipelagic baselines enclose pursuant to Article 47. Article 50 provides that an archipelagic State may draw closing lines to delimit internal waters in accordance with Articles 9-11.

UNCLOS Article 1(1)(2) defines the Authority cited in UNCLOS Article 82(4).

Section 12 defines "atoll;" § 23, "chart" or "nautical chart;" § 28, "coast;" § 31, "coastal State;" § 79, "harbor works" or facility (port);" § 81, "high seas;" § 93, "line;" § 105, "mile" or "nautical mile;" § 140, "reef;" § 147, "rock;" § 160, "sedimentary rock;" § 176, "straight line, straight baseline; straight archipelagic baseline."[353]

§ 17. *Bearing, abbreviated BRG*

In UNCLOS analysis, "bearing," abbreviated BRG, means the direction from a reference station, usually from 000 degrees at the reference direction, clockwise through 360 degrees.

Comment

In LOAC-governed situations under the "other rules of international law" clauses in UNCLOS, a different definition may apply. The same may be the situation if the UN Charter supersedes UNCLOS or if jus cogens norms apply.[354]

The Former ECDIS Glossary, page 2, defined "bearing" as "[t]he direction from a reference station, usually from 000 degrees at the

[353] *See also* Churchill & Lowe 51–52, 120–26; Roach & Smith ch. 4; Noyes, *Definitions* 322–23 & Part III.D.3; Walker, *Consolidated Glossary* 233–39.

[354] *See* Parts III.B-III.D and § 132, defining "other rules of international law."

reference direction, clockwise through 360 degrees." The newer ECDIS Glossary does not define "bearing."

Section 14 defines "azimuth;" § 76, "geographic coordinates," "geographical coordinates" or "coordinates;" § 90, "latitude;" § 97, "longitude."[355]

§ 18. *Bed*

A synonym for "sea-bed" or "seabed;" *see* § 157.

§ 19. *Benefit of mankind as a whole, or benefit of humankind as a whole*

In UNCLOS analysis, "benefit of mankind as a whole," or its gender neutral equivalent, "benefit of humankind as a whole," must be interpreted irrespective of the geographical location of States, whether coastal or land-locked, and taking into particular consideration the interests and needs of developing States and of peoples who have not attained full independence or other self-governing status recognized by the United Nations in accordance with UN General Assembly Resolution 1514 and other relevant Assembly resolutions, including Resolution 2749. There must also be consideration that the term appears only in UNCLOS Articles related to the Area, marine scientific research in the Area, and objects of historical or archeological value found in the Area. Activities in the Area must, as provided in UNCLOS Part XI, be carried out to foster healthy development of the world economy and balanced growth of international trade, and to promote international cooperation for all countries', especially developing countries', overall development, with a view to ensuring enhancement of the common heritage for the benefit of mankind as a whole.

Comment

In LOAC-governed situations under the "other rules of international law" clauses in UNCLOS, a different definition may apply. The same may be the situation if the UN Charter supersedes UNCLOS or if jus cogens norms apply.[356]

---

[355] *See also* DOD Dictionary 66; Walker, *ECDIS Glossary* 242–43, 2003–04 ABILA Proc. 214.

[356] *See* Parts III.B-III.D and § 132, defining "other rules of international law."

The phrase, "benefit of mankind as a whole," for which this *Report* offers a gender-neutral equivalent, "benefit of humankind as a whole," appears in the UNCLOS preamble and in Articles 140(1), 143(1), 149 and 150(i).

The preamble speaks of "benefit of mankind as a whole" in citing UN General Assembly Resolution 2749 (1970). Resolution 2749 "solemnly declared *inter alia* that the area of the sea-bed beyond the limits of national jurisdiction, as well as its resources, are the common heritage of mankind, the exploration and exploitation of which shall be carried out for the benefit of mankind as a whole, irrespective of the geographic location of States[.]"[357]

Article 140(1) declares:

> Activities in the Area shall, as specifically provided for in this Part [XI, concerning the Area], be carried out for the benefit of mankind as a whole, irrespective of the geographical location of States, whether coastal or land-locked, and taking into particular consideration the interests and needs of developing States and of peoples who have not attained full independence or other self-governing status recognized by the United Nations in accordance with General Assembly resolution 1514(XV) [the Declaration on Principles of International Law Concerning Friendly Relations and Cooperation Among States] and other relevant ... Assembly resolutions.[358]

Article 143(1) declares that marine scientific research in the Area must be carried out "exclusively for peaceful purposes and for the benefit of mankind as a whole, in accordance with Part XIII [UNCLOS's MSR principles]." Article 149 requires that objects of an archeological and historical nature found in the Area must be preserved or disposed of "for the benefit of mankind as a whole, particular regard being paid to the preferential rights of the State or country of origin, or the State of cultural origin, or the State of historical and archeological origin." Article 150(i) requires that activities in the Area must, as provided in Part XI, be carried out to foster healthy development of the world economy and balanced growth of international trade, and to promote international cooperation for all countries', especially developing countries', overall development, with a view to ensuring "development of the common heritage for the benefit of mankind as a whole."

---

[357] For preamble analysis, *see* 1 Commentary 450–67; for text of Resolution 2749, *see* 10 ILM 220 (1971).

[358] *See* Jennings & Watts § 105 for general analysis of the Resolution.

In 1967 space law treaties had begun to use using similar phrases with respect to benefitting mankind as a whole.[359] No 1958 LOS Convention has language regarding benefit of mankind or humankind as a whole.

Although commentators declare that a modern definition of "common heritage" may include additional concepts,[360] application of the LOS through UNCLOS and the 1994 Agreement, with their limitations to Area development, may mean that common heritage for the LOS may be different from that for, *e.g.*, space law.

Section 9 defines "area" and "Area;" § 34, "common heritage of mankind" or "common heritage of humankind;" § 100, "marine scientific research."

§ 20. *Black box*

A synonym for "voyage data recorder;" *see* § 197.

§ 21. *BRG*

Abbreviation for "bearing;" *see* § 17, Bearing.

§ 22. *Cap*

"Cap" has different meanings in UNCLOS when the word is used in the navigational context or when analyzing the law of the continental shelf:

(a) When used in navigation pursuant to UNCLOS, "cap" means a submarine feature with a rounded cap-like top.

---

[359] Convention on Principles Governing the Activities of States in the Exploration and Use of Outer Space, Including the Moon and Other Celestial Bodies, Jan. 27, 1967, pmbl., art. 1, 18 UST 2410, 610 UNTS 205 (COPUOS) (common interest of all mankind in progress of space exploration; exploration, use of outer space, including the Moon and other celestial bodies, shall be carried out for benefit and in interests of all countries, irrespective of their degree of economic or scientific development, and shall be the province of all mankind); Convention on International Liability for Damage Caused by Space Objects, Mar. 29, 1972, pmbl., 24 UST 2389, 961 UNTS 187 (Space Liability Convention) (common interest of all mankind in furthering exploration, use of outer space for peaceful purposes); Agreement Governing Activities of States on the Moon and Other Celestial Bodies, Dec. 5, 1979, art. 11, 1363 UNTS 3 (Moon Treaty) (Moon, its natural resources common heritage of mankind, subject to international regime to be established). *See also* Jennings & Watts ch. 7.

[360] *E.g.*, Christopher C. Joyner, *Legal Implications of the Concept of the Common Heritage of Mankind*, 35 Int'l & Comp. L.Q. 190 (1986). *See also* 2007–08 ABILA Proc. 171–73.

(b) When used in navigation pursuant to UNCLOS, "cap" may also mean a feature on land with a rounded cap-like top, usually on a promontory visible from the sea and so stated on navigational charts.
(c) In UNCLOS Article 76(6), when referring to the continental shelf, "cap" means a submerged plateau or flat area of considerable extent, dropping off abruptly on one or more sides.

Comment

In LOAC-governed situations under the "other rules of international law" clauses in UNCLOS, a different definition may apply. The same may be the situation if the UN Charter supersedes UNCLOS or if jus cogens norms apply.[361]

Consolidated Glossary ¶ 14 defines "cap" as a "submarine feature with a rounded cap-like top. [It also means] … a plateau or flat area of considerable extent, dropping off abruptly on one or more sides."[362] Former Glossary ¶ 14 defined "cap" as a "feature with a rounded cap-like top," omitting the word "submarine." Although the Former Glossary did not say so, its first definition seemed to refer to a feature on land near the sea. The second, in § 22(c) and the same in both Glossaries, refers to sea bottom features. The single UNCLOS reference to "cap" supports this view.

UNCLOS Article 76(6), discussed in connection with § 15's definition for "bank; bank(s)," says its provision "does not apply to submarine elevations that are natural components of the continental margin, such as its plateaus, rises, caps, banks and spurs." There appears to be no 1958 LOS Convention or UNCLOS reference to "cap" as the first Glossary statement defines it, unless UNCLOS Article 76(6) includes that meaning of "cap."

Besides the submarine feature, mariners may recall personal experience with nautical charts that use "cap" to refer to land promontories used to fix positions in navigation, perhaps referring to a "cape" in a language other than English. Section 3(b) offers this as a second definition.

---

[361] *See* Parts III.B-III.D and § 132, defining "other rules of international law."

[362] *Accord,* 2 Commentary ¶ 76.18(I), p. 880. *Annex 1* 322, concerned with continental shelf issues, defines "cap" as "[a] submarine feature with a rounded caplike top; also defined as a plateau or flat area of considerable extent, dropping off abruptly on one or more sides."

"Cap" may also refer to mariner headgear, *e.g.*, an officer's cap as distinguished from a sailor's hat. The custom of the sea may require or recommend touching a cap, or removing it, in salute or courtesy.

Section 23 defines "chart" or "nautical chart;" § 126, "ocean space" or "sea;" § 127, "oceanic plateau."[363]

§ 23. *Chart; nautical chart*

"Chart" or "nautical chart" as used in UNCLOS is a map specially designed to meet the needs of marine navigation. A chart depicts such information as depth of water, nature of the sea-bed, configuration and nature of the coast, and dangers and aids to navigation, in a standardized format. UNCLOS provisions may require different scales of charts, coastal State recognition of a chart, publicity standards and depository rules.

Comment

In LOAC-governed situations under the "other rules of international law" clauses in UNCLOS, a different definition may apply. The same may be the situation if the UN Charter supersedes UNCLOS or if jus cogens norms apply.[364]

Consolidated Glossary ¶ 15 defines "chart" as a "nautical chart specially designed to meet the needs of marine navigation. It includes such information as depths of water, nature of the seabed, configuration and nature of the coast, dangers and aids to navigation, in a standardised format; also called simply, Chart." Using the same word in the definition creates a tautology.

Although "chart" almost invariably refers to a depiction of water areas, often as related to land areas and designed to meet needs of marine navigation,[365] "map" usually refers to depiction of land areas or land and water areas.[366]

---

[363] *See also* 2007–08 ABILA Proc. 173–75; 2 Commentary ¶¶ 76.1–76.18(a), 76.18(I), at 880; NWP 1-14M Annotated ¶ 1.6 & Fig. A1-2; 1 O'Connell ch. 13; 2 *id.* ch. 18A; Restatement (Third) §§ 511–12; Noyes, *Definitions* 322–23 & Part III.D.3; Walker, *Consolidated Glossary* 239–40.

[364] *See* Parts III.B–III.D and § 132, defining "other rules of international law."

[365] 2 Commentary ¶ 5.4(c); 2 O'Connell 646–47. *Annex 1* 322, defines "chart" as "[a] special-purpose map generally meet the needs of marine navigation; also called *nautical chart* or *navigational chart*." (italics in original).

[366] *Cf.* 2 O'Connell 645. DOD Dictionary 423 defines "plot" inter alia as "Map, chart, or graph representing data of any sort."

UNCLOS and the Territorial Sea Convention recite "chart," often with qualifications, but they do not define the word. Because UNCLOS provisions recite different standards for charts, the last sentence has been added to the definition of "chart." No LOS Convention uses the word "map."

In connection with the territorial sea, UNCLOS Articles 5-6 refer to "large-scale charts officially recognized by the coastal State." Territorial Sea Convention Article 3 uses similar language. UNCLOS Article 16(1) requires showing lines of territorial sea delimitation "on charts of a scale or scales adequate for showing their position;" Article 16(2) requires due publicity for these charts, which must be deposited with the UN Secretary-General.

UNCLOS does not have chart requirements for the contiguous zone; *see* Article 33.

Under UNCLOS Article 75, when coastal States proclaim EEZ, it must be shown on "charts of a scale or scales adequate for ascertaining [the] ... position [of EEZ outer limit lines and Article 74 lines of delimitation]." The State must give due publicity to such charts and must deposit a copy with the Secretary-General.

UNCLOS Article 76(9) requires a State proclaiming a continental shelf to deposit with the Secretary-General "charts" and other information permanently describing the shelf's outer limits; the Secretary-General must give due publicity to this.[367] Subject to other rules in UNCLOS Part V on the shelf, UNCLOS Article 84 requires that shelf outer limit lines and Article 83 lines of delimitation must be shown on "charts of a scale or scales adequate for ascertaining their position." Coastal States must give due publicity to such charts and must deposit copies with the Secretary-General and a copy showing the outer limits of the shelf with the Authority Secretary-General.

UNCLOS Article 47(8) requires an archipelagic State to show archipelagic baselines on "charts of a scale or scales adequate for ascertaining their position. Under Article 47(9) that State must give due publicity to these charts and must deposit a copy of these with the UN Secretary-General.

Under UNCLOS Article 22(4), coastal States must "clearly indicate sea lanes and traffic separation schemes [in the territorial sea] on

---

[367] COCS *Second Report*, Conclusion 13, p. 236 declares that a coastal State may no longer change its previously-filed Article 76(9) outer limit lines unless another State successfully challenges them.

charts to which due publicity shall be given." UNCLOS Article 41(6) recites the same standard for sea lanes and traffic separation schemes in straits; Article 53(10) has the same rules for archipelagic States.

UNCLOS Article 134(3) says requirements concerning deposit of and publicity given to charts showing limits of the Area are in UNCLOS Part VI, which declares continental shelf rules, thereby incorporating UNCLOS Articles 76(9) and 84 by reference.

UNCLOS Article 1(1)(2) defines the "Authority." While defining "basepoint" and "point," § 16 discusses baselines. Section 3 defines "aid(s) to navigation;" "navigational aid(s);" facility (navigational);" § 24, "chart datum;" § 25, "chart symbol;" § 28, "coast;" § 31, "coastal State;" § 54, "due notice," "appropriate publicity" and "due publicity;" § 93, "line;" § 126, "ocean space" or "sea;" § 133, "outer limit;" § 150, "routing system;" § 154, "scale;" § 157, "sea-bed" "seabed," or "bed;" § 176, "straight line, straight baseline; straight archipelagic baseline;" § 192, "traffic separation scheme."[368]

§ 24. *Chart datum*

In UNCLOS analysis, "chart datum" means the vertical datum reflecting the tidal level to which depths on a nautical chart refer. While there is no universally agreed chart datum level, under International Hydrographic Conference Resolution A 2.5, it is a plane so low that the tide will seldom fall below it.

Comment

In LOAC-governed situations under the "other rules of international law" clauses in UNCLOS, a different definition may apply. The same may be the situation if the UN Charter supersedes UNCLOS or if jus cogens norms apply.[369]

Consolidated Glossary ¶ 92 defines "chart datum" in defining "tide" as "[t]he tidal level to which depths on a nautical chart are referred to constitutes a vertical datum called chart datum." The Glossary notes that "While there is no universally agreed chart datum level, under an

[368] *See also* Churchill & Lowe 37, 53, 120–26, 149, 267–69; 2 Commentary ¶¶ 5.1–5.3, 5.4(c)–5.4(d), 6.1–6.6, 6.7(e), 16.1–16.8(e), 22.1–22.9, 41.1–41.8, 47.1–47.8, 47.9(m), 53.1–53.8, 53.9(*l*), 75.1–75.5(d), 76.1–76.18(a), 76.18(*l*), 84.1–84.9(c); DOD Dictionary 327 ("map;" "map chart;"); NWP 1-14M Annotated ¶ 1.3.1; 1 O'Connell 205–06; 2 *id.* 636, 645–47; Roach & Smith ¶ 4.5.3; Noyes, *Definitions* 322–23 & Part III.D.3; Walker, *Consolidated Glossary* 240–42.

[369] *See* Parts III.B-III.D and § 132, defining "other rules of international law."

International Hydrographic Conference Resolution (A 2.5) it 'shall be a plane so low that the tide will seldom fall below it.' "

"Chart datum" does not appear as a term in any LOS Convention.

Section 23 defines "chart" or "nautical chart;" § 25, "chart symbol;" § 75, "geodetic datum;" § 93, "line;" § 98, "low water line or low water mark;" § 189, "tide."[370]

§ 25. *Chart symbol*

As used in UNCLOS analysis, "chart symbol" means a character, letter, line style, or similar graphic representation used on a chart to indicate some object, characteristic, etc.

Comment

In LOAC-governed situations under the "other rules of international law" clauses in UNCLOS, a different definition may apply. The same may be the situation if the UN Charter supersedes UNCLOS or if jus cogens norms apply.[371]

The Former ECDIS Glossary, page 3, defined "chart symbol" as "[a] character, letter, line style, or similar graphic representation used on a *chart* to indicate some *object*, characteristic, etc." The newer ECDIS Glossary does not define "chart symbol."

Section 23 defines "chart" or "nautical chart;" § 24, "chart datum;" § 93, "line;" § 125, "object;" § 176, "straight line; straight baseline; straight archipelagic baseline."[372]

§ 26. *Closing line*

"Closing line" is a dividing line between the internal waters and the territorial seas of a coastal State enclosing a river mouth, a bay or a harbor; or a dividing line for the archipelagic waters of an archipelagic State as stated in UNCLOS Articles 9–11 and 50.

Comment

In LOAC-governed situations under the "other rules of international law" clauses in UNCLOS, a different definition may apply. The same

---

[370] *See also* 2007–08 ABILA Proc. 177–78; NWP 1-14M Annotated ¶ 1.3.1 n.12; Walker, *Consolidated Glossary* 242–43.

[371] *See* Parts III.B-III.D and § 132, defining "other rules of international law."

[372] *See also* DOD Dictionary 328 ("map reference"); Walker, *ECDIS Glossary* 243, 2003–04 ABILA Proc. 214–15.

may be the situation if the UN Charter supersedes UNCLOS or if jus cogens norms apply.[373]

Consolidated Glossary ¶ 16 defines "closing line," citing UNCLOS Articles 9–11 and 50, as a "dividing line between the internal waters and the territorial seas of a coastal State enclosing a river mouth ..., a bay ... or a harbor ...; of the archipelagic waters of an archipelagic State. ..." Former Glossary ¶ 16 defined "closing line" as "[a] line that divides the internal waters and territorial seas of a coastal State or the archipelagic waters of an archipelagic State. It is most often used in the context of establishing the baseline at the entrance to rivers ..., bays ..., and harbors. ..."

UNCLOS Article 9, and its counterpart in Territorial Sea Convention Article 14, refer to a "straight line across the mouth of the river ..." where it enters the sea. UNCLOS Article 10(4), and its counterpart in Territorial Sea Convention Article 7(4), refer to a "closing line" across the entrance to a bay more than 24 miles across. UNCLOS Article 11, and its counterpart in Territorial Sea Article 8, establishing rules for ports, do not mention lines of any kind. UNCLOS Article 50 allows an archipelagic State to draw "closing lines" to delimit its internal waters in accordance with UNCLOS Articles 9–11. Other UNCLOS and Territorial Sea Convention provisions refer to "baselines" or "lines" for the territorial sea, contiguous zone, EEZ, continental shelf, archipelagic States or the Area. The phrase "closing line" is not used in those provisions.

Section 16 defines "base point" or "point" in discussing baselines; § 93, "line;" § 126, "ocean space" or "sea;" § 143, "river;" § 176, "straight line; straight baseline; straight archipelagic baseline."[374]

§ 27. *CMG*

Abbreviation for "course made good," § 42.

§ 28. *Coast*

"Coast" is the edge or margin of land next to the sea.

---

[373] *See* Parts III.B-III.D and § 132, defining "other rules of international law."

[374] The *Annex 1* 322 definition is almost the same as the Glossary definition. *See also* Churchill & Lowe ch. 2; 2 Commentary ¶¶ 9.1–9.5(e), 10.1–10.4, 10.5(d), 11.1–11.5(d); NWP 1-14M ¶ 1.3.3 & Figs. 1-2 - 1-4; 1 O'Connell 352–53, 381–84, 389; 2 *id.* 647–48; Restatement (Third) §§ 511–12; Walker, *Consolidated Glossary* 243–44.

Comment

In LOAC-governed situations under the "other rules of international law" clauses in UNCLOS, a different definition may apply. The same may be the situation if the UN Charter supersedes UNCLOS or if jus cogens norms apply.[375]

Consolidated Glossary ¶ 17 defines "coast" as the "edge or margin of land next to the sea." Former Glossary ¶ 17 defined "coast" as "The sea-shore. The narrow strip of land in immediate contact with any body of water, including the area between high- and low-water lines."

Section 2 defines "adjacent coasts;" § 31, "coastal State;" § 32, "coastal warning;" § 89, "land territory" or "land domain;" § 93, "line;" § 98, "low water line" or "low water mark;" § 126, "ocean space" or "sea;" § 130, "opposite coasts."

§ 29. *Coast Pilot*

See Sailing directions, Coastal Pilots or Coast Pilot, § 153.

§ 30. *Coastal Pilots*

See Sailing directions, Coastal Pilots or Coast Pilot, § 153.

§ 31. *Coastal State*

"Coastal State" is a State from whose coast or baselines the breadth of the territorial sea is measured, those baselines being determined in accordance with UNCLOS Articles 5–7, 9–10 and 47.

Comment

In LOAC-governed situations under the "other rules of international law" clauses in UNCLOS, a different definition may apply. The same may be the situation if the UN Charter supersedes UNCLOS or if jus cogens norms apply.[376]

UNCLOS does not explain "coastal State." A commentary declares: "It is that State from the coast or baselines of which the breadth of the territorial sea is measured ..."[377]

---

[375] *See* Parts III.B-III.D and § 132, defining "other rules of international law;" *see also* DOD Dictionary 94 ("coastal frontier" in military operations).

[376] *See* Parts III.B-III.D and § 132, defining "other rules of international law."

[377] 2 Commentary ¶ 1.29.

UNCLOS refers to "coastal State" in many provisions, *e.g.*, Articles 2 (coastal State sovereignty over land territory, internal waters, archipelagic waters in the case of archipelagic States, territorial sea and airspace above the territorial sea and territorial sea's bed and subsoil), 5, 7, 14 (coastal State determination of baselines), 6 (rules for reefs), 15 (adjacent coastal State determination of baselines), 16(2) (coastal State obligations to publish charts or lists of geographic coordinates of baselines, deposit them with UN Secretary-General), 19 (definition of innocent passage in coastal State territorial sea), 21 (coastal State authority to adopt laws, regulations relating to innocent passage), 22 (coastal State authority to impose sea lanes, traffic separation schemes in its territorial sea), 24 (coastal State duties with regard to innocent passage), 25 (coastal State rights of protection), 27–28 (coastal State criminal, civil jurisdiction over foreign ships in coastal State territorial waters), 30 (coastal State's right to require warship to leave its territorial waters if warship does not comply with coastal State laws, regulations concerning territorial sea passage), 31 (flag State obligation for loss, damage to coastal State for warship noncompliance with territorial sea passage), 33 (coastal State discretion to establish contiguous zone), 56 (coastal State rights, jurisdiction, duties, required to have due regard for other States' rights, duties, consistent with Convention), 58 (coastal, other States' high seas rights, and due regard obligation), 59 (coastal State and obligation to resolve EEZ conflicts), 60 (coastal State exclusive right to construct, authorize and regulate construction, operation, use of artificial islands and the like; establishment of safety zones), 61 (coastal State determination of allowable catch of living resources in its EEZ), 62 (coastal State promotion of optimum utilization of resources in its EEZ), 63 (rules where species occurs in more than one coastal State's EEZ), 65 (same with respect to highly migratory species), 65 (coastal State authority to prohibit, limit, regulate exploitation of marine mammals in its EEZ), 67 (rules for catadromous species in coastal State EEZ), 69 (landlocked States' rights in coastal State EEZ), 70 (geographically disadvantaged States' rights in coastal State EEZ), 73 (coastal State measures for exercising sovereign exploration, etc. rights), 75(2) (coastal State obligations to publish EEZ charts or geographic coordinates, deposit them with UN Secretary-General), 76 (rules for coastal States and continental shelf), 77 (coastal State rights over continental shelf), 78 (coastal State continental shelf rights do not affect airspace, waters over the shelf),

79 (rights of States to lay submarine cables, pipelines on continental shelf subject to coastal State consent), 81 (exclusive coastal State right to regulate continental shelf drilling), 82 (payment rules for exploiting non-living resources beyond 200 nautical miles), 84 (coastal State obligations to publish EEZ charts or geographic coordinates, deposit them with UN Secretary-General), 85 (coastal State tunnelling rights), 111 (coastal States and hot pursuit rules), 208(1) (coastal State obligation to adopt laws, regulations regarding marine environmental pollution), 211(6)(c) (additional coastal State laws regarding pollution), 216(1)(a) (coastal State enforcement of rules against dumping within its territorial sea), 220 (coastal State enforcement of pollution laws regarding its territorial sea or EEZ), 228(1) (time limitation, exceptions on bringing proceedings to impose penalties); 234 (coastal States' rights to adopt laws, regulations for ice-covered areas), 246 (MSR and coastal State EEZ, continental shelf), 248 (States', international organizations' duty to provide coastal State of MSR projects in coastal State's EEZ, continental shelf), 253 (coastal State's right to suspend MSR), 254 (neighboring land-locked, geographically disadvantaged States' rights to MSR and coastal State), 297(1) (dispute resolution procedures concerning interpretation, application of Convention in certain cases); 303 (coastal State rights to archeological, historical objects).

UNCLOS Article 124 defines "land-locked State."

The 1958 LOS Conventions do not define "coastal State," although there are many references to the term, *e.g.*: Territorial Sea Convention Articles 2 (coastal State sovereignty over airspace, territorial sea, bed, subsoil), 3 (baseline determination by coastal State), 4(6) (rules for coastal State delimitation of baselines), 9 (roadstead rules), 14(4) (coastal State and innocent passage), 15 (coastal State obligations with respect to innocent passage), 16 (coastal State authority where passage is not innocent; suspension of innocent passage), 17 (compliance with coastal State innocent passage rules), 19–20 (coastal State criminal, civil jurisdiction), 24 (coastal State authority to declare contiguous zone); High Seas Convention Article 23 (coastal States and hot pursuit rules); Fishing Convention Articles 6-7 (coastal State special interest in maintaining, regulating productivity of living resources in adjacent high seas areas); Shelf Convention Articles 2-5 (coastal State sovereignty, rights, obligations with regard to the continental shelf).

Section 16 defines "base point" or "point" in discussing baselines; § 28, "coast;" § 81, "high seas;" § 93, "line;" § 176, "straight line; straight baseline; straight archipelagic baseline."[378]

§ 32. *Coastal warning*

As used in UNCLOS analysis, "coastal warning" means a navigational warning promulgated by a national coordinator covering a coastal region or a portion thereof.

Comment

In LOAC-governed situations under the "other rules of international law" clauses in UNCLOS, a different definition may apply. The same may be the situation if the UN Charter supersedes UNCLOS or if jus cogens norms apply.[379]

The Former ECDIS Glossary, page 3, defined "coastal warning" as "[a] *navigational warning* promulgated by a national co-ordinator covering a coastal region or a portion thereof." The newer ECDIS Glossary does not define "coastal warning."

Section 2 defines "adjacent coasts;" § 4, "alarm;" § 28, "coast;" § 31, "coastal State;" § 44, "danger to navigation;" § 45, "danger to overflight;" § 76, "geographic coordinates," "geographical coordinates" or "coordinates;" § 118, "navigational warning;" § 121, "notice to airmen;" § 122, "notice to mariners;" § 130, "opposite coasts;" § 199, "warning."[380]

§ 33. *COG*

Abbreviation for "course over ground," § 43.

§ 34. *Common heritage of mankind or common heritage of humankind*

In UNCLOS analysis the principle of the "common heritage of mankind," or its gender neutral equivalent, "the common heritage of humankind," is defined as the international regime designed to ensure equitable exploitation of the resources of the Area for the benefit of all

---

[378] *See also* 2007–08 ABILA Proc. 180–83; Churchill & Lowe ch. 2; Walker, *Defining* 353.

[379] *See* Parts III.B-III.D and § 132, defining "other rules of international law."

[380] *See also* Walker, *ECDIS Glossary* 243–44, 2003–04 ABILA Proc. 215.

countries, especially developing States. The UNCLOS common heritage principle applies only to the Area, *i.e.*, the seabed and the ocean floor and the subsoil thereof, beyond national jurisdiction limits as defined in UNCLOS Article 1(1). Equitable exploitation of Area resources pursuant to the UNCLOS common heritage principle is further subject to rules in UNCLOS Part XI and the 1994 Agreement and as developed by Area agencies. Common heritage principles in other international agreements, *e.g.*, those governing outer space, are not necessarily the same as the UNCLOS common heritage principle.

Comment

In LOAC-governed situations under the "other rules of international law" clauses in UNCLOS, a different definition may apply. The same may be the situation if the UN Charter supersedes UNCLOS or if jus cogens norms apply.[381]

"Common heritage of mankind," for which this *Report* offers a gender-neutral equivalent, "common heritage of humankind," is in the UNCLOS preamble, which cites UN General Assembly Resolution 2749 (1970). Resolution 2749 "solemnly declared *inter alia* that the area of the sea-bed beyond the limits of national jurisdiction, as well as its resources, are the common heritage of mankind, the exploration and exploitation of which shall be carried out for the benefit of mankind as a whole, irrespective of the geographic location of States[.]"[382] Article 125(1) declares that landlocked States have the right of access to and from the sea for exercising Convention rights, including freedom of the high seas and the common heritage of mankind, thus linking UNCLOS provisions on landlocked States to its Articles governing the Area.[383]

The Area, defined in Article 1(1) as the sea-bed and ocean floor and subsoil thereof beyond the limits of national jurisdiction,[384] and Area resources are the common heritage of mankind, according to Article 136. Article 150(i) requires that activities in the Area must, as

[381] *See* Parts III.B-III.D and § 132, defining "other rules of international law."

[382] For preamble analysis, *see* 1 Commentary 450–67; for text of Resolution 2749, *see* 10 ILM 220 (1971).

[383] 3 Commentary ¶ 125.9(d). Article 124(1)(a) defines a landlocked State as a State that has no sea-coast.

[384] Article 1(1) corresponds to the first phrase of operative paragraph 1 of Resolution 2749. "As foreshadowed in the sixth paragraph of the preamble … one of the objects of this Convention is to develop the principles … in that Declaration [Resolution 2749]." 2 Commentary ¶ 1.17.

provided in Part XI, be carried out to foster healthy development of the world economy and balanced growth of international trade, and to promote international cooperation for all countries', especially developing countries', overall development, with a view to ensuring "development of the common heritage [sic] for the benefit of mankind as a whole." Article 155(2) charges the Area Review Conference, established under Area governance articles, with ensuring maintenance of "the principle of the common heritage of mankind, the international regime designed to ensure equitable exploitation of the resources of the Area for the benefit of all countries, especially the developing States …" Article 311(6) declares that States Parties agree there shall be no amendments to the basic principle relating to the common heritage of mankind in Article 136 and that they shall not be party to any agreement in derogation of Article 136. The UNCLOS common heritage principle is a theme running through UNCLOS Part XI, which with the 1994 Agreement establishes other rules and principles regarding the Area.

The common heritage principle for the law of the sea had its beginnings in the 1967 address by Malta's Ambassador Avid Pardo in the UN General Assembly in which he called for a treaty allocating deep seabed resources for the common heritage of mankind.[385] At about the same time space law treaties began using similar phrases,[386] although these treaties do not include the qualifying language of UNCLOS Article 155(2) with respect to common heritage, *i.e.*, "the principle of the common heritage of mankind, the international regime designed to ensure equitable exploitation of the resources of the Area for the benefit of all countries, especially the developing States …" It would therefore seem that the LOS common heritage principle differs from its space law cousins in these respects:

(1) The UNCLOS common heritage principle applies only to the Area, *i.e.*, the seabed and the ocean floor and the subsoil thereof, beyond national jurisdiction limits as defined in UNCLOS Article 1(1).

---

[385] Churchill & Lowe 226.

[386] COPUOS, note 359, pmbl., art. 1 (exploration, use of outer space, including the Moon and other celestial bodies, shall be carried out for benefit and in interests of all countries, irrespective of their degree of economic or scientific development, and shall be the province of all mankind); Space Liability Convention, note 359, pmbl. (common interest of all mankind in furthering exploration, use of outer space for peaceful purposes); Moon Treaty, note 359, art. 11 (Moon, its natural resources are common heritage of mankind, subject to international regime to be established). *See also* Jennings & Watts ch. 7.

(2) The UNCLOS common heritage principle means the equitable exploitation of Area resources for the benefit of all States, with especial concern for developing States.
(3) Equitable exploitation of Area resources pursuant to the UNCLOS common heritage principle is further subject to rules in UNCLOS Part XI and the 1994 Agreement and rules developed by Area agencies.
(4) States cannot unilaterally appropriate, under UNCLOS Article 137(1) and as § 6 defines "appropriate" and "appropriation," resources protected under the common heritage of mankind principle.
(5) A common management system among UNCLOS and 1994 Agreement parties for resources protected under the common heritage of mankind principle.
(6) Universal participation among UNCLOS and 1994 Agreement parties, subject to UNCLOS and 1994 Agreement rules.
(7) Resource conservation and protection of the marine environment as UNCLOS and the 1994 Agreement require.

The Committee's definition has been developed is advanced on these theses, with primary language taken from UNCLOS Article 155(2), and with a gender neutralized equivalent, the "common heritage of humankind."[387]

Although commentators declare that a modern definition of "common heritage" may include additional concepts,[388] application of the LOS through UNCLOS and the 1994 Agreement, with their limitations to Area development, may mean that common heritage for the LOS may be different from that for, *e.g.*, space law.[389]

Section 9 defines "area" and "Area;" § 6, "appropriate" and "appropriation;" § 19, "benefit of mankind as a whole" or "benefit of humankind as a whole;" § 81, "high seas;" § 157, "sea-bed," "seabed" or "bed."

§ 35. *Competent international organization or competent international organizations*

Because of different usages in different UNCLOS provisions, "competent international organization" or "competent international organizations" are defined separately by usage where UNCLOS does not specify the particular competent international organization or competent international organizations:

387 *See also* Churchill & Lowe ch. 12; Jennings & Watts §§ 350–52.
388 *E.g.*, Joyner, note 360.
389 *See* note 360 and accompanying text; *see also* 2007–08 ABILA Proc. 183–86.

(a) "The competent international organization," as used in UNCLOS Articles 22, 41 and 60, means the International Maritime Organization (IMO) or its successor. "The competent international organization," as used in UNCLOS Article 53, means the IMO or its successor with respect to ships' navigation, and the International Civil Aviation Organization (ICAO) or its successor with respect to overflight navigation and also to international straits transit passage under UNCLOS Article 39(3)(a).
(b) "The competent international organization," as used in UNCLOS Part XII, means IMO or its successor with respect to issues of preventing, reducing and controlling vessel-source pollution; dumping at sea; safety of navigation and routing systems; and design, construction, equipment and manning of vessels. The International Atomic Energy Agency (IAEA) or its successor is "the competent international organization" with respect to issues involving radioactive substances.
(c) In UNCLOS Article 220(7), which is within Part XII, because of the qualifying clause "unless otherwise agreed," reference to "the competent international organization" means that other international organizations may be involved.
(d) In UNCLOS Article 223, which is within Part XII, "the competent international organization" means that international organization which is the competent one for the purposes of Article 223, on the basis of which proceedings were instituted.
(e) In UNCLOS Article 265, "competent international organization" does not necessarily mean IMO or its successor, but rather a particular international organization, global, regional or subregional, involved in a marine scientific research project and subject to Article 265 interim measures principles.
(f) "A competent international organization," as used in UNCLOS Article 297, may mean IMO or any organization other than IMO.
(g) "Competent international organizations, whether subregional, regional or global," as used in UNCLOS, Articles 61 and 119, means the Food and Agriculture Organization (FAO) or its successor as the "global" organization; "subregional" or "regional" organizations mean subregional or regional fishery bodies, whether they are subject to FAO or its successor or independent of them.
(h) "Competent international organizations," as used in UNCLOS Parts XII-XIV and Annex II, Article 3(2), means global, regional and subregional international organizations.

Comment

In LOAC-governed situations under the "other rules of international law" clauses in UNCLOS, a different definition may apply. The same may be the situation if the UN Charter supersedes UNCLOS or if *jus cogens* norms apply.[390]

The phrase "or its successor" in § 35 accounts for a possibility that IMO, ICAO, FAO or other organizations may change in purposes, principles and functions, so that another international organization would be considered "the competent international organization" in the future.[391]

The phrases "competent international organization" or "competent international organizations" appear in many UNCLOS provisions without specifying the particular organization or organizations: Articles 22(3)(a), 41(4), 41(5), 53(9), 60(3), 60(5), 61(2), 61(5), 119(2), 197, 198, 199, 200, 201, 202, 204(1), 205, 207(4), 208(5), 210(4), 211(1), 211(2), 211(3), 211(5), 211(6)(a), 212(3), 213, 214, 216(1), 217(1), 217(4), 217(7), 218(1), 220(7), 222, 223, 238, 239, 242(1), 243, 244(1), 244(2), 246(3), 246(5), 246(5)(d), 248, 249(1), 251, 252, 252(b), 253(1)(b), 253(4), 253(5), 254(1), 254(2), 254(3), 254(4), 256, 257, 262, 263(1), 263(2), 263(5), 265, 266(1), 268, 269, 271, 272, 273, 275(1), 275(2), 276(2), 278 and 297(1)(c), and in Annex II, Article 3(2). References to "competent international organization" or "competent international organizations" appear in 9 of 17 Parts of UNCLOS, *i.e.*, Article 22(3)(a), Part II, Territorial Sea and Contiguous Zone; Articles 41(4)–41(5), Part III, Straits Used for International Navigation; Article 53(9), Part IV, Archipelagic States; Articles 60(3)–61(5), Part V, EEZ; Article 119(2), Part VII, High Seas; Articles 197–223, Part XII, Protection and Preservation of the Marine Environment; Articles 238–65, Part XIII, MSR; Articles 266(1)–78, Part XIV, Development and Transfer of Marine Technology; Article 297(1)(c), Part XV, Settlement

---

[390] *See* Parts III.B-III.D and § 132, defining "other rules of international law."

[391] *Cf. Competent*, note 321, p. 79. UNCLOS art. 123, dealing with enclosed or semi-enclosed seas, recites the duty of States bordering and enclosed or semi-enclosed sea to try to cooperate directly or through an appropriate regional organization ... "(d) to invite ... other interested States or international organizations to cooperate with them in furtherance of art. 123's provisions. *Competent* p. 84 lists FAO, the International Atomic Energy Agency (IAEA), IHO, IMO, International Oceanographic Commission (IOC) of UNESCO, UN Development Programme (UNDP), UN Enviromental Programme (UNEP), World Meterological Organization (WMO) and the World Bank as international organizations.

of Disputes. Annex II provides for establishing a Commission on the Limits of the Continental Shelf. Among the 1958 LOS Conventions, "competent international organizations" only appears in High Seas Convention Article 25; States must take into account these organizations' standards and regulations in preventing pollution of the seas from dumping of radioactive waste and must cooperate with them in taking measures for preventing pollution of the seas or air space above them resulting from activities with radioactive materials or other harmful agents.[392]

Review of commentaries on these UNCLOS provisions reveals different international organizations are considered the "competent international organization[s]" for different articles. The generic meaning for "international organization" is not clear; a proposal to define "international organization" as an intergovernmental organization, following the Vienna Convention on the Law of Treaties definition, was not adopted.[393]

> The meaning of the plural expression [the competent international organizations] will clearly be dependent on time, place and circumstance (an observation equally applicable to the singular expression in [A]rticle 223). It also allows States to interact with different international intergovernmental organizations in given circumstances. The meaning of the singular expression, however, is more circumscribed. In dealing with applicable rules, standards and recommended practices and procedures, the expression "*the* competent international organization is frequently encountered in articles adopted by the both the Second … and the Third Committee[s, dealing with navigation and safety rules], and this normally refers to … (IMO). Elsewhere in the Convention, however, the

[392] By contrast, sometimes the Convention names the UN, a UN organ, a UN specialized agency, or an UNCLOS-related international organization: UNCLOS arts. 16(2) (UN), 75(2) (UN), 76(8) (UN), 76(9) (UN), 83(4) (International Seabed Authority [ISBA]), 84(1) (ISBA), 84(2) (UN, ISBA), 143(3)(b) (IAEA, IHO, IOC, ISBA, UNEP, UNESCO, WMO), 143(3)(c) (same), 163(13) (UN, IAEA, International Labour Organisation [ILO], IMO, IOC, UNCTAD. UNDP, UNEP, WMO, World Trade Organization), 273 (ISBA inter alia); *id.* Annex II art. 3(2) (IHO, International IOC); *id.* Annex VIII art. 3(e) (FAO, IMO, IOC, UNEP; *see also Competent*, note 321, pp. 81–95. Following the principle that this Report does not define anew terms that UNCLOS defines, § 35 does not offer additional international organizations for these UNCLOS provisions if the Convention names the organization or organizations, *e.g.*, UNCLOS art. 16(2) (coastal States' duties to deposit charts or geographical coordinates of territorial sea). *See* Part III.A.

[393] 4 Commentary ¶ XII.17 (citation omitted), referring to Vienna Convention, art. 2(1)(I); *see also* Reparation for Injuries Suffered in Service of the United Nations, 1949 ICJ 174, 179, 185 (adv. op.); Aust 395, 398–99; McNair 269–70; Restatement (Third) § 221.

> singular expression refers to whichever international organization is competent in the circumstances. It was generally understood in the [Law of the Sea] Conference, in both the Second ... and the Third Committee[s], that the IMO is "the competent international organization" with regard to the prevention, reduction and control of vessel-source pollution ...; dumping at sea; the safety of navigation and routeing systems; and the design, construction, equipment and manning of vessels. ... [T]he International Atomic Energy Agency is the competent international organization with respect to radioactive substances.[394]

Commentaries on specific UNCLOS provisions bear out this general statement.[395]

"IMO is recognized as the only international organization responsible for establishing and adopting measures on an international level concerning the routeing of ships ..." in territorial sea innocent passage, the subject of Article 22(3)(a).[396] (The UNCLOS Article 17–32 nonsuspendable innocent passage regime, and therefore IMO as the competent international organization to establish and adopt sea lanes, applies to straits used for international navigation but excluded from straits transit passage under Article 38[1], or those straits used for international navigation between a part of the high seas or an EEZ and a foreign State's territorial sea).[397] The same is true for routing systems IMO designates for straits transit passage, the subject of UNCLOS Articles 41(4)–41(5), and for archipelagic sea lanes passage, where IMO designates sea lanes and routes, the subject of Article 53(9).[398] For aircraft exercising rights of archipelagic overflight, Article 53(9) does not apply; the International Civil Aviation Organization (ICAO) Rules of

---

394 4 Commentary ¶ XII.17, inter alia citing Statute of International Atomic Energy Agency, Oct. 26, 1956, 8 UST 1093, 276 UNTS 3 (other citations omitted). IMO "has a wide competence in matters affecting shipping and has adopted a detailed and technical approach to its work. Its committees ... have played a prominent role in drawing up regulations concerning navigation and pollution." Over 40 IMO-drafted conventions and protocols, many with wide State acceptance, are in force. *See generally* Churchill & Lowe 23, 264–77, 333, 339–56; 2 O'Connell 771–80, 831–36, 997–1015. The IAEA sponsored Convention on Civil Liability for Nuclear Damage, 2 ILM 727 (1963). Churchill & Lowe 23, 362.

395 To the extent merchant ship crews' working conditions affect safety of navigation, International Labor Organization-sponsored treaties could have an impact. Churchill & Lowe 270; 2 O'Connell 831.

396 *Competent*, note 321, p. 81; 2 Commentary ¶ 22.8(d); *see also* Churchill & Lowe 95 n. 59.

397 *Cf.* 2 Commentary ¶¶ 45.1, 45.8(a)–45.8(c).

398 *Competent*, note 321, p. 81 (IMO the competent international organization); Churchill & Lowe 106, 108, 127–28 (same); 2 Commentary ¶¶ 41.9(c)–41.9(d), 53.1, 53.9(k)–53.9(*l*).

the Air apply to these flights.[399] Similarly, ICAO Rules of the Air apply to civil aircraft in straits passage under Article 39(3)(a); State aircraft "will normally comply with such safety measures and will at all times operate with due regard for the safety of navigation."[400]

IMO is also recognized as the competent international organization for UNCLOS Articles 60(3) and 60(5), dealing with removing artificial islands, installations and structures, and safety zones around them.[401] (Article 208, requiring coastal States to adopt laws and regulations to prevent, reduce and control pollution of the marine environment, refers to Article 60.[402] Article 246(5)(b), which addresses EEZ and continental shelf MSR, also refers to Article 60.[403])

On the other hand, commentators note the different thrust of UNCLOS Articles 61(2) and 61(5),[404] dealing with "competent international organizations, whether subregional, regional or global," for conservation and management measures and exchange of available scientific information, catch and fishing effort statistics and other data relevant to conserving fish stocks:

> In paragraph 2, the expression "competent international organization, whether subregional, regional or global" must be carefully distinguished from the expression "competent international organization" used in the articles ... relating to navigation and preservation and protection of the marine environment. In those provisions, the expression normally refers to the [IMO]. ... In dealing with the harmonization of references to subregional, regional and global organizations, ... "except with respect to article 61," the term "competent international organizations" is sufficient to refer to global organizations or to both global and other organizations ...
>
> ... [FAO] is not in the same position with respect to fisheries, [conservation of which is within the ambit of Article 61]. The FAO Committee on Fisheries constitute[d, in 1993] the only intergovernmental forum in which fishery problems are examined periodically on a worldwide basis, and could, in some respects, be considered a global organization to which

---

399 2 Commentary ¶¶ 53.9(k)–53.9(*l*); *see also* Churchill & Lowe 173–74.

400 *See also Competent*, note 321, p. 81.

401 *Competent*, note 321, p. 82; 2 Commentary ¶¶ 60.15(f), 60.15(h); *see also* Churchill & Lowe 155, 167–68, 170.

402 2 Commentary ¶ 60.15(*l*); 4 *id.* ¶ 208.10(a).

403 2 *id.* ¶ 60.15(m); *see also* notes 396–98 and accompanying text.

404 "What is much less certain is whether the coastal State's fishery management duties ... in articles 61 and 62 have become part of customary law." Churchill & Lowe 290 (citations omitted).

> [A]rticle 61 refers. Alongside this Commission, there are a number of regional fishery bodies both inside and outside FAO, the activities of which are of more direct relevance to the actual management of fishery resources.[405]

Article 119(2)'s similar reference to "competent international organizations, whether subregional, regional or global," in the context of high seas conservation of living resources, must be read in the same light as the references in Articles 61(2) and 61(5), *i.e.*, the primary reference should be to FAO, along with regional fishery bodies inside and outside FAO.[406] The same should be true for highly migratory species under Article 64(1)[407] and marine mammals under Article 65.[408] FAO, the World Bank and regional and subregional organizations are international organizations assisting landlocked States under Article 65.[409]

There are more references to "the competent international organization" or "competent international organizations" in UNCLOS Part XII, Protection and Preservation of the Marine Environment, than any other Part of UNCLOS. First, as a general matter, Part XII references to "competent international organizations" include global organizations or global and other organizations.[410] Second, however, if the singular "competent international organization" is used, IMO has been considered "the competent international organization" with regard to prevention, reduction and control of vessel-source pollution; dumping at sea; safety of navigation and routing systems; and design, construction, equipment and manning of vessels. IAEA has been considered "the competent international organization" with respect to radioactive substances.[411]

The first is true for references to "competent international organizations," in the plural, in UNCLOS Article 197,[412] commentary for which

---

[405] 2 Commentary ¶ 61.12(e) (citations omitted); *see also id.* ¶ 61.12(j); *Competent*, note 321, p. 82; *cf.* Churchill & Lowe 294–96.

[406] *Cf. Competent*, note 321, p. 83 (also listing IOC); Churchill & Lowe 297–305, 313; 4 Commentary ¶¶ 119.1, 119.7(e); *see also* 2 *id.* ¶¶ 61.12(e), 61.12(j), 61.12(k); note 400 and accompanying text.

[407] *Competent*, note 321, p. 82.

[408] *Id.* (also listing International Whaling Commission, UNEP).

[409] *Id.*

[410] 4 Commentary ¶ XII.17, at 16 (citation omitted).

[411] *Id.* ¶ XII.17; *see also* Churchill & Lowe 333 (treaties governing pollution from ships adopted under IMO auspices), 339–70, 394–96; notes 389–96, 399, 402 and accompanying text.

[412] 4 Commentary ¶ 197.7.

mentions IMO but does not exclude other organizations, *i.e.*, global or other organizations.[413] The same drafting pattern for "competent international organizations" appears in commentaries for Articles 198–99, 200–01, 204(1), 205 and 214,[414] but not in those for Articles 202, 210(4), 212(3), 216 and 222, and indirectly in Articles 207, 208 and 213 commentaries.[415] Article 200 commentary refers to IMO and other organizations.[416] Article 212 commentary (atmospheric pollution) refers to ICAO.[417]

UNCLOS Articles 211(1)–11(3), 211(5) and 211(6)(a), by contrast, refer to "the competent international organization" in the singular; IMO was "the" organization that was meant:

> only one international intergovernmental organization — [IMO] ... — is competent for ... establishing international rules and standards to prevent, reduce and control pollution of the marine environment from vessels, and for adopting, where appropriate, routeing systems designed to minimize the threat of accidents which might cause pollution of the marine environment.

However,

> Regional organizations, whose specific competence in the part of the sea concerned is generally acknowledged and recognized, especially by the flag State, and whose decisions are compatible with the Convention, could assist in the implementation of the international rules and standards, the elaboration of regional rules and standards and the

[413] *See* 4 Commentary ¶ 197.3. *Competent*, note 321, p. 85 lists FAO, IAEA, ICAO, IHO, IOC, ISBA, UNEP, UNIDO, WHO and WMO besides IMO.

[414] 4 Commentary ¶¶ 198.1, 199.1, 199.5, 200.6, 201.5, 204.7, 205.5, 214.7(a). *Competent*, note 318, pp. 85–88 lists FAO, IAEA, IHO, IMO, IOC, ISBA and UNEP for UNCLOS art. 198; FAO, IAEA, IHO, IMO, IOC, ISBA, UNEP and WMO for art. 199; FAO, IAEA, ICAO, IHO, IMO, IOC, UNEP, UNESCO, UNIDO, WHO and WMO for art. 200; FAO, IAEA, ICAO, IHO, IMO, IOC, UNEP, UNESCO, WHO and WMO for art. 201; FAO, IAEA, ICAO, IHO, IMO, IOC, UNCTAD, UNEP, UNIDO, UNESCO, WHO and WMO for art. 202; IAEA, IMO and UNEP for art. 214.

[415] *Compare* 4 Commentary ¶ 207.4 *with id.* ¶ 207.5; *see id.* ¶ 208.10(e), referring to *id.* ¶ 207.5; *id.* ¶ 213.7(f), referring to *id.* 207.7(d). *Competent*, note 321, pp. 85–88, lists IAEA, ICAO, IHO, ILO, IMO, IOC, UNEP, UNIDO and WHO for UNCLOS art. 207(4); IAEA, IHO, ILO, IMO, IOC, UNEP and UNIDO for art. 208(5); IAEA, ICAO, IMO, IOC, UNEP and WHO for art. 210(4); IAEA, ICAO, IMO, UNEP and UNIDO for art. 213.

[416] 4 Commentary ¶ 200.1 (referring inter alia to IMCO, FAO).

[417] *Id.* ¶¶ 212.9(a)–212.9(c); *Competent*, note 321, p. 88, refers to IAEA, ICAO, IMO, IOC, UNEP and WMO for art. 212(3).

> establishment of regional monitoring systems, the dissemination of information and the promotion of technical cooperation.[418]

Similarly, commentary for Article 217, referring thrice to "the competent international organization," says IMO is the organization that establishes international rules and standards for vessel compliance with marine environmental pollution standards.[419] Article 218 commentary, also referring to "the competent international organization," does not elucidate the rationale, however. Article 220(7), by referring to "the competent international organization or as otherwise agreed," suggests cooperation not only with IMO but also with FAO and bodies associated with it.[420] A flag State could also conclude an agreement with a coastal State.

Although UNCLOS Article 223 refers to "the competent international organization," "that does not imply that in principle only one international organization can be competent for the purposes of this [A]rticle [223]. It refers to that international organization which was the competent one for the purposes of that provision of the Convention on the basis of which the proceedings were instituted."[421]

Thus although there seems to be no negotiating history or commentary for a few UNCLOS Part XII provisions, data from the rest confirms the view that "the competent international organization" means the IMO and only the IMO, except in UNCLOS Article 220(7), where the qualifying phrase, "or as otherwise agreed," signals a possibility of cooperation with other international organizations. Article 223 documentation, dealing with enforcement, indicates UNCLOS negotiators did not mean to confine the meaning of "the competent international organization" to IMO. For the phrase "competent international organizations" in Part XII, it seems reasonably clear that regional and subregional organizations are also meant.[422]

---

[418] 4 Commentary ¶ 211.15(d); *see also id.* ¶ 211.2 (IMCO's earlier work), 211.15(g) (IMO contact with States); *Competent*, note 321, p. 87.

[419] 4 Commentary ¶ 217.8(b); *see also Competent*, note 321, p. 88.

[420] 4 Commentary ¶ 220.1; *see also id.* ¶ 220.11(k). Nevertheless, *Competent*, note 321, p. 89 just lists IMO.

[421] IMO was reported to have considered the need for special procedures for submitting evidence by the IMO in UNCLOS art. 223 proceedings. 4 Commentary ¶ 223.9(a) (citation omitted).

[422] This has been the result in practice. *Competent*, note 321, p. 89 lists FAO, IAEA, ICAO, IHO, ILO, IOC, ISBA, UNEP, WHO and WMO besides IMO.

There are equally as many references to "competent international organization" or "competent international organizations" in UNCLOS Part XIII, providing for MSR. The Part XII pattern of definition[423] for "competent international organizations" continues in Part XIII. They can include governmental and nongovernmental organizations. Part XIII's use of the term "refer[s] to whichever organization or organizations are conducting" MSR. The Intergovernmental Oceanographic Commission (IOC), part of UNESCO, works with FAO on fisheries; the IAEA, on marine environmental protection; the IHO and WMO; and UNEP, particularly on global ocean monitoring and marine pollution research and monitoring programs. IOC has cooperative arrangements with regional groups, *e.g.*, Comision Permanente del Pacifico Sur and the international Commission for the Scientific Exploration of the Mediterranean Sea. IOC also has agreements with NGOs like the International Council for the Exploration of the Seas and the Scientific Committee on Oceanic Research, the latter part of the International Council of Scientific Unions.[424]

Commentaries and organization tables for UNCLOS Articles 238,[425] 239,[426] 243,[427] 244,[428] 246,[429] 247,[430] 248,[431] 249,[432] 251,[433] 252,[434] 253,[435]

---

[423] *See* notes 408–20 and accompanying text.

[424] 4 Commentary ¶ XIII.14; *see also* Churchill & Lowe 412, 415–18.

[425] 4 Commentary ¶ 238.11(c), listing the International Sea-Bed Authority established in UNCLOS art. 143; the UN and competent specialized agencies; the IAEA; the IOC; UNEP; possible NGOs. *Competent*, note 321, p. 89, lists FAO, IAEA, IHO, IMO, IOC, ISBA, UNEP, UNESCO and WMO.

[426] *Competent*, note 321, p. 90, lists FAO, IAEA, IHO, IMO, IOC, ISBA, the UN, UNDP, UNEP, UNESCO, WHO, WMO and the World Bank.

[427] 4 Commentary ¶ 243.7(b); *Competent*, note 321, p. 90, lists FAO, IAEA, IHO, IMO, IOC, ISBA, the UN, UNDP, UNEP, UNESCO, WHO, WMO and the World Bank.

[428] 4 Commentary ¶¶ 244.9(a)–244.9(b); *Competent*, note 321, p. 90, lists FAO, IAEA, IHO, IMO, IOC, ISBA, UNEP, UNESCO, WHO and WMO.

[429] *Competent*, note 321, p. 90, lists FAO, IAEA, IHO, IMO, IOC, UNEP, UNESCO and WMO.

[430] *Id.* p. 91 lists FAO, IAEA, IHO, IMO, IOC, ISBA, UNEP, UNESCO and WMO.

[431] *Id.* lists FAO, IAEA, IHO, IMO, IOC, UNEP, UNESCO and WMO.

[432] *Id.* lists FAO, IAEA, IHO, IMO, IOC, UNEP, UNESCO and WMO.

[433] *Id.* lists FAO, IAEA, IHO, IMO, IOC, ISBA, the UN, UNEP, UNESCO and WMO. 4 Commentary ¶ 251.4 says there is no indication of what are the "competent" international organizations, but IOC plays leading role in implementing art. 251.

[434] *Competent*, note 321, p. 91 lists FAO, IAEA, IHO, IMO, IOC, UNEP, UNESCO and WMO; *see also* 4 Commentary ¶ 252.9(a).

[435] *Competent*, note 321, p. 91 lists FAO, IAEA, IHO, IMO, IOC, UNEP, UNESCO and WMO.

254,[436] 256,[437] 257,[438] 261,[439] 262[440] and 263[441] underscore the possible diversity of organizations. Commentary for Article 242(1) lacks similar references; however, given this article's provenance within Part XIII's context,[442] where other commentaries note the variety of organizations that can participate, the same meaning for "competent international organizations" should attach to Articles 239, 242(1), 246, 248, 249(1), 253, 254 and 263.

UNCLOS Article 265 lacks the article "the" before "competent international organization." There is no commentary on the omission; since Article 265 refers to "the State or competent international organization" authorized to conduct an MSR project, Article 265's context[443] might lead to the conclusion that "competent international organization" in Article 265 does not mean IMO as in other contexts,[444] but rather a particular international organization, whether global, regional or subregional, involved in an MSR project and subject to Article 265 interim measures issues. Practice has been otherwise, however.[445]

---

436 *Id.* pp. 91–92 lists FAO, IAEA, IHO, IMO, IOC, UNEP, UNESCO and WMO.

437 4 Commentary ¶ 256.7(c) (reference to "competent international organizations" indicates UNCLOS art. 256 applies to "any and all such organizations" wishing to conduct MSR in maritime zones beyond national jurisdictional limits that are capable of doing so). *Competent*, note 321, p. 92 lists FAO, IAEA, IHO, IMO, IOC, ISBA, UNEP, UNESCO and WMO.

438 4 Commentary ¶ 257.6(b) & n. 2 (reference to WMO programs). *Competent*, note 321, p. 92 lists FAO, IAEA, IHO, IMO, IOC, UNEP, UNESCO and WMO as art. 257 participants.

439 4 Commentary ¶ 261.5 n. 2 (IMO Secretariat's opinion IMO "would appear to be the most appropriate body for developing the international rules and standards to ensure safety at sea;" also reference to ICAO, International Telecommunication Union [ITU], IOC, IHO, others, citing Implications of the United Nations Convention on the Law of the Sea, 1982, for the International Maritime Organization (IMO): Study by the Secretariat of IMO, IMO Doc. LEG/MISC/1, ¶ 127 [1986, *reprinted in* 3 Netherlands Institute for the Law of the Sea, International Organizations and the Law of the Sea: Documentary Yearbook 340, 388 [1987]).

440 4 Commentary ¶¶ 261.5 n. 2, 262.5 & n. 3 (air safety under ICAO; safety at sea under IMO; internationally agreed warning signals under ITU). *Competent*, note 318, p. 92 lists FAO, IAEA, ICAO, IMO, IMO, IOC, ISBA, UNEP, UNESCO and WMO.

441 *Competent*, note 321, p. 93 lists FAO, IAEA, IHO, IMO, IOC, ISBA, UNEP, UNESCO and WMO.

442 Vienna Convention art. 31(1); *see also* Kasikili/Sedudu Island (Botswana v. Namibia), 1999 ICJ 1045, 1059 (Dec. 13) (Art. 31 customary law); Aust 234–35; Restatement (Third) § 325(1); Sinclair 119–27.

443 Vienna Convention art. 31(1); *see also* note 55 and accompanying text.

444 *See* notes 391–96, 399, 409 and accompanying text.

445 *Competent*, note 321, p. 93 lists FAO, IAEA, IHO, IOC, ISBA, UNEP, UNESCO and WMO in addition to IMO.

Commentaries to UNCLOS, Part XIV, Development and Transfer of Marine Technology, follow the pattern of Parts XII and XIII for defining "competent international organizations." Commentaries to or tables for Articles 266(1),[446] 268,[447] 269,[448] 271,[449] 272,[450] 273,[451] 275,[452] 276[453] and 278[454] note the variety of possible organizations.

Article 297(1)(c), in UNCLOS Part XV, Settlement of Disputes, refers to "a competent international organization." There appears to be no commentary on this. However, Article 297(1)(c) refers to "specified international rules and standards for the protection and preservation

---

[446] 4 Commentary ¶ 266.7(a) (phrase "broad enough to embrace any international intergovernmental organization ... competent to render the requested assistance, whether by virtue of its general characteristics and sphere of activity, or ... its regional association"). *Competent*, note 321, p. 93 lists FAO, IAEA, IHO, IMO, IOC, ISBA, UNCTAD, UNDP, UNEP, UNESCO, UNIDO, WIPO, WMO and the World Bank.

[447] 4 Commentary ¶ 268.5(d) (IMO steps to implement art. 268[d]; no evidence IMO the only competent international organization). This has been the practice. Besides IMO, these organizations have operated under Article 268 powers: FAO, IAEA, IHO, IOC, ISBA, UNCTAD, UNDP, UNEP, UNESCO, UNIDO, WIPO, WMO and the World Bank. *Competent*, note 321, p. 93.

[448] *Competent*, note 321, p. 93 lists FAO, IAEA, IHO, IMO, IOC, ISBA, UNCTAD, UNDP, UNEP, UNESCO, UNIDO, WIPO, WMO and the World Bank as participating organizations. 4 Commentary ¶¶ 269.2–269.3 suggest that "competent international organizations" is a shorthand version of "cooperation at the international, regional and sub-regional levels."

[449] *Competent*, note 321, p. 94 lists FAO, IAEA, IHO, IMO, IOC, ISBA, UNCTAD, UNEP, UNESCO, UNIDO, WIPO and WMO as cooperating organizations.

[450] *Id.* lists FAO, IAEA, IHO, IMO, IOC, ISBA, UNCTAD, UNDP, UNEP, UNESCO, UNIDO, WIPO, WMO and the World Bank. 4 Commentary ¶¶ 272.1–272.2 suggest "competent international organizations" is shorthand for "organizations in this field [of transfer of technology], including any regional or international programmes;" UNCLOS art. 272 says States "shall endeavour to ensure that competent international organizations co-ordinate their activities, including any regional or global programmes. ..."

[451] *Competent*, note 321, p. 94 lists IOC, UNCTAD, UNDP, UNEP, UNESCO, UNIDO, WIPO and the World Back in addition to ISBA, named in Art. 273. *See also* 4 Commentary ¶ 273.9(e) ("'competent international organization' refers to any international organization ... competent in the circumstances present; in Part XIV, however, it does not have the same specific connotation that it has in Part XII").

[452] *Competent*, note 321, p. 94 lists FAO, IAEA, IOC, ISBA, UNDP, UNEP, UNESCO, UNIDO, WMO and the World Bank as participants.

[453] 4 Commentary ¶¶ 276.5–276.6 suggest that "competent international organizations" is a shorthand version of "competent regional organizations, [and] international organizations. ..."

[454] *Competent*, note 321, p. 95 lists FAO, IAEA, IHO, IMO, IOC, ISBA, UNCTAD, UNDP, UNEP, UNESCO, UNIDO, WIPO, WMO and the World Bank; *see also* 4 Commentary ¶ 278.4(a) (art. 278 "addressed to 'competent international organizations,' ... those referred to in Part XIII [Articles 238–65] as well as those in Part XIV[;] ... not possible to indicate in general terms the competent international organizations which the article has in mind").

of the marine environment which are applicable to the coastal State and which have been established ... through a competent international organization ... in accordance with this Convention." Under UNCLOS Part XII, providing for protection and preservation of the marine environment, when "the competent international organization" is used, IMO is considered "the competent international organization" for prevention, reduction and control of vessel-source pollution; dumping at sea; safety of navigation and routing systems; and design, construction, equipment and manning of vessels. IAEA is considered the "competent international organization" for radioactive substances.[455] Since Article 297 refers to protection and preservation of the marine environment, and UNCLOS Part XII commentaries accord a meaning to "the competent international organization," logically "a competent international organization" in Article 297(1)(c) should have the same meaning as "the competent international organization" in Part XII. In practice WMO and UNEP have shared competence.[456]

UNCLOS Annex II, Article 3(2) allows the Commission on the Limits of the Continental Shelf to cooperate with the IOC, IHO and "other competent international organizations." Article 3(2) commentary[457] does not say whether "other" organizations might include regional, subregional or nongovernmental organizations. However, given the apparent construction of "the competent international organizations" as including these, it is consistent to accord the same definition to Article 3(2).[458]

Section 7 defines "appropriate international organization" or "appropriate international organizations;" § 31, "coastal State;" § 81, "high seas;" § 141, "regional organization" or "sub-regional organization;" § 163, "ship" or "vessel."[459]

§ 36. *Compilation*

As used in UNCLOS analysis, in cartography "compilation" means selection, assembly and graphic presentation of all relevant information

455 *See* notes 391–98, 401, 404, 411 and accompanying text.

456 *Competent*, note 321, p. 95.

457 2 Commentary ¶ A.II.10(c).

458 *Competent*, note 321, p. 83 lists IHO, IOC and the ISBA.

459 *See also* 2007–08 ABILA Proc. 183–200; Churchill & Lowe 22–24, 95 n.2, 108–09, 127–28, 173, 276–77, 297, 302–04, 313, 321–22, 334, 336, 364, 368, 371–75, 380–81, 415–16; Walker, *Last Round* 158–68.

required for preparation of a new map or chart or a new edition thereof. Such information may be derived from other maps or charts, aerial photographs, surveys, new data and other sources.

Comment

In LOAC-governed situations under the "other rules of international law" clauses in UNCLOS, a different definition may apply. The same may be the situation if the UN Charter supersedes UNCLOS or if jus cogens norms apply.[460]

The Former ECDIS Glossary, page 4, defined "compilation" as "[i]n cartography, the selection, assembly, and graphic presentation of all relevant information required for the preparation of a new map/chart or a new edition thereof. Such information may be derived from other maps/charts, aerial photographs, surveys, new data, and other sources." The newer ECDIS Glossary does not define "compilation."

Section 23 defines "chart" or "nautical chart;" § 24, "chart datum;" § 54, "due notice," "appropriate publicity," and "due publicity."[461]

§ 37. *Continental rise*

As used in UNCLOS Articles 76(3) and 76(6), "rise," *i.e.*, the "continental rise," is a submarine feature which is that part of the continental margin lying between the continental slope and the deep ocean floor. It usually has a gradient of 0.5 degrees or less and a generally smooth surface consisting of sediment.

Comment

In LOAC-governed situations under the "other rules of international law" clauses in UNCLOS, a different definition may apply. The same may be the situation if the UN Charter supersedes UNCLOS or if jus cogens norms apply.[462]

Consolidated Glossary ¶ 20 defines the "continental rise" as a "submarine feature which is that part of the continental margin lying between the continental slope and the deep ocean floor; simply

[460] *See* Parts III.B-III.D and § 132, defining "other rules of international law."

[461] *See also* Churchill & Lowe 37, 53, 149; Walker, *ECDIS Glossary* 244, 2003–04 ABILA Proc. 215–16.

[462] *See* Parts III.B-III.D and § 132, defining "other rules of international law."

called the Rise in [UNCLOS]. It usually has a gradient of 0.5E or less and a generally smooth surface consisting of sediment." Former Glossary ¶ 20 defined the "continental rise" as "[a] submarine feature which is a part of the continental margin lying between the continental slope and the abyssal plain. It is usually a gentle slope with gradients of 1/2 degree or less and a generally smooth surface consisting of sediments."[463]

UNCLOS Article 76(3) defines the continental margin as "the submerged prolongation of the land mass of the coastal State, and consist[ing] of the seabed and subsoil of the [continental] shelf, the slope and the rise. It does not include the deep ocean floor with its oceanic ridges or the subsoil thereof." UNCLOS Article 76(6), setting a 350-mile outer continental shelf limit, says its terms do not apply to "submarine elevations that are natural components of the continental margin, such as its plateaux, rises, caps, banks and spurs." UNCLOS does not refer to "continental rise" or otherwise refer to "rise." There are no comparable Shelf Convention provisions.

UNCLOS does not use the term "abyssal plain." Article 1(1)(1), defining the Area, includes "the sea-bed and ocean floor and subsoil thereof, beyond the limits of national jurisdiction[,]" as does the Preamble, referring to U.N. General Assembly Resolution 2749, Declaration of Principles on the Seabed and Ocean Floor (Dec. 17, 1970).[464] UNCLOS Article 76(3) refers to the "deep ocean floor." Article 56(3), reciting EEZ rights, says rights related to the "sea-bed and subsoil thereof shall be exercised in accordance with Part VI[,]" referring to the law of the continental shelf. The basic shelf definition, Article 76(1), refers to "the sea-bed and subsoil of the submarine areas that extend beyond its territorial sea throughout the natural prolongation of its land territory to the outer edge of the continental margin ..." This might be compared with a geological definition of the continental shelf:

> ... [T]he continental shelf is only one part of the submerged prolongation of land territory offshore. It is the inner-most of three geomorphological areas — the continental slope and the continental rise are the other two — defined by changes in the angle at which the seabed drops off toward the deep ocean floor. The shelf, slope and rise, taken together,

---

[463] *Accord*, 2 Commentary ¶ 76.18(d).

[464] 25 U.N. GAOR Supp. No. 28, at 24, ¶¶ 1–4, 9 (1970); *see also* Restatement (Third) § 523 r.n.2.

are known as the continental margin. Worldwide, there is a wide variation in the breadths of these areas.[465]

UNCLOS Article 77(4) says continental shelf natural resources include "mineral and other non-living resources of the sea-bed and subsoil …" Article 194(3)(c) includes among measures dealing with marine pollution sources those designed to minimize pollution from installations and devices used in exploring or exploiting "sea-bed and subsoil" natural resources.

The Shelf Convention has no comparable provisions.

Section 16 discusses UNCLOS Articles 76(3) and 76(6) in connection with baselines and basepoints. Section 38 defines "continental slope;" § 47, "deep ocean floor;" § 67, "foot of the continental slope;" § 93, "line;" § 157, "sea-bed," "seabed" or "bed;" § 162, "shelf;" § 176, "straight line; straight baseline; straight archipelagic baseline."[466]

§ 38. *Continental slope*

"Continental slope" or "slope," as used in UNCLOS Article 76, means that part of the continental margin lying between the continental shelf and the continental rise. The continental slope may not be uniform or abrupt and may locally take the form of terraces. The continental slope's gradients are usually greater than 1.5 degrees.

Comment

In LOAC-governed situations under the "other rules of international law" clauses in UNCLOS, a different definition may apply. The same may be the situation if the UN Charter supersedes UNCLOS or if jus cogens norms apply.[467]

Consolidated Glossary ¶ 22 defines the "continental slope as "[t]hat part of the continental margin that lies between the shelf and the rise[, s]imply called the slope in [UNCLOS] Art. 76.3. The slope may not be

---

465 Roach & Smith ¶ 8.1, citing Offshore Consultants, Inc., Navigational Restrictions Within the New LOS Context: Geographical Implications for the United States 22–23 (L.M. Alexander ed. Dec. 1986).

466 *See also* 2007–08 ABILA Proc. 200–02; Churchill & Lowe chs. 2, 12, pp. 148–50; 2 Commentary ¶¶ 76.1–76.17, 76.18(d) & Fig. 2; NWP 1-14M Annotated ¶ 1.6 & Fig. A1-2; Restatement (Third) §§ 511–12, 515; Noyes, *Definitions* 322–23 & Part III.D.3; Walker, *Consolidated Glossary* 244–45.

467 *See* Parts III.B-III.D and § 132, defining "other rules of international law."

uniform or abrupt, and may locally take the form of terraces. The gradients are usually greater than 1.5E."[468]

UNCLOS Article 76(3), defines the continental margin as "the submerged prolongation of the land mass of the coastal State, and consist[ing] of the seabed and subsoil of the [continental] shelf, the slope and the rise. It does not include the deep ocean floor with its oceanic ridges or the subsoil thereof." Article 76(4)(a)(ii) requires a coastal State to establish the outer edge of the continental margin wherever the margin extends beyond 200 nautical miles from the baselines from which the territorial sea's breadth is measured by "a line delineated in accordance with [Article 76(7)] by reference to fixed points not more than 60 nautical miles from the foot of the continental slope." (Article 76[4][a][i] gives another measuring option, not relevant to this analysis.) Article 76(4)(b) says that "in the absence of evidence to the contrary," "the foot of the continental slope shall be determined as the point of maximum change in the gradient."[469] Article 76(1) defines the continental shelf. This might be compared with a geomorphological definition of the continental shelf:

> ... [T]he continental shelf is only one part of the submerged prolongation of land territory offshore. It is the inner-most of three geomorphological areas — the continental slope and the continental rise are the other two — defined by changes in the angle at which the seabed drops off toward the deep ocean floor. The shelf, slope and rise, taken together, are known as the continental margin. Worldwide, there is a wide variation in the breadths of these areas.[470]

The ILA Committee on the Outer Continental Shelf comments:

> Article 76(4)(b) ... provides that in the absence of evidence to the contrary, the foot of the continental slope shall be determined as the point of

[468] *Accord*, 2 Commentary ¶ 76.18(d). Former Glossary ¶ 22 differs slightly from the 2006 version.

[469] Article 76(4)(b) does not indicate what "evidence to the contrary" consists of. "As the article is concerned with the definition of the foot of the slope it will concern evidence, which indicates that the foot is located at another point than the point of maximum change in gradient at the base of the continental slope." Committee on Legal Issues of the Outer Continental Shelf, *Report*, in ILA, Report of the Seventy-First Conference Held in Berlin 16–21 August 2004, at 773, 793–94 (2004), reported a need for further consideration by the Committee. 2 Commentary ¶ 76.18(e) observes that the phrase implies that there may be special circumstances requiring applying alternative means for determining the foot of the continental slope.

[470] Roach & Smith ¶ 8.1, citing Offshore Consultants, Inc., note 465, pp. 22–23.

> maximum change in the gradient at its base. The reference to these two approaches to determine the foot of the slope indicates that the foot of the slope can be determined on the basis of geomorphological and/or geological characteristics.
> Article 76(4)(b) does not establish a precedence between the two approaches … A coastal State may opt to present evidence to the contrary to locate the foot of the slope, or, if such evidence is not available, present evidence on the maximum change of gradient at the foot of the slope.[471]

See also the *Comment* for § 16, "basepoint" or "point."

The Shelf Convention has no comparable provisions.

Section 16 discusses lines while defining "basepoint" or "point." Section 26 defines "closing line;" § 37, "continental rise;" § 47, "deep ocean floor;" § 67, "foot of the continental slope;" § 93, "line;" § 105, "mile" or "nautical mile;" § 157, "sea-bed," "seabed" or "bed;" § 176, "straight line; straight baseline; straight archipelagic baseline."[472]

§ 39. *Contributions in kind*

In UNCLOS Article 82(1), "contributions in kind" means a coastal State's remitting the extracted nonliving resources which are the equivalent in monetary value to payments due; the in-kind contributions serve as substitutes for payments.

Comment

In LOAC-governed situations under the "other rules of international law" clauses in UNCLOS, a different definition may apply. The same may be the situation if the UN Charter supersedes UNCLOS or if jus cogens norms apply.[473]

UNCLOS Article 82(1) requires a coastal State to make "payments or contributions in kind in respect of the exploration of the non-living resources of the continental shelf beyond 200 nautical miles from the baselines from which the breadth of the territorial sea is measured." Article 82(2) declares that

---

471 COCS *Second Report*, Conclusion 4, p. 222.

472 *See also* Churchill & Lowe, chs. 2, 12, pp. 148–50; 2 Commentary ¶¶ 76.1–76.17, 76.18(d) & Fig. 2; NWP 1-14M Annotated ¶ 1.6 & Fig. A1-2; Restatement (Third) §§ 511–12, 515; Noyes, *Definitions* 322–23 & Part III.D.3; Walker, *Consolidated Glossary* 246–47.

473 *See* Parts III.B-III.D and § 132, defining "other rules of international law."

> payments and contributions shall be made annually with respect to all production at a site after the first five years of production at that site. For the sixth year, the rate of payment or contribution shall be 1 percent of the value or volume of production at the site. The rate shall increase by 1 percent for each subsequent year until the twelfth year and shall remain at 7 percent thereafter. Production does not include resources used in connection with exploitation.

Article 82(3) exempts a developing State which is a net importer of a mineral resource produced from its continental shelf from making such payments or contributions. Article 82(4) requires that payments or contributions shall be made through the Authority, which must distribute them to UNCLOS parties on the basis of equitable sharing criteria, taking into account developing States' interests and needs, particularly the least developed and the land-locked among them.

"Contribution" or "contributions" appear in UNCLOS Articles 160, 162 171, 173 and 184 and in UNCLOS Annex 4, Articles 11(1)(b) and 11(3)(d). UNCLOS Annex 3, Article 6(3) speaks of "financial contributions." UNCLOS Article 124 defines "land-locked State."

"Contributions in kind" seems to have originated in a 1975 U.S. proposal:

> The coastal State shall make payments or in its discretion, equivalent contributions in kind of the resource itself in respect of the exploitation of the non-living resources of the continental shelf beyond 200 nautical miles, from the baselines from which the breadth of the territorial sea is measured.[474]

This seems to have been shortened to the Article 82(1) format of "payments or contributions in kind in respect of the exploration of the non-living resources of the continental shelf beyond 200 nautical miles from the baselines from which the breadth of the territorial sea is measured."[475] There are two possible interpretations: (1) the drafters meant the same thing as the 1975 U.S. proposal when they finalized Article 87(2), *i.e.*, if oil is extracted, the only option is oil as an in-kind contribution; or (2) the drafters meant any in-kind contribution of non-living resources, *e.g.*, if oil and mineral nodules are extracted, the in-kind payment can be oil, even though the nodules are the real value. In view of the drafting history, it would seem that the first option is probably what the drafters meant.

---

[474] 2 Commentary ¶ 82.5, p. 938; *see also* 2007–08 ABILA Proc. 204–06.

[475] *Id.* ¶¶ 82.5, p. 938–82.12(a).

The 2008 ILA Committee on the Outer Continental Shelf *Report on Article 82 of the 1982 UN Convention on Law of the Sea (UNCLOS)* published 12 *Conclusions* related to "contributions in kind" and UNCLOS Article 82:

... 1: The obligation to make "payments or contributions in kind" rests solely with the "coastal State" and not with any other entity that may be involved in the exploitation of the non-living resources of the [outer continental shelf].

... 2: The term "all" production at a site refers to the gross, rather than net, value of the total production of the non-living resources obtained from that site.

... 3: Whereas the actual designation of a production "site" for the exploitation of the non-living resources beyond [the] 200 [nautical mile] limit is within the discretion of the coastal State concerned, the exercise of this discretion does not allow the coastal State to escape its obligation under Article 82(1) to make "payments or contributions" for the exploitation of any non-living resources from the continental shelf beyond the 200 [nautical mile] limit.

... 4: The coastal State can decide the method it will use to calculate "the rate of payment or contribution" under Article 82(2), subject to communicating this method to the International Sea-bed Authority [ISA] as the designated recipient for these "payments or contributions in kind."

... 5: The coastal State has the choice of making "payments or contributions in kind" to fulfil its obligation under Article 82, but it cannot decide to make a combined "payment" and "contribution in kind."

... 6: As it is the coastal State that has to make the required "payments or contributions in kind," it follows that it is only this State and no other State(s) or inter-governmental or commercial entities (such as the ISA, or the companies involved in the actual production of the non-living resources concerned) that has the discretion to decide on the form in which the payments or contributions will take; the method by which such payments and/or contributions are delivered to the ISA; and exactly when such payments and/or contributions will be made to the ISA on an annual basis. Neither the ISA, "through" which this payment and/or contribution is made, nor any of the recipient "State Parties" of these payments or contributions, can overturn the discretion afforded to the coastal State in this respect. However, as the designated recipient of the payments or contributions made, the ISA can express its view on the latter two issues: the method and timing of the payments and/or contributions, to the coastal State concerned. Furthermore, the coastal State's discretion as to the form, method and timing of the payments or contributions is circumscribed by general principles of "good faith" and "non-abuse" of rights, as well as generally applied international industrial standards and procedures.

... 7: The coastal State should report on its implementation of the obligations under Article 82, especially in respect of ... three issues: a) the starting date for exploitation of the non-living resources from the OCS [Outer Continental Shelf]; b) the total annual production of the non-living resources from the OCS for ... calculating the value or volume of the "payments or contributions in kind" required to be made "through" the ISA, under Article 82(4); c) the method applied by the coastal State for determining the value or volume of the "payments or contributions in kind" to be made.

... 8: Notwithstanding the possible legal implications of the inconsistent use of "non-living" and "mineral" resources between Articles 82(1) and 82(3), developing States that are net importers of the resources concerned are exempt from making the required payments or contributions in kind under Articles 82(1) and 82(2).

... 9: The term: "resources" in the last sentence of Article 82(3) is to be read as being limited to the introduction or re-introduction of physical elements such as water or gas that are utilized to directly assist in the exploitation of the non-living resources concerned.

... 10: The procedure through which the "equitable sharing criteria" is to be developed by the ISA for the distribution of the payments or contributions under Article 82 must be pursued separately from the criteria for the equitable sharing of the financial and other economic benefits from mining activities within the Area, because of the need to prioritize the "least developed and land-locked developing States within this set of criteria (for Article 82 payments or contributions).

... 11: Regardless of whether the interests of "peoples" or "territories" that have not achieved full independence are taken into account in the development of the "equitable sharing criteria" within the ISA, these entities will not be able to benefit from the payments or contributions in kind made by coastal States under Article 82, until they become "States Parties" to the 1982 UNCLOS.

... 12: In the event of disputes arising from the interpretation and application of Article 82, the scope for the ISA to engage the coastal State within the dispute settlement procedures of the 1982 UNCLOS is limited to seeking an advisory opinion from the Sea-Bed Disputes Chamber: States Parties on the other hand, can utilize the dispute settlement procedures under Part XV [of UNCLOS] against the coastal State concerned to "settle any dispute between them concerning the interpretation or application of this Convention."[476]

---

[476] International Law Association Committee on the Outer Continental Shelf, *Report on Article 82 of the 1982 UN Convention on Law of the Sea (UNCLOS)*, in International Law Association, Report of the Seventy-Third Conference Held in Rio de Janeiro, Brazil 17–21 August 2008, at 1044, 1050–62 (2008) (emphasis and italics omitted; ILA Report cited as ILA 73d Conf. Rep.).

The *Report*, and particularly *Conclusion* 5, is consistent with the Committee definition.

Section 9 defines "Area" and "area;" § 28, "coast;" § 31, "coastal State;" § 51, "developing State(s);" § 105, "mile" and "nautical mile."

§ 40. *Coordinates*

See Geographic coordinates, § 76.

§ 41. *Course*

As used in UNCLOS analysis, "course" means the horizontal direction in which a vessel is intended to be steered, expressed as an angular distance from north clockwise through 360 degrees.

Comment

In LOAC-governed situations under the "other rules of international law" clauses in UNCLOS, a different definition may apply. The same may be the situation if the UN Charter supersedes UNCLOS or if jus cogens norms apply.[477]

The Former ECDIS Glossary, page 5, defined "course" as "[T]he horizontal direction in which a vessel is intended to be steered, expressed as an angular distance from north clockwise through 360 degrees." The newer ECDIS Glossary does not define "course."

Section 42 defines "course made good;" § 43, "course over ground;" § 163, "ship" or "vessel."[478]

§ 42. *Course made good, abbreviated as CMG*

As used in UNCLOS analysis, "course made good," abbreviated CMG, means the single resultant direction from a vessel's point of departure to its point of arrival at any given time.

Comment

In LOAC-governed situations under the "other rules of international law" clauses in UNCLOS, a different definition may apply. The same

[477] *See* Parts III.B-III.D and § 132, defining "other rules of international law."

[478] *See also* DOD Dictionary 133; Walker, *ECDIS Glossary* 244–45, 2003–04 ABILA Proc. 216–17.

may be the situation if the UN Charter supersedes UNCLOS or if jus cogens norms apply.[479]

The Former ECDIS Glossary, page 5, defined "course made good" as "[t]he single resultant direction from a vessel's point of departure to its point of arrival at any given time." The newer ECDIS Glossary does not define "course made good."

Section 16 defines "basepoint" or "point;" § 41, "course;" § 43, "course over ground;" § 163, "ship" or "vessel."[480]

§ 43. *Course over ground, abbreviated as COG*

As used in UNCLOS analysis, "course over ground," abbreviated COG, means the direction of a vessel's path actually followed, usually a somewhat irregular line.

Comment

In LOAC-governed situations under the "other rules of international law" clauses in UNCLOS, a different definition may apply. The same may be the situation if the UN Charter supersedes UNCLOS or if jus cogens norms apply.[481]

The Former ECDIS Glossary, page 5, defined "course over ground," abbreviated as COG, as "[t]he direction of a vessel's path actually followed, usually a somewhat irregular line." The newer ECDIS Glossary does not define "course over ground."

Section 41 defines "course;" § 42, course made good;" § 93, "line;" § 94, "line of delimitation;" § 163, "ship" or "vessel;" § 176, "straight line," "straight baseline" and "straight archipelagic baseline."[482]

§ 44. *Danger to navigation*

"Danger to navigation" as used in UNCLOS Article 24(2) and as incorporated by reference in Articles 54 and 121, means a hydrographic feature, a condition violating Articles 60 or 80 and as incorporated

---

479 *See* Parts III.B-III.D and § 132, defining "other rules of international law."

480 *See also* Churchill & Lowe ch. 2; Walker, *ECDIS Glossary* 245, 2003–04 ABILA Proc. 217. DOD Dictionary, Appx. A, *Abbreviations and Acronyms*, p. A-29, defines COG as "center of gravity" or "continuity of government."

481 *See* Parts III.B-III.D and § 132, defining "other rules of international law."

482 *See also* Churchill & Lowe ch. 2; Walker, *ECDIS Glossary* 245–46, 2003–04 ABILA Proc. 217–18.

by reference in Articles 54 and 121, or an environmental condition that might hinder, obstruct, endanger or otherwise prevent safe navigation.

Comment

In LOAC-governed situations under the "other rules of international law" clauses in UNCLOS, different definitions may apply. The same may be the situation if the UN Charter supersedes UNCLOS or if jus cogens norms apply.[483]

Consolidated Glossary ¶ 23 defines "danger to navigation" as a "hydrographic feature or environmental condition that might hinder, obstruct, endanger or otherwise prevent safe navigation." Former Glossary ¶ 23 defined "danger to navigation" as "[a] hydrographic feature or environmental condition that might operate against the safety of navigation." The Glossary does not define "danger to overflight;" § 45 defines this term.

UNCLOS Article 24(2), following the Territorial Sea Convention Article 15(2) rule, requires a coastal State to give "appropriate publicity to any danger to navigation, of which it has knowledge, within its territorial sea." UNCLOS Article 44 requires "States bordering straits … [to] give appropriate publicity to any danger to navigation or overflight within or over the strait of which they have knowledge. There shall be no suspension of transit passage." A State declaring an EEZ must, under Article 60(3), have a permanent warning system for artificial islands, installations or structures in its EEZ. Article 80 applies this rule to the continental shelf, echoing Shelf Convention Article 5(5). UNCLOS Article 121 applies the UNCLOS rules to an island's territorial sea, EEZ or shelf. Article 54, governing archipelagic States' rights and duties, applies Article 44, thereby requiring an archipelagic State to give appropriate publicity to any danger to navigation or overflight within or over archipelagic sea lanes of which the archipelagic State has knowledge. Article 225 says that States in enforcing environmental laws or regulations "shall not endanger the safety of navigation or otherwise create any hazard to a vessel. …"

UNCLOS does not define "danger to navigation" or "danger to overflight." UNCLOS differentiates between navigation, relating to vessels, and overflight, relating to aircraft operations while in flight.

---

[483] *See* Parts III.B-III.D and § 132, defining "other rules of international law."

See, e.g., Articles 87(1)(a) (freedom of navigation), 87(1)(b) (freedom of overflight); *see also* High Seas Convention Articles 2(1), 2(4) (freedom of navigation, freedom to fly over the high seas). There is no right, analogous to straits transit or archipelagic waters passage, of aircraft innocent passage through the territorial sea. *See* UNCLOS Articles 2, 19(2)(e); Territorial Sea Convention Articles 1-2, 14.[484]

Section 28 defines "coast;" § 31, "coastal State;" § 81, "high seas."

§ 45. *Danger to overflight*

"Danger to overflight" as used in UNCLOS Article 44 and as incorporated by reference in Articles 54 and 121, means a hydrographic feature, a condition violating Articles 60 or 80 and as incorporated by reference in Articles 54 and 121, an environmental condition, or any other obstruction that UNCLOS does not authorize that might hinder, obstruct, endanger or otherwise prevent safe overflight as UNCLOS permits.

Comment

In LOAC-governed situations under the "other rules of international law" clauses in UNCLOS, different definitions may apply. The same may be the situation if the UN Charter supersedes UNCLOS or if jus cogens norms apply.[485]

The final phrase, "as permitted by UNCLOS," continues the prohibition against territorial sea overflight but would allow high seas overflight while forbidding dangers to overflight there. *See* Articles 2, 19(2)(e); Territorial Sea Convention Articles 1-2, 14, 87(1)(a), 87(1)(b); High Seas Convention Articles 2(1), 2(4). Freedom of high seas overflight, subject to regulations in UNCLOS and the 1958 LOS Conventions for the contiguous zone, EEZ, continental shelf or the Area, remains for those sea areas. *See* UNCLOS Articles 1(1)(1), 33, 58, 78, 87, 134;

---

[484] *See also* Convention on International Civil Aviation, Dec. 7, 1944, art. 1, 61 Stat. 1180, 15 UNTS 295; Joint Statement on Uniform Interpretation of Rules of International Law Governing Innocent Passage, Sept. 23, 1989, USSR-U.S., ¶¶ 3–7, 89 Dep't St. Bull. 25, 26 (Nov. 1989), 28 ILM 1444 (1989) (Joint Statement); Churchill & Lowe 100, 155, 168, 271; 2 Commentary ¶¶ 2.1–2.8(f), 19.1–19.9, 19.10(b), 19.10(f), 19.11, 21.12, 24.1–24.7(a), 24.7(c), 24.7(e)-24.8, 54.1–54.7(b), 60.1–60.15(m), 80.1–80.9; 3 *id.* ¶¶ 121.1–121.12(c); DOD Dictionary 144 ("danger area"); NWP 1–14M Annotated ¶¶ 1.4.2, 1.4.3, 1.5.2, 1.6–1.8, 2.3.2–2.3.2.4, 2.3.4–2.3.4.2, 2.5.1; Walker, *Consolidated Glossary* 247–49.

[485] *See* Parts III.B-III.D and § 132, defining "other rules of international law."

Territorial Sea Convention Article 24(1); Shelf Convention Article 3; High Seas Convention Article 2(4).

Consolidated Glossary ¶ 23 defines "danger to navigation" as a "hydrographic feature or environmental condition that might hinder, obstruct, endanger or otherwise prevent safe navigation." Former Glossary ¶ 23 defined "danger to navigation" as "[a] hydrographic feature or environmental condition that might operate against the safety of navigation." The Glossary does not define "danger to overflight."

UNCLOS Article 24(2), following the Territorial Sea Convention Article 15(2) rule, requires a coastal State to give "appropriate publicity to any danger to navigation, of which it has knowledge, within its territorial sea." UNCLOS Article 44 requires "States bordering straits … [to] give appropriate publicity to any danger to navigation or overflight within or over the strait of which they have knowledge. There shall be no suspension of transit passage." A State declaring an EEZ must, under Article 60(3), have a permanent warning system for artificial islands, installations or structures in its EEZ. Article 80 applies this rule to the continental shelf, echoing Shelf Convention Article 5(5). UNCLOS Article 121 applies the UNCLOS rules to an island's territorial sea, EEZ or shelf. Article 54, governing archipelagic States' rights and duties, applies Article 44, thereby requiring an archipelagic State to give appropriate publicity to any danger to navigation or overflight within or over archipelagic sea lanes of which the archipelagic State has knowledge. Article 225 says that States in enforcing environmental laws or regulations "shall not endanger the safety of navigation or otherwise create any hazard to a vessel …"

UNCLOS does not define "danger to navigation" or "danger to overflight." UNCLOS differentiates between navigation, relating to vessels, and overflight, relating to aircraft operations while in flight. *See, e.g.*, Articles 87(1)(a) (freedom of navigation), 87(1)(b) (freedom of overflight); *see also* High Seas Convention Articles 2(1), 2(4) (freedom of navigation, freedom to fly over the high seas). It is therefore appropriate to define the terms separately; *see* § 44, defining "danger to navigation." There is no right, analogous to straits transit or archipelagic waters passage, of aircraft innocent passage through the territorial sea. *See* UNCLOS Articles 2, 19(2)(e); Territorial Sea Convention Articles 1-2, 14.[486]

---

[486] *See also* Convention on International Civil Aviation, note 484, art. 1; Joint Statement, note 484, ¶¶ 3–7; Churchill & Lowe 100, 155, 168, 271;

Section 28 defines "coast;" § 31, "coastal State;" § 81, "high seas."

§ 46. *Datum (vertical) or vertical datum*

In UNCLOS analysis, "datum (vertical)" or "vertical datum" means any level surface, *e.g.*, mean sea level, taken as a surface of reference from which elevations may be reckoned.

Comment

In LOAC-governed situations under the "other rules of international law" clauses in UNCLOS, a different definition may apply. The same may be the situation if the UN Charter supersedes UNCLOS or if jus cogens norms apply.[487]

Former ECDIS Glossary, page 6, defined "datum (vertical)" as "[a] ny level surface (e.g. sea mean sea level) taken as a surface of reference from which to reckon elevations." The newer ECDIS Glossary does not define "datum (vertical)."

Section 24 defines "chart datum;" § 75, "geodetic datum;" § 126, "ocean space" or "sea."[488]

§ 47. *Deep ocean floor*

As used in UNCLOS Article 76(3), "deep ocean floor" means the surface lying at the bottom of the deep ocean with its oceanic ridges, beyond the continental margin.

Comment

In LOAC-governed situations under the "other rules of international law" clauses in UNCLOS, a different definition may apply. The same may be the situation if the UN Charter supersedes UNCLOS or if jus cogens norms apply.[489]

---

2 Commentary ¶¶ 2.1–2.8(f), 19.1–19.9, 19.10(b), 19.10(f), 19.11, 21.12, 24.1–24.7(a), 24.7(c), 24.7(e)-24.8, 54.1–54.7(b), 60.1–60.15(m), 80.1–80.9; 3 *id.* ¶¶ 121.1–121.12(c); DOD Dictionary 144; NWP 1-14M Annotated ¶¶ 1.4.2, 1.4.3, 1.5.2, 1.6–1.8, 2.3.2–2.3.2.4, 2.3.4–2.3.4.2, 2.5.1; Walker, *Consolidated Glossary* 247–49.

[487] *See* Parts III.B-III.D and § 132, defining "other rules of international law."

[488] *See also* DOD Dictionary 145 (noting plural is "datums," not "data" and that another military definition is the last known position of a submarine or suspected submarine after contact with it has been lost); Walker, *ECDIS Glossary* 246, 2003–04 ABILA Proc. 218.

[489] *See* Parts III.B-III.D and § 132, defining "other rules of international law."

Consolidated Glossary ¶ 24 defines "deep ocean floor" as "[t]he surface lying at the bottom of the deep ocean with its oceanic ridges, beyond the continental margin."[490]

UNCLOS's Preamble cites UN General Assembly Resolution 2749, which inter alia declared that the area of the seabed and subsoil and the subsoil thereof, beyond the limits of national jurisdiction, as well as its resources, are the common heritage of humankind, the exploration and exploitation of which shall be carried out for the benefit of humankind as a whole, irrespective of the geographical location of States. UNCLOS Article 1(1)(1) defines the Area as the seabed and ocean floor and subsoil thereof beyond the limits of national jurisdiction. Article 76(3) defines the continental margin as "the submerged prolongation of the land mass of the coastal State, and consist[ing] of the seabed and subsoil of the [continental] shelf, the slope and the rise. It does not include the deep ocean floor with its oceanic ridges or the subsoil thereof."

Section 16 discusses UNCLOS Articles 76(3) and 76(6) in connection with baselines and basepoints. Section 37 defines "continental rise;" § 38, "continental slope;" § 67, "foot of the continental slope;" § 126, "ocean space" or "sea;" § 128, "oceanic ridge;" § 157, "sea-bed," "seabed" or "bed;" § 176, "straight line; straight baseline; straight archipelagic baseline;" § 182, "submarine ridge."[491]

§ 48. *Delimitation*

See line of delimitation, § 94.

§ 49. *Delta*

As used in UNCLOS Article 7(2), "delta" means a tract of alluvial land enclosed and traversed by the diverging mouths of a river.

Comment

In LOAC-governed situations under the "other rules of international law" clauses in UNCLOS, a different definition may apply. The same

[490] *Accord,* 2 Commentary ¶ 76.18(d).

[491] *See also* Churchill & Lowe 148–50; 2 Commentary ¶¶ 76.1–76.17, 76.18(d) & Fig. 2; NWP 1-14M Annotated ¶ 1.6 & Fig. A1-2; Restatement (Third) § 523; Noyes, *Definitions* 322–23 & Part III.D.3; Walker, *Consolidated Glossary* 249–50.

may be the situation if the UN Charter supersedes UNCLOS, or if jus cogens norms apply.[492]

Consolidated Glossary ¶ 26 defines "delta" as "[a] tract of alluvial land enclosed and traversed by the diverging mouths of a river."[493]

UNCLOS Article 7(2) says that where because of the presence of a delta and other natural conditions the coastline is highly unstable, the appropriate points [for the baseline(s)] may be selected along the furthest seaward extent of the low-water line and, notwithstanding subsequent regression of the low-water line, the straight baselines shall remain effective until changed by the coastal State in accordance with" UNCLOS. However, Article 9, following Territorial Sea Convention Article 13, says that if a river flows directly into the sea, the baseline is a straight line across the river mouth between points on the low-water line of its banks.

Section 16 discusses baselines while defining "basepoint" or "point;" § 26 defines "closing line" and also discusses these lines; § 28 defines "coast;" § 31, "coastal State;" 93, "line;" § 108, "mouth" (of a river); § 143, "river;" § 176, "straight line; straight baseline; straight archipelagic baseline."[494]

§ 50. *Dependent species*

See Associated species, § 11.

§ 51. *Developing State(s)*

In UNCLOS, "developing State(s)," which is synonymous with an earlier and not presently preferred term, "less-developed States," means States whose economies only support low standards of living and are in the early stages of development. Only normal conditions and not such factors as exceptionally favorable conditions for a country's exports should be taken into account in determining developing State status. "Early stages of development" should apply even to somewhat advanced economies that are industrializing to free themselves from dependence

---

[492] *See* Parts III.B-III.D and § 132, defining "other rules of international law."

[493] *Accord*, 2 Commentary ¶ 7.9(a).

[494] *See also* Churchill & Lowe 37–38, 55–56; 2 Commentary ¶¶ 7.9.1–7.9(d), 9.1–9.5(e); NWP 1-14M Annotated ¶ 1.3.4; 1 O'Connell 221–30, 398 n.12; 2 *id.* 682–83; Restatement (Third) §§ 511–12; Walker, *Consolidated Glossary* 250–51.

on primary production. Any characterization of a country as a developing State must take into account criteria established by UNCLOS or UN organs or agencies.

Comment

In LOAC-governed situations under the "other rules of international law" clauses in UNCLOS, a different definition may apply. The same may be the situation if the UN Charter supersedes UNCLOS or if jus cogens norms apply.[495]

The term "developing State(s)" appears in many UNCLOS articles and legal contexts. The 1958 LOS Conventions do not use the term.

Article 61, dealing with conservation of EEZ living resources, requires States imposing conservation and management measures under Article 61(2) to ensure, under Article 61(3), that such measures also maintain or restore populations of harvested species that can produce maximum sustainable yield, as qualified inter alia by the special requirements of developing States, while taking into account various factors, *e.g.*, fishing patterns. Article 62(2) requires a coastal State to determine its capacity to harvest its EEZ living resources. If the coastal State does not have the capacity to harvest the entire catch, it must, through treaties, laws or other regulations, give other States access to the surplus allowable catch, "having particular regard to … articles 69 and 70, especially in relation to the developing States mentioned therein." (Articles 69 and 70 establish terms for landlocked and geographically disadvantaged States.) Article 62(3) requires that a coastal State, in giving EEZ access to other States, must take into account all relevant factors, including, inter alia, developing States' requirements in the subregion or location in harvesting part of the surplus.

Article 82(3) declares that a developing State that is a net importer of a mineral resource produced from its continental shelf is exempt from making payments or contributions in respect of that resource extracted from its continental shelf beyond 200 nautical miles.

With respect to high seas fishing and the allowable catch and establishing other conservation measures for high seas living resources, Article 119(1)(a) requires states to take measures designed, on the best scientific evidence available to the States concerned, to maintain or

---

[495] *See* Parts III.B-III.D and § 132, defining "other rules of international law."

restore populations of harvested species at levels which can produce the maximum sustainable yield, "as qualified by relevant environmental and economic factors, including the special requirements of developing States," and other factors.

As to the maritime environment, Article 202 requires States, directly or through competent international organizations, to promote scientific, educational, technical and other assistance to developing States for the protection and preservation of the marine environment and prevention, reduction and control of marine pollution. States must provide appropriate assistance, "especially to developing States," for minimizing effects of major incidents that may cause serious pollution of the marine environment, and concerning preparation of environmental assessments. Article 203 gives developing States preference in international organizations in allocating appropriate funds and technical assistance and use of those organizations' specialized services, for preventing, reducing and controlling pollution of the marine environment or minimizing its effects. With respect to land-based source pollution, Article 207(4) requires States, acting especially through competent international organizations, to endeavor to establish global and regional rules, standards and recommended practices and procedures to prevent, reduce and control pollution of the marine environment from these sources, taking into account inter alia the economic capacity of developing States.

With respect to marine scientific research, Article 244(2) requires States, individually and in cooperation with other States and competent international organizations, to actively promote scientific data and information flow and knowledge transfer resulting from MSR, "especially to developing States, as well as the strengthening of the autonomous [MSR] capabilities of developing States through, *inter alia*, programs to provide adequate education and training of their technical and scientific personnel." Article 276(1) requires States, in coordination with competent international organizations, the International Sea-Bed Authority[496] and national marine scientific and technological research institutions, to promote establishing regional marine scientific and technological research centers, particularly in developing States, to stimulate and advance the conduct of MSR by developing States and foster transfer of marine technology.

---

[496] UNCLOS art. 1(2) defines the "Authority."

Articles 140(1), 143(3)(b), 144(1)(b), 144(2)(a), 144(2)(b), 148, 150, 150(d), 152(2), 155(1)(f), 155(2), 173(2)(c), 273, 274, 276(1); Articles 5(3)(e), 8, 9(2), 13(1)(d), 15 and 17(1)(b)(xi) of UNCLOS Annex 3; Articles 12(3)(b)(ii) and 13(4)(d) of UNCLOS Annex 4; and Articles 3(b) and 12(a)(ii) of UNCLOS Resolution II govern developing States' activities with respect to the Area. UNCLOS Articles 160(2)(f)(i) and 160(2)(k) recite special concerns for developing States in the Area Assembly's powers and functions. Articles 161(1)(c), 161(1)(d), 161(2)(b) and 162(2)(o)(i) provide for special Area Council representation and consideration of developing States' interests and needs. Under UNCLOS Article 164(2)(d) the Economic Planning Commission must propose to the Council for submission to the Assembly a compensation system or other measures of economic adjustment assistance for developing States which suffer adverse effects caused by activities in the Area.

With respect to development and transfer of marine technology, UNCLOS Articles 144(2)(a) and 144(2)(b) require the Authority and states parties to cooperate in promoting technology and scientific knowledge transfer relating to Area activities so that the Enterprise and states parties may benefit. Access of developing States to relevant technology, under fair and reasonable terms and conditions, is required. States and the Authority must provide opportunities for training personnel from developing States in marine science and technology and for their full participation in Area activities. UNCLOS Part XIV, Development and Transfer of Marine Technology, also has special provisions for developing States in Articles 266(2), 269(a), 271–73, 274 and 276(1), as does UNCLOS Annex 3, Article 17(1)(b)(xi).

The 1994 Agreement, Annex, § 5, ¶ 2, declares that Annex 3, Article 5 shall not apply to States parties to the Agreement. This underscores the point that the 1994 Agreement must be read alongside UNCLOS.

A Restatement (Third) reporters' note discusses evolution of "developing States" from the former term, "less-developed States":

> ... The GATT speaks of "less-developed" states, although "developing" is now preferred. Article XVIII refers to economies "which can only support low standards of living and are in the early stages of development." Interpretative Notes and Article XVIII specify: (1) that only normal conditions and not such factors as exceptionally favorable conditions for a country's exports should be taken into account in determining its

> status; and (2) that "early stages of development" should apply even to somewhat advanced economies … industrializing … to free themselves from dependence on primary production.[497]

The issue of developing States or countries cuts across much of today's international law besides the law of the sea and economic advancement.[498] Although UNCLOS does not explain "developing States," the term is in common use, and the United Nations has its established criteria for determining States within this category.[499] Any definition for the term should refer to UN and UNCLOS organs' or agencies' criteria.

Section 9 defines "area" and "Area;" § 28, "coast;" § 31, "coastal State;" § 39, "contributions in kind;" § 65, "fishing;" § 81, "high seas;" § 100, "marine scientific research;" § 162, "shelf."

§ 52. *Distress*

"Distress," as used in UNCLOS Articles 18, 39, 98 and 109, and as incorporated by reference in UNCLOS Articles 45 and 54, means an event of grave necessity, such as severe weather or mechanical failure in a ship or aircraft; or a human-caused event, such as a collision with another ship or aircraft. The necessity must be urgent and proceed from such a state of things as may be supposed to produce in the mind of a skillful mariner or aircraft commander a well-grounded apprehension of the loss of the vessel or aircraft and its cargo, or for the safety or lives of its crew or its passengers. A claimant may not raise a defense of distress if the claimant caused the event of grave necessity, except in cases involving protection of human life or human safety. Distress and "force majeure," defined in § 68, may overlap; force majeure situations primarily refer to external causes affecting a ship, an aircraft or a crew or passengers of either.

Comment

In LOAC-governed situations under the "other rules of international law" clauses in UNCLOS, a different definition may apply. The same

---

[497] Restatement (Third) § 810 r.n. 1, citing John H. Jackson, World Trade and the Law of GATT 651–53 (1969).

[498] *See generally* Jennings & Watts § 106 (New International Economic Order analysis); 2 Simma 908 (analyzing UN Charter arts. 55[a]–55[b]).

[499] 4 Commentary ¶ 606.6(b).

may be the situation if the UN Charter supersedes UNCLOS or if jus cogens norms apply.[500]

UNCLOS Article 18(2) requires territorial sea innocent passage be "continuous and expeditious. However, passage includes stopping and anchoring, but only in so far as the same are incidental to ordinary navigation or are rendered necessary by *force majeure* or distress or for ... rendering assistance to persons, ships or aircraft in danger or distress." Similarly, Territorial Sea Convention Article 14(3) declares that "Passage includes stopping and anchoring, but only in so far as the same are incidental to ordinary navigation or are rendered necessary by *force majeure* or by distress."[501]

UNCLOS Article 39(1)(c), relating to duties of ships and aircraft during straits transit passage, requires ships and aircraft while exercising the right of transit passage to "refrain from any activities other than those incident to their normal modes of continuous and expeditious transit unless rendered necessary by *force majeure* or by distress[.]" These are considered customary rules.[502]

UNCLOS Article 45(1)(a) applies the territorial sea innocent passage regime to straits excluded from transit passage by Article 38(1)(a). Article 45(1)(b) applies the territorial sea innocent passage regime to straits between a part of the high seas or an EEZ and a foreign State's territorial sea.[503]

UNCLOS Article 54 incorporates Article 39 *mutatis mutandis* to archipelagic sea lanes passage.[504]

UNCLOS Article 98(1) commands every State to require the master of a ship flying its flag,

> in so far as he can do so without serious danger to the ship, the crew or the passengers:
> (a) to render assistance to any person found at sea in danger of being lost;
> (b) to proceed with all possible speed to the rescue of persons in distress, if informed of their need for assistance, in so far as such action may be reasonably expected of him;

---

[500] *See* Parts III.B-III.D and § 132, defining "other rules of international law."

[501] Restatement (Third) § 513 cmt. a also recites this principle, citing UNCLOS art. 18(2) and Territorial Sea Convention art. 14(3).

[502] Restatement (Third) § 513 cmt. j, citing UNCLOS art. 39(1)(c).

[503] Presumably Restatement (Third) § 513 cmt. a would apply these rules to UNCLOS art. 45(1)-governed straits, although cmt. a does not cite UNCLOS art. 45.

[504] Presumably Restatement (Third) § 513 cmt. j would apply this principle to archipelagic sea lanes passage as well, although cmt. j does not cite UNCLOS art. 54.

(c) after a collision, to render assistance to the other ship, its crew and its passengers and, where possible, to inform the other ship of the name of his own ship, its port of registry and the nearest port at which it will call.

High Seas Convention Article 12(1) is identical.

UNCLOS Article 109(2) excludes distress call transmissions from its "unauthorized broadcasting" definition.

Other treaties underscore a requirement to render assistance to those in distress in peace or war.[505]

Commentaries on UNCLOS Articles 18(2), 39(1)(c), 45, 54, 98 and 109 negotiations do not elucidate the meaning of "distress."[506] Commentary to Article 39(1)(c), dealing with transit passage distress situations, inquired whether Article 39(1)(c) includes stopping and anchoring if necessary in distress situations, and whether Article 39(1)(c) includes the danger or distress to other "persons, ships or aircraft." As to the first question, the commentary would say that stopping and anchoring under these situations is covered, as it would be in an innocent passage situation. The second answer is "less obvious," but would fall within the "tradition of going to the aid of persons in distress is as old as maritime navigation itself, and is regarded as an obligation by vessels and aircraft of all flags. ... Elementary considerations of humanity also dictate that a ship go to the aid of persons in distress."[507] Presumably this humanity principle also applies to aircraft's going to the aid of persons in distress.

---

[505] *E.g.*, Convention for Unification of Certain Rules of Law with Respect to Assistance & Salvage at Sea, art. 11, Sept. 23, 1910, 37 Stat. 1658; International Convention on Salvage, art. 10, Apr. 28, 1989, TIAS —, 1953 UNTS 193; International Convention on Maritime Search & Rescue, Annex, ch. 2, ¶ 2.1.10, Apr. 27, 1979, TIAS 11093, 1405 UNTS 97; International Convention for Safety of Life at Sea, Annex, ch. 5, reg. 10, Nov. 1, 1974, 32 UST 47, 1184 UNTS 2. The rule is the same in armed conflict situations. Protocol I Additional to the Geneva Conventions of 12 August 1949, and Relating to Protection of Victims of International Armed Conflicts, arts. 8(b), 10, 33, June 8, 1977, 1125 UNTS 3; Convention for Amelioration of Condition of Wounded, Sick and Shipwrecked Members of Armed Forces at Sea, art. 12, Aug. 12, 1949, 6 UST 3217, 75 UNTS 85; *see also* C. John Colombos, The International Law of the Sea § 369 (6th ed. 1967); NWP 1-14M Annotated ¶ 3.2.1–3.2.2; Walker, The Tanker 422; Guy S. Goodwin-Gill, *Refugees and Responsibility in the Twenty-First Century: More Lessons Learned from the South Pacific*, 12 Pac. Rim L. & Pol. J. 23, 31–32 (2003).

[506] 2 Commentary ¶¶ 18.1–18.6(e), 39.1–39.10(*l*), 45.1–45.8(c), 54.1–54.7(b); 3 *id.* ¶¶ 98.1–98.11(g),109.1–109.8(f).

[507] 2 *id.* ¶ 39.10(g), inter alia citing UNCLOS art. 98; High Seas Convention art. 12; *see also* Churchill & Lowe 81, 107; 3 Commentary ¶ 1; NWP 1-14M Annotated ¶ 3.2.2.1.

Thus in combination with UNCLOS Article 18, "the duty to render assistance exists throughout the ocean, whether in the territorial sea, in straits used for international navigation, in archipelagic waters, in the exclusive economic zone or on the high seas. Assistance is to be given to any person, ship or aircraft in distress."[508]

Cases in the British and U.S. courts, international arbitrations and commentators have considered and defined distress situations. The British High Court of Admiralty offered this test: "It must be an urgent distress; it must be something of grave necessity; [*e.g.*] ... where a ship is said to be driven in by stress of weather." A party claiming distress cannot have caused the situation giving rise to the claim.[509] The Supreme Court of the United States accepted this test, adding that "the necessity must be urgent and proceed from such a state of things as may be supposed to produce in the mind of a skillful mariner a well-grounded apprehension of the loss of the vessel and cargo, or of the lives of the crew."[510] Mechanical breakdown, fuel exhaustion or action of a foreign flag warship or mutineers all can be predicates for a necessity claim.[511] If a ship must enter a port or internal waters to save human life, that vessel has a right of entry under international law. Whether distress entry to save property, if human life is not at risk, will justify a distress defense is questionable, at least where there is a serious pollution risk incident to entry.[512] The same may be true if a ship, *e.g.*, enters the territorial sea to assist a downed aircraft in distress.[513] On the other hand, aircraft in distress have a right of entry into the territorial sea to seek refuge on land.[514]

Force majeure and distress may also be defenses to claims of breach of treaty obligations. The International Law Commission *Articles on State Responsibility* include provisions for force majeure and distress. Article 23, Force Majeure, provides:

> 1. The wrongfulness of an act of a State not in conformity with an international obligation of that State is precluded if the act is due to *force majeure*, that is the occurrence of an irresistible force or of an

---

[508] 3 Commentary ¶ 98.11(g), p. 177; *see also* 2 O'Connell 853–54.

[509] The Eleanor, 165 Eng. Rep. 1058, 1068 (High Ct. Adm. 1809).

[510] The New York, 16 U.S. (3 Wheat.) 59, 68 (1818); *accord*, NWP 1–14M Annotated ¶ 3.2.2. *See also* The Brig Concord, 13 U.S. (9 Cranch) 387, 388 (1815).

[511] *See generally* Colombos, note 505, §§ 353–54; 2 O'Connell 855–57.

[512] Churchill & Lowe 63.

[513] NWP 1–14M Annotated ¶ 2.3.2.5 n.35.

[514] *Id.* ¶ 4.4, referring to *id.* 3.2.2.1.

unforeseen event, beyond the control of the State, making it materially impossible in the circumstances to perform that obligation.
2. Paragraph 1 does not apply if:
   (a) the situation of *force majeure* is due, either alone or in combination with other factors, to the conduct of the State invoking it; or
   (b) the State has assumed the risk of that situation occurring.[515]

Similarly, but not identically, Article 24, Distress, provides:

1. The wrongfulness of an act of a State not in conformity with an international obligation of that State is precluded if the author of the act in question has no other reasonable way, in a situation of distress, of saving the author's life or the lives of other persons entrusted to the author's care.
2. Paragraph 1 does not apply if:
   (a) the situation of distress is due, either alone or in combination with other factors, to the conduct of the State invoking it; or
   (b) the act in question is likely to create a comparable or greater peril.[516]

Article 24 *Commentary* explains the difference:

> Article 24 [reciting standards for distress] deals with the specific case where an individual whose acts are attributable to the State is in a situation of peril, either personally or in relation to persons under his or her care. The article precludes the wrongfulness of conduct adopted by the State agent in circumstances where the agent had no other reasonable way of saving life. Unlike … *force majeure* …, a person acting under distress is not acting involuntarily, even though the choice is effectively nullified by the situation of peril. Nor is it a case of choosing between compliance with international law and other legitimate interests of the State, such as characteristic situations of necessity under article 25. The interest concerned is the immediate one of saving people's lives, irrespective of their nationality.[517]

Article 24 *Commentary* cites UNCLOS Articles 18, 39(1)(c), 98 and 109 but does not cite Article 54, as well as Territorial Sea Convention Article 14(3).[518] Article 24 would limit coverage to situations where

---

[515] ILC Responsibility Articles, art. 23, p. 183, *reprinted in* Crawford p. 170.

[516] ILC Responsibility Articles, art. 24, p. 189, *reprinted in* Crawford p. 174.

[517] ILC Responsibility Articles, art. 24, cmt. 1, p. 189, *reprinted in* Crawford p. 174, citing Oliver J. Lissistzyn, *The Treatment of Aerial Intruders in Recent Practice in International Law*, 47 AJIL 588 (1953), and referring to ILC Responsibility Articles, art. 25, p. 194, *reprinted in* Crawford p. 178. For "force majeure" analysis, *see* § 68.

[518] ILC Responsibility Articles, art. 24, cmt. 5, p. 192, *reprinted in* Crawford p. 176, citing UNCLOS arts. 18, 39(1)(c), 98, 109.

human life is at stake and would deny the defense if the State claiming distress, alone or in combination "with others," causes or induces the situation.[519] "Distress can only preclude wrongfulness where the interests sought to be protected (*e.g.*, the lives of passengers or crew) clearly outweigh the other interests at stake in the circumstances," citing, *e.g.*, the example of a military aircraft carrying explosives that might cause a disaster by making an emergency landing. Distress does not apply if the succoring act is likely to create a comparable or greater peril, but "'comparable or greater peril' must be assessed in the context of the overall purpose of saving lives."[520] The *Commentary* notes that although the principal use of the defense has been in maritime and aerial incidents where there has been stress of weather or after mechanical or navigational failure, the distress claim is not limited to such cases.[521]

Limiting distress as the ILC does to cases involving saving human life, citing the defense in the context of maritime incidents on or over the oceans, is an unfortunate limitation for distress situations involving the law of the sea. Prior decisional law and state practice under the law of the sea suggest a broader application to situations involving safety as well as possible loss of human life, and loss of property, although the defense's validity in property-saving contexts is mixed.[522] To be sure, different standards may apply in other contexts, *e.g.*, self-defense under the Charter, other situations under Charter law, or jus cogens situations,[523] but the distress defense should be allowed in UNCLOS-governed situations involving possible property loss, unless the actor claiming distress caused the circumstances giving rise to a claim; distress would be allowed in circumstances where two actors are or may be responsible, *e.g.*, a collision of ships where both may be liable under the predominant divided damages rule in admiralty law, and one vessel is so heavily damaged it must invoke distress. The exception to the

---

[519] ILC Responsibility Articles, art. 24, cmts. 6, 8, pp. 192, 193, *reprinted in* Crawford pp. 176, 177, excluding the defense's validity in Rainbow Warrior (N.Z. v. Fr.), 20 R.I.A.A. 217, 254–55 (Arb. Trib.1990).

[520] ILC Responsibility Articles, art. 24, cmt. 10, p. 194, *reprinted in* Crawford p. 177.

[521] ILC Responsibility Articles, art. 24, cmts. 2–4, pp. 189–91, *reprinted in* Crawford pp. 174–75. 2007–08 ABILA Proc. did not publish a definition for distress. This definition resulted from circulation of drafts among ABILA LOS Committee members and other commentators. *See also* DOD Dictionary 169 ("distressed person"), 336 ("mayday," a distress call).

[522] *See* notes 505–10 and accompanying text.

[523] *See* notes 515–20 and accompanying text. *Rainbow Warrior* may be best explained in this context.

foregoing would be a case involving threat to human life, including severe injury. The example might be serious injuries or a threat to safety aboard both ships in a collision situation.

With ILC Article 23 in mind, the Committee definition accepts principles laid down in the principal cases discussing distress and applies them to aircraft as well as ships. The definition also adds concern for the safety of the crew, as distinguished from their lives, and concern for the safety or lives of passengers, as part of the definition. It is not enough to save human life; humans must be put in a place of safety as well. The last sentence departs from the older cases to give an exception to the rule that a claimant may not raise a defense of distress if the claimant caused an event that creates a grave necessity. It can be raised in cases involving protecting human life or human safety, even though the claimant's action precipitated the event, *e.g.*, negligently failing to take on enough fuel to complete a flight or voyage.

Section 68 defines "force majeure;" § 81, "high seas;" § 161, "serious act of pollution;" § 163, "ship" or "vessel;" § 177, "strait" or "straits."

§ 53. *Drying reef*

As used in UNCLOS Articles 47(1) and 47(7), "drying reef" means that part of a reef which is above water at low tide but is submerged at high tide.

Comment

In LOAC-governed situations under the "other rules of international law" clauses in UNCLOS, a different definition may apply. The same may be the situation if the UN Charter supersedes UNCLOS or if jus cogens norms apply.[524]

Consolidated Glossary ¶ 74 defines "drying reef" as "[t]hat part of a reef which is above water at low tide but submerged at high tide."[525]

UNCLOS Article 47(1) allows an archipelagic State to draw straight archipelagic baselines joining the outermost points of the archipelago's outermost islands and drying reefs, provided that the main islands are included within such baselines and an area in which the ratio of the area of the water to the area of the land, including atolls, is between 1 to 1 and 9 to 1.

---

[524] *See* Parts III.B-III.D and § 132, defining "other rules of international law."

[525] *Accord*, 2 Commentary ¶ 47.9(b).

Article 47(7) says that to compute the ratio of water to land under Article 47(1), land areas may include waters lying within islands' and atolls' fringing reefs, including that part of a steepsided oceanic plateau enclosed or nearly enclosed by a chain of limestone islands and drying reefs lying on the plateau perimeter.

Section 12 defines "atoll;" § 69, "fringing reef;" § 98, "low water line" or "low water mark;" § 127, "oceanic plateau;" § 140, "reef;" § 147, "rock;" § 160, "sedimentary rock;" § 176, "straight line; straight baseline; straight archipelagic baseline." In defining "basepoint" or "point," § 16 discusses baselines.[526]

§ 54. *Due notice, appropriate publicity, and due publicity*

(a) As used in UNCLOS, "due notice," "appropriate publicity" and "due publicity" mean communication of a given action for general information through appropriate authorities within a reasonable amount of time in a suitable manner.

(b) Besides communication to concerned States and international organizations as UNCLOS requires through diplomatic or other designated channels, more immediate dissemination to mariners and airmen may be achieved by passing information directly to national hydrographic offices or analogous national government offices for inclusion in governments' Notices to Mariners (NOTMARs) or Notices to Airmen (NOTAMs) as appropriate.

Comment

The second paragraph follows the Consolidated Glossary ¶ 28 suggestion, discussed in this *Comment*, adding references to international organizations, analogous governmental offices for those countries that do not have separate hydrographic offices for Notices to Mariners (NOTMARs) or have offices dealing with Notices to Airmen (NOTAMs). Those exercising freedoms of overflight stand on the same footing of needing due notice through NOTAMs as mariners through NOTMARs.

In LOAC-governed situations under the "other rules of international law" clauses in UNCLOS, a different definition may apply. The same

---

[526] *See also* Churchill & Lowe ch. 2, pp. 120–26; 2 Commentary ¶¶ 47.1–47.9(c), 47.9(*l*); NWP 1-14M Annotated ¶ 1.3.5; 1 O'Connell 185–96; Restatement (Third) § 511; Walker, *Consolidated Glossary* 251–52.

may be the situation if the UN Charter supersedes UNCLOS or if jus cogens norms apply.[527]

Consolidated Glossary ¶ 28, like Former Glossary ¶ 27, defines "due publicity" as "[n]otification of a given action for general information through appropriate authorities within a reasonable amount of time in a suitable manner." The Glossary does not define "due notice" or other similar terms. It adds a suggestion: "In addition to notification to concerned States through diplomatic channels, more immediate dissemination to mariners may be achieved by passing the information directly to national Hydrographic Offices for inclusion in their Notices to Mariners."

UNCLOS Articles 16(2), 47(9), 75(2) and 84(2) requires States to give "due publicity" to charts or lists of geographic coordinates, as well as depositing copies of these, with the UN Secretary-General, for their baselines measuring the territorial sea and lines delimiting them under Articles 7, 9, 10, 12 and 15; for their archipelagic State baselines; for their EEZ outer limit lines; and for their continental shelf outer lines. Article 76(9) requires coastal States to deposit charts and relevant information, including geodetic data, permanently describing the outer limits of its continental shelf, with the Secretary-General. The Secretary-General must give "due publicity" to these charts and relative information. Article 21(3) requires "due publicity" to coastal State laws and regulations, adopted in conformity with UNCLOS and "other rules of international law," relating to innocent passage through the territorial sea, permitted under Articles 21(1) and 21(2). Article 22(4) requires "due publicity" of charts clearly indicating sea lanes and traffic separation schemes. Under Article 53(7), an archipelagic State may, when circumstances require, after giving "due publicity," substitute sea lanes or traffic separation schemes for those previously designated or prescribed. Article 53(10) requires archipelagic states to clearly indicate the axis of sea lanes and traffic separation schemes they designate or prescribe on charts; they must give "due publicity" to these charts.

Article 41(2) allows States bordering straits, when circumstances require, after giving "due publicity," to substitute other sea lanes or traffic separation schemes for those previously designated or prescribed. Article 41(6) requires these States to clearly indicate sea lanes or traffic separation schemes they designate or prescribe on charts "to which

[527] *See* Parts III.B-III.D and § 132, defining "other rules of international law."

due publicity shall be given." Under Article 42(3) these States must give "due publicity" to their laws and regulations governing transit straits passage permitted by Articles 42(1), 42(2) and 44. Under Article 54 these rules apply *mutatis mutandis* to archipelagic sea lanes passage.

Under Article 211(3) States establishing particular requirements for preventing, reducing and controlling marine environmental pollution as a condition for foreign vessel entry into their ports or internal waters or for an offshore terminal call must give "due publicity" to these requirements and must communicate them to the competent international organization.

Territorial Sea Convention Article 9 requires "due publicity" to be given to charts "clearly demarcat[ing]" roadsteads outside the territorial sea.

UNCLOS Article 60(3) requires "[d]ue notice" of construction of artificial islands, installations or structures in the EEZ; Article 60(5) requires "due notice" of safety zones around these artificial islands, installations or structures. Article 60(3) also requires "[a]ppropriate publicity" of the depth, position and dimensions of any installations or structures not entirely removed. Article 80 applies these rules *mutatis mutandis* to the continental shelf. Article 62(5) requires a coastal State establishing an EEZ to give "due notice" of its conservation and management laws and regulations. Article 51(2) requires an archipelagic State to allow maintaining and replacing existing submarine cables after receiving "due notice" of the cables' location and intention to repair or replace them. Article 147(2)(a) requires "due notice" of erection, emplacement and removal of installations in the Area.

Shelf Convention Article 5(5) requires "[d]ue notice" of construction of installations on the continental shelf.

Section 10 defines "artificial island;" § 16, "basepoint" or "point" in discussing baselines; § 23, "chart" or "nautical chart;" § 26, "closing line;" § 28, "coast;" § 31, "coastal State;" § 35, "competent international organization;" § 93, "line;" § 121, "notice to airmen;" § 122, "notice to mariners;" § 146, "roadstead" or "roads;" § 176, "straight line; straight baseline; straight archipelagic baseline;" § 179, "submarine cable;" § 192, "traffic separation scheme."[528]

---

[528] *See also* 2007–08 ABILA Proc. 217–20; Churchill & Lowe 53, 100, 124, 168, 239; 2 Commentary ¶¶ 16.1–16.7, 16.8(c)–16.8(e), 21.1–21.10, 21.11(h), 21.12, 22.1–22.9, 41.1–41.8, 41.9(b), 42.1–42.9, 42.10(j), 42(10)(*l*), 47.1–47.8, 47.9(m), 51.1–51.6, 51.7(g)-51.7(I), 53.1–53.8, 53.9(*l*), 54.1–54.7(b), 60.1–60.15(c), 60.15(e)-60.

§ 55. *Due publicity*

See Due notice, § 54.

§ 56. *Due regard*

(a) "Due regard," as used in UNCLOS Article 87, is a qualification of the rights of States in exercising freedoms of the high seas. "Due regard" requires all States, in exercising their high seas freedoms, to be aware of and consider the interests of other States in using the high seas, and to refrain from activities that interfere with the exercise by other States of the freedom of the high seas. States are bound to refrain from any acts that might adversely affect the use of the high seas by nationals of other States. Article 87 recognizes that all States have the right to exercise high seas freedoms and balances consideration for the rights and interests of all States in this regard.
(b) In UNCLOS Article 79, "due regard" means that in addition to the due regard that a State laying pipelines or cables must show to others exercising high seas freedoms, it must also be aware of and consider the interests of other States that have previously laid pipelines or cables and must balance its rights and interests against other States' high seas freedoms and the rights and interests of other States with respect to cables or pipelines already laid.
(c) In UNCLOS Article 27(4), "due regard" means that a State conducting an arrest aboard a foreign ship in territorial sea passage must be aware of and consider the interests of other States whose ships are navigating in that territorial sea and must balance its rights and interests against the rights and interests of States conducting territorial sea passage.
(d) In UNCLOS Article 39(3)(a), "due regard" means that a State aircraft in straits transit passage must at all times be operated with awareness and consideration of safety of navigation, by air and by other modes, in the strait. The State aircraft's rights and interests in operating in straits transit passage must be balanced against the

---

15(f), 60.15(h), 62.1–62.16(a), 62.16(k)-62.16(*l*), 75.1–75.4, 75.5(c)-75.5(d), 76.1–76.18(a), 76.18(*l*), 84.1–84.9(c); 4 *id.*, ¶¶ 211.1–211.15(f); DOD Dictionary 443 ("public information"); Noyes, *Definitions* 322–23 & Part III.D.3; Walker, *Consolidated Glossary* 252–54.

rights and interests of other States in navigating the strait by air and by other modes.

(e) In UNCLOS Article 234, "due regard" means that in ice-covered areas that are part of the EEZ of a coastal State, which in adopting and enforcing nondiscriminatory laws and regulations for preventing, reducing and controlling marine pollution from ships, must be aware of and consider the right to navigation and the protection and preservation of the marine environment in that ice-covered part of its EEZ. That coastal State must balance these laws and regulations against the rights and interests of other States to navigate, and be obliged under UNCLOS to protect and preserve the marine environment, in that ice-covered part of its EEZ.

(f) In UNCLOS Article 56(3), "due regard" means that a coastal State, in exercising its rights and performing its duties in its EEZ, must be aware of and consider the rights and duties of other States in its EEZ. The coastal State must balance its rights and duties against the rights and duties of other States in its EEZ.

(g) In UNCLOS Article 58(3), "due regard" means that other States, in exercising their rights and performing their duties, must inter alia be aware of and consider the rights and duties of the coastal State in its EEZ. Other States must balance their rights and duties against the rights and duties of the coastal State in its EEZ.

(h) In UNCLOS Article 60(3), "due regard" means that a coastal State in removing artificial islands, installations or structures in its EEZ must be aware of and consider the rights and duties of other States in fishing, protecting the maritime environment, and other matters covered by UNCLOS in its EEZ.

(i) In UNCLOS Article 66(3)(a), "due regard" means that with respect to fishing beyond EEZ limits, the States concerned must maintain consultations with a view to agreement on terms and conditions of such fishing and must be aware of and consider the conservation requirements and needs of the State of origin in respect of anadromous fish stocks. States concerned must place in the balance the conservation requirements and needs of the State of origin of these fish stocks in these consultations.

(j) In UNCLOS Article 142(1), "due regard" means that with respect to resource deposits in the Area which lie across limits of national jurisdiction, the Authority and other States mining or otherwise having an interest in Area resource deposits must be aware of and consider the rights and legitimate interests of any coastal State across whose jurisdiction such resource deposits lie. The Authority and those States must balance their interests against the rights and legitimate interests of those coastal States.

(k) In UNCLOS Article 148, "due regard" means that when there is promotion of developing States' participation in activities in the Area as UNCLOS Part XI and the 1994 Agreement provide, there must be awareness and consideration of those developing States' special interests and needs. Those special interests and needs must be placed in the balance when developing States' participation in activities in the Area are promoted.

(l) In UNCLOS Article 267, "due regard" means that when States promote, develop and transfer marine technology, they must be aware of and consider all legitimate interests, including the rights and duties of holders, suppliers and recipients of marine technology. Those legitimate interests, including the rights and duties of holders, suppliers and recipients of marine technology, must be placed in the balance when States promote development and transfer of marine technology. All relevant circumstances must be taken into consideration.

(m) In UNCLOS Article 161(4), "due regard" means that with respect to the desirability of rotation of Area Authority Council membership, those who decide on Council membership must be aware of and consider rotating Council membership. They must balance the rotation criterion in considering other legitimate factors for Council membership.

(n) In UNCLOS Annex IV, Article 5(1), "due regard" means that with respect to the principle of equitable geographical distribution in electing Area Enterprise Governing Board members, those who decide on Board membership must be aware of and consider all legitimate factors, including equitable geographical distribution. They must balance the equitable geographical distribution criterion when considering other legitimate factors for electing Board members.

(o) In UNCLOS Annex IV, Article 5(2), "due regard" means that with respect to the principle of rotation of Area Enterprise Governing Board membership, those who decide on Board membership must be aware of and consider rotating Board membership. They must balance the rotation criterion in considering other legitimate factors for Board membership.

(p) In UNCLOS Article 162(2)(d), "due regard" to economy and efficiency means that decision makers must be aware of and consider the economy and efficiency criteria along with other legitimate factors. Economy and efficiency must be balanced with other legitimate factors.
(q) In UNCLOS Article 163(2), "due regard" to economy and efficiency means that the Area Council must be aware of and consider economy and efficiency criteria along with other legitimate factors in increasing the size of the Area Economic Planning Commission and the Area Legal and Technical Commission. Economy and efficiency must be balanced with other legitimate factors.
(r) In UNCLOS Article 167(2) and in UNCLOS Annex IV, Article 7(3), "due regard" means that with respect to the importance of recruiting and retaining Authority staff on as wide a geographic basis as possible, subject to the paramount consideration for securing the highest standards of efficiency, competence, and integrity, those who recruit and retain Authority staff must be aware of and consider the importance of recruiting and retaining Authority staff on as wide a geographic basis as possible, but subject to the paramount consideration for securing the highest standards of efficiency, competence and integrity. Recruiting and retaining on as wide a geographic basis as possible must be thrown into the balance along with the paramount consideration for securing the highest standards of efficiency, competence, and integrity.
(s) In UNCLOS Annex II, Article 2(1), "due regard" means that with respect to the need to ensure equitable geographical representation States parties to UNCLOS, in electing members of the Commission on the Limits of the Continental Shelf, must be aware of and consider equitable geographic representation on the Commission. Equitable geographic representation must be balanced against other legitimate factors in electing Commission members.

Comment

As the subdivision of § 55 into subsections 55(a)–55(s) suggests, the meaning of "due regard" depends on the context in which it is invoked. In LOAC-governed situations under the "other rules of international law" clauses in UNCLOS, a different definition may apply. The same may be the situation if the UN Charter supersedes UNCLOS or if *jus cogens* norms apply.[529]

The phrase "due regard" appears in UNCLOS Articles 27(4), 39(3)(a), 56(2), 58(3), 60(3), 66(3)(a), 79(5), 87(2), 142(1), 148, 161(4), 162(2)(d), 163(2), 167(2), 234 and 267; Appendixes II, Article 2(1); IV, Articles 5(1) and 5(2).

UNCLOS Article 87(2) declares that high seas freedoms Article 87(1) lists — inter alia freedoms of navigation and overflight, to lay submarine cables and pipelines (subject to Part VI, governing the continental shelf), to construct artificial islands and other installations permitted under international law (also subject to Part VI), of fishing (subject to Articles 116-20), and scientific research (subject to Parts VI and XIII [governing MSR]) — "shall be exercised by all States with due regard of the interests of other States in their exercise of the freedom of the high seas, and ... with due regard for the rights under [the] Convention with respect to activities in the Area." This UNCLOS due regard rule applies, under Articles 1(1), 3, 33, 55, 58, 76(1), 78, 121 and 135 to high seas areas claimed by coastal States as part of their contiguous zones, continental shelves or EEZs, or those high seas otherwise under Area cognizance, except as otherwise governed by UNCLOS, in, *e.g.*, Articles 56(3), 58(3), 60(3), 66(3)(a), 142(1), 148 and 234.[530] High Seas Convention Article 2, similarly listing high seas freedoms, declares that they "shall be exercised by all States with reasonable regard to the interests of other States in their exercise of the freedom of the high seas."[531] The High Seas Convention reasonable regard rule applies, under Territorial Sea Convention Article 24; Shelf Convention Article 3; and the Fishing Convention to high seas areas a coastal State claims as part of its contiguous zone, continental shelf or fishery zone respectively. The Convention on International Civil Aviation requires States parties, when issuing regulations for their State aircraft, to have "due regard" for civil aircraft navigation safety.[532]

---

[529] *See* Parts III.B-III.D and § 132, defining "other rules of international law."

[530] *Cf.* 3 Commentary ¶ 87.9(m).

[531] Fisheries Jurisdiction (U.K. v. Ice.), 1974 I.C.J. 3, 22, 29, held Article 2 and the rest of the High Seas Convention generally declaratory of established principles of international law; *see also* High Seas Convention, pmbl.; Restatement (Third) §§ 521(3), 514 r.n. 3.

[532] Convention on International Civil Aviation, note 484, art. 3(d); *see also* Restatement (Third) § 521 cmt. d.

UNCLOS Article 87(2) commentary explains "due regard":

> ... [T]he requirement of "due regard" is a qualification of the rights of States in exercising the freedoms of the high seas. The standard of "due regard" requires all States, in exercising their high seas freedoms, to be aware of and consider the interests of other States in using the high seas, and to refrain from activities that interfere with the exercise by other States of the freedom of the high seas. As the ILC[, which prepared drafts of the 1958 LOS Conventions,] stated in its Commentary in 1956, "States are bound to refrain from any acts that might adversely affect the use of the high seas by nationals of other States." The construction in paragraph 2 recognizes that all States have the right to exercise high seas freedoms, and balances consideration for the rights and interests of all States in this regard.[533]

Article 87(2)'s "due regard" formulation evolved from the High Seas Convention Article 2 "reasonable regard" language, through an intermediate draft phrase of "due consideration."[534]

UNCLOS Article 79(5) requires that States laying submarine cables or pipelines "shall have due regard to cables or pipelines already in position."[535] High Seas Convention Article 26(3) has a similar provision, requiring States laying cables or pipelines to "pay due regard" to those already in position on the seabed.[536] States exercising the high seas freedom to lay pipelines and cables, besides having due regard for other States in those States' exercise of their high seas freedoms, must also have due regard for cables and pipelines already on the seabed.

UNCLOS Article 27(4), governing arrests aboard a foreign ship in territorial sea passage, requires that "local authorities shall have due regard to the interests of navigation,"[537] language similar to that

---

533 3 Commentary ¶ 87.8(*l*) (footnote omitted); *see also* Brownlie 226; Churchill & Lowe 206, 264; Jennings & Watts § 285, p. 729 ("reasonable regard;" "weighting of freedoms may change with circumstances and with time"); NWP 1-14M Annotated ¶ 2.4.3 & n. 65 ("reasonable regard" of High Seas Convention, "due regard of [UNCLOS] "are one and the same and require any using nation to be cognizant of the interests of the interests of others in using a high seas area, and to abstain from nonessential, exclusive uses which substantially interfere with the exercise of other nations' high seas freedoms"); 1 O'Connell 57–58 ("reasonableness of competing uses"); 2 *id.* 796, 798–99 (same; "due regard"); Restatement (Third) § 521(3) ("reasonable regard"); Walker, The Tanker 536–39; Bernard H. Oxman, *The Regime of Warships Under the United Nations Convention on the Law of the Sea,* 24 Va. J. Int'l L. 809, 837–38 (1984) ("due regard"); Robertson, *The "New,"* note 81, p. 297.

534 3 Commentary ¶ 87.8(*l*) n. 32; *see also* Churchill & Lowe 206.

535 *See also* 2 Commentary ¶ 79.8(e).

536 *See also id.* ¶ 79.2.

537 *See also id.* ¶ 27.8(e).

in Territorial Sea Convention Article 19(4).[538] UNCLOS Article 39(3)(a), addressing duties of aircraft during straits transit passage, requires State aircraft to "at all times operate with due regard for the safety of navigation,"[539] a "principle applicable to the high seas generally."[540] In ice-covered areas, coastal States may, under Article 234, adopt and enforce nondiscriminatory laws and regulations for preventing, reducing, and controlling marine pollution from ships within their EEZ limits, but "[s]uch laws shall have due regard to navigation and the protection and preservation of the marine environment ..."[541]

Article 56(3) requires that a coastal State, in exercising its rights and performing its duties in its EEZ, "shall have due regard to the rights and duties of other States ..." Article 58(3) requires other States, in exercising their rights and performing their duties in the EEZ, inter alia "shall have due regard to the rights and duties of the coastal State ..."[542] Article 60(3) requires that a coastal State removing artificial islands, installations or structures in its EEZ "shall have due regard to fishing, the protection of the marine environment and the rights and duties of other States."[543] Article 66(3)(a), regulating anadromous fish stocks, provides with respect to fishing beyond an EEZ's outer limits, "States concerned shall maintain consultations with a view to ... agreement on terms and conditions of such fishing giving due regard to the conservation requirements and the needs of the State of origin in respect of these stocks."[544] Commentators note that "[t]he concept of 'due regard' in the Convention balances the obligations of ... the coastal State and other States within the EEZ."[545]

Article 142(1), in Part XI, providing for the Area, requires that "Activities in the Area with respect to resource deposits in the Area

---

[538] *See also id.* ¶ 27.2.

[539] *See also id.* ¶¶ 39.10(k)–39.10(*l*) (state aircraft not automatically subject to the Rules of the Air, promulgated by ICAO, like civil aircraft; State aircraft should normally comply with such safety measures and should always operate with due regard for safety of navigation, not merely aerial navigation).

[540] Restatement (Third) § 521 cmt. d; *see also* notes 498–99 and accompanying text.

[541] *See also* 4 Commentary ¶¶ 234.1 (art. 234 a *lex specialis*), 234.5(a), 234.5(e).

[542] *See also* 2 *id.* ¶¶ 56.4–56.7; Roach & Smith 175.

[543] *See also* 2 Commentary ¶¶ 60.11, 60.14, 60.15(f); NWP 1-14M Annotated ¶ 2.4.2.

[544] *See also* 2 Commentary ¶¶ 66.3–66.8, 66.9(c)–66.9(d).

[545] Roach & Smith 175; *see also* Brownlie 202 ("delicate balancing process"); Jennings & Watts § 342, p. 803; Restatement (Third) § 514, cmt. e & r.n. 3; Robertson, *The "New,"* note 81, p. 285.

which lie across limits of national jurisdiction, shall be conducted with due regard to the rights and legitimate interests of any coastal State across whose jurisdiction such deposits lie." Article 148 recites in part that "The effective participation of developing States in activities in the Area shall be promoted as specifically provided for in this Part [XI], having due regard to their special interests and needs …"

Article 267 requires States, in promoting development and transfer of marine technology, to "have due regard for all legitimate interests, including, inter alia, the rights and duties of holders, suppliers and recipients of marine technology." "The expression 'due regard' … implies that all the relevant circumstances are to be taken into consideration."[546]

UNCLOS applies the due regard principle to Area governance and management and to the Commission on the Limits of the Continental Shelf. Article 161(4), providing for Area Authority Council membership, requires that "due regard should be paid to the desirability of rotation of membership." Similarly, Annex IV, Article 5(1), in the Statute of the Enterprise for the Area, requires in electing Enterprise Governing Board members, "due regard" shall be paid to the principle of equitable geographical distribution; Article 5(2) requires that "due regard shall be paid to the principle of rotation of membership." UNCLOS Article 162(2)(d) requires the Area Council to establish subsidiary organs, "with due regard to economy and efficiency;" "due account" must be taken of the principle of equitable geographical distribution and special interests. Article 163(2) allows the Council to increase the size of the Economic Planning Commission or the Legal and Technical Commission, but with "due regard to economy and efficiency." Article 167(2) enjoins "due regard" to be paid to the importance of recruiting and retaining the Authority staff on as wide a geographic basis as possible, subject to the paramount consideration for securing the highest standards of efficiency, competence and integrity; Annex IV, Article 7(3) echoes this standard. Annex II, Article 2(1) requires Commission on the Limits of the Continental Shelf membership to be elected from among UNCLOS parties, "having due regard to the need to ensure equitable geographical representation."[547]

The *San Remo Manual* on the LOAC at sea has adopted "due regard" formulations for regulating belligerent rights and duties in naval

---

[546] 4 Commentary, ¶ 267.3(b), at 682; *see also id.* ¶¶ 267.1–267.2.

[547] *See also* 2 *id.* ¶ A.II.10(b).

warfare, to which the law of the sea is subject through UNCLOS's and the 1958 LOS Conventions' "other rules" clauses,[548] and neutrals' rights and duties under the law of the sea.[549]

Commentators have noted another elusive term, "comity," which has at least five meanings: a species of accommodation, not unrelated to morality but distinguishable from it; a synonym for international law; an equivalent to private international law, or in U.S. usage, conflict of laws; a policy basis for and source of particular conflicts rules; and as the reason for and source of international law.[550] Comity and due regard may be considered related. An often-cited case from the Supreme Court of the United States said:

> Comity, in the legal sense, is neither a matter of absolute obligation … nor of mere courtesy and good will … [I]t is the recognition which one nation allows within its territory to the legislative, executive or judicial acts of another nation, having due regard both to international duty and convenience and to the rights of its own citizens or of other persons who are under the protection of its laws.[551]

Whatever might be said about the nature of comity and its relationship with "due regard," UNCLOS elevates "due regard" to a positive command of law in its provisions. Thus although warships may exchange salutes on the high seas as a matter of courtesy and good will, they must exercise reciprocal due regard under UNCLOS or the High Seas Convention for each vessel's high seas freedoms.

"Due regard" has two components. The first is awareness and consideration of either State's interest(s) or other factor(s); the second is balancing the interest(s) or factor(s) into analysis for a decision. Although commentators suggest this should occur in a negotiation process,[552] perhaps leading to an agreement subsidiary to UNCLOS,[553] awareness, consideration and balancing can occur in ad hoc, practical situations as well, *e.g.*, situations among vessels on the high seas under

---

548 *See* Parts III.B-III.D and § 132, defining "other rules of international law."

549 San Remo Manual ¶¶ 12, 34, 36, 88, 106(c); *see also id.* ¶ 37 ("take care" to avoid damaging cables, pipelines not exclusively serving belligerent); Parts III.B-III.D and § 132, defining "other rules of international law."

550 Brownlie 28; *see also* Jennings & Watts § 17; Restatement (Third) §§ 101, cmt. e; 403, cmt. a.

551 Hilton v. Guyot, 159 U.S. 113, 163–64 (1895).

552 Churchill & Lowe 206 (also suggesting third party dispute settlement).

553 UNCLOS, arts. 311(2)–311(6); *see also* notes 42–46 and accompanying text.

UNCLOS Article 87 not covered by COLREGS, *i.e.*, the Collision Regulations.[554]

Section 28 defines "coast;" § 31, "coastal State;" § 81, "high seas;" § 156, "sea-bed," "seabed" or "bed."[555]

§ 57. *Entity*

In UNCLOS analysis, "entity" means any concrete or abstract thing of interest, including associations of things. In the latter situations, "entity" may appear in the plural.

Comment

In LOAC-governed situations under the "other rules of international law" clauses in UNCLOS, a different definition may apply. The same may be the situation if the UN Charter supersedes UNCLOS or if jus cogens norms apply.[556]

Former ECDIS Glossary, page 9, defined "entity" as "[a]ny concrete or abstract thing of interest, including associations of things." The newer ECDIS Glossary does not define "entity." Section 64 defines "feature object;" § 73, "geo object."[557]

§ 58. *Equidistance line; equidistant line; median line*

In UNCLOS analysis, an "equidistance line," synonymous with "equidistant line" or "median line," means a line every point of which is equally distant from the nearest points on the baselines of two States.

Comment

UNCLOS Article 15 uses the term "equidistant," but the definition has been more broadly stated to take into account agreements contemplated

---

[554] Convention on International Regulations for Preventing Collisions at Sea, note 281, replacing International Regulations for Preventing Collisions at Sea, note 281, for most States. *See* TIF 379–80. Many mariners know these treaties as the Collision Regulations or COLREGS. UNCLOS arts. 21(1)(a), 22(1), 39(2)(a), 41, 42(1)(a), 60(3), 94(3), 98(2), 147(2)(c), 194(3)(b), 194(3)(c), 194(3)(d), 225, 242(2), 262 authorize promulgation of safety at sea rules, sometimes by international agreement and sometimes by coastal States, an example of the latter being innocent passage rules. *See also* Roach & Smith 382–86. Agreements like COLREGS cannot be inconsistent with the Convention. UNCLOS art. 311.

[555] *See also* 2007–08 ABILA Proc. 220–28; Churchill & Lowe 98, 108, 169, 170, 173–74, 205–06, 264; Walker, *Last Round* 168–77, 2005–06 ABILA Proc. 57–66.

[556] *See* Parts III.B–III.D and § 132, defining "other rules of international law."

[557] *See also* Walker, *ECDIS Glossary* 246–47, 2003–04 ABILA Proc. 218–19.

by, *e.g.*, UNCLOS Articles 74, 83 or 134(4), or Shelf Convention Articles 6(1), 6(2).

In LOAC-governed situations under the "other rules of international law" clauses in UNCLOS, a different definition may apply. The same may be the situation if the UN Charter supersedes UNCLOS or if jus cogens norms apply.[558]

Consolidated Glossary ¶¶ 31, 59 define "equidistance line" or "median line" as a "line every point of which is equidistant from the nearest points of two States." Former Glossary ¶¶ 29, 51 define "equidistance line" or "median line" as a "line every point of which is equidistant from the nearest points on the baselines of two or more States between which it lies."

UNCLOS Article 15 inter alia provides that when two States' coasts are opposite or adjacent to each other, unless there is an agreement between them, neither State may extend its territorial sea "beyond the median line every point of which is equidistant from the nearest points on the baselines" from which the territorial sea's breadth is measured. Territorial Sea Convention Article 12(1) recites the same formula, omitting the agreement exception. Shelf Convention Articles 6(1) and 6(2) have the same formula as in UNCLOS Article 15, but the analogous UNCLOS continental shelf and EEZ provisions, UNCLOS Articles 74, 83 and 134(4), do not.

Section 16 defines "basepoint" or "point" and discusses baselines; § 26, "closing line;" § 93, "line;" § 176, "straight line; straight baseline; straight archipelagic baseline."[559]

§ 59. *Equidistant line*

See Equidistance line, § 58.

§ 60. *Estuary*

As used in UNCLOS Articles 1(1)(4) and 207(1), "estuary" means the tidal mouth of a river where the seawater is measurably diluted by the fresh water from the river.

---

[558] *See* Parts III.B–III.D and § 132, defining "other rules of international law."

[559] *See also* Churchill & Lowe ch. 2, p. 183; 2 Commentary ¶¶ 15.1–15.12(d); 2 O'Connell 637–39; Restatement (Third) § 511; Walker, *Consolidated Glossary* 254–55.

Comment

In LOAC-governed situations under the "other rules of international law" clauses in UNCLOS a different definition may apply. The same may be the situation if the UN Charter supersedes UNCLOS or if jus cogens norms apply.[560]

Consolidated Glossary ¶ 32 defines "estuary" as the "tidal mouth of a river, where the seawater is measurably diluted by the fresh water from the river." Former Glossary ¶ 30 defined "estuary" as the "tidal mouth of a river, where the tide meets the current of fresh water."[561] Commentators note the difficult problem between a river directly entering the sea and one entering through an estuary. "Nor is it always easy to determine exactly where the mouth of a river is located, especially on a coast with an extensive tidal range." The result has been claims for lines drawn by coastal States across estuaries that have been protested by other States.[562] Waters to the landward side of these lines, if drawn properly under the LOS, are part of internal waters under UNCLOS Article 8(1) and Territorial Sea Convention Article 5(1).[563]

UNCLOS Article 1(1)(4) defines "pollution of the marine environment" as

> introduction by man, directly or indirectly, of substances or energy into the marine environment, including estuaries, which results or is likely to result in such deleterious effects as harm to living resources and marine life, hazards to human health, hindrance to marine activities, including fishing and other legitimate uses of the sea, impairment of quality for use of sea water and reduction of amenities[.]

Article 207(1) requires States to adopt laws and regulations "to prevent, reduce and control pollution of the marine environment from land-based sources, including rivers, estuaries, pipelines and outfall structures, taking into account internationally agreed rules, standards and recommended practices and procedures."

The definition includes those bodies of water denominated "river," where ocean tides meet fresh water, *e.g.*, the River Plate between Argentina and Uruguay.

---

[560] *See* Parts III.B–III.D and § 132, defining "other rules of international law."

[561] *Accord*, 2 Commentary ¶ 1.22, p. 42.

[562] Churchill & Lowe 46–47 (citing example of Argentina's River Plate claims, Uruguay, U.K., U.S. protests).

[563] *Id.* 60; 2 Commentary §§ 8.1, 8.6.

Section 28 defines "coast;" § 31, "coastal State;" § 93, "line;" § 108, "mouth" (of a river); § 143, "river;" § 176, "straight line, straight baseline, straight archipelagic baseline;" § 189, "tide."[564]

§ 61. *Facility (Navigational)*

See Aid(s) to navigation, § 3.

§ 62. *Facility (Port)*

See Harbor works, § 79

§ 63. *Feature*

In UNCLOS analysis, "feature" means a representation of a real world phenomenon, *e.g.*, a particular cardinal buoy represented through a symbol on a chart.

Comment

In LOAC-governed situations under the "other rules of international law" clauses in UNCLOS, a different definition may apply. The same may be the situation if the UN Charter supersedes UNCLOS or if jus cogens norms apply.[565]

The Former ECDIS Glossary, page 10, defined "feature" as "[r]epresentation of a real world phenomenon," giving as an example, "a particular cardinal buoy represented through a symbol on a chart." The ECDIS Glossary, page 4, has the same definition for "feature," without the example.

Section 23 defines "chart" or "nautical chart;" § 64, "feature object."[566]

§ 64. *Feature object*

In UNCLOS analysis, "feature object" means an object which contains non-locational information about real-world entities.

---

[564] *See also* 2 Commentary ¶¶ 1.1–1.15, 1.1.24; 4 *id.* ¶¶ 207.1–207.7(a); NWP 1-14M Annotated ¶ 1.3.4 & n.24; 1 O'Connell 221–25; Restatement (Third) §§ 511–12; Walker, *Consolidated Glossary* 255–56.

[565] *See* Parts III.B-III.E and § 132, defining "other rules of international law."

[566] *See also* Walker, *ECDIS Glossary* 247, 2003–04 ABILA Proc. 219.

Comment

In LOAC-governed situations under the "other rules of international law" clauses in UNCLOS, a different definition may apply. The same may be the situation if the UN Charter supersedes UNCLOS or if jus cogens norms apply.[567]

Former ECDIS Glossary, page 10, defined "feature object " as "[a]n *object* which contains the non-locational information about real-world *entities*." The newer ECDIS Glossary, page 4, has the same definition.

Section 57 defines "entity;" § 63, "feature;" § 125, "object."[568]

§ 65. *Fishing*

In UNCLOS analysis, "fishing" refers to the action of extracting living resources from ocean areas, including the water column and the soil and subsoil of the seabed. Extraction methods include using nets, seines, lines, traps, dredging or dragging.

Comment

In LOAC-governed situations under the "other rules of international law" clauses in UNCLOS, a different definition may apply. The same may be the situation if the UN Charter supersedes UNCLOS or if jus cogens norms apply.[569]

Under UNCLOS Article 87, fishing is a high seas freedom, subject to conditions UNCLOS prescribes, other rules of international law, the principle of due regard for others' exercising their high seas freedoms, the principle of due regard for rights with respect to activities in the Area, and Articles 116–20, which lay down rules for conserving and management of high seas living resources, including marine mammals. Articles 58 and 61–73, declaring the EEZ is a high seas area subject to coastal State jurisdiction and sovereign rights for exploring, exploiting, conserving and managing EEZ living natural resources in the water column and the seabed and its subsoil, also lays down detailed rules for

---

567 *See* Parts III.B-III.D and § 132, defining "other rules of international law."

568 *See also* Walker, *ECDIS Glossary* 247–48, 2003–04 ABILA Proc. 219–20.

569 *See* Parts III.B-III.D and § 132, defining "other rules of international law." *E.g.*, Hague Convention (XI) Relative to Certain Restrictions with Regard to the Exercise of the Right of Capture in Naval War, Oct. 18, 1907, art. 3, 36 Stat. 2396, has rules on immunity of certain fishing boats from capture during armed conflict. These principles might be quite different from UNCLOS rules related to fishing boat seizures. Still other rules might apply in Charter or jus cogens-governed situations.

EEZ fishing. As in the Shelf Convention, UNCLOS Article 77 allows a coastal State declaring a continental shelf sovereign rights for exploring and exploiting shelf natural resources, which include living organisms belonging to sedentary species on the seabed or its subsoil. Under UNCLOS Article 19(2)(i) any fishing activities by a foreign flag vessel exercising innocent passage are considered prejudicial to the peace, good order, or security of the coastal State. The same rules apply under Articles 52(1) and 53 to archipelagic sea lanes passage.

Like UNCLOS, High Seas Convention Article 2(2) declares fishing is a high seas freedom subject to the reasonable regard principle for others' exercising high seas freedoms. The Fishing Convention lays down rules for high seas fishing near coastal States' territorial seas and principles for agreements among States whose nationals fish the same high seas areas. Also like UNCLOS, Shelf Convention Article 2 includes within coastal State shelf sovereignty sedentary living organisms on or beneath the continental shelf. Article 5(1) declares that exploration of the continental shelf may not result in unjustifiable interference with navigation, fishing, or conservation of high seas resources.

Nowhere does any LOS treaty define "fishing." However, it seems safe to say that fishing is concerned with living resources. UNCLOS and the Shelf Convention both differentiate between living and nonliving resources, *e.g.*, the difference between oysters and oil on the seabed and the subsoil beneath the seabed. UNCLOS is replete with references to and regulation of catching living resources in ocean areas. All LOS treaties refer to catch, *i.e.*, affirmative action to extract living resources from ocean areas. Therefore, any definition must be limited to extraction of living resources from ocean areas.[570]

Section 9 defines "area" and "Area;" § 28, "coast;" § 31, "coastal State;" § 81, "high seas;" § 126, "ocean space" or "sea;" § 157, "sea-bed," "seabed" or "bed;" § 184, "subsoil;" § 185, "superjacent waters" or "water column."

§ 66. *Flag state*

"Flag State" is a State whose flag a ship flies and is entitled to do so under UNCLOS.

---

[570] What is a living resource is not free from doubt. *See, e.g.*, Craig H. Allen, *Protecting the Oceanic Gardens of Eden: International Law Issues in Deep-Sea Vent Resource Conservation and Management*, 13 Georgetown Int'l Envt'l L. Rev. 563 (2001). *See also* 2007–08 ABILA Proc. 233–34.

Comment

In LOAC-governed situations under the "other rules of international law" clauses in UNCLOS, a different definition may apply. The same may be the situation if the UN Charter supersedes UNCLOS or if jus cogens norms apply.[571]

UNCLOS does not define "flag State," although the term's meaning can be deduced from UNCLOS Articles 91 and 94[572] or High Seas Convention Article 5(1). Articles 1 and 2 of the Ship Registration Convention, not in force, define "flag State" as "a State whose flag a ship flies and is entitled to fly" and indicate that the flag State must "exercise effectively its jurisdiction and control over such ships with regard to identification and accountability of ship owners and operators as well as with regard to administrative, technical, economic and social matters."[573] Since the Ship Registration Convention is not in force, its additional requirements ("a State … social matters.") have been omitted. These qualifications will govern States party to that Convention when it is in force and will govern all except persistently objecting States if Ship Registration Convention standards are accepted as custom. Until then, nonparty registry States may choose to apply definitions different from Ship Registration Convention Article 2 if they are consistent with other obligations under the conventional or customary law of the sea. In this regard UNCLOS Article 91 requires UNCLOS States parties to establish a "genuine link" between a registry State and the vessel. Similarly, High Seas Convention Article 5(1) establishes "genuine link" standards for States party to that Convention, *e.g.*, the United States,[574] that are not UNCLOS parties.

Special rules apply to warships. Under UNCLOS Article 29,

> For the purposes of [UNCLOS], "warship" means a ship belonging to the armed forces of a State bearing the external marks distinguishing such ships of its nationality, under the command of an officer duly commissioned by the government of the State and whose name appears in the appropriate service list or its equivalent, and manned by a crew which is under regular armed forces discipline.

---

571 *See* Parts III.B-III.D and § 132, defining "other rules of international law."

572 2 Commentary ¶ 1.30.

573 *Id.*; 3 *id.* ¶ 91.9(e); 4 *id.* ¶ 217.8(j), citing Ship Registration Convention, arts. 1–2; *see also* Churchill & Hedley 6, § 5.1.1; Churchill & Lowe 208–09, 255–56, 273–74, 286.

574 *See* TIF 395.

High Seas Convention Article 8(2) is similar, referring to "naval forces" instead of "armed forces" and "Navy List" instead of "appropriate service list or its equivalent."[575]

LOAC standards may differ from those under the LOS. The definition of a warship is the same under the LOS and the LOAC.[576] However, customary naval warfare rules declare that belligerents may consider the fact that a merchant vessel flying an enemy State's flag is conclusive evidence of its enemy character, and the fact that a merchant vessel flying a neutral flag is prima facie evidence of its neutral character.[577] This is but one example of the point made for all definitions; *i.e.*, a different standard may apply during armed conflict. UN Charter-governed obligations, *e.g.*, actions in individual or collective self-defense or pursuant to Security Council decisions, and jus cogens principles, may also require different standards.[578]

Section 72 defines "genuine link;" § 163, "ship" or "vessel."[579]

---

[575] Although Oil Platforms (Iran v. U.S.), 2003 ICJ 161 (Nov. 6) concerned a U.S. reparations counterclaim for an attack on *U.S.S. Samuel B. Roberts*, a U.S. warship, the case did not consider whether *Roberts* was a warship. Iran apparently conceded this issue.

[576] *Compare* UNCLOS, art. 29 *and* High Seas Convention, art. 8(2) *with* Hague Convention VII Relating to Conversion of Merchant Ships into War-Ships, Oct. 18, 1907, arts. 2–5, 205 Consol. T.S. 319, Schindler & Toman 1065. The United States and some other States are not parties, although most naval powers are. *See Signatures, Ratifications, Accessions, id.* 1068–70. Treaty succession principles for former colonies, now independent States, and to separating or dividing States (*e.g.*, Austria-Hungary, Russia) may bind still more countries. *See generally* Brownlie 661–66; Committee on Aspects of the Law of State Succession, *Final Report*, in ILA 73d Conf. Rep., note 473, pp. 250, 360–62 (2008) (*Final Report*); Jennings & Watts § 62, pp. 211–13; Symposium, *State Succession in the Former Soviet Union and in Eastern Europe*, 33 Va. J. Int'l L. 253 (1993); George K. Walker, *Integration and Disintegration in Europe: Reordering the Treaty Map of the Continent*, 6 Transnat'l Law. 1 (1993). The Convention's warship rules are now customary law. NWP 1-14M Annotated ¶ 2.1.1 (citing inter alia Hague VII arts. 2–5, UNCLOS art. 29, High Seas Convention art. 8(2); San Remo Manual ¶ 13(g) (same).

[577] Just because a merchant ship flies a neutral flag does not necessarily establish neutral character. Declaration Concerning the Laws of War, Feb. 26, 1909, art. 57, Schindler & Toman 1111, 1120; NWP 1-14M Annotated ¶ 7.5; San Remo Manual ¶¶ 112, 113. Oil Platforms, note 575, 2003 ICJ, p. 215 distinguished between a U.S.-flagged tanker, *Sea Isle City*, formerly of non-U.S. registry, for which the United States had standing to claim reparations, and *Texaco Caribbean*, a U.S. beneficially owned but Panama-registered tanker that was not flying a U.S. ensign when attacked, for which the United States could not claim.

[578] *See* Parts III.B-III.D and § 132, defining "other rules of international law."

[579] *See also* Churchill & Lowe 208–09, discussing S.S. Lotus, 1927 PCIJ, Ser. A, No. 10, 208 and the superseding International Convention for Unification of Certain Rules Relating to Penal Jurisdiction in Matters of Collision or Other Incidents of Navigation, May 10, 1952, 439 UNTS 233, now superseded by the High Seas Convention and

§ 67. *Foot of the continental slope*

As used in UNCLOS Article 76, "foot of the continental slope" means the point where the continental slope meets the continental rise or, if there is no rise, the deep ocean floor.

Comment

In LOAC-governed situations under the "other rules of international law" clauses in UNCLOS, a different definition may apply. The same may be the situation if the UN Charter supersedes UNCLOS or if jus cogens norms apply.[580]

Consolidated Glossary ¶ 36 now quotes UNCLOS Article 76(4)(b) and defines "foot of the continental slope" as "In the absence of evidence to the contrary, the foot of the continental slope shall be determined as the point of maximum change of gradient at its base." The Glossary adds:

> It is the point where the continental slope meets the continental rise or, if there is no rise, the deep ocean floor. To determine the maximum change of gradient requires adequate bathymetry covering the slope and a reasonable extent of the rise, from which a series of profiles may be drawn and the point of maximum change of gradient located.

Former Consolidated Glossary ¶ 34 recited UNCLOS Article 76(4)(b) and says the continental slope "is the point where the continental slope meets the continental rise or, if there is no rise, the deep ocean floor," adding the same quoted material.[581]

UNCLOS Articles 76(4)(a)(i) and 76(4)(a)(ii) use the continental slope as a point of reference for the continental margin. Article 76(4)(b) says that absent contrary evidence, "the foot of the continental slope shall be determined as the point of maximum change in the gradient at its base."

UNCLOS on the jurisdictional issue for States party to the latter treaties; Walker, *Definitions* 204–05.

[580] *See* Parts III.B-III.D and § 132, defining "other rules of international law."

[581] Although the practice of this analysis is to exclude definitions UNCLOS supplies, *see* notes 17–31 and accompanying text, the definition for "foot of the continental slope" has been retained because of its prior publication as a different definition in material connected with this study. Walker, *Consolidated Glossary* 256–57.

In defining "basepoint" or "point," § 16 discusses UNCLOS Article 76. Section 37 defines "continental rise;" § 38, "continental slope;" § 47, "deep ocean floor."[582]

§ 68. *Force majeure*

"Force majeure," as used in UNCLOS Articles 18 and 39, as incorporated by reference in UNCLOS Articles 45 and 54, and as used in analyzing other UNCLOS provisions like Articles 98 and 109, means an event of grave necessity, such as severe weather or mechanical failure in a ship or aircraft, or a human-caused event, such as a collision with another ship or aircraft. The situation of force majeure must be urgent and proceed from such a state of things as may be supposed to produce in the mind of a skillful mariner or aircraft commander a well-grounded apprehension of the loss of the vessel or aircraft and its cargo, or for the safety or lives of its crew or its passengers. A claimant may not raise a defense of force majeure if the claimant substantially caused the event of force majeure, except in cases involving protection of human life or human safety. Force majeure and "distress," defined in § 52, may overlap; force majeure situations primarily refer to external causes affecting a ship, an aircraft or a crew or passengers of either.

Comment

In LOAC-governed situations under the "other rules of international law" clauses in UNCLOS, a different definition may apply. The same may be the situation if the UN Charter supersedes UNCLOS or if jus cogens norms apply.[583]

UNCLOS Article 18(2) requires territorial sea innocent passage to be "continuous and expeditious. However, passage includes stopping and anchoring, but only in so far as the same are incidental to ordinary navigation or are rendered necessary by *force majeure* or distress or for … rendering assistance to persons, ships or aircraft in danger or distress." Similarly, Territorial Sea Convention Article 14(3) declares that "Passage includes stopping and anchoring, but only in so far as the

---

[582] *See also* Churchill & Lowe chs. 2, 12, pp. 148–50; 2 Commentary ¶¶ 76.1–76.18(a), 76.18(e)–76.18(g); NWP 1-14M Annotated ¶ 1.6 & Fig. A1-2; Restatement (Third) §§ 511, 515, 523; Noyes, *Definitions* 322–23 & Part III.D.3.

[583] *See* Parts III.B-III.D and § 132, defining "other rules of international law."

same are incidental to ordinary navigation or are rendered necessary by *force majeure* or by distress."[584]

UNCLOS Article 39(1)(c), relating to duties of ships and aircraft during straits transit passage, requires ships and aircraft while exercising the right of transit passage to "refrain from any activities other than those incident to their normal modes of continuous and expeditious transit unless rendered necessary by *force majeure* or by distress[.]" These are considered customary rules.[585]

UNCLOS Article 45(1)(a) applies the territorial sea innocent passage regime to straits excluded from transit passage by Article 38(1)(a). Article 45(1)(b) applies the territorial sea innocent passage regime to straits between a part of the high seas or an EEZ and a foreign State's territorial sea.[586]

UNCLOS Article 54 incorporates Article 39 *mutatis mutandis* to archipelagic sea lanes passage.[587]

UNCLOS Article 98(1) commands every State to require the master of a ship flying its flag,

> in so far as he can do so without serious danger to the ship, the crew or the passengers:
> (a) to render assistance to any person found at sea in danger of being lost;
> (b) to proceed with all possible speed to the rescue of persons in distress, if informed of their need for assistance, in so far as such action may be reasonably expected of him;
> (c) after a collision, to render assistance to the other ship, its crew and its passengers and, where possible, to inform the other ship of the name of his own ship, its port of registry and the nearest port at which it will call.

High Seas Convention Article 12(1) is identical. Although Article 98(1) does not recite force majeure as Article 98(1)(b) does for distress, force majeure might the predicate for a distress situation Article 98 contemplates.

---

584 Restatement (Third) § 513 cmt. a also recites this principle, citing UNCLOS art. 18(2) and Territorial Sea Convention art. 14(3).

585 Restatement (Third) § 513 cmt. j, citing UNCLOS art. 39(1)(c).

586 Presumably Restatement (Third) § 513 cmt. a would apply these rules to UNCLOS art. 45(1)-governed straits, although cmt. a does not cite UNCLOS art. 45.

587 Presumably Restatement (Third) § 513 cmt. j would apply this principle to archipelagic sea lanes passage as well, although cmt. j does not cite UNCLOS art. 54.

Similarly, UNCLOS does not cite force majeure in Article 109, which refers to distress as an exception to its definition of "unauthorized broadcasting."[588]

Treaties underscore a requirement to render assistance to those in distress in peace or war.[589] Some treaties recite special rules for force majeure situations during armed conflict.[590] Others recite terms like force majeure or vis major, perhaps referrring to act of God or the like, as defenses to liability in municipal law-based maritime litigation.[591]

Commentaries on UNCLOS Articles 18(2), 39(1)(c), 45, 54, 98 and 109 negotiations do not elucidate the meaning of "force majeure."[592]

---

[588] *See generally* Part IV.D § 52, defining "distress."

[589] Convention for Unification of Certain Rules of Law with Respect to Assistance and Salvage at Sea, note 505, art. 11; International Convention on Salvage, note 505, art. 10; International Convention on Maritime Search and Rescue, Annex, ch. 2, note 505, ¶ 2.1.10; International Convention for the Safety of Life at Sea, Annex, ch. 5, note 505, reg. 10. The rule is the same in armed conflict situations. Protocol I Additional to the Geneva Conventions of 12 August 1949, and Relating to the Protection of Victims of International Armed Conflicts, arts. 8(b), 10, 33; Convention for Amelioration of the Condition of Wounded, Sick and Shipwrecked Members of Armed Forces at Sea, note 505, art. 12; *see also* Colombos, note 505, § 369; NWP 1-14M Annotated ¶¶ 3.2.1–3.2.2; Walker, The Tanker 422; Goodwin-Gill, note 505, pp. 31–32.

[590] During the eighteenth century there was a practice of releasing enemy warships forced into enemy ports by stress of weather, *i.e.*, force majeure. That is no longer consistent with international law. 2 O'Connell 858. Hague Convention VI Relating to Status of Enemy Merchant Ships at Outbreak of Hostilities, art. 2, Oct. 18, 1907, 105 Consol. T.S. 305, Schindler & Toman 1059, declares that a merchant ship unable, owing to force majeure, to leave an enemy port within times the Convention, Article 1, sets, may not be confiscated. The belligerent may only detain it, without paying compensation, but subject to restoration after the war, or requisition it upon payment of compensation. Hague VI is considered in disuetude. San Remo Manual ¶ 136, cmt. 136.2; *cf.* 2 O'Connell 858. Hague Convention XIII Concerning Rights & Duties of Neutral Powers in Naval War, art. 21, Oct. 18, 1907, 36 Stat. 2415, declares: "A prize may only be brought into a neutral port on account of unseaworthiness, stress of weather, or want of fuel or provisions. It must leave as soon as the circumstances which justified its entry ... end. If it does not, the neutral Power must employ the means at its disposal to release it with its officers and crew and to intern the prize crew." Similarly, *id.* art. 14 says that a belligerent warship may not prolong its stay in a neutral port beyond the permissible time [24 hours under *id.* art. 13, or in accordance with local regulations] except on account of damage or stress of weather. It must depart as soon as the cause of the delay ... end[s]." *See also* NWP 1-14M Annotated, ¶¶ 7.3.2–7.3.2.1; 2 O'Connell 858; San Remo Manual ¶ 21.

[591] *E.g.*, International Convention for Unification of Certain Rules Relating to Bills of Lading for Carriage of Goods by Sea, art. 4, Aug. 25, 1924, 51 Stat. 233, 120 LNTS 155 (perils of the sea, acts of God, acts of war, acts of public enemies, restraint of princes, quarantines, etc.).

[592] 2 Commentary ¶¶ 18.1–18.6(e), 39.1–39.10(*l*), 45.1–45.8(c), 54.1–54.7(b); 3 *id.* ¶¶ 98.1–98.11(g), 109.1–109.8(f). DOD Dictionary 415 defines "perils of the sea" as "Accidents and dangers peculiar to maritime activities, such as storms, waves, and

Commentary to Article 39(1)(c), dealing with transit passage distress situations, inquired whether Article 39(1)(c) includes stopping and anchoring if necessary in force majeure situations, and whether Article 39(1)(c) includes the danger or distress to other "persons, ships or aircraft." As to the first question, the commentary would say that stopping and anchoring under these situations is covered, as it would be in an innocent passage situation. The second answer is "less obvious," but would fall within the "tradition of going to the aid of persons in distress is as old as maritime navigation itself, and is regarded as an obligation by vessels and aircraft of all flags. … Elementary considerations of humanity also dictate that a ship go to the aid of persons in distress."[593] Presumably this humanity principle also applies to aircraft's going to the aid of persons in distress. Thus in combination with UNCLOS Articles 18 and 98, "the duty to render assistance exists throughout the ocean, whether in the territorial sea, in straits used for international navigation, in archipelagic waters, in the exclusive economic zone or on the high seas. Assistance is to be given to any person, ship or aircraft in distress."[594]

Cases in the British and U.S. courts, international arbitrations and commentators have considered and defined distress situations, some of which were caused by outside forces, the usual predicate for a force majeure claim. The British High Court of Admiralty offered this test: "It must be an urgent distress; it must be something of grave necessity; [*e.g.*] … where a ship is said to be driven in by stress of weather." A party claiming distress cannot have caused the situation giving rise to the claim.[595] The Supreme Court of the United States accepted this test, adding that "the necessity must be urgent and proceed from such a state of things as may be supposed to produce in the mind of a skillful mariner a well-grounded apprehension of the loss of the vessel and cargo, or of the lives of the crew."[596] Mechanical breakdown, fuel exhaustion or action of a foreign flag warship or mutineers all can be

---

wind; collision; grounding; fire smoke and noxious fumes; flooding, sinking and capsizing; loss of propulsion or steering; and any other hazards resulting from the unique environment of the sea."

593 2 Commentary ¶ 39.10(g), inter alia citing UNCLOS art. 98; High Seas Convention art. 12; *see also* Churchill & Lowe 81, 107; 3 Commentary ¶ 1; NWP 1-14M Annotated ¶¶ 2.3.2.1 note 25; 3.2.2.1.

594 3 Commentary ¶ 98.11(g), p. 177; *see also* 2 O'Connell 853–54.

595 The Eleanor, 165 Eng. Rep. 1058, 1068 (High Ct. Adm. 1809).

596 The New York, 16 U.S. (3 Wheat.) 59, 68 (1818); *accord*, NWP 1-14M Annotated ¶ 3.2.2. *See also* The Brig Concord, 13 U.S. (9 Cranch) 387, 388 (1815).

predicates for a necessity claim.[597] As is apparent from these examples, some claims may fall more easily, linguistically speaking, under force majeure, implying an outside force. If a ship must enter a port or internal waters to save human life, that vessel has a right of entry under international law. Whether distress entry to save property, if human life is not at risk, will justify a defense is questionable, at least where there is a serious pollution risk incident to entry.[598] The same may be true if a ship, *e.g.*, enters the territorial sea to assist a downed aircraft in distress.[599] On the other hand, aircraft in distress have a right of entry into the territorial sea to seek refuge on land.[600]

Force majeure and distress may be defenses to claims of breach of treaty obligations. The International Law Commission *Articles on State Responsibility* include provisions for force majeure and distress. Article 23, Force Majeure, provides:

> 1. The wrongfulness of an act of a State not in conformity with an international obligation of that State is not precluded if the act is due to *force majeure*, that is the occurrence of an irresistible force or of an unforeseen event, beyond the control of the State, making it materially impossible in the circumstances to perform that obligation.
> 2. Paragraph 1 does not apply if:
>   (a) the situation of *force majeure* is due, either alone or in combination with other factors, to the conduct of the State invoking it; or
>   (b) the State has assumed the risk of that situation occurring.[601]

Similarly, but not identically, Article 24, Distress, provides:

> 1. The wrongfulness of an act of a State not in conformity with an international obligation of that State is not precluded if the author of the act in question has no other reasonable way, in a situation of distress, of saving the author's life or the lives of other persons entrusted to the author's care.
> 2. Paragraph 1 does not apply if:
>   (a) the situation of distress is due, either alone or in combination with other factors, to the conduct of the State invoking it; or
>   (b) the act in question is likely to create a comparable or greater peril.[602]

---

597 *See generally* Colombos, note 505, §§ 353–54; 2 O'Connell 855–57.

598 Churchill & Lowe 63.

599 NWP 1-14M Annotated ¶ 2.3.2.5 n.35.

600 *Id.* ¶ 4.4, referring to *id.* ¶ 3.2.2.1.

601 ILC Responsibility Articles, art. 23, p. 183, *reprinted in* Crawford p. 170.

602 ILC Responsibility Articles, art. 24, p. 189, *reprinted in* Crawford p. 174.

Article 24 *Commentary* explains the difference:

> Article 24 [reciting distress standards] deals with the specific case where an individual whose acts are attributable to the State is in a situation of peril, either personally or in relation to persons under his or her care. The article precludes the wrongfulness of conduct adopted by the State agent in circumstances where the agent had no other reasonable way of saving life. Unlike … *force majeure* …, a person acting under distress is not acting involuntarily, even though the choice is effectively nullified by the situation of peril. Nor is it a case of choosing between compliance with international law and other legitimate interests of the State, such as characteristic situations of necessity under article 25. The interest concerned is the immediate one of saving people's lives, irrespective of their nationality.[603]

Article 23 *Commentary* adds:

> *Force majeure* … involves a situation where the State in question is in effect compelled to act in a manner not in conformity with the requirements of an international obligation incumbent upon it. [It] … differs from … distress … or necessity (Article 25) because the conduct of the State which would otherwise be internationally wrongful is involuntary or at least involves no element of free choice.[604]

Under the ILC Articles,

> … [*F*]*orce majeure* … only arises where three elements are met: (a) the act … must be brought about by an irrestible force or an unforeseen event, (b) which is beyond the control of the State concerned, and (c) which makes it materially impossible in the circumstances to perform the obligation. … "[I]rresistible" qualifying … "force" emphasizes that there must be a constraint which the State was unable to avoid or oppose by its own means. To have been "unforeseen: the event must have been neither foreseen nor of an easily foreseeable kind. … [T]he "irresistible force" or "unforeseen event" must be causally linked to the situation of material impossibility as indicated by … "due to *force majeure* … making it materially impossible."

Subject to Article 23(2), if these elements are met, the defense remains as long as the force majeure situation exists.[605]

---

603 ILC Responsibility Articles, art. 24, cmt. 1, p. 189, *reprinted in* Crawford p. 174, citing Oliver J. Lissistzyn, *The Treatment of Aerial Intruders in Recent Practice in International Law*, 47 AJIL 588 (1953), and referring to ILC Responsibility Articles, art. 25, p. 194, *reprinted in* Crawford p. 178.

604 ILC Responsibility Articles, art. 23, cmt. 1, p. 183, *reprinted in* Crawford p. 170, referring to, arts. 24, 25, pp. 189, 194, *reprinted in* Crawford pp. 174, 178. For "distress" analysis, *see* Part IV.B § 52.

605 ILC Responsibility Articles, art. 23, cmt. 2, p. 183, *reprinted in* Crawford p. 170.

"Material impossibility of performance giving rise to *force majeure* may be due to a natural or physical event (e.g., stress of weather which may divert State aircraft into the territory of another State, earthquakes, floods or drought) or to human intervention (e.g., loss of control over a portion of the State's territory as a result of ... insurrection ... " or a third State's military operations in that territory, or a combination of the two. Certain duress or coercion situation may also amount to force majeure if Article 23 requirements are met. " ... [T]he situation must be irresistible, so that the State concerned has no real possibility of escaping its effects." Force majeure does not include circumstances where performance of an obligation has just become more difficult; it does not cover a State's neglects or defaults, even if the resulting injury was accidental and unintended.[606]

According to the ILC, impossibility of performance, a ground for treaty termination, and force majeure, a defense to performance of an international obligation, whether stated in an international agreement or in, *e.g.*, customary law, are different. "The degree of difficulty associated with *force majeure* ... precluding wrongfulness, though considerable, is less than is required by [Vienna Convention] article 61 for termination of a treaty on grounds of supervening impossibility." Force majeure claims have failed where the defense involved difficulty of performance, but a claim of material impossibility has been successful where, *e.g.*, an aircraft strays across a national border due to damage to or loss of control of the aircraft due to bad weather.[607]

ILC Article 23 *Commentary* cites UNCLOS Article 18(2) and Territorial Sea Convention Article 14(3) as recognizing the basic principle in Article 23. Unlike the ILC analysis for "distress," the *Commentary* does not cite other UNCLOS provisions citing or related to force majeure.[608] Presumably the same standards apply to other UNCLOS provisions. International tribunals have accepted the principle,[609]

[606] ILC Responsibility Articles, art. 23, cmt. 3, p. 184, *reprinted in* Crawford p. 170.

[607] ILC Responsibility Articles, art. 23, cmts. 4–5, p. 185, *reprinted in* Crawford p. 171, inter alia citing Vienna Convention art. 61; Project Case, note 185, 1997 ICJ, p. 63.

[608] ILC Responsibility Articles, art. 23, cmt. 6, p. 186, *reprinted in* Crawford p. 172; *see also* UNCLOS arts. 39(1)(c), 45(1)(a), 54, 98(1), 109; Part IV.B § 52.

[609] ILC Responsibility Articles, art. 23, cmt. 7, p. 186, *reprinted in* Crawford p. 177, inter alia citing Payment of Various Serbian Loans (Fr. v. Km. of Serbs, Croats & Slovenes), 1929 PCIJ (Ser. A), No. 20, pp. 30, 33–40; Brazilian Loans (Fr. v. Brazil), 1929 PCIJ, Ser. A, No. 21, pp. 47, 120; Rainbow Warrior, note 519, 20 R.I.A.A., p. 253.

as have international commercial arbitral tribunals. It may qualify as a general principle of law.[610]

Article 23(2)(a) declares that the force majeure defense does not apply if the situation of force majeure is due alone or in combination with other factors, to the conduct of the State invoking force majeure. The ILC Article follows the pattern of the Vienna Convention on the impossibility of performance defense, except that the situation must be "due" to the invoking State's sole action. If the invoking State contributed to the situation of material impossibility by an act taken in good faith and did not itself make the event any less unforeseen, and which in hindsight might have been done differently, the Article 23(2)(a) exception does not apply. The invoking State's role in the occurrence of force majeure must be "substantial."[611] Although a State may assume the risk of force majeure and thereby forfeit the defense later under Article 23(2)(b), the assumption of risk must be "unequivocal and directed towards those to whom the obligation is owed."[612]

Unlike the Article 24 provision for distress, the ILC rubric for force majeure says nothing about human life and the like. In the context of the law of the sea, this seems to be a serious omission.

As the foregoing analysis demonstrates, the distress and force majeure concepts overlap, force majeure principally referring to external causes affecting a ship, an aircraft or a crew or passengers of either. However, since UNCLOS refers to the terms separately, a separate definition is in order.

The definition accepts principles laid down in the principal cases and commentaries discussing force majeure and applies them to aircraft as well as ships. The definition also adds concern for the safety of the crew, as distinguished from their lives, and concern for the safety or lives of passengers, as part of the definition. It is not enough to save human life; humans must be put in a place of safety as well. The last sentence departs from the older cases to give an exception to the rule

---

[610] ILC Responsibility Articles, art. 23, cmt. 8, p. 187, *reprinted in* Crawford p. 173, inter alia citing UNCITRAL Convention on Contracts for the International Sale of Goods, art. 79, Apr. 11, 1980, TIAS No. —, 1489 UNTS 58; Denkavit N.V. v. Belgium, 1987 Eur. Ct. H.R. 565; Commission v. Italy, 1985 Eur. Ct. H.R. 2629; George H. Aldrich, The Jurisprudence of the Iran-United States Claims Tribunal (1996); *see also* ICJ Stat. art. 38(1).

[611] ILC Responsibility Articles, art. 23, cmt. 9, p. 188, *reprinted in* Crawford p. 173, inter alia citing Vienna Convention art. 61; Libya Arab Foreign Inv. Co. v. Republic of Burundi, 96 I.L.R. 279, 318 (Arb. Tribunal 1994) (force majeure rejected).

[612] ILC Responsibility Articles, art. 23, cmt. 10, p. 188, *reprinted in* Crawford p. 173.

that a claimant may not raise a defense of force majeure if the claimant "substantially" caused an event that creates a grave necessity. In this regard the definition follows ILC Article 23(2)(a),[613] except that it can be raised in cases involving protecting human life or human safety, even though the claimant's action precipitated the event, *e.g.*, negligently failing to take on enough fuel to complete a flight or voyage, or in the case of a collision with a State vessel where the State vessel's action was deliberate. The Committee decided to omit the equivalent of ILC Article 23(2)(b), assumption of risk.[614]

Section 52 defines "distress;" § 81, "high seas;" § 159, "seaworthy," "seaworthiness;" § 161, "serious act of pollution;" § 163, "ship" or "vessel;" § 177, "strait" or "straits."

§ 69. *Fringing reef*

As used in UNCLOS Articles 6 and 47(7), "fringing reef" means a reef attached directly to the shore or continental land mass, or located in their immediate vicinity.

Comment

In LOAC-governed situations under the "other rules of international law" clauses in UNCLOS, a different definition may apply. The same may be the situation if the UN Charter supersedes UNCLOS or if jus cogens norms apply.[615]

Consolidated Glossary ¶ 66 defines "fringing reef" as "[a] reef attached directly to the shore or continental land mass, or located in their immediate vicinity."

UNCLOS Article 6 says that in the cases of islands on atolls or islands having fringing reefs, the baseline for measuring the territorial sea's breadth is the seaward low-water line of the reef, as shown by the appropriate signal on charts the coastal State officially recognizes. Article 47(7) says that to compute the water-land ratio under Article 47(1), land areas may include waters lying within islands' and atolls' fringing reefs, including that part of a steepsided oceanic plateau

---

[613] *See* note 611 and accompanying text.

[614] *See* note 612 and accompanying text. 2007–08 ABILA Proc. did not publish a definition for force majeure. This definition was derived by correspondence among ABILA LOS Committee members and other commentators.

[615] *See* Parts III.B-III.D and § 132, defining "other rules of international law."

enclosed or nearly enclosed by a chain of limestone islands and drying reefs lying on the plateau perimeter.

Section 12 defines "atoll;" § 23, "chart" or "nautical chart;" § 28, "coast;" § 31, "coastal State;" § 53, "drying reef;" § 93, "line;" § 98, "low water line" or "low water mark;" § 127, "oceanic plateau;" § 140, "reef;" § 176, "straight line; straight baseline; straight archipelagic baseline." In defining "basepoint" or "point," § 16 discusses baselines.[616]

§ 70. *Generalization*

In UNCLOS analysis, "generalization" means the concentration on more significant facts, and omission of less important detail when compiling charts, to avoid overloading them where chart space is limited.

Comment

In LOAC-governed situations under the "other rules of international law" clauses in UNCLOS, a different definition may apply. The same may be the situation if the UN Charter supersedes UNCLOS or if jus cogens norms apply.[617]

Former ECDIS Glossary, page 10, defined "generalization" as "[t]he omission of less important detail when compiling a *chart*. Its purpose is to avoid overloading charts where space is limited." The newer ECDIS Glossary does not define "generalization."

The § 70 definition adds "chart" before "space" to avoid confusion with, *e.g.*, "ocean space" or "sea," defined in § 126.

Section 23 defines "chart" or "nautical chart."[618]

§ 71. *Generally accepted*

See Applicable, § 5.

§ 72. *Genuine link*

"Genuine link" in UNCLOS Article 91 means more than mere registration of a ship with a State; "genuine link" requires, *e.g.*, connections

---

[616] *See also* Churchill & Lowe 51–52, 120–26; 2 Commentary ¶¶ 6.1–6.7(e), 47.1–47.8, 47.9(*l*); 1 O'Connell 185–96; NWP 1-14M Annotated ¶ 1.3.5; Restatement (Third) §§ 511–12; Walker, *Consolidated Glossary* 257–58.

[617] *See* Parts III.B-III.D and § 132, defining "other rules of international law."

[618] *See also* Walker, *ECDIS Glossary* 248, 2003–04 ABILA Proc. 220.

between a flag State under whose laws a ship is registered such that the flag State has the ability to exercise effective jurisdiction and control over the ship when registration is granted; connections between the flag, *i.e.*, registry, State and the ship's crew; connections between the flag, *i.e.*, registry, State and the ship's officers; or connections between the flag, *i.e.*, registry, State and the ship's beneficial owners.

Comment

In LOAC-governed situations under the "other rules of international law" clauses in UNCLOS, a different definition may apply. The same may be the situation if the UN Charter supersedes UNCLOS, or if jus cogens norms apply.[619] Section 130, defining "flag state," illustrates the point for possible differences between the LOS and the LOAC.

This attempts to recombine standards in High Seas Convention Article 5(1), as restated in UNCLOS Articles 91 and 94(1). It leaves to practice pursuant to UNCLOS Article 94, to decide what is effective exercise and control of a ship's administrative, technical and social matters, and perhaps to treaties,[620] on these matters. What is appropriate exercise and control is a matter of national laws, but in any case it must be effective exercise and control. Moreover, a State whose nationals comprised the entire crew, or the entire wardroom of ship's officers, could not claim a genuine link if that State is not the flag, *i.e.*, registry, State.[621]

"Genuine link" appears in UNCLOS Article 91(1):

> Every State shall fix the conditions for the grant of its nationality to ships, for the registration of ships in its territory, and for the right to fly its flag. Ships have the nationality of the State whose flag they are entitled to fly. There must exist a genuine link between the State and the ship.

Article 94(1), carrying over language from the High Seas Convention, Article 5(1), declares: "Every State shall effectively exercise its jurisdiction and control in administrative, technical and social matters over ships flying its flag." Ensuing Article 94 provisions elaborate on

[619] *See* Parts III.B-III.D and § 132, defining "other rules of international law."
[620] Noyes, *Definitions* 316.
[621] This definition differs from earlier drafts. *Compare* Walker, *ECDIS Glossary* 228–31, 2003–04 ABILA Proc. 197–201 and Walker, *Definitions* 208 *with* Walker, *Defining* 357, 2001–02 ABILA Proc. 162–65. Noyes, *Treaty* 380–83, 2001–02 ABILA Proc. 189–93 and Noyes, *Definitions* 314–16 ably critiques the issue.

these requirements.[622] Article 217 imposes environmental enforcement requirements on registry States.[623] High Seas Convention Article 5(1) has similar language:

> Each State shall fix the conditions for the grant of its nationality to ships, for the registration of ships in its territory, and for the right to fly its flag. Ships have the nationality of the State whose flag they are entitled to fly. There must be a genuine link between the State and the ship; in particular, the State must effectively exercise its jurisdiction and control in administrative, technical and social matters over ships flying its flag.

Neither treaty defines "genuine link." A principal difference between them is their scope; UNCLOS applies its Article 91/94 terms in all ocean areas, while the High Seas Convention only governs the high seas.[624] Both treaties leave it to States to fix specific registry requirements in their discretion.[625]

Among the High Seas Convention languages, translation of the Spanish text suggests the same meaning as "genuine link" in the English language version. The French language version translates to "substantial" or "significant" link, suggesting some difference of meaning. The same distinction seems true for UNCLOS Article 91(1).[626]

The High Seas Convention preparatory works the International Law Commission developed suggest that mere administrative formality, *i.e.*, registry only or grant of a certificate of registry without submitting to registry State control, does not satisfy that Convention's "genuine link" requirement. States would be free to establish their own conditions for registration, however.[627] The 1958 UN Conference on the Law of the Sea added the "particularly ..." language, but there was disagreement on whether the requirement of effective exercise of jurisdiction and control was "an indispensable, if not necessarily the only, element of the genuine link (the traditional maritime States' view), or whether

[622] High Seas Convention art. 10 was a source for UNCLOS arts. 94(3), 94(5). Churchill & Hedley, p. 6, §§ 3.3.2, 4.1, 4.3, 4.6; 3 Commentary ¶¶ 91.9(c), 94.2; *see also* Oude Elferink, note 235, pp. 43–44. The Committee also acknowledges the comments of Todd Jack, a Committee member.

[623] *See also* Churchill & Hedley § 4.6; 4 Commentary ¶¶ 217.8(a)–217.8(j).

[624] 3 Commentary ¶¶ 91.9(f), 94.8(*l*).

[625] *Id.* ¶ 91.9(b).

[626] Churchill & Hedley §§ 3.2 p. 11, 4.2 p. 42, confessing lack of ability in other official UNCLOS languages. UNCLOS art. 320 lists five equally authentic texts: Arabic, Chinese, English, French, Russian and Spanish.

[627] Churchill & Hedley § 3.3.1, p. 19; 3 Commentary ¶¶ 91.9(b)–91.9(c); Oude Elferink, note 235, pp. 46–48.

the requirement was independent of the genuine link (flag of convenience States' view)."[628] Preparatory work leading to UNCLOS does not explain why the High Seas Convention Article 5(1) "particularly" language was dropped, to be reinserted in similar language in UNCLOS Article 94(1). There is no explanation of how this shift affects the meaning of "genuine link."[629]

> Nevertheless, one observation may be made and a possible conclusion drawn. It would not seem permissible to deduce from the difference between Article 5 ... and Article 91 ... that the effective exercise of flag State jurisdiction is no longer an element in the genuine link. It does not seem that the drafters of the 1982 Convention had any intention, when deleting the effective exercise of jurisdiction phrase, of affecting the meaning of ... "genuine link."[630]

The negotiating history confirms this view. The transfer appears to have been a drafting decision, so that the same language would not appear in Article 91 and Article 94(1).[631] The Ship Registration Convention would give substance to a definition of genuine link, but its low ratification rate suggests that it would not be appropriate to copy that Convention's terms into a definition now.[632]

Most but not all international court decisions considering High Seas Convention Article 5(1) appear to support a view that mere registry is not enough for a genuine link.[633] Commentators divide on the issue; more recent analyses say that more than just registry is necessary to establish a genuine link.[634]

Whether more than pro forma registry is necessary to establish a genuine link under UNCLOS is not free of doubt. However, because of transfer of High Seas Convention Article 5(1)'s "particularly" language from UNCLOS Article 91 to Article 94, and elaboration of

---

[628] Churchill & Hedley § 3.3.2, pp. 20–21.

[629] *Id.* § 4.3, pp. 45–46.

[630] *Id.* § 4.3, pp. 46–47.

[631] 3 Commentary ¶¶ 91.9(c), 94.8(b).

[632] Churchill & Hedley § 5.1.1; 3 Commentary ¶ 91.9(e); 4 *id.* ¶ 217.8(j), citing and discussing the Ship Registration Convention.

[633] National court decisions were not considered in the analysis. Churchill & Hedley §§ 3.4-3.4.2, 4.4-4.4.2; *see also* Walker, The Tanker 293.

[634] Churchill & Hedley §§ 3.5, 3.6, 4.5, 4.6 (genuine link requirement has same meaning as in High Seas Convention), Part 6; *see also* Churchill & Lowe 257–62 (noting confusion among commentators, courts); Walker, The Tanker 293–95 (supporting view that satisfying genuine link requirement imposes more obligations on States than mere registry); Oude Elferink, note 235, pp. 58–63.

requirements in Articles 94(2)-94(7), some of which were derived from High Seas Convention Article 10, and what seems the weight of recent decisional and commentator authority, it would appear that a "genuine link" requires more than nominal registry. What is enough for satisfying the genuine link must be considered on a case-by-case basis.

It has been argued that "genuine link" could mean "ability to exercise jurisdiction and control" rather than effective exercise of jurisdiction and control.[635]

Section 66 defines "flag State;" § 81, "high seas;" § 163, "ship" or "vessel."[636]

§ 73. *Geo object*

In UNCLOS analysis, "geo object" means a feature object carrying the a real world entity's descriptive characteristics.

Comment

In LOAC-governed situations under the "other rules of international law" clauses in UNCLOS, a different definition may apply. The same may be the situation if the UN Charter supersedes UNCLOS or if jus cogens norms apply.[637]

Former ECDIS Glossary, page 10, defined "geo object" as "[a] *feature object* which carries the descriptive characteristics of a real world *entity*[,]" noting that positional information is provided through the spatial object. The newer ECDIS Glossary, page 5, definition is the same without the notation.

Section 57 defines "entity;" § 64, "feature object;" § 125, "object;" § 168, "spatial object."[638]

§ 74. *Geodetic data*

In UNCLOS analysis, "geodetic data" means parameters defining geodetic or astronomical reference systems and their mutual relations; horizontal, vertical and/or three dimensional coordinates of points

---

635 Noyes, *Treaty* 380–83, 2001–02 ABILA Proc. 189–93, responding to Walker, *Defining* 355–57, 2001–02 ABILA Proc. 162–65; *see also* Noyes, *Definitions* 314–16, responding to Walker, *Defining II* 205–08; Churchill & Hedley § 6, pp. 70–71.

636 *See also* Walker, *ECDIS Glossary* 228–31, 2003–04 ABILA Proc. 197–201.

637 *See* Parts III.B-III.D and § 132, defining "other rules of international law."

638 *See also* Walker, *ECDIS Glossary* 248–49, 2003–04 ABILA Proc. 220–21.

referred to such systems; observations of high precision from which such coordinates may be derived; ancillary data such as gravity, deflections of the vertical or geoid separation at points or areas referred to such systems.

Comment

In LOAC-governed situations under the "other rules of international law" clauses in UNCLOS, a different definition may apply. The same may be the situation if the UN Charter supersedes UNCLOS or if jus cogens norms apply.[639]

Consolidated Glossary ¶ 39 defines "geodetic data" as

> Parameters defining geodetic or astronomical reference systems and their mutual relations; horizontal, vertical and/or three dimensional coordinates of points referred to such systems; observations of high precision from which such coordinates may be derived; ancillary data such as gravity, deflections of the vertical or geoid separation at points or areas referred to such systems.

Former Consolidated Glossary ¶ 35 defined "geodetic data" as "[i]nformation concerning points established by a geodetic survey, such as descriptions for recovery, coordinate values, height above sea level and orientation."

UNCLOS Article 76(9) requires a coastal State to deposit with the UN Secretary-General charts and relevant information, including geodetic data, permanently describing the outer limits of its continental shelf. Although the term seems to appear only in UNCLOS Article 76(9), the § 72 definition is more inclusive, to take into account UNCLOS-related agreements that may use the term.

Section 9 defines "Area" and "area;" § 16, "basepoint" or "point;" § 23, "chart" or "nautical chart;" § 28, "coast;" § 31, "coastal State;" § 75, "geodetic datum;" § 125, "ocean space" or "sea." [640]

§ 75. *Geodetic datum*

In UNCLOS analysis, "geodetic datum" means the horizontal datum or horizontal reference datum. A datum defines the basis of a coordinate

---

[639] *See* Parts III.B-III.D and § 132, defining "other rules of international law."

[640] *See also* Churchill & Lowe 149–50; 2 Commentary ¶ 76.1–76.18(a), 76.18(*l*); NWP 1-14M Annotated ¶ 1.6; Noyes, *Definitions* 322–23 & Part III.D.3; Walker, *Consolidated Glossary* 258–59.

system. A local or regional geodetic datum is normally referred to an origin whose coordinates are defined. The datum is associated with a specific reference which best fits the surface (geoid) of the area of interest. A global geodic datum is now related to the center of the Earth's mass; its associated spheroid is a best fit to the known size and shape of the whole Earth.

Comment

In LOAC-governed situations under the "other rules of international law" clauses in UNCLOS, a different definition may apply. The same may be the situation if the UN Charter supersedes UNCLOS or if jus cogens norms apply.[641]

Consolidated Glossary ¶ 40 defines "geodetic datum:"

> A geodetic datum positions and orients a geodetic reference system in relation to the geoid and the astronomical reference system.
> A local or regional datum takes a reference ellipsoid to best fit the geoid in its (limited) area of interest and its origin of Cartesian coordinates will usually be displaced from the mass-center of the Earth — but, if well oriented, it will have its Cartesian axes parallel to those of the astronomical reference system.
>
> A global datum will normally take the most recent international geodetic reference system (currently GRS 80) — which is designed to best fit the global geoid, it will therefore seek to place its origin of Cartesian coordinates at the mass-center of the Earth, with its Cartesian axes well oriented.

Former Consolidated Glossary ¶ 36 defined "geodetic datum:"

> A datum defines the basis of a coordinate system. A local or regional geodetic datum is normally referred to an origin whose coordinates are defined. The datum is associated with a specific reference which best fits the surface (geoid) of the area of interest. A global geodic datum is now related to the center of the Earth's mass, and its associated spheroid is a best fit to the known size and shape of the whole Earth.

The Former Glossary also said: "[G]eodetic datum is also known as the horizontal datum or horizontal reference datum," commenting: "The position of a point common to two different surveys executed on different geodetic datums will be assigned two different sets of geographical coordinates. It is important, therefore, to know what geodetic

[641] *See* Parts III.B-III.D and § 132, defining "other rules of international law."

datum has been used when a position is defined[,]" and that "[t]he geodetic datum must be specified when lists of geographical coordinates are used to define the baselines and the limits of some zones of jurisdiction[,]" citing UNCLOS Articles 16(1), 47(8), 75(1) and 84(1).

The Committee decided to keep the definition in Former Glossary ¶ 36.

UNCLOS Article 16(1) refers to a list of geographical coordinates of points, which specify the geodetic datum, as an alternative for charts showing territorial sea baselines as stated in Articles 7, 9, 10, and lines of delimitation in Articles 12 and 15. Article 47(8) gives the same option for archipelagic baselines. Article 75(1) gives the same option for EEZ outer limit lines and lines of delimitation. Article 84(1) gives the same option for continental shelf outer limit lines and lines of delimitation.

In defining "basepoint" or "point," § 16 discusses baselines. Section 23 defines "chart" or "nautical chart;" § 74, "geodetic data; § 93, "line;" § 94, "line of delimitation;" § 176, "straight line, straight baseline, straight archipelagic baseline."[642]

§ 76. *Geographic coordinates, geographical coordinates, or coordinates*

(a) As used in UNCLOS Articles 16, 47, 75, 84 and 134, "geographical coordinates" most commonly means angular parameters of latitude and longitude that define the position of a point on the Earth's surface and which, in conjunction with a height, similarly define positions vertically above or below such a point. Latitude is expressed in degrees, minutes, and seconds, or decimals of a minute, from 0 degrees to 90 degrees north or south of the Equator. Lines or circles joining points of equal latitude are known as "parallels of latitude" or "parallels." Longitude is expressed in degrees, minutes and seconds or decimals of a minute, from 0 degrees to 180 degrees east or west of the Greenwich meridian. Lines joining points of equal longitude are known as "meridians." Rectangular geographical coordinates that are unambiguous, such as those on the Universal Transverse Mercator Grid (quoting the appropriate

---

[642] *See also* Churchill & Lowe ch. 2; 2 Commentary ¶¶ 16.1–16.8(b), 47.1–47.8, 47.9(m), 84.1–84.9(a); 2 O'Connell 635–37, 648–49; Walker, *Consolidated Glossary* 259–60.

zone number), Marsden Squares or Polar Grid Coordinates, may also be used under UNCLOS.

(b) "Geographic coordinates" is synonymous with "geographical coordinates."

(c) "Coordinates" as used in UNCLOS Annex III, Articles 8 and 17(2)(a), is synonymous with "geographical coordinates" or "geographic co-ordinates" found elsewhere in UNCLOS.

Comment

In LOAC-governed situations under the "other rules of international law" clauses in UNCLOS, a different definition may apply. The same may be the situation if the UN Charter supersedes UNCLOS or if jus cogens norms apply.[643]

Consolidated Glossary ¶ 42 defines "geographical coordinates" as "Angular parameters of latitude and longitude which define the position of a point on the Earth's surface and which, in conjunction with a height, similarly define positions vertically above or below such a point." Former Glossary ¶ 37 defined "geographical coordinates" as "[u]nits of latitude and longitude which define the position of a point on the Earth's surface with respect to the ellipsoid of reference."

Consolidated Glossary ¶ 88 and Former Glossary ¶ 79 say that "[t]he most common system of co-ordinates are those of latitude and longitude, although rectangular co-ordinates on the Universal Transverse Mercator Grid (quoting the appropriate zone number), Marsden Squares, Polar Grid Co-ordinates, etc. are also unambiguous."

Consolidated Glossary ¶ 42 and Former Glossary ¶ 37 note that latitude is expressed in degrees, minutes and seconds or decimals of a minute, from 0 degrees to 90 degrees north or south of the Equator. Lines or circles joining points of equal latitude are known as "parallels of latitude" or "parallels." Longitude is expressed in degrees, minutes and seconds or decimals of a minute, from 0 degrees to 180 degrees east or west of the Greenwich meridian. Lines joining points of equal longitude are known as "meridians."

Sections 90 and 97 define "latitude" and "longitude."

UNCLOS Article 16(1) refers to a list of geographical coordinates of points, which specify the geodetic datum, as an alternative for charts

[643] *See* Parts III.B-III.D and § 132, defining "other rules of international law;" *see also* DOD Dictionary 127, 228.

showing territorial sea baselines as stated in Articles 7, 9, 10, and lines of delimitation in Articles 12 and 15. Article 16(2) requires a coastal State to give these lists of geographical coordinates due publicity and to deposit a copy of each list with the UN Secretary-General. Articles 47(8) and 47(9) offer the same option and impose the same requirements for archipelagic baselines. Article 75 offers the same option and imposes the same requirements for EEZ outer limit lines and lines of delimitation. Article 84 offers the same option and imposes the same requirements for continental shelf outer limit lines and lines of delimitation. Article 134(3) refers to Articles 1(1)(1) and 84 and governs deposit of and publicity for lists with respect to the Area. UNCLOS Annex III, Articles 8 and 17(2)(a) refer to the unmodified word "coordinates," although the context strongly suggests that "geographic coordinates" are meant.

Section 16 defines "basepoint" or "point" and discusses baselines; § 23, "chart" or "nautical chart;" § 28, "coast;" § 31, "coastal State;" § 75, "geodetic datum;" § 93, "line;" § 176, "straight line; straight baseline; straight archipelagic baseline."[644]

§ 77. *Geographical coordinates*

See "Geographic coordinates," § 76.

§ 78. *Geometric primitive*

In UNCLOS analysis, "geometric primitive" means one of the three basic geometric units of representation: area, line and point.

Comment

In LOAC-governed situations under the "other rules of international law" clauses in UNCLOS, a different definition may apply. The same may be the situation if the UN Charter supersedes UNCLOS or if jus cogens norms apply.[645]

Former ECDIS Glossary, page 11, defined "geometric primitive" as "[o]ne of the three basic geometric units of representation: *point,*

---

[644] *See also* Churchill & Lowe ch. 2; 2 Commentary ¶¶ 16.1–16.8(e), 47.1–47.8, 47.9(m), 75.1–75.5(d), 84.1–84.9(c); DOD Dictionary 127, 228; Restatement (Third) § 511; Walker, *Consolidated Glossary* 259–60.

[645] *See* Parts III.B-III.D and § 132, defining "other rules of international law."

line and *area*." The newer ECDIS Glossary, page 5, definition is the same.

Section 9 defines "Area" and "area;" § 16, "basepoint or point;" § 93, "line;" § 94, "line of delimitation;" § 176, "straight line, straight baseline, straight archipelagic baseline."[646]

§ 79. *Harbor works; facility (port)*

As used in UNCLOS Article 11, "harbor works" or "port facility" means permanent human-made structures built along the coast which form an integral part of the harbor system such as jetties, moles, quays, or other port facilities, coastal terminals, wharves, piers, breakwaters, sea walls, etc.

Comment

In LOAC-governed situations under the "other rules of international law" clauses in UNCLOS, a different definition may apply. The same may be the situation if the UN Charter supersedes UNCLOS or if jus cogens norms apply.[647]

Consolidated Glossary ¶ 44 and Former Glossary ¶ 38 define "harbor works" as "[p]ermanent man-made structures built along the coast which form an integral part of the harbor system such as jetties, moles, quays, or other port facilities, coastal terminals, wharves, breakwaters, sea walls, etc."[648] "Port facility" has the same meaning.

UNCLOS Article 11 says that for delimiting the territorial sea, "the outermost permanent harbor works which form an integral part of the harbor system are regarded as forming part of the coast. Offshore installations and artificial islands shall not be considered as permanent harbor works." Territorial Sea Convention Article 8 says that for delimiting the territorial sea, "the outermost permanent harbor works which form an integral part of the harbor system shall be regarded as forming

---

[646] *See also* Churchill & Lowe chs. 2, 12; Walker, *ECDIS Glossary* 249, 2003–04 ABILA Proc. 221.

[647] *See* Parts III.B-III.D and § 132, defining "other rules of international law."

[648] *Accord,* 2 Commentary ¶ 11.5(c). DOD Dictionary 447 defines "quay" as "A structure of solid construction along a shore or bank that provides berthing and generally provides cargo-handling facilities. A similar facility of open construction is called a wharf." *Id.* 595 defines "wharf" as "A structure built of open rather than solid construction along a shore or a bank that provides cargo-handling facilities. A similar facility of solid construction is called a quay."

part of the coast." As Section 16 demonstrates, territorial sea baselines anchored in coastal points are the predicate for delimiting, *e.g.*, the contiguous zone, the EEZ and the continental shelf.[649]

In defining "basepoint" and "point," § 16 discusses baselines. Section 3 defines "aid(s) to navigation, navigational aid(s), facility (navigational);" § 28, "coast;" § 31, "coastal State;" § 93, "line;" § 176, "straight line, straight baseline, straight archipelagic baseline."[650]

§ 80. *Heading*

In UNCLOS analysis, "heading" means the direction in which a vessel is pointed, expressed as an angular distance from north clockwise through 360 degrees; it is a constantly changing value as a vessel yaws across its course due to the effects of sea, wind, etc.

Comment

In LOAC-governed situations under the "other rules of international law" clauses in UNCLOS, a different definition may apply. The same may be the situation if the UN Charter supersedes UNCLOS or if jus cogens norms apply.[651]

Former ECDIS Glossary, page 11, defined "heading" as "[t]he direction in which a vessel is pointed, expressed as an angular distance from north clockwise through 360 degrees. A constantly changing value as a

[649] *See also* Consolidated Glossary 62.

[650] *See also* Churchill & Lowe 47–48, 51; 2 Commentary ¶¶ 11.1–11.5(d); DOD Dictionary 18 ("air facility" is "An installation from which air operations may be or are being conducted"), 199 ("facility" is a "real property entity consisting of one or more of the following: a building, a structure, a utility system, pavement, and underlying land"), 237 ("harbor" is "A restricted body of water, an anchorage, or other limited coastal water area and its mineable approaches, from which shipping operations are projected or supported. Generally, a harbor is part of a base, in which case the harbor defense force forms a component element of the base defense force established for the local defense of the base and its included harbor."), 550 ("terminal" is "A facility designed to transfer cargo from one means of conveyance to another. [Conveyance is the piece of equipment used to transport cargo, *i.e.*, railcar to truck or truck to truck. This is as opposed to mode, which is the type of equipment.])," 551 ("terminal operations" means "The reception, processing, and staging of passengers; the receipt, transit, storage, and marshalling of cargo; and the manifesting and forwarding of cargo and passengers to destination"), 592 ("water terminal" means "A facility for berthing ships simultaneously at piers, quays, and/or working anchorages, normally located within sheltered coastal waters adjacent to rail, highway, air, and/or inland water transportation networks"); NWP 1-14M Annotated ¶ 1.3.6; 1 O'Connell 385; Restatement (Third) §§ 511-12; Roach & Smith ¶ 4.4.3; Walker, *Consolidated Glossary* 262–63.

[651] *See* Parts III.B-III.D and § 132, defining "other rules of international law."

vessel yaws back and forth across the course due to the effects of sea, wind, etc." "[B]ack and forth" following "yaws" is redundant and has been deleted from the definition above. When a vessel yaws, it moves laterally back and forth from its course and heading. The newer ECDIS Glossary does not define "heading."

Section 41 defines "course;" § 42, "course made good;" § 43, "course over ground;" § 126, "ocean space" or "sea;" § 163, "ship" or "vessel."[652]

§ 81. *High seas*

In UNCLOS analysis, "high seas" means all parts of the surface and water column of ocean space or the sea that are not included in the territorial sea or in the internal waters of a State. The exclusive economic zone is sui generis but is part of the high seas with respect to high seas freedoms, including those UNCLOS Article 87 does not name specifically.

Comment

In LOAC-governed situations under the "other rules of international law" clauses in UNCLOS, a different definition may apply. The same may be the situation if the UN Charter supersedes UNCLOS or if jus cogens norms apply.[653]

UNCLOS often refers to the high seas, but the Convention does not define the term. The High Seas Convention, Article 1, defines "high seas" as meaning "all parts of the sea that are not included in the territorial sea or in the internal waters of a State." Commentators have said that "Given the emphasis in [UNCLOS] on establishing functional regimes for different maritime areas. it became unnecessary to include a formal definition of the 'high seas.' "[654]

Articles 86-120, UNCLOS Part VII, recite general provisions governing the high seas and rules for conserving and managing high seas living resources.

---

[652] *See also* Walker, *ECDIS Glossary* 249–50, 2003–04 ABILA Proc. 221–22. DOD Dictionary 601 defines "yaw": "1. The rotation of an aircraft, ship, or missile about its vertical axis so as to cause the longitudinal axis of the aircraft, ship, or missile to deviate from the flight line or heading in its horizontal plane. 2. Angle between the longitudinal axis of a projectile at any moment and the tangent to the trajectory in the corresponding point of flight of the projectile."

[653] *See* Parts III.B-III.D and § 130, defining "other rules of international law."

[654] 3 Commentary ¶ 86.11(a) (footnote omitted).

Article 86 says that Part VII's provisions apply to all parts of the sea not included in a State's EEZ, territorial sea or internal waters, or in an archipelagic State's archipelagic waters. Article 86 does not entail abridging freedoms all States enjoy in the EEZ under UNCLOS Article 58.[655] Article 58(1) declares that in the EEZ all States enjoy, subject to relevant provisions of the Convention, high seas freedoms of navigation, overflight and laying of submarine cables and pipelines, "and other internationally lawful uses of the sea related to these freedoms, such as those associated with the operation of ships, aircraft and submarine cables and pipelines, and compatible with the other provisions of" UNCLOS. Article 58(2) declares that UNCLOS Articles 88-115, "and other pertinent rules of international law," apply to the EEZ insofar as they are not incompatible with UNCLOS Articles 55-75, *i.e.*, the UNCLOS rules for the EEZ. Article 58(3) requires States in exercising rights and duties under the Convention to "have due regard to the rights and duties of the coastal State and shall comply with the laws and regulations adopted by the coastal state in accordance with the provisions of [UNCLOS] and other rules of international law in so far as they are not incompatible with [Articles 55-75]."[656]

Article 87 declares that "The high seas are open to all States, whether coastal or land-locked.[657] Freedom of the high seas is exercised under

[655] UNCLOS arts. 55–75 govern the EEZ; *id.* arts. 2–33, the territorial sea and contiguous zone; *id.* art. 8, territorial waters; *id.* arts. 46–54, archipelagic States and archipelagic waters.

[656] *See also* 3 Commentary ¶¶ 86.11(b)–86.11(c); Restatement (Third) § 514(2). International Committee on the Exclusive Economic Zone, *The Freedom of the High Seas and the Exclusive Economic Zone*, International Law Association, Report of the Sixty-First Conference Held at Paris: August 26th to September 1st, 1984, at 183, 193, 194–95 (1985) concluded that

> it is extremely difficult to sustain the thesis that the Exclusive Economic Zone is part of the high seas. The words "specific legal regime" could only mean that whatever may be the legal regime of the Exclusive Economic Zone it is different from both the territorial sea and from the high seas. It is a zone which partakes of the characteristics of both regimes but belongs to neither.

See also Churchill & Lowe ch. 9. However, 3 Commentary ¶¶ 86.11(b)–86.11(c), referring to *id.* ¶¶ VII.6–VII.7, comes to a different conclusion, agreeing with the ILA Committee that although the EEZ is sui generis, the EEZ is part of the high seas with respect to high seas freedoms, including those not named specifically in UNCLOS art. 87(1). *See also* UNCLOS art. 58; 2 Commentary ¶¶ 58.1–58.10(e). The *Report* takes no position on the issue, which continues to divide States and commentators. *See, e.g.*, Churchill & Lowe 170–76.

[657] UNCLOS art. 124(1)(a) defines "land-locked State" as a State that has no sea coast. Section 31 defines "coastal State."

the conditions laid down by this Convention and by other rules of international law." Freedom of the high seas

> comprises, *inter alia*, both for coastal and land-locked States:
> (a) freedom of navigation;
> (b) freedom of overflight;
> (c) freedom to lay submarine cables and pipelines, subject to Part VI[, Articles 76-85, related to the continental shelf];
> (d) freedom to construct artificial islands and other installations permitted under international law, subject to Part VI [Articles 76-85, related to the continental shelf];
> (e) freedom of fishing, subject to section 2 [Articles 116-20, dealing with high seas fishing];
> (f) freedom of scientific research, subject to Parts VI and XIII [Articles 76-85, 238-65, related to the continental shelf and marine scientific research].

All States must exercise high seas freedoms "with due regard for" other States' interests in their exercise of high seas freedoms, "and also with due regard for" rights under UNCLOS for Area activities. High Seas Convention Article 2 recites a shorter nonexclusive list of high seas freedoms, the "other rules of international law" derogation, and an analogous "reasonable regard" principle.[658]

Article 88 declares that "The high seas shall be reserved for peaceful purposes."[659] Under Article 89, which follows High Seas Convention Article 2, no State "may validly purport to subject any part of the high seas to its sovereignty."[660] UNCLOS Article 90, echoing High Seas Convention Article 4, declares that all States, coastal or land-locked, may sail ships flying their flags on the high seas.[661]

Articles 91-94 lay down rules for ships' nationality, jurisdiction over ships flagged under a State, ships flagged under two or more States, special rules for ships operating under the UN, its specialized agencies or the IAEA, and flag State duties.[662] Articles 95-96, echoing High Seas

---

[658] *See also* 3 Commentary ¶¶ 87.1–87.2, 87.9(a)–87.9(m); Restatement (Third) § 521.

[659] *See also* 3 Commentary ¶ 88.1, referring to UNCLOS, pmbl.'s reference to "peaceful uses of the seas and oceans;" *id.* ¶¶ 88.7(a)–88.7(d); Restatement (Third) § 521 cmt. b; Parts III.B-III.D and § 132, defining "other sources of international law," and further analysis of "peaceful purposes."

[660] *See also* 3 Commentary ¶¶ 89.1, 89.9(a)–89.9(d); Restatement (Third) § 521.

[661] *See also* 3 Commentary ¶¶ 90.1–90.2, 90.8(a)–90.8(d).

[662] *Compare* High Seas Convention arts. 5–7; *see also* § 130, defining "flag State."

Convention articles 8-9, declare the rules that warships, or ships owned or operated by a State and used only on government non-commercial service on the high seas have complete immunity from the jurisdiction of any State other than the flag State.[663] UNCLOS Article 97 recites rules for penal jurisdiction or other navigational incidents on the high seas.[664] Article 98, similar to High Seas Convention Article 12, declares duties for rendering high seas assistance.[665] UNCLOS Articles 99-109 recite rules related to transport of slaves, piracy on the high seas, drug shipments and unauthorized broadcasting from the high seas.[666] Article 110 states the approach and visit rules for the high seas, and Article 111 declares rules for hot pursuit and can be compared with High Seas Convention Articles 22-23.[667] UNCLOS Articles 112-15, like High Seas Convention Articles 26-29, recite submarine cable and pipeline rules.[668]

Article § 116, echoing Article 87(1)(e), declares that all States have the right for their nationals to fish on the high seas, but this right is qualified by those States' treaty obligations, rights and duties as well as the interests of coastal States "provided for, *inter alia,* in [UNCLOS A] rticle 63[2], ... and [A]rticles 64 to 67; and the provisions of [Articles 116-20]." Article 63(2) regulates fish stocks within a coastal State's EEZ "and in an area beyond and adjacent to the zone ..." Articles 64-67 state rules for highly migratory species, marine mammals and anadromous stocks, *i.e.,* fish stocks that spend part of their lives in rivers. The rest of Part VII, § 2, Articles 117-20, declares rules for States' duties

---

663 *See also* 3 Commentary ¶¶ 95.1–95.2, 95.6(a)–95.6(c), 96.1, 96.10(a)–96.10(d); Restatement (Third) § 522.

664 *Compare* High Seas Convention art. 11; International Convention for the Unification of Certain Rules Relating to Penal Jurisdiction in Matters of Collision or Other Incidents of Navigation, May 10, 1952, 439 UNTS 233; *see also* 3 Commentary ¶¶ 97.1–97.2, 97.8(a)–97.8(d).

665 *See also* 3 Commentary ¶¶ 98.1 (general customary rule), 98.11(a)–98.11(g).

666 Apart from no provision for unauthorized high seas broadcasting or seizure of drugs, High Seas Convention arts. 13–21 recite the same or similar rules. *See also* 3 Commentary ¶¶ 99.1–99.2, 99.6(a)–99.6(c), 100.1–100.2, 100.7(a)–100.7(d), 101.1, 101.8(a)–101.8(I), 102.1, 102.6(a), 103.1–103.2, 103.5(a)–103.5(c), 104.1–104.2, 104.5(a)–104.5(c), 105.1–105.2, 105.10(a)–105.10(c), 106.1–106.2, 106.6(a)–106.6(c), 107.1–107.2, 107.7(a)–107.7(d), 108.1, 108.8(a)–108.8(c), 109.1–109.2, 109.8(a)–109.8(f).

667 *See also* 3 Commentary ¶¶ 110.1–110.2, 110.11(a)–110.11(h); 111.1–111.2, 111.9(a)–111.9(I); Restatement (Third) §§ 513, cmt. g; 522.

668 *See also* 3 Commentary ¶¶ 112.1–112.2, 112.8(a)–112.8(d); 113.1–113.2, 113.7(a)–113.7(e); 114.1–114.2, 114.7(a)–114.7(c), 115.1–115.2, 115.7(a)–115.7(d); Part IV.B, § 179, "submarine cable;" § 181, "submarine pipeline."

with respect to their nationals for conserving high seas living resources, States' cooperation in high seas living resources conservation and management, and high seas conservation and management of marine mammals under Article 65.[669]

Other UNCLOS provisions relate to its high seas regime.

Article 135 declares that nothing in Part XI, *i.e.*, Articles 133-91, which along with the 1994 Agreement deals with the Area, "nor any rights granted or exercised pursuant thereto [*i.e.*, pursuant to Part XI] shall affect the legal status of the waters superjacent to the Area or that of the air space above those waters."[670]

UNCLOS continental shelf provisions do not refer to the high seas. However, when the basic definition of the continental shelf in Article 76(1), *i.e.*, the seabed and subsoil of submarine areas beyond a coastal State's territorial waters, is combined with Articles 87(1)(c), 87(1)(d), 87(1)(f), and these rules in Article 78, it is clear that the UNCLOS continental shelf regime does not affect the sea surface or the water column above the continental shelf:

1. The rights of the coastal State over the continental shelf do not affect the legal status of the superjacent waters or of the air space above those waters.
2. The exercise of the rights of the coastal State over the continental shelf must not infringe or result in any unjustifiable interference with navigation and other rights and freedoms of other States as provided in this Convention.

These provisions follow Continental Shelf Convention Articles 1 and 3, as well as UNCLOS Article 135, dealing with the legal status of the water column and sea surface in the Area.[671]

UNCLOS provisions deal with routes to or from the high seas.

UNCLOS Article 7(6) provides that a State may not apply a straight baseline system in such a manner as to cut off another State's territorial sea from the high seas or an EEZ; Territorial Sea Convention Article 4(5) is the same with respect to the territorial sea but does not cover an EEZ.[672]

---

[669] Fishing Convention arts. 1–14 might be compared. *See also* 3 Commentary ¶¶ 116.1–116.2, 116.9(a)–116.9(g), 117.1–117.2, 117.9(a)–117.9(c), 118.1–118.2, 118.7(a)–118.7(g), 119.1, 119.7(a)–119.7(e), 120.1, 120.5(a)–120.5(d).

[670] *See also* 3 Commentary ¶ 86.11(d).

[671] *See also* 2 Commentary ¶¶ 76.1–76.2, 76.18(a)–76.18(b), 78.1–78.2, 78.8(a)–78.8(d), 3 *id.* 86.11(d); Restatement (Third) § 515(2).

[672] *See also* 2 Commentary ¶¶ 7.9(h)–7.9(I).

UNCLOS Article 36 declares that Articles 34-45 do not apply to a strait used for international navigation if a route through the high seas or through an EEZ "of similar convenience" exists with respect to navigational and hydrographic characteristics. In this case other relevant Parts of UNCLOS, including provisions related to navigation and overflight, apply.[673] The UNCLOS straits transit passage regime, Articles 37-44, applies to straits used for international navigation between one part of the high seas or an EEZ and another part of the high seas or an EEZ, according to Article 37.[674] Article 38(1) declares that in straits covered by Article 37 all ships and aircraft enjoy the right of transit passage,

> which shall not be impeded; except that, if the strait is formed by an island of a State bordering the strait and its mainland, transit passage shall not apply if there exists seaward of the island a route through the high seas or ... an [EEZ] ... of similar convenience with respect to navigational and hydrographical characteristics.

Article 38(2) defines transit passage:

> the exercise in accordance with [Articles 34-45] ... of the freedom of navigation and overflight solely for the purpose of continuous and expeditious transit of the strait between one part of the high seas or an [EEZ] ... and another part of the high seas [or an EEZ]. ... However, ... continuous and expeditious transit does not preclude passage through the strait for ... entering, leaving or returning from a State bordering the strait, subject to the conditions of entry to that State.[675]

Article 45(1)(b), dealing with straits between a part of the high seas or an EEZ and the territory of a foreign State, declares that the right of innocent passage as recited in Articles 17-32 applies to these straits used for international navigation. Territorial Convention Article 16(4), without differentiating among different kinds of straits, declares: "There shall be no suspension of the innocent passage of foreign straits which are used for international navigation between one part of the high seas and another part of the high seas or the territorial sea of a foreign state."[676]

UNCLOS Article 47(5) declares that archipelagic baselines may not be applied by an archipelagic State, defined in Article 46(a), so as to cut

---

673 *See also id.* ¶¶ 36.1, 36.7(a)–36.7(e).

674 *See also id.* ¶¶ 37.1, 37.7(a)–37.7(c).

675 *See also id.* ¶¶ 38.1, 38.8(a)–38.8(f).

676 *See also id.* ¶¶ 45.1–45.2, 45.8(a)–45.8(c).

off another State's territorial sea from the high seas or the EEZ. Article 53(3) defines archipelagic sea lanes passage as the exercise, in accordance with UNCLOS, "of the rights of navigation and overflight in the normal mode solely for … continuous, expeditious and unobstructed transit between one part of the high seas or an [EEZ] … and another part of the high seas or an [EEZ] …"[677]

UNCLOS Article 125(1) guarantees land-locked States right of access to and from the sea for exercising Convention rights, "including those relating to the freedom of the high seas and the common heritage of mankind. To this end, land-locked States shall enjoy freedom of transit through the territory of transit States by all means of transport."[678]

The definition of high seas used here follows High Seas Convention Article 1, substituting "the surface and water column of ocean space or the sea and airspace above this surface" for "the sea" to make it clear that exceptions in § 126 for "ocean space or the sea" do not apply. The last sentence declares that the EEZ, although sui generis, is part of the high seas with respect to high seas freedoms, including those not named specifically in UNCLOS Article 87.

In defining "basepoint" and "point," § 16 discusses baselines. Section 9 defines "area" and "Area;"; § 10, "artificial island;" § 28, "coast;" § 31, "coastal State;" § 34, "common heritage of mankind" or "common heritage of humankind;" § 56, "due regard;" § 66, "flag State;" § 72, "genuine link;" § 83, "hydrographic survey;" § 93, "line;" § 100, "marine scientific research;" § 126, "ocean space or sea;" § 132, "other rules of international law;" § 143, "river;" § 176, "straight line, straight baseline, straight archipelagic baseline;" § 177, "strait, straits;"§ 179, "submarine cable;" § 181, "submarine pipeline;" § 185, "superjacent waters" or "water column."[679]

---

[677] *See also id.* ¶¶ 46.1, 46.6(a), 47.1, 47.9(g), 53.1, 53.9(c)–53.9(f).

[678] UNCLOS arts. 124(1)(b) defines "transit State" as "a State, with or without a seacoast, situated between a land-locked State and the sea, through whose territory traffic in transit passes." *Id.* art. 124(1)(c) defines "traffic in transit;" *id.* art. 124(1)(d) defines "means of transport." Section 31 defines "coastal State." The High Seas Convention art. 3 regime is different and relies on required agreements between a coastal State and a landlocked State. *See also* 3 Commentary ¶¶ 124.1, 124.8(a), 124.8(c)–124.8(e), 125.1–125.2, 125.9(a)–125.9(e).

[679] *See also* 2007–08 ABILA Proc. 250–58; NWP 1-14M Annotated ¶¶ 1.5–1.5.3; 2 O'Connell chs. 21, 23.3, 24.A.2, 24.C. "High seas" can have a different municipal law definition. *See, e.g.*, State v. Jack, 125 P.3d 311, 315–16 (Alaska 2005) (high seas, for U.S. state statute's purposes, includes foreign territorial waters, inter alia citing

§ 82. *Historic bay*

As used in UNCLOS Article 10(6), "historic bay" means a bay over which a coastal State has publicly claimed and exercised jurisdiction, and this jurisdiction has been acquiesced in by other States. Historic bays need not meet requirements prescribed in the UNCLOS Article 10(2) definition of "bay."

Comment

In LOAC-governed situations under the "other rules of international law" clauses in UNCLOS, a different definition may apply. The same may be the situation if the UN Charter supersedes UNCLOS or if jus cogens norms apply.[680]

The § 82 definition appears to follow the U.S. position, discussed below, shortening "open, effective, long term, and continuous exercise of authority" to "publicly claimed and exercised" and otherwise following the Glossary formulation. Other States may have different views. Given continuing controversy over certain water areas' eligibility for historic bay status, the definition does not list historic bays.

Consolidated Glossary ¶ 45 refers to UNCLOS Article 10(6), saying UNCLOS has not defined the term; "[h]istoric bays need not meet the requirements prescribed in the definition of 'bay' ... in [UNCLOS] Art. 10.2." Former Glossary ¶ 39 defined "historic bay" as "those [bays] over which the coastal State has publicly claimed and exercised jurisdiction[,] and this jurisdiction has been accepted by other States. Historic bays need not meet the requirements prescribed in the definition of "bay" contained in [UNCLOS,] article 10(2)."

UNCLOS Articles 10(1)-10(5) establish rules for bays belonging to a single State. If a bay as defined in UNCLOS has a closing line of a distance not exceeding 24 nautical miles between two low-water marks, a closing line may be drawn between two low-water marks; waters thus enclosed are considered internal waters under Article 10(4). Under Article 2(1) internal waters are part of a coastal State's sovereign territory. If the distance between the low-water marks is more than 24 nautical miles, Article 10(5) requires that a straight

U.S. case law). DOD Dictionary 396 defines "open ocean" as "Ocean limit defined as greater than 12 nautical miles (nm) from shore, as compared with high seas that are over 200 nm from shore."

680 *See* Parts III.B-III.D and § 132, defining "other rules of international law."

baseline of 24 nautical miles must be drawn within the bay to enclose the maximum area of water with a line of that length. Territorial Sea Convention Articles 1(1), 7(1)-7(5) recite the same rules.[681]

UNCLOS Article 10(6) and Territorial Sea Convention Article 7(6) say the "foregoing provisions do not apply to so-called 'historic bays,' or in any case where the system of straight baselines provided for in [UNCLOS Article 7, Territorial Sea Convention Article 4] is applied." UNCLOS Article 15, providing rules for opposite and adjacent territorial seas, excepts from its application "where it is necessary by reason of historic title or other special circumstances to delimit the territorial sea of the two States in a way that is at variance therewith." Territorial Sea Convention Article 12(1) has a similar exception.

UNCLOS Article 298(1)(a) allows a State signing, ratifying or acceding to the Convention, "or at any time thereafter … without prejudice to the obligations" under Articles 279-85, to declare it does not accept the UNCLOS compulsory dispute resolution procedures, Articles 286-96, with respect to disputes concerning interpretation of Article 15 relating to sea boundary delimitations or those involving historic bays or titles. After UNCLOS is in force for a State, a declaring State must submit to UNCLOS Annex V § 2 conciliation unless it reaches agreement with States concerned. After conciliators report, States parties must reach agreement based on the report. If there is no agreement, the States must submit the question to an Article 286-96 dispute resolution procedure, unless they otherwise agree. The Article 298 procedure does not apply if settlement methods under a binding bilateral or multilateral agreement are in force.

What are "historic bays" has been a subject of controversy; the UNCLOS Article 298(1) exception for them and historic title cases illustrates the issue's sensitivity. U.S. policy is that

> To meet the international standard for establishing a claim to a historic bay, a nation must demonstrate its open, effective, long term, and continuous exercise of authority over the bay, coupled with acquiescence by foreign nations in the exercise of that authority. The United States has taken the position that an actual showing of acquiescence by foreign nations in such a claim is required, as opposed to a mere absence of opposition.[682]

---

[681] For commentary and illustrations, *see* NWP 1–14 Annotated ¶ 1.3.3 & Figs. 1-2 - 1-4.

[682] *Id.* ¶ 1.3.3.1, inter alia citing Assistant Legal Adviser for Ocean Affairs Bernard H. Oxman, Sept. 17, 1973 memorandum, Law of the Sea and International Waterways,

Other countries' policies may be different. Controversial historic bay claims include Argentina's and Uruguay's for Rio de la Plata; Australia's for Anxious Bay, Encounter Bay, Lacepede Bay and Rivoli Bay; Cambodia's for the Gulf of Thailand; Canada's for Hudson Bay; India and Sri Lanka's for Palk Bay and the Gulf of Manaar; Italy's for the Gulf of Taranto; Libya's for the Gulf of Sidra (Sirte); Panama's for the Gulf of Panama; the Gulf of Riga and Peter the Great Bay; and Vietnam's for the Gulfs of Tonkin and Thailand.[683]

Section 2 defines "adjacent coasts;" 28, "coast;" 31, "coastal State;" § 93, "line;" § 98, "low water line or low water mark;" § 107, "mouth" (of a bay); § 130, "opposite coasts;" § 176, "straight line, straight baseline, straight archipelagic baseline."[684]

§ 83. *Hydrographic survey*

(a) In UNCLOS analysis, "hydrographic survey" means the science of measuring and depicting those parameters necessary to describe the precise nature and configuration of the seabed and coastal strip, its geographical relationship to the land mass, and the characteristics and dynamics of the sea. Hydrographic surveys are among the "surveys" UNCLOS Articles 19(2)(j), 21(1)(g), 40, 45, 54 and 121(2) contemplate.

(b) Hydrographic surveys may be necessary to determine the features that constitute baselines or basepoints and their geographical position.

Comment

In LOAC-governed situations under the "other rules of international law" clauses in UNCLOS, a different definition may apply. The same

---

1973 Digest § 2, at 244 (1974) (U.S. historic bays position); L.F.E. Goldie, *Historic Bays in International Law — An Impressionistic Overview*, 11 Syracuse J. Int'l L. & Com. 205, 221–23, 248, 259 (1984); United States v. Alaska, 422 U.S. 184, 200 (1975). Fisheries (U.K. v. Norway), 1951 ICJ 116, 138–39 would say toleration is sufficient; *see also* United States v. Alaska, 521 U.S. 1, 11 (1997); United States v. Maine, 475 U.S. 89, 95 n.10 (1986); United States v. Louisiana, 470 U.S. 93, 101–02 (1985); Churchill & Lowe 41–46; 2 Commentary ¶¶ 10.1–10.6; 1 O'Connell chs. 9A, 10–11; 2 *id.*, pp. 647–48; Restatement (Third) § 511, cmt. f & r.n.5; Roach & Smith ch. 3, ¶¶ 4.5–4.5.2.

683 Churchill & Lowe 44–45; NWP 1-14 Annotated ¶ 1.3.3.1 n.23 & Table A1-14; Roach & Smith §§ 3.3-3.3.10. References in these sources discuss claims of the former USSR with respect to the Gulf of Riga and Peter the Great Bay. Since 1991 and the Soviet Union's dissolution, the claimant States have changed.

684 *See also* 2007–08 ABILA Proc. 258–60; Walker, *Consolidated Glossary* 263–65.

may be the situation if the UN Charter supersedes UNCLOS or if jus cogens norms apply.[685]

Consolidated Glossary ¶ 46 and Former Glossary ¶ 40 define "hydrographic survey" as "[t]he science of measuring and depicting those parameters necessary to describe the precise nature and configuration of the seabed and coastal strip, its geographical relationship to the land mass, and the characteristics and dynamics of the sea." The Glossary adds: "Hydrographic surveys may be necessary to determine the features that constitute baselines or basepoints and their geographical position."

UNCLOS Article 19(2)(j) says that a foreign ship's passage is considered prejudicial to coastal State peace, good order or security, *i.e.*, it is not innocent passage, if it engages in carrying out "research" (otherwise not qualified) or "survey" (also otherwise not qualified) activities in the territorial sea. Article 21(1)(g) provides that a coastal State may adopt laws and regulations, in conformity with UNCLOS relating to innocent passage through the territorial sea and for MSR and hydrographic surveys. In other words, a coastal State may allow hydrographic surveys in its territorial sea pursuant to UNCLOS; if there are no coastal State laws or regulations governing these surveys, conducting them violates the UNCLOS innocent passage regime. Article 121(2) incorporates the territorial sea regime by reference for islands. Territorial Sea Convention Article 14 has no specific prohibition on surveys during innocent passage. Article 14(4) says "[p]assage is innocent so long as it is not prejudicial to the peace, good order or security of the coastal State. Such passage shall take place in conformity with [Articles 14-23] and other rules of international law." Article 17 requires foreign ships in innocent passage to comply with laws and regulations of the coastal State in conformity with Articles 14-23 and other rules of international law and, in particular, with laws and regulations relating to transport and navigation. Article 21 applies these rules to government ships operated for commercial purposes. As to government ships operated for non-commercial purposes, Article 22(1) applies these rules as well, but Article 22(2) says that with exceptions in Articles 21 and 22(1), nothing in Articles 14-23 affects immunities that government non-commercial ships enjoy under Articles

[685] *See* Parts III.B-III.D and § 132, defining "other rules of international law."

14-23 or other rules of international law. Article 10(2) says an island's territorial sea is measured by Articles 1-13.[686]

UNCLOS Article 40 forbids MSR and hydrographic survey activities during straits transit passage without prior authorization of States bordering straits. Article 45 imposes an innocent passage regime on straits covered by Article 38(1) and straits between a part of the high seas or an EEZ and a foreign State's territorial sea, thereby incorporating Articles 19(2)(j) and 21(1)(g) by reference. Article 54 incorporates Article 40 by reference for archipelagic sea lanes passage, thereby forbidding hydrographic survey activity during archipelagic sea lanes passage without the archipelagic State's prior authorization. Territorial Sea Convention Article 16(4) says the innocent passage regime for straits used for international navigation between one part of the high seas and another part of the high seas or the territorial sea of a foreign State may not be suspended.

UNCLOS Annex III, Article 17(2)(b)(ii), governing rules, regulations, and procedures for exercise of the Authority's functions in the Area, says that these rules, regulations and procedures must fully reflect objective criteria, inter alia, for duration of exploration operations to permit a thorough survey of a specific area.

Section 16 defines "basepoint" or "point" while discussing baselines. Section 28 defines "coast;" § 31, "coastal State;" § 93, "line;" § 132, "other rules of international law;" § 157, "sea-bed," "seabed" or "bed;" § 163, "ship" or "vessel;" § 176, "straight line, straight baseline, straight archipelagic baseline."[687]

§ 84. *Indicator*

In UNCLOS analysis, "indicator" means visual indication giving information about the condition of a system or equipment.

---

[686] *See also* Consolidated Glossary 63.

[687] *See also* Joint Statement, note 484, ¶ 3; Churchill & Lowe 108, 127, 404–05; 2 Commentary ¶ 19.1–19.9, 19.10(j), 19.11, 21.1–21.11(a), 21.11(d), 40.1–40.9(d), 45.1–45.8(c), 54.1–54.7(b); 3 *id.* ¶¶ 121.1–121.11, 121-12(b); DOD Dictionary 250 ("hydrographic reconnaissance" is "Reconnaissance of an area of water to determine depths, beach gradients, the nature of the bottom, and the location of coral reefs, rocks, shoals, and manmade obstacles"); NWP 1–14M Annotated ¶¶ 2.3.2–2.3.2.4, 2.3.3–2.3.3.2, 2.3.4.2, 2.4.2.1–2.4.3; 1 O'Connell ch. 7; 2 *id.* 867–74, 959–65, 1026–33; Restatement (Third) §§ 511-13; Walker, *Consolidated Glossary* 266–68.

Comment

In LOAC-governed situations under the "other rules of international law" clauses in UNCLOS, a different definition may apply. The same may be the situation if the UN Charter supersedes UNCLOS or if jus cogens norms apply.[688]

Former ECDIS Glossary, page 12, defined "indicator" as "[v]isual indication giving information about the condition of a system or equipment." The newer ECDIS Glossary does not define "indicator."

Section 4 defines "alarm;" § 199, "warning."[689]

§ 85. *Installation (offshore)*

See Artificial island, § 10.

§ 86. *International nautical mile*

See Mile or nautical mile, § 105.

§ 87. *Isobath*

(a) Under UNCLOS Article 76(5) and in general UNCLOS analysis, "isobath" means a line representing the horizontal contour of the seabed at a given depth.
(b) "Isobath" can also refer to lines depicting pressure gradients on weather charts or maps.

Comment

In LOAC-governed situations under the "other rules of international law" clauses in UNCLOS, a different definition may apply. The same may be the situation if the UN Charter supersedes UNCLOS or if jus cogens norms apply.[690]

Consolidated Glossary ¶ 51, echoing Former Glossary ¶ 44, defines "isobath" as "[a] line representing the horizontal contour of the seabed at a given depth." Although not so defined in the Glossary, "isobath"

---

[688] *See* Parts III.B–III.D and § 132, defining "other rules of international law."

[689] *See also* DOD Dictionary 259 (definitions for "indications," "indications and warning"); Walker, *ECDIS Glossary* 250, 2003–04 ABILA Proc. 222.

[690] *See* Parts III.B–III.D and § 132, defining "other rules of international law."

can also refer to lines depicting pressure gradients on weather charts or maps.

UNCLOS Article 76(5) requires that fixed points comprising the line of the outer limits of the continental shelf on the seabed, drawn under Articles 76(4)(a)(i) and 76(4)(a)(ii), either may not exceed 350 nautical miles from the baselines from which the territorial sea's breadth is measured or may not exceed 100 nautical miles from the 2500-meter isobath, which is a line connecting the depth of 2500 meters. Although only UNCLOS Article 76(5) recites the term, "isobath" is a term of general usage and might appear on charts and other documents UNCLOS requires.

In defining "basepoint" and "point," § 16 discusses baselines. Section 23 defines "chart" or "nautical chart;" § 93, "line;" § 105, "mile" or "nautical mile;" § 126, "ocean space" or "sea;" § 157, "sea-bed," "seabed" or "bed;" § 176, "straight line, straight baseline, straight archipelagic baseline."[691]

§ 88. *Land domain*

See Land territory, § 89.

§ 89. *Land territory; land domain*

"Land territory" as used in UNCLOS Articles 2(1), 76(1), or "land domain" as used in Article 7(3), means islands and continental land masses above water at high tide, and land connected to these masses and uncovered between high and low tide. When land territory or land domain under this definition is submerged, it becomes subject to law of the sea rules, *e.g.*, those in Article 8(1) for internal waters or UNCLOS Articles 76-85 for the continental shelf. Land territory or land domain also includes rivers, streams, lakes, ponds and the like within islands or continental land masses that do not connect with the sea through internal waters or rivers flowing into the sea.

Comment

In LOAC-governed situations under the "other rules of international law" clauses in UNCLOS, a different definition may apply. The same

[691] *See also* Churchill & Lowe 148–50; 2 Commentary ¶¶ 76.1–78.18(a), 76.18(h); NWP 1-14M Annotated ¶ 1.6 & Fig. A1-2; 1 O'Connell 443–49; Restatement (Third) §§ 511-12, 515, 523; Noyes, *Definitions* 322–23 & Part III.D.3; Walker, *Consolidated Glossary* 268.

may be the situation if the UN Charter supersedes UNCLOS or if jus cogens norms apply.[692]

Consolidated Glossary ¶ 52, following Former Glossary ¶ 45, defines "land territory" as "[a] general term in the Convention that refers to both insular and continental land masses that are above water at high tide," citing UNCLOS Articles 2(1) and 76(1). It does not define "land domain," to which Article 7(3) refers.

UNCLOS Article 2(1) declares that sovereignty of a coastal State extends, "beyond its land territory and internal waters and, in the case of an archipelagic State [defined in Article 46(a)], its archipelagic waters [defined in Article 46(b)], to an adjacent belt of sea, described as the territorial sea." Article 76(1) says the continental shelf of a coastal State comprises the seabed and subsoil of submarine areas extending beyond its territorial sea "throughout the natural prolongation of its land territory to the outer edge of the continental margin, or to 200 nautical miles from baselines from which the territorial sea's breadth is measured where the continental margin's outer edge does not extend up to that distance.

Measurement for territorial sea baselines begins at the low-water line, UNCLOS Articles 5, 6, 7(2), and 9 declare, as do Territorial Sea Convention Articles 3, 13. UNCLOS Articles 7(4) and 13 define and set rules for low-tide elevations, as does Territorial Sea Convention Article 11; if a low-tide elevation is beyond the territorial sea's breadth from the mainland or an island, it has no territorial sea of its own On the other hand, a low-tide elevation is wholly or partly within the breadth of the territorial sea, its low-water line may be used as a territorial sea baseline. The regime of bays, UNCLOS Articles 10(3)-10(5), refer to low-water marks; Territorial Sea Convention Articles 7(3)-7(5) also do so. UNCLOS appears to refer to the high tide line only in defining an island, Article 121(1); Territorial Sea Convention Article 10(1) also does so.

UNCLOS Article 8(1) says waters on the landward side of territorial sea baselines are part of a coastal State's internal waters, except in the case of archipelagic States. Territorial Sea Convention Article 5(1) states the same rule, omitting reference to archipelagic States. Under UNCLOS Article 49, archipelagic States have sovereignty over archipelagic waters defined in Article 47, subject to rules in Articles 46-54. Article 50 allows archipelagic States to draw closing lines for its internal waters in

[692] *See* Parts III.B-III.D and § 132, defining "other rules of international law."

accordance with Articles 9-11. Article 7(3) inter alia says sea areas within straight baselines "must be sufficiently closely linked to the land domain to be subject to the regime of internal waters." Territorial Sea Convention Article 4(2) uses the same language.

If the Glossary high-tide rule is adopted, the result can be a belt of land that appears between high and low tide that could be said to be subject to an internal waters regime at high tide and while there is sea covering it, and a land regime at low tide when no water covers it. The Glossary definition does not account for waters within the land mass, *e.g.*, rivers, streams lakes or ponds that have no outlet to the sea through rivers or other internal waters. An example is the U.S. Great Salt Lake. Nor does it account for drying reefs, defined in § 53 as "that part of a reef which is above water at low tide but is submerged at high tide."

It would seem that a definition of land territory should refer to the high-water mark, but with a transition to LOS criteria (*e.g.*, internal waters) when land between the low and high water marks is covered with water. It would seem, also, that the definition should include waters that are not connected to rivers or internal waters as defined in UNCLOS.

Section 16 defines "basepoint" and "point" and discusses baselines. Section 28 defines "coast;" § 53, "drying reef;" § 93, "line;" § 98, "low water line" or "low water mark;" § 126, "ocean space" or "sea;" § 143, "river;" § 157, "sea-bed," "seabed" or "bed;" § 176, "straight line, straight baseline, straight archipelagic baseline;" § 189, "tide."[693]

§ 90. *Latitude, parallels of latitude or parallels*

In preparing geographic coordinates or geographical coordinates and for similar purposes under UNCLOS, latitude is expressed in degrees, minutes and seconds, or decimals of a minute, from 0 degrees to 90 degrees north or south of the Equator. Lines or circles joining points of equal latitude are known as "parallels of latitude" or "parallels."

Comment

In LOAC-governed situations under the "other rules of international law" clauses in UNCLOS, a different definition may apply. The same

[693] *See also* 2007–08 ABILA Proc. 264–66; 2 Commentary ¶¶ 2.1–2.8(c), 7.1–7.8, 7.9(e), 76.1–76.18(b); NWP 1-14M Annotated ¶ 1.4.1; Restatement (Third) §§ 511-12, 515; Walker, *Consolidated Glossary* 269–70.

may be the situation if the UN Charter supersedes UNCLOS or if jus cogens norms apply.[694]

In defining "geographical coordinates," or "geographic coordinates," § 76 notes that Consolidated Glossary ¶ 42 and Former Glossary ¶ 37 say latitude is expressed in degrees, minutes and seconds or decimals of a minute, from 0 degrees to 90 degrees north or south of the Equator. Lines or circles joining points of equal latitude are known as "parallels of latitude" or "parallels." No LOS Convention refers to "latitude," but its meaning is critical to understanding geographical coordinates, geographic coordinates, and charts generally. Although Consolidated Glossary ¶ 63 lists "parallel of latitude" separately, a separate definition seems unnecessary.

UNCLOS Article 76(7) requires a coastal State to delineate the outer limits of its continental shelf, where that shelf extends beyond 200 nautical miles from the baselines from which the territorial sea's breadth is measured, "by straight lines not exceeding 60 nautical miles in length, connecting fixed points, defined by coordinates of latitude and longitude."

Section 16, discussing baselines, defines "basepoints" and "points;" § 23 defines "chart" or "nautical chart;" § 31, "coastal State;" § 76, "geographic coordinates," "geographical coordinates" or "coordinates;" § 93, "line;" § 97, "longitude;" § 105, "mile" or "nautical mile;" § 162, "shelf;" § 176, "straight line, straight baseline, straight archipelagic baseline."[695]

§ 91. *Leg*

In UNCLOS analysis, "leg" means a line connecting two waypoints.

Comment

In LOAC-governed situations under the "other rules of international law" clauses in UNCLOS, a different definition may apply. The same may be the situation if the UN Charter supersedes UNCLOS or if jus cogens norms apply.[696]

---

[694] *See* Parts III.B-III.D and § 132, defining "other rules of international law."

[695] *See generally* 2007–08 ABILA Proc. 266–67; Churchill & Lowe ch. 2, pp. 148–50; 2 O'Connell ch. 16; Noyes, *Definitions* 322–23 & Part III.D.3; Walker, *Consolidated Glossary* 270–71.

[696] *See* Parts III.B-III.D and § 132, defining "other rules of international law."

Former ECDIS Glossary, page 13, defined "leg" as "[a] line connecting two *waypoints*." The newer ECDIS Glossary, page 6 definition is the same.

Section 93 defines "line;" § 94, "line of delimitation;" § 176, "straight line; straight baseline; straight archipelagic baseline;" § 201, "waypoint."[697]

§ 92. *Light list*

See List of lights, § 95.

§ 93. *Line*

In UNCLOS analysis, "line" means a one-dimensional geometric primitive of an object that specifies location.

Comment

In LOAC-governed situations under the "other rules of international law" clauses in UNCLOS, a different definition may apply. The same may be the situation if the UN Charter supersedes UNCLOS or if jus cogens norms apply.[698]

Former ECDIS Glossary, page 13, defined "line" as "[t]he one-dimensional *geometric primitive* of an *object* that specifies location." The newer ECDIS Glossary, page 6, defines "line" as "*a* one-dimensional GEOMETRIC PRIMITIVE of an OBJECT that specifies location." The Committee definition follows the latter ECDIS definition.

Section 78 defines "geometric primitive;" § 94, "line of delimitation;" § 125, "object;" § 176, "straight line, straight baseline, straight archipelagic baseline."[699]

§ 94. *Line of delimitation*

In UNCLOS analysis, "line of delimitation" means a line drawn on a map or chart depicting the separation of any type of maritime jurisdiction. A line of delimitation may result from unilateral action or from agreement of States.

---

[697] *See generally* Churchill & Lowe ch. 2; Walker, *ECDIS Glossary* 250–51, 2003–04 ABILA Proc. 222–23.

[698] *See* Parts III.B-III.D and § 132, defining "other rules of international law."

[699] *See also* Churchill & Lowe ch. 2; Walker, *ECDIS Glossary* 251, 2003–04 ABILA Proc. 223.

Comment

In LOAC-governed situations under the "other rules of international law" clauses in UNCLOS, a different definition may apply. The same may be the situation if the UN Charter supersedes UNCLOS or if jus cogens norms apply.[700]

Consolidated Glossary ¶ 47 defines "line of delimitation" as "[a] line drawn on a map or chart depicting the separation of any type of maritime jurisdiction," noting that "[a] line of delimitation may result … from unilateral action or from bilateral agreement and, in some cases, the State(s) concerned may be required to give due publicity." Reference to "publicity" has been dropped in § 92. Section 94 refers to "agreement of States" instead of bilateral agreements in the Glossary definition; sometimes more than bilateral agreements may be involved.

UNCLOS refers to lines of delimitation in many contexts: territorial sea, Articles 15, 16(1), 60(8), 147(2)(e), 259; archipelagic State internal waters, Article 50; the EEZ, Article 74, 75(1), 147(2)(e), 259; continental shelf, Article 76(10), 83, 134(4), 147(2)(e), 259 and Annex II, Article 9; territorial sea, EEZ or shelf opposite or adjacent coasts, Articles 15, 74(1), 76(10), 83(1), 134(4) and Annex II, Article 9; special circumstances or historic title, Article 15; disputes regarding delimitations, Article 298(1)(a)(i), 298(a)(iii) and Annex II, Article 9. Article 208(1), requiring coastal States to adopt laws to prevent, reduce and control pollution from artificial islands, etc., cross-references to Article 60, which is also incorporated into Article 246(5)(b), which allows coastal States to withhold consent to MSR under certain conditions. Some Articles also require filing with international organizations, *e.g.*, the UN Secretary-General, besides giving due publicity.

Territorial Sea Convention Article 8 also refers to delimiting or delimitation, as does Shelf Convention Article 6(3).

Section 16, in discussing baselines, defines "basepoint" and "point;" § 23 defines "chart" or "nautical chart;" § 28, "coast;" § 31, "coastal State;" § 55, "due notice," "appropriate publicity" and "due publicity;" § 93, "line;" § 176, "straight line, straight baseline, straight archipelagic baseline."[701]

---

[700] *See* Parts III.B-III.D and § 132, defining "other rules of international law."

[701] *See also* 2 Commentary ¶¶ 15.1–15.12(d), 16.1–16.8(b), 50.1–50.6(b), 60.1–60.15(c), 60.15(k)–60.15(m), 74.1–74.11(f), 75.1–75.5(d), 76.1–76.18(a), 76.18(m), 83.1–83.19(b); 4 *id.* ¶¶ 208.1–208.10(d), 246.1–246.17(f); 2 O'Connell ch. 16; Restatement (Third) §§ 511–12, 514–17; Noyes, *Definitions* 322–23 & Part III.D.3; Walker, *Consolidated Glossary* 271–72.

§ 95. *List of lights or light list*

In UNCLOS analysis, "list of lights" or "light list" means a publication, issued by a marine administration, that tabulates navigational lights, with their locations, candle powers, characteristics, etc. to assist in their identification, and details of any accompanying fog signal. A list of lights may contain other information useful to a navigator.

Comment

In LOAC-governed situations under the "other rules of international law" clauses in UNCLOS, a different definition may apply. The same may be the situation if the UN Charter supersedes UNCLOS or if jus cogens norms apply.[702]

Former ECDIS Glossary, page 13, defined "List of Lights" or "light list" as "[a] publication tabulating navigational lights, with their locations, candle powers, characteristics, etc. to assist in their identification, and details of any accompanying fog signal. A list of lights may contain other information useful to a navigator. ...," noting its issuance by a marine administration. The newer ECDIS Glossary does not define "List of Lights."

Section 3 defines "aid(s) to navigation" and "navigational aid(s);" § 96, "List of Radio Signals."[703]

§ 96. *List of Radio Signals*

In UNCLOS analysis, "List of Radio Signals" means a publication, issued by a marine organization, that tabulates and combines particulars of coast radio stations, port radio stations, radio direction finding systems, radiobeacons, etc., as well as other information on radio services useful to a navigator,

Comment

In LOAC-governed situations under the "other rules of international law" clauses in UNCLOS, a different definition may apply. The same may be the situation if the UN Charter supersedes UNCLOS or if jus cogens norms apply.[704]

---

[702] *See* Parts III.B-III.D and § 132, defining "other rules of international law."

[703] *See also* Walker, *ECDIS Glossary* 251–52, 2003–04 ABILA Proc. 223–24.

[704] *See* Parts III.B-III.D and § 132, defining "other rules of international law."

Former ECDIS Glossary, page 13, defined "List of Radio Signals" as "[a] publication tabulating and combining particulars of: coast radio stations, port radio stations, radio direction finding systems, radiobeacons, etc., as well as other information on radio services useful to a navigator," noting that this publication is issued under authority of a marine administration. The newer ECDIS Glossary does not define "List of Radio Signals."

UNCLOS Article 39(3)(b) requires aircraft in straits transit passage to monitor the radio frequency assigned by the competent internationally designated air traffic control authority or the appropriate international distress radio frequency. Article 94(3)(c) requires every State to take measures for vessels flying its flag to ensure safety at sea with regard to use of signals and maintenance of communications. Article 94(4)(b) says these measures include those necessary to ensure "that each ship is in the charge of a master and officers who possess appropriate qualifications ... in ... communications ..., and that the crew is appropriate in qualification and numbers for the ... equipment of the ship. Article 94(4)(c) says these measures include those necessary to ensure "that the master, officers and, to the extent appropriate, the crew are fully conversant with and required to observed the applicable international regulations concerning ... maintenance of communications by radio."[705]

Section 95 defines "list of lights" or "light list;" § 137, "port;" § 163, "ship" or "vessel."

§ 97. *Longitude; meridian or meridians*

In preparing geographical coordinates or geographic coordinates and for similar purposes under UNCLOS, longitude is expressed in degrees, minutes and seconds, or decimals of a minute, from 0 degrees to 180 degrees east or west of the Greenwich meridian. Lines joining points of equal longitude are known as "meridians."

Comment

In LOAC-governed situations under the "other rules of international law" clauses in UNCLOS, a different definition may apply. The same

---

[705] *See also* 2 Commentary ¶¶ 39.1–39.9, 39.10(k)–39.10(*l*); 3 *id.* ¶¶ 94.1–94.7, 94.8(d), 94.8(h); Walker, *ECDIS Glossary* 252, 2003–04 ABILA Proc. 224–25.

may be the situation if the UN Charter supersedes UNCLOS or if jus cogens norms apply.[706]

In defining "geographic coordinates," "geographical coordinates" or "coordinates," § 76 notes that Consolidated Glossary ¶ 42 and Former Glossary ¶ 37 say that longitude is expressed in degrees, minutes and seconds or decimals of a minute, from 0 degrees to 180 degrees east or west of the Greenwich meridian. Lines joining points of equal longitude are known as "meridians."

UNCLOS Article 76(7) requires a coastal State to delineate the outer limits of its continental shelf, where that shelf extends beyond 200 nautical miles from the baselines from which the territorial sea's breadth is measured, "by straight lines not exceeding 60 nautical miles in length, connecting fixed points, defined by coordinates of latitude and longitude."

Section 16, discussing baselines, defines "basepoints" and "points;" § 23, "chart" or "nautical chart;" § 31, "coastal State;" § 90, "latitude;" § 93, "line;" § 105, "mile" or "nautical mile;" § 162, "shelf;" § 176, "straight line; straight baseline; straight archipelagic baseline."[707]

§ 98. *Low water line or low water mark*

(a) In UNCLOS, the phrases "low-water line" and "low-water mark" are synonymous. They mean the intersection of the plane of low water with the shore, or the line along a coast or beach to which the sea recedes at low tide.
(b) It is the normal practice for the low-water line to be shown as an identifiable feature on nautical charts unless the scale is too small to distinguish it from the high-water line or where there is no tide so that the high and low water lines are the same.
(c) The actual water level taken as low water for charting purposes is known as the level of chart datum.

Comment

In LOAC-governed situations under the "other rules of international law" clauses in UNCLOS, a different definition may apply. The same

[706] *See* Parts III.B-III.D and § 132, defining "other rules of international law."

[707] *See generally* 2007–08 ABILA Proc. 271; Churchill & Lowe ch. 2, pp. 148–50; 2 O'Connell ch. 16; Noyes, *Definitions* 322–23 & Part III.D.3; Walker, *Consolidated Glossary* 273.

may be the situation if the UN Charter supersedes UNCLOS or if jus cogens norms apply.[708]

Consolidated Glossary ¶ 56, echoing Former Glossary ¶ 50, defines "low-water line" or "low-water mark" as "[t]he intersection of the plane of low water with the shore[, or t]he line along a coast, or beach, to which the sea recedes at low water." Both Glossaries also note:

> It is the normal practice for the low-water line to be shown as an identifiable feature on nautical charts unless the scale is too small to distinguish it from the high-water line or where there is no tide so that the high and low water lines are the same. The actual water level taken as low-water for charting purposes is known as the level of chart datum.[709]

Measurement for territorial sea baselines begins at the low-water line, UNCLOS Articles 5, 6, 7(2), and 9, as it does in Territorial Sea Convention Articles 3, 13. UNCLOS Articles 7(4) and 13 define and set rules for low-tide elevations, as does Territorial Sea Convention Article 11; if a low-tide elevation is beyond the territorial sea's breadth from the mainland or an island, it has no territorial sea of its own On the other hand, if a low-tide elevation is wholly or partly within the breadth of the territorial sea, its low-water line may be used as a territorial sea baseline. The regime for bays, UNCLOS Articles 10(3)-10(5), refers to low-water marks; the Territorial Sea Convention regime for bays, Articles 7(3)-7(5), also does so.

Hydrographers report that regression of low-water marks is a rare phenomenon.[710] However, determining where low-water marks should be can be less than an exact science.[711]

Section 87, defining "land territory" and "land domain," discusses these and related UNCLOS provisions. Section 23 defines "chart" or

---

[708] *See* Parts III.B-III.D and § 132, defining "other rules of international law."

[709] *Accord*, 2 Commentary ¶ 5.4(b).

[710] *Id.* ¶ 7.9(c).

[711] Before the LOS Conventions, which reflect recent State practice, high tide was the benchmark in some quarters. There are at least 11 choices of tide level for hydrological purposes. Low tide for hydrological purposes may therefore not be the same as the juridical definition. Other authorities distinguish "mean low water" from "low low water." *See generally* 1 O'Connell 173–83; *see also* Churchill & Lowe 33 n. 4, 53. As Section 105 comments that in defining "mile" and "nautical mile," Murphy's Law of Measurements suggests that disputes will always occur between competing claims for the low tide line.

"nautical chart;" § 31, "coastal State;" § 91, "line;" § 124, "ocean space" or "sea;" § 174, "straight line; straight baseline; straight archipelagic baseline."[712]

§ 99. *Low water mark*

See Low water line, § 98.

§ 100. *Marine scientific research, abbreviated MSR*

In UNCLOS analysis, marine scientific research, abbreviated MSR, means those activities undertaken in ocean space to expand scientific knowledge of the marine environment and its processes.

Comment

In LOAC-governed situations under the "other rules of international law" clauses in UNCLOS, a different definition may apply. The same may be the situation if the UN Charter supersedes UNCLOS or if jus cogens norms apply.[713]

Although UNCLOS Part XIII, Marine Scientific Research, consists of 27 detailed articles, the Convention does not define "marine scientific research." Research of UNCLOS negotiations reveals a variety of approaches, which ended by omission of a definition in the Convention.[714]

Canada proposed a definition to Subcommittee III of the Sea-Bed Committee in 1972: "Marine scientific research is any study, whether fundamental or applied, intended to increase knowledge about the marine environment, including all its resources and living organisms, and embraces all related scientific activity."[715] The next year four East European States submitted this "explanation of the term 'scientific research in the world ocean'":

---

[712] *See also* Churchill & Lowe 32–33; 2 Commentary ¶¶ 5.1–6.7(e), 7.1–7.9(a), 7.9(c)–7.9(d), 7.9(f), 9.1–9.5(e), 10.1–10.5(f), 13.1–13.5(b); DOD Dictionary 217 ("foreshore"); NWP 1-14M Annotated ¶ 1.3.1; 1 O'Connell 173–83, 398–99; 2 *id.* 635; Restatement (Third), §§ 511–12; Roach & Smith ¶ 4.4.1; Walker, *Consolidated Glossary* 273–75.

[713] *See* Parts III.B-III.D and § 132, defining "other rules of international law."

[714] In proceeding with a definition, the Committee is mindful of the hazards of advancing one where the Convention is silent; *see* Parts III.D-III.D.

[715] 4 Commentary ¶ 238.3, quoting Canada's working paper submitted to Sub-Committee III of the Sea-Bed Committee, A/AC.138/SC.III/L.18 (1972).

> … any fundamental or applied research and related experimental work, conducted by States and their juridical and physical persons, as well as by international organizations, which does not aim directly at industrial exploitation but is designed to obtain knowledge of all aspects of the natural processes and phenomena occurring in ocean space, on the seabed and in the subsoil thereof, which is necessary for the peaceful activity of States for the further development of navigation and other forms of utilization of the sea and also utilization of the air space above the world ocean.[716]

In 1974 Trinidad and Tobago submitted a draft definition:

> (a) Marine scientific research is any study or investigation of the marine environment and experiments related thereto;
> (b) Marine scientific research is of such a nature as to preclude any clear or precise distinction between pure scientific research and industrial or other research conducted with a view to commercial exploitation or military use.[717]

Also in 1974, a consolidated alternative text described marine scientific research as "any study of, and related to experimental work in, the marine environment designed to increase man's knowledge and conducted for peaceful purposes" but was limited to areas beyond national jurisdiction. Freedom to conduct MSR in areas where coastal States would enjoy economic rights over resources was recognized only in relation to research not connected with exploration for, or the exploitation of, natural resources.[718] That year Egypt introduced a different approach:

> Scientific research lends itself to all investigations dealing with natural phenomena in the marine environment and the atmosphere there above, as well as to promotion of methodology for abatement of marine pollution and other abnormalities. Scientific research is contradictory [sic] to all non-peaceful aspects, and does not cover activities aimed at the direct exploitation of the marine resources.[719]

In 1975 nine Socialist States offered this formula: "'Marine scientific research' means any study of, or related experimental work in, the

[716] 4 Commentary ¶ 238.4, quoting in part draft art. 1 submitted by four Eastern European States to Sub-Committee III of the Sea-Bed Committee, A/A.138/SC. III/L.31 (1973).

[717] 4 Commentary ¶ 238.6, quoting art. 1 of Trinidad and Tobago draft articles, A/CONF.62/C.3/L.9 (1974), 3 Off. Rec. 252 (1974).

[718] 4 Commentary ¶ 238.6, p. 445, referring to arts. 1, 3, A/CONF.62/C.3/L.17 (1974), 3 Off. Rec. 263–65 (1974).

[719] 4 Commentary ¶ 238.6, p. 445, quoting Egypt's informal paper, 1974, CRP/ Sc.Res./12 (1974).

marine environment that is designed to increase man's knowledge and is conducted for peaceful purposes."[720] Article 1 of Part III of the Informal Single Negotiating Text had a short definition: "Marine scientific research means any study or related experimental work designed to increase man's knowledge of the marine environment."[721] The Informal Group of Juridical Experts proposed a revised Article 1: "*For the purpose of this Convention*, marine scientific research means any study or related experimental work designed to increase *mankind's* knowledge of the marine environment *including its resources*."[722] In 1977 a definition provision was not in the Informal Consolidated Negotiating Text; in 1978 there was insufficient support for reinserting one.[723] Commentators summarize the result:

> The [later] definitions ... remain useful as examples of the use of the term 'marine scientific research' for purposes of the Convention. At the very least, the development of the relevant texts demonstrates that the general right to conduct marine scientific research, recognized in [UNCLOS] article 238, may have a different substantive content in relation to different maritime zones.[724]

UNCLOS Articles 245–57 establish different rules for different ocean areas, *e.g.*, the territorial sea and the EEZ. UNCLOS Article 87(1)(f) recognizes MSR as a high seas freedom, subject to rules in Part XIII and provisions governing the continental shelf, Part VI. UNCLOS Article 240(a) repeats a theme of some draft articles: "[M]arine research shall be conducted exclusively for peaceful purposes." Article 88 echoes this principle: "The high seas shall be reserved for peaceful purposes."[725]

Commentators have given definitions; the ECDIS and Consolidated Glossaries do not define MSR. In 2006 an ABILA LOS Committee member offered this meaning for MSR: "Marine scientific research is the general term most often used to describe those activities undertaken in the ocean and coastal waters to expand scientific knowledge

---

[720] 4 Commentary ¶ 238.7, quoting draft art. 1 of nine Socialist States, 1975, A/CONF.62/C.3/L.26, 4 Off. Rec. 213 (1975).

[721] 4 Commentary ¶ 238.7, quoting draft art. 1, Informal Single Negotiating Text, Part III (1975), A/CONF.62/WP.8/Part III, 4 Off. Rec. 171, 177 (1975).

[722] 4 *id.* ¶ 238.7, p. 447 (emphasis in original).

[723] 4 *id.* ¶¶ 238.9, 238.10.

[724] 4 *id.* ¶ 238.10.

[725] *See also* UNCLOS art. 301; Part III.B and § 132, defining "other rules of international law."

of the marine environment and its processes."[726] Another definition has been advanced: "Marine scientific research includes activities undertaken in the ocean and coastal waters to expand knowledge of the marine environment for peaceful purposes, and includes: oceanography, marine biology, geological/geophysical scientific surveying, as well as other activities with a scientific purpose."[727] Other commentators, recognizing that UNCLOS does not define the term, would say that MSR does not include hydrography, and note that the Convention differentiates between pure and applied research in Convention-designated areas, *e.g.*, the EEZ.[728] States differ on whether military surveys are lawful; in view of Convention provisions for high seas use and MSR for peaceful purposes, an inference is that military surveys are lawful, so long as they do not contravene the peaceful purposes MSR and high seas regimes.[729]

Although MSR is also a customary high seas freedom, custom parallels the Shelf Convention in its Article 5(8) prohibition on MSR without coastal State permission, which qualifies Convention Article 5(1). Similarly, consent must be obtained for MSR in a coastal State's EEZ, archipelagic waters, or territorial sea.[730]

The Committee decided to adopt its member's general definition, modified slightly, taking the view that the kind of MSR UNCLOS authorizes in different sea areas is covered by the Convention's terms, including Article 240(a)'s "peaceful purposes" requirement.

Section 28 defines "coast;" § 31, "coastal State;" § 81, "high seas;" § 126, "sea" and "ocean space."

---

[726] J. Ashley Roach, *Defining Scientific Research: Marine Data Collection*, in Myron H. Nordquist et al. eds., Law, Science and Ocean Management 541, 543 (2007), citing comparison of UNCLOS arts. 243, 246(3) and Alfred H.A. Soons, Marine Scientific Research and the Law of the Sea 124 (1982); *see also* Roach & Smith 425 (same; United States accepts definition).

[727] NWP 1-14M Annotated ¶ 2.4.2.1.

[728] Churchill & Lowe 405.

[729] *Id.* 411; *see also* Part III.B and § 132, defining "other rules of international law." The United States recognizes that coastal State consent must be given for MSR in that State's EEZ, but a coastal State cannot regulate hydrographic surveys or military surveys beyond its territorial sea. A coastal State cannot require notification of these activities. NWP 1-14M Annotated ¶ 2.4.2.2; Roach & Smith ¶¶ 15.1.2–15.1.3.

[730] Churchill & Lowe 401–11; Jennings & Watts §§ 3348–49; Roach & Smith ¶¶ 15.2, 15.4–15.4.4. DOD Dictionary, Appendix A, *Abbreviations and Acronyms*, p. A-98 defines MSR as "main supply route," "maritime support request," or "mission support request."

§ 101. *Maritime safety information, abbreviated MSI*

In UNCLOS analysis, "maritime safety information," abbreviated MSI, means navigational and meteorological warnings, meteorological forecasts, distress alerts, and other urgent safety-related messages broadcasted to ships.

Comment

In LOAC-governed situations under the "other rules of international law" clauses in UNCLOS, a different definition may apply. The same may be the situation if the UN Charter supersedes UNCLOS or if jus cogens norms apply.[731]

Former ECDIS Glossary, page 14, defined "maritime safety information," abbreviated as MSI, as "[n]avigational and meteorological warnings, meteorological forecasts, distress alerts and other urgent safety related messages broadcast to ships." The newer ECDIS Glossary does not define "maritime safety information."

Section 3 defines "aid(s) to navigation" and "navigational aid(s);" § 54, "due notice," "appropriate publicity," and "due publicity;" § 137, "port;" § 163, "ship" or "vessel;" § 199, "warning."[732]

§ 102. *Maximum sustainable yield*

"Maximum sustainable yield," as used in UNCLOS Articles 61 and 119, means that level of abundance of population of a living resource that will assure maintaining or restoring that living resource. It is one of the primary objectives of conservation measures taken by a State.

Comment

In LOAC-governed situations under the "other rules of international law" clauses in UNCLOS, a different definition may apply. The same may be the situation if the UN Charter supersedes UNCLOS or if jus cogens norms apply.[733]

"Maximum sustainable yield" appears in UNCLOS Article 61(3), dealing with EEZ living resources conservation:

---

[731] *See* Parts III.B-III.D and § 132, defining "other rules of international law."
[732] *See also* Walker, *ECDIS Glossary* 253, 2003–04 ABILA Proc. 225–26.
[733] *See* Parts III.B-III.D and § 132, defining "other rules of international law."

> ... Such [coastal State conservation and management measures] shall also be designed to maintain or restore populations of harvested species at levels which can produce the maximum sustainable yield, as qualified by relevant environmental and economic factors ..., and taking into account fishing patterns, the interdependence of stocks and any generally recommended international minimum standards ...

The term is also in UNCLOS Article 119(1)(a), dealing with high seas living resources conservation:

> ... In determining the allowable catch and establishing other conservation measures for the living resources of the high seas, States shall:
>
> ... take measures ... designed, on the best scientific evidence available to the States concerned, to maintain or restore populations of harvested species at levels which can produce the maximum sustainable yield, as qualified by relevant environmental and economic factors, ..., and taking into account fishing patterns, the interdependence of stocks and any generally recommended international minimum standards ...

"Maximum sustainable yield" applies to a coastal State's EEZ and the high seas under UNCLOS Articles 61 and 119. By contrast, "optimum utilization," defined in § 129, applies only to a coastal State's EEZ under UNCLOS Article 62(1).

Fishing Convention Article 2 provides:

> ... [T]he expression "conservation of the living resources of the high seas" means the aggregate of the measures rendering possible the optimum sustainable yield from those resources ... to secure a maximum supply of food and other marine products. Conservation programmes should be formulated with a view to securing in the first place a supply of food for human consumption.

UNCLOS Article 61(3) commentary elucidates the meaning of "maximum sustainable yield":

> [Maximum sustainable yield] refers to the levels of [living resource] population abundance, the maintenance or restoration of which is one of the primary objectives of the conservation measures ... taken by the coastal State. The English text [of Article 61(3)] uses ... "as qualified" by various other factors, embracing relevant and economic aspects ... The French text [of Article 61(3)] — "*eu egard*" (having regard to) — expresses the thrust of this position....
>
> ... "[M]aximum sustainable yield" incorporates the concept of the allowable catch, and is central to article 61. References to the allowable catch are not yet common in national legislation, and there is no established practice for determining it. Most States manage their fisheries using a combination of biological and economic considerations. Where legislation is framed in biological terms, it is difficult to reach any

> conclusion as to the practical application of those criteria, above all because in many instances fish are caught in multi-species fisheries where it is virtually impossible to achieve simultaneously the maximum sustainable yield of the different species. Most major coastal States manage their fisheries to accomplish multiple economic and political objectives, while attempting through national measures (which may themselves originate in appropriate international bodies) to avoid serious overexploitation.[734]

Article 119(1)(a) commentary says the same definition for "maximum sustainable yield" as in Article 61(3) is meant for Article 119(1)(a).[735] It is a flexible concept.[736]

Section 28 defines "coast;" § 31, "coastal State;" § 81, "high seas;" § 131, "optimum utilization."[737]

§ 103. *Median line*

See Equidistance line, § 58.

§ 104. *Meridian or meridians*

See Longitude, § 97.

§ 105. *Mile or nautical mile*

"Mile" or "nautical mile," wherever appearing in UNCLOS, means the international nautical mile, *i.e.,* 1852 meters or 6076.115 feet, corresponding to 60 nautical miles per degree of latitude.

Comment

In LOAC-governed situations under the "other rules of international law" clauses in UNCLOS, a different definition may apply. The same may be the situation if the UN Charter supersedes UNCLOS or if jus cogens norms apply.[738]

UNCLOS and the 1958 LOS Conventions do not define "mile." According to one commentary, the UNCLOS negotiators understood

---

734 2 Commentary ¶¶ 61.12(g)–61.12(h) (italics in original).

735 3 *id.* ¶ 119.7(c).

736 Jennings & Watts § 334; *see also* 1 O'Connell 564–55.

737 *See also* Churchill & Lowe 296–97; Walker, *Last Round* 177–79, 2005–06 ABILA Proc. 66–68.

738 *See* Parts III.B-III.D and § 132, defining "other rules of international law."

that a nautical mile of 1852 meters or 6080 feet was meant, *i.e.*, 60 nautical miles per degree of latitude.[739] (O'Connell notes, however, that although the U.S. figure was 6080.2 feet, this equals 1853.248 meters.[740]) Although "absence of a formal definition may be more in accord with modern marine cartography,"[741] lack of any definition may sow seeds of claims well beyond the contemplation of UNCLOS because of different definitions of "mile"[742] and resulting protests,[743] even though differences can be relatively minute.[744] Since 1959 the current international nautical mile has been 6076.115 feet or 1852 meters.[745] Consolidated Glossary ¶¶ 49, 60, 64, following Consolidated Glossary ¶¶ 52, 56 include "mile" within its definition of "nautical mile" and define a nautical mile as a unit of distance equal to 1852 meters, noting the International Hydrographic Organization adopted this definition. *Annex 1* also defines a nautical mile as 1852 meters.

Absent a more precise definition than the developing international rule, § 103 accepts 6,076.115 feet or 1852 meters as the definition for "mile" and "nautical mile." It has been suggested that the appositive phrase, "60 nautical miles per degree of latitude," may not be necessary.[746] Because § 88 defines "latitude," and because many mariners sometimes think of "mile" in terms of latitude equivalency, the

---

[739] 2 Commentary ¶ 1.27.

[740] 2 O'Connell 644.

[741] 2 Commentary ¶ 1.27.

[742] 2 O'Connell 643–45 lists six different possibilities, some with multiple measurements: Roman or Italian mile, 1472, 1478 or 1482 meters; English statute mile, 1609.3 meters; international geographic mile used in Scandinavia, 7420 meters or 4.6 English statute miles; Prussian mile, 7531.9 meters; Norwegian mile, 7529 meters or 4.68 English statute miles; Admiralty mile, 1853.2 meters. In navigational situations not calling for pinpoint accuracy, many mariners use 2000 yards as the equivalent of a mile, or a mile per minute of latitude.

[743] Protests on other LOS issues, but not on defining "mile," have been numerous before and after UNCLOS' ratification. *See generally* Roach & Smith.

[744] *E.g.*, 0.237 kilometers over 200 miles is the difference between the U.K. Admiralty measurement and the measurement using 1852 meters to the nautical mile. 2 O'Connell 644. Nevertheless, Murphy's Law of Measurements suggests that if there will be a dispute, *e.g.*, over a sunken treasure ship, it will be within those 237 meters.

[745] Spain uses 1850 meters, and the United Kingdom would seem to use 1855 meters, based on a marine Admiralty league of 20 leagues to a degree of latitude, or 5565 meters and 3.4517 English statute miles per league. The Scandinavian league of 7420 meters is based on 15 leagues per degree of latitude. The French metric equivalent, 1852 meters to the mile, is gaining currency in legislation and in international organizations. *Id.* 644–45. Any measurement is inexact for all of the Earth; it is an oblate spheroid and not a perfect sphere. *See generally id.* 639–43. The United States has adopted the international nautical mile equivalent to 1852 meters or 6076.11549 feet. DOD Dictionary 372.

[746] Noyes, *Treaty* 372–73, 2001–02 ABILA Proc. 181–82.

decision is to keep the appositive. The definition has been expanded to include the words "nautical mile" as well as "mile," in accordance with the Consolidated Glossary. UNCLOS and common parlance refer to both.

Section 90 defines "latitude."[747]

§ 106. *Monetary penalties only; monetary penalties*

(a) As used in UNCLOS Articles 230(1) and 230(2), "monetary penalties only" excludes imposing corporal punishment, including imprisonment, for violations of national laws and regulations or applicable international rules and standards for the prevention, reduction and control of pollution of the marine environment, committed by foreign vessels, unless there is an applicable international agreement between the States concerned. In the case of wilful and serious act of pollution in the territorial sea, as an exception the coastal State may impose imprisonment but no other form of corporal punishment.

(b) As used in UNCLOS Annex 3, Articles 5(4), 18(2) and 18(3), "monetary penalties" should receive the same construction as in UNCLOS Articles 230(1) and 230(2), *i.e.*, no corporal punishment and no imprisonment (*e.g.*, for contempt of court in failing to perform a contract) unless other options in Annex 3, Articles 5(4), 18(2) and 18(3) apply in a particular case, or an applicable international agreement provides otherwise.

Comment

In LOAC-governed situations under the "other rules of international law" clauses in UNCLOS, a different definition may apply. The same may be the situation if the UN Charter supersedes UNCLOS or if jus cogens norms apply.[748]

UNCLOS Articles 230(1) and 230(2) provide:

> 1. Monetary penalties only may be imposed with respect to violations of national laws and regulations or applicable international rules and standards for the prevention, reduction and control of pollution of the marine environment, committed by foreign vessels beyond the territorial sea.

---

[747] *See also* Noyes, *Treaty* 372–73, 2001–02 ABILA Proc. 181–82; Walker, *Defining* 357–59, 2001–02 ABILA Proc. 165–66; *id.*, *Definitions II* 208–10, 2003–04.

[748] *See* Parts III.B-III.D and § 132, defining "other rules of international law."

2. Monetary penalties only may be imposed with respect to violations of national laws and regulations or applicable international rules and standards for the prevention, reduction and control of pollution of the marine environment, committed by foreign vessels in the territorial sea, except in the case of a wilful and serious act of pollution in the territorial sea.

Commentators, reviewing Article 230's negotiating history, declare that the "only monetary penalties" provision of Article 230(1) means that all forms of corporal punishment, including imprisonment, are excluded for violations occurring beyond the territorial sea, unless there is an agreement between the States concerned.[749] On the other hand, with respect to violations occurring in the territorial sea, "*as an exception*," coastal States may impose nonmonetary penalties if there is "a wilful and serious act" of pollution in the territorial sea. "[I]t is taken for granted that the penalties imposed by the coastal State may not include 'any other form of corporal punishment.' "[750] Presumably concerned States could establish different rules by agreement. Whether "monetary penalties only" includes injunctions or administrative orders has been debated. An injunction or similar relief might be an ancillary part of a judgment giving monetary penalties, and an administrative order might decree a monetary payment. On the other hand, the letter of Article 230 speaks in terms of monetary penalties with no reference to these alternatives; under standard construction principles this would exclude other penalties. The Committee takes no position on the issue.

UNCLOS Annex 3, Articles 5(4), 18(2), and 18(3) provide in pertinent part with respect to penalties imposed on contractors for breach of contract in Area operations:

> [5]4. Disputes concerning undertakings required by [Article 5(3)], like other provisions of the contracts, shall be subject to compulsory settlement in accordance with Part XI [of UNCLOS, dealing with the Area] and, in cases of violation of these undertakings, suspension or termination of the contract or monetary penalties may be ordered in accordance with article 18 of this Annex.
>
> [18]2. In the case of any violation of the contract not covered by [Article 18(1)(a), providing for suspending or terminating the contract], or in lieu of suspension or termination under [Article 18(1)(a), the

[749] 4 Commentary ¶ 230.9(b).

[750] *Id.* ¶ 230.9(c), referring to UNCLOS arts. 19(2)(h), 27(5), 73.

> [International Sea-Bed] Authority may impose upon the contractor monetary penalties proportionate to the seriousness of the violation.
>
> [18]3. Except for emergency orders under [UNCLOS] article 162, paragraph 2(w), the Authority may not execute a decision involving monetary penalties ... until the contractor has been awarded a reasonable opportunity to exhaust the judicial remedies available ... pursuant to Part XI.[751]

The same construction applied to UNCLOS Article 230(1) should be applied to these Annex provisions.[752]

Section 9 defines "area" and "Area;" § 28, "coast;" § 31, "coastal State;" § 161, "serious act of pollution;" § 163, "ship" or "vessel."

§ 107. *Mouth (of a bay)*

In UNCLOS analysis "mouth" of a bay means the entrance to the bay from the ocean, including bays described in UNCLOS, Articles 10(2)–10(6), bays excluded from Article 10 coverage because they belong to more than one State, "historic bays" as provided in Article 10(6), or bays in which the UNCLOS Article 7 system of straight baselines applies.

Comment

In LOAC-governed situations under the "other rules of international law" clauses in UNCLOS, a different definition may apply. The same may be the situation if the UN Charter supersedes UNCLOS or if jus cogens norms apply.[753]

Consolidated Glossary ¶ 61, echoing Former Glossary ¶ 53, defines "mouth" of a bay as "the entrance to the bay from the ocean." The Glossary further comments that UNCLOS Article 10(2)

> states "a bay is a well-marked indentation," and the mouth of that bay is "the mouth of the indentation." UNCLOS Articles 10(3), 10(4) and 10(5) refer to "natural entrance points of a bay." Thus i[t] can be said that the mouth of a bay lies between its natural entrance points. In other words, the mouth of a bay is its entrance. Although some States have developed standards by which to determine natural entrance points to bays, no international standards have been established.

---

751 UNCLOS art. 1(2) defines "Authority" as the International Sea-Bed Authority.

752 *See* notes 749–50 and accompanying text.

753 *See* Parts III.B-III.D and § 132, defining "other rules of international law."

The Glossary definition seems to focus too narrowly in its elaboration. Any definition of a bay "mouth" should be understood to also include those excluded from UNCLOS Article 10 coverage.

Besides bays described in UNCLOS Articles 10(2)–10(5), Article 10(1) limits Article 10 coverage to bays, the coast of which belongs to a single State; *i.e.*, Article 10 does not govern bays belonging to more than one State. Article 10(6) excludes from Article 10 coverage "so-called 'historic bays,' or in any case where the system of straight baselines provided for in [Article] 7 is applied. Territorial Sea Convention Article 7 is similar to UNCLOS Article 10.

Not all bodies of waters that are labeled "gulf" or "bay" are considered "bays" within the meaning of the LOS Conventions; the latter are "juridical bays," as distinguished from "geographic bays."[754] The Bay of Bengal in the Indian Ocean is an example of a geographic bay.

Section 16 discusses baselines in connection with defining "basepoint" or "point;" § 82 defines "historic bay;" § 93, "line;" § 108, "mouth" (of a river); § 176, "straight line, straight baseline, straight archipelagic baseline."

§ 108. *Mouth (of a river)*

In UNCLOS Article 9, "mouth" of a river means the place of discharge of a stream into the ocean.

Comment

In LOAC-governed situations under the "other rules of international law" clauses in UNCLOS, a different definition may apply. The same may be the situation if the UN Charter supersedes UNCLOS or if jus cogens norms apply.[755]

Consolidated Glossary ¶ 62, echoing Former Glossary ¶ 54, defines "mouth" of a river as "[t]he place of discharge of a stream into the ocean."

UNCLOS Article 9 provides that "[i]f a river flows directly into the sea, the baseline shall be a straight line across the mouth of the river between points on the low-water line of its banks." Territorial Sea Convention Article 13 is the same, except that "low-tide" is used instead of the term "low-water" in UNCLOS Article 9.

---

[754] *See generally* Churchill & Lowe 41–46; 2 Commentary ¶¶ 10.1–10.6; NWP 1-14M Annotated ¶ 1.3.3 & Figs. 1-2–1.4; 1 O'Connell chs. 9A, 10–11; 2 *id.* 647–48; Restatement (Third) § 511, cmt. f & r.n.5; Walker, *Consolidated Glossary* 275–76.

[755] *See* Parts III.B-III.D and § 132, defining "other rules of international law."

Commenting on UNCLOS Article 9, the Glossary and Former Glossary say in part: "Note that the French text of the Convention [,Article 9] is 'si un fleuve se jette dans la mer sans former d'estuaire. …'" and that "[n]o limit is placed on the length of the line to be drawn." The fact that the river must flow "directly into the sea" suggests that the mouth should be well marked, but otherwise the comments on the mouth of a bay apply equally to the mouth of a river.

Section 16, in discussing baselines, defines "basepoint" or "point;" § 60 defines "estuary;" § 93, "line;" § 97, "low water line" or "low water mark;" § 107, "mouth" (of a bay); § 126, "ocean space" or "sea;" § 143, "river;" § 176, "straight line, straight baseline, straight archipelagic baseline."[756]

§ 109. *MSI*

Abbreviation for Maritime safety information, § 101.

§ 110. *MSR*

Abbreviation for Marine scientific research, § 100.

§ 111. *Natural prolongation*

As used in UNCLOS Article 76(1), "natural prolongation" refers to the natural extension of a coastal State's land territory to define that coastal State's continental shelf. To establish which areas are part of the natural prolongation, the starting point is that State's land territory. The connection between the land territory and the natural prolongation can be geomorphological and/or geological.

Comment

In LOAC-governed situations under the "other rules of international law" clauses in UNCLOS, a different definition may apply. The same may be the situation if the UN Charter supersedes UNCLOS or if jus cogens norms apply.[757]

The ILA Committee on Legal Issues of the Outer Continental Shelf defines "natural prolongation" as used in UNCLOS Article 76(1):

> Article 76(1) … refers to the natural prolongation of the land territory to define the continental shelf. To establish which areas are comprised by

[756] *See also* Churchill & Lowe 46–47; 2 Commentary ¶¶ 9.1–9.5(e); NWP 1-14M Annotated ¶ 1.3.4; 1 O'Connell 221–30, 398; Restatement (Third) §§ 511-12; Roach & Smith ¶ 4.4.4; Walker, *Consolidated Glossary* 276–77.

[757] *See* Parts III.B-III.D and § 132, defining "other rules of international law."

> the reference to natural prolongation, the starting point is the land territory. The connection between the land territory and the natural prolongation can be geomorphological and/or geological. One of the implications of the definition of the continental shelf by reference to natural prolongation is that the continental shelf may consist of areas that are either continental and/or oceanic in origin.[758]

UNCLOS Article 76(1) is the basic definition for the continental shelf and differs from the Shelf Convention Article 1 definition.[759]

The ABILA LOS Committee accepted this definition but tightened its wording, omitting the final sentence, "An implication of defining the continental shelf by referring to natural prolongation is that the [continental] shelf may consist of areas that are either continental and/ or oceanic in origin."

Section 9 defines "Area" and "area;" § 28, "coast;" § 31, "coastal State;" § 89, "land territory" or "land domain;" § 126, "ocean space" or "sea."

§ 112. *Natural resources*

In UNCLOS analysis, "natural resources" means the living organisms and nonliving matter in a given ocean area or space. UNCLOS provisions may qualify this definition, *e.g.*, in UNCLOS Article 77(4) governing the continental shelf, which defines "natural resources" as the mineral and other non-living resources of the seabed and subsoil together with living organisms belonging to sedentary species, *i.e.*, organisms which, at the harvestable stage, are immobile on or under the seabed or are unable to move except in constant physical contact with the seabed or the subsoil.

Comment

In LOAC-governed situations under the "other rules of international law" clauses in UNCLOS, a different definition may apply. The same may be the situation if the UN Charter supersedes UNCLOS or if jus cogens norms apply.[760]

---

758 COCS *Second Report*, Conclusion 2, p. 217.

759 *See also* 2007–08 ABILA Proc. 286–90; Brownlie 205–20; 2 Commentary ¶¶ 76.1–76.2, 76.18(a)–76.18(b); Churchill & Lowe 148–50; Jennings & Watts §§ 314–26; 2 O'Connell ch. 18A; Restatement (Third) § 517; Roach & Smith ch. 8; Part IV.B § 16.

760 *See* Parts III.B-III.D and § 132, defining "other rules of international law."

The term "natural resources" appears in different contexts in UNCLOS, depending on the ocean area.

As to the EEZ, UNCLOS Article 56(1)(a) declares the coastal State has sovereign rights for exploring and exploiting, conserving and managing "the natural resources, whether living or non-living, of the waters subjacent to the seabed and of the seabed and its subsoil, and with regard to other activities for the economic exploitation and exploration of the zone, such as the production of energy from the water, currents and winds." Article 56(3) adds that Article 56 seabed and subsoil rights must be exercised in accordance with UNCLOS Part VI, *i.e.*, terms governing the continental shelf. The Article 56 expression "natural resources, whether living or non-living" applying to the EEZ contrasts with "natural resources" in UNCLOS Article 77, governing the continental shelf.

With respect to the continental shelf, UNCLOS Article 77(1) declares that the coastal State exercises sovereign rights for exploring the shelf and exploiting shelf natural resources. Article 77(4) defines shelf natural resources: "the mineral and other non-living resources of the seabed and subsoil together with living organisms belonging to sedentary species, [*i.e.*] ... organisms which, at the harvestable stage, ... are immobile on or under the seabed or are unable to move except in constant physical contact with the seabed or the subsoil." Article 79(2) says the coastal State may not impede laying or maintaining of submarine cables or pipelines, subject to that State's right inter alia "to take reasonable measures for ... the exploitation of its natural resources ..."[761] Because of UNCLOS Articles 68 and 77, "living organisms belonging to sedentary species" come within the continental shelf regime and not the EEZ regime according to one commentator; another says these organisms come within the EEZ regime.[762] It would seem that the proper interpretation is that these species come within the continental shelf regime if a State claims an EEZ. A continental shelf may extend beyond 200 nautical miles, the outer limit of an EEZ; *see* UNCLOS Articles 57, 76. (One can imagine a bottom-crawler species' surprise if it emerged into an entirely different regime when it crossed the 200-mile dividing line. If the continental shelf regime applies across the board, the rules are the same as to whether the bottom-crawler is

---

[761] *See also* § 56, defining "due regard" and similar terms.

[762] *Compare* 2 Commentary ¶ 56.11(c) (within shelf regime) *with* Jennings & Watts § 348 (within EEZ regime).

fair game.) Under Article 77(4), if a State does not claim a continental shelf, the continental shelf regime still applies. If a State claims an EEZ but has not claimed a continental shelf, the EEZ regime applies to the breadth of the EEZ, and the continental shelf regime applies to the continental shelf, whether claimed or not, under UNCLOS.

UNCLOS Article 71(1) and 71(4) provisions are similar to Shelf Convention Articles 2(1), 2(4). Article 5(1) declares that exploitation of shelf natural resources must not result in unjustifiable interference with navigation, fishing or conservation of the sea's living resources or any interference with fundamental oceanographic or other scientific research carried out with the intention of open publication. Article 5(2) allows States to build installations on the shelf and declare safety zones to explore and exploit shelf natural resources. Article 5(7) requires a coastal State to undertake all appropriate measures in the safety zones to protect the sea's living resources from harmful agents.

UNCLOS Article 193 gives States "the sovereign right to exploit their natural resources pursuant to their environmental policies and in accordance with their duty to protect and preserve the marine environment."[763]

As to the Area, UNCLOS Article 145(b) requires the International Sea-Bed Authority to adopt rules, regulations and procedures for inter alia "protection and conservation of the natural resources of the Area and the prevention of damage to the flora and fauna of the marine environment."[764] Since UNCLOS Article 1(1) defines the Area as "the seabed and ocean floor and subsoil thereof beyond the limits of national jurisdiction," Article 145(b) should be interpreted to mean only the natural resources of the seabed and ocean floor and subsoil thereof beyond the limits of national jurisdiction, and not the natural resources of the water column above the Area.

No commentator seems to have defined "natural resources." Because UNCLOS Article 77 regulates living organisms and non-living resources, including minerals, it would seem that a broad definition of "natural resources" would include all living organisms and non-living matter ("matter" instead of "resources" avoids a tautology), including minerals, in an area of ocean space covered by particular provisions.

---

[763] UNCLOS art. 192 declares the general obligation of States "to preserve and protect the marine environment."

[764] *See also* UNCLOS art. 1(2), defining "Authority" as the International Sea-Bed Authority.

By parity of reasoning, EEZ natural resources include all living organisms and all non-living matter within ocean areas covered by UNCLOS's EEZ provisions. Continental shelf natural resources would include living organisms and non-living matter on and below the continental shelf as Article 77 provides. Area natural resources would include living organisms and non-living matter in the Area as it is defined in Article 1(1). Elsewhere, in other ocean areas UNCLOS governs, a general rule for environmental protection applies; *e.g.*, in the territorial sea, coastal States may explore and exploit natural resources, *i.e.* all living organisms and nonliving matter, under their environmental policies as territorial sea sovereign, but they have an UNCLOS Article 193 duty to protect and preserve the marine environment.

Section 9 defines "Area" and "area;" § 28, "coast;" § 31, "coastal State;" § 126, "ocean space" or "sea."

§ 113. *Nautical chart*

See Chart, § 23.

§ 114. *Nautical mile*

See Mile or nautical mile, § 105.

§ 115. *Navarea*

In UNCLOS analysis, "Navarea" means a geographical sea area established for the purpose of coordinating the transmission of radio navigational warnings.

Comment

In LOAC-governed situations under the "other rules of international law" clauses in UNCLOS, a different definition may apply. The same may be the situation if the UN Charter supersedes UNCLOS or if jus cogens norms apply.[765]

Former ECDIS Glossary, page 15, defined "Navarea" as "[a] geographical sea area established for the purpose of co-ordinating the transmission of radio *navigational warnings*." The newer ECDIS Glossary does not define "Navarea."

---

765 *See* Parts III.B-III.D and § 132, defining "other rules of international law."

Section 3 defines "aid(s) to navigation" or "navigational aid(s);" § 9, "Area" and "area;" § 54, "due notice," appropriate publicity," and "due publicity;" § 95, "List of Radio Signals;" § 101, "Maritime Safety Information," abbreviated MSI; § 116, "Navarea warning;" § 117, "navigational warning;" § 126, "ocean space" or "sea;" § 199, "warning."[766]

§ 116. *Navarea warning*

In UNCLOS analysis, "Navarea warning" means a navigational warning issued by the Navarea coordinator for the Navarea.

Comment

In LOAC-governed situations under the "other rules of international law" clauses in UNCLOS, a different definition may apply. The same may be the situation if the UN Charter supersedes UNCLOS or if jus cogens norms apply.[767]

Former ECDIS Glossary, page 15, defined "Navarea warning" as "[a] *navigational warning* issued by the Navarea co-ordinator for the *Navarea*." The newer ECDIS Glossary does not define "Navarea warning."

Section 54 defines "due notice," "appropriate publicity," and "due publicity;" § 115, "Navarea;" § 118, "navigational warning;" § 199, "warning."[768]

§ 117. *Navigational aid(s)*

See Aid(s) to navigation, § 3.

§ 118. *Navigational warning*

In UNCLOS analysis, "navigational warning" means a broadcast message containing urgent information relating to safe navigation.

Comment

In LOAC-governed situations under the "other rules of international law" clauses in UNCLOS, a different definition may apply. The same

---

[766] *See also* Churchill & Lowe ch. 12; Walker, *ECDIS Glossary* 253–54, 2003–04 ABILA Proc. 226.

[767] *See* Parts III.B-III.D and § 132, defining "other rules of international law."

[768] *See also* Walker, *ECDIS Glossary* 254–55, 2003–04 ABILA Proc. 226–27.

may be the situation if the UN Charter supersedes UNCLOS or if jus cogens norms apply.[769]

Former ECDIS Glossary, page 15, defined "navigational warning" as "[a] broadcast message containing urgent information relating to safe navigation." The newer ECDIS Glossary does not define "navigational warning."

Section 3 defines "aid(s) to navigation" or "navigational aid(s);" § 53, "due notice," "appropriate publicity," and "due publicity;" § 199, "warning."[770]

§ 119. *NOTAM*

See Notice to airmen, § 121.

§ 120. *Notice*

See Appropriate notice, § 8; Due notice, § 54.

§ 121. *Notice to airmen, abbreviated NOTAM*

In UNCLOS analysis, "notice to airmen," abbreviated as NOTAM, means a periodical notice issued by maritime administrations, or other competent authorities, regarding changes in aids to aerial navigation, dangers to aerial navigation, and, in general all such information as affects nautical charts, sailing directions, light lists, and other nautical or aerial navigation publications.

Comment

In LOAC-governed situations under the "other rules of international law" clauses in UNCLOS, a different definition may apply. The same may be the situation if the UN Charter supersedes UNCLOS, or if jus cogens norms apply.[771]

The ECDIS Glossary does not define "notice to airmen." This definition is based on § 122, Notice to mariners, abbreviated NtM or NOTMAR.

Section 3 defines "aid(s) to navigation" and "navigational aid(s);" § 23, "chart" and "nautical chart;" § 44, "danger to navigation;" § 45, "danger

[769] *See* Parts III.B-III.D and § 132, defining "other rules of international law."
[770] *See also* Walker, *ECDIS Glossary* 254, 2003–04 ABILA Proc. 227.
[771] *See* Parts III.B-III.D and § 132, defining "other rules of international law."

to overflight;" § 54, "due notice," "appropriate publicity" and "due publicity;" § 95, "list of lights" or "light list;" § 153, "sailing directions."[772]

§ 122. *Notice to mariners, abbreviated NtM or NOTMAR*

In UNCLOS analysis, "notice to mariners," abbreviated as NtM or NOTMAR, means a periodical notice issued by maritime administrations, or other competent authorities, regarding changes in aids to navigation, dangers to navigation, important new soundings, and, in general all such information as affects nautical charts, sailing directions, light lists, and other nautical publications.

Comment

In LOAC-governed situations under the "other rules of international law" clauses in UNCLOS, a different definition may apply. The same may be the situation if the UN Charter supersedes UNCLOS or if jus cogens norms apply.[773]

Former ECDIS Glossary, page 16, defined "notice to mariners," abbreviated as NtM or NOTMAR, as "[a] periodical notice issued by maritime administrations, or other competent authorities, regarding changes in aids to navigation, dangers to navigation, important new soundings, and, in general all such information as affects nautical charts, sailing directions, light lists and other nautical publications." The newer ECDIS Glossary does not define "notice to mariners."

Section 3 defines "aid(s) to navigation" and "navigational aid(s);" § 23, "chart" or "nautical chart;" § 44, "danger to navigation;" § 45, "danger to overflight;" § 54, "due notice," "appropriate publicity" and "due publicity;" § 95, "list of lights" or "light list;" § 121, "notice to airmen;" § 153, "sailing directions," "Coast Pilot" or "Coastal Pilot."[774]

§ 123. *NOTMAR*

See Notice to mariners, § 122.

---

[772] *See also* Walker, *ECDIS Glossary* 255, 2003–04 ABILA Proc. 227–28. DOD Dictionary 384 defines "notice to airmen" similarly: "A notice containing information concerning the establishment, condition, or change in any aeronautical facility, service, procedures, or hazard, the timely knowledge of which is essential to personnel concerned with flight operations. Also called NOTAM."

[773] *See* Parts III.B-III.D and § 132, defining "other rules of international law."

[774] *See* Walker, *ECDIS Glossary* 255–56, 2003–04 ABILA Proc. 228–29. DOD Dictionary does not define "notice to mariners," but *id.* Appendix A, *Abbreviations and Acronyms*, p. A-107 defines NOTMAR as "notice to mariners."

§ 124. *NtM*

See Notice to mariners, § 122.

§ 125. *Object*

In UNCLOS analysis, "object" means an identifiable set of information. An object may have characteristics and may be related to other objects. It does not include archeological and historical "objects" protected by UNCLOS Article 303.

Comment

In LOAC-governed situations under the "other rules of international law" clauses in UNCLOS, a different definition may apply. The same may be the situation if the UN Charter supersedes UNCLOS or if jus cogens norms apply.[775]

Former ECDIS Glossary, page 16, defined "object" as "[a]n identifiable set of information. An object may have *attributes* and may be related to other objects." The newer ECDIS Glossary, page 7, definition is the same.

UNCLOS Article 303(1) declares: "States have the duty to protect objects of an archaeological and historical nature found at sea and shall cooperate for this purpose." Use of "object" in UNCLOS Article 303 is not within the § 125 definition.

Section 13 defines "attributes;" § 64, "feature object."[776]

§ 126. *Ocean space or sea*

"Ocean space" or "sea" as used in UNCLOS analysis means the water surface and water column as those water areas that are regulated by UNCLOS provisions. Depending on a particular ocean space or sea area, "ocean space" or "sea" may also include the seabed. "Ocean space" or "sea" may include the air column superjacent to a given water surface of an ocean space or sea area governed by UNCLOS; the law of the air column over these ocean spaces or sea areas is governed in part by UNCLOS (*e.g.*, high seas overflight as a freedom of the seas) and in part by other law, *e.g.*, air law.

---

[775] *See* Parts III.B-III.D and § 132, defining "other rules of international law."

[776] *See also* 2007–08 ABILA Proc. 294; Walker, *ECDIS Glossary* 256, 2003–04 ABILA Proc. 229.

Comment

In LOAC-governed situations under the "other rules of international law" clauses in UNCLOS, different definitions may apply. The same may be the situation if the UN Charter supersedes UNCLOS or if jus cogens norms apply.[777]

UNCLOS does not define "sea" or "ocean space."[778] Because UNCLOS deals with sea areas ranging from the high seas to internal waters, UNCLOS measures "ocean space" or the "sea" from given distances from land, regardless of the technical legal or physical classification of those ocean spaces. A "saltiness" or salinity definition is not useful; some "ocean space" or "sea" areas, *e.g.*, some internal waters covered by UNCLOS may be brackish or largely freshwater in nature.

Research uncovered no institutional or commentator definitions for "ocean space" or "sea." The ABILA LOS Committee approved the revised definition published above.[779] The second sentence of the definition covers situations of a seabed outside the Area, *see* UNCLOS Article 1(1), where, *e.g.*, a coastal State has not claimed to the limit for a continental shelf that Article 76 permits, and the seabed off a coastal State between the edge of Article 76's limit and the seabed within the Area. The third sentence declares applicability of air law where UNCLOS does not apply. UNCLOS Article 2(2), following Territorial Sea Convention Article 2, declares that coastal State sovereignty extends to the airspace over the coastal State's territorial sea. UNCLOS Article 34(1) inter alia declares that straits passage shall not in other respects affect the exercise by States bordering straits of their sovereignty or jurisdiction over their airspace. Article 49(2) declares that archipelagic state sovereignty extends to airspace over archipelagic waters. Article 56(1)(a) declares the coastal State has sovereign rights with regard to other activities for EEZ economic exploitation and exploration, *e.g.*, energy production "from … winds[.]" Articles 58(1)

[777] *See* Parts III.B-III.D and § 132, defining "other rules of international law."

[778] 2 Commentary ¶ 1.26.

[779] Horace B. Robertson, Jr., Professor Emeritus, Duke University School of Law and a former U.S. UNCLOS delegation member, recommended revising the first draft; the Committee gratefully acknowledges this recommendation and accepts it for the definition. *Compare* Walker, *Defining* 358–59 (original text and analysis) *with* Walker, *Definitions* 210–11 (revised text and analysis); *see also* 2007–08 ABILA Proc. 294–96. DOD Dictionary 331 defines "maritime domain" as "The oceans, seas, bays, estuaries, islands, coastal areas, and the airspace above these, including the littorals."

and 87(1), the latter following High Seas Convention Article 2, refer to overflight rights in the EEZ and over the high seas.

Section 9 defines "area" and "Area;" § 28, "coast;" § 31, "coastal State;" § 47, "deep ocean floor;" § 81, "high seas;" § 127, "oceanic plateau;" § 128, "oceanic ridge;" § 157, "sea-bed," "seabed" or "bed;" § 185, "superjacent waters" or "water column."

§ 127. *Oceanic plateau*

As used in UNCLOS Article 47(7), "oceanic plateau" means a comparatively flat-topped elevation of the seabed which rises steeply from the ocean floor on all sides and is of considerable extent across the summit.

Comment

In LOAC-governed situations under the "other rules of international law" clauses in UNCLOS, a different definition may apply. The same may be the situation if the UN Charter supersedes UNCLOS or if jus cogens norms apply.[780]

Consolidated Glossary ¶ 67, echoing Former Glossary ¶ 59, defines "oceanic plateau" as "[a] comparatively flat-topped elevation of the sea-bed which rises steeply from the ocean floor on all sides, and is of considerable extent across the summit."

UNCLOS Article 47(7), part of the UNCLOS rules for archipelagic States, provides: "For the purpose of computing the ratio of water to land under [Article 47(1)], land areas may include waters lying within the fringing reefs of islands and atolls, including that part of a steep-sided oceanic plateau which is enclosed or nearly enclosed by a chain of limestone islands and drying reefs lying on the perimeter of the plateau." The Glossary recites a similar but not identical recitation of Article 47(7).

Section 12 defines "atoll;" § 47, "deep ocean floor;" § 53, "drying reef;" § 69, "fringing reef;" § 126, "ocean space" and "sea;" § 140, "reef;" § 157, "sea-bed," "seabed" or "bed."[781]

---

[780] *See* Parts III.B-III.D and § 132, defining "other rules of international law."

[781] Geographic archipelagoes may not qualify as juridical archipelagoes under UNCLOS. *See generally* Churchill & Lowe 120–26; 2 Commentary ¶¶ 47.1–47.8, 47.9(*l*); NWP 1-14M Annotated ¶¶ 1.4.3, 1.6 & Fig. A1-2; 1 O'Connell ch. 6; Restatement (Third) §§ 511–12, 515, 523; Walker, *Consolidated Glossary* 277–78.

§ 128. *Oceanic ridge*

As used in UNCLOS Article 76(3), "oceanic ridge" means a long elevation of the ocean floor with irregular or smooth topography and smooth sides. "Oceanic ridge" is not synonymous with "submarine ridge," defined in § 182.

Comment

In LOAC-governed situations under the "other rules of international law" clauses in UNCLOS, a different definition may apply. The same may be the situation if the UN Charter supersedes UNCLOS or if jus cogens norms apply.[782]

Consolidated Glossary ¶ 68, echoing Former Glossary ¶ 60, defines "oceanic ridge" as "[a] long elevation of the ocean floor with either irregular or smooth topography and smooth sides."[783]

UNCLOS Article 76(3), defining the continental margin, says "[i]t does not include the deep ocean floor with its ridges or the subsoil thereof." The ILA Committee on Legal Issues of the Outer Continental Shelf comments on "oceanic ridges":

> Article 76(3) ... provides that the continental margin does not include the deep ocean floor with its oceanic ridges or the subsoil thereof. Article 76(6) ... provides that on submarine ridges the outer limit of the continental shelf shall not exceed 350 nautical miles from the baselines. Article 76(6) does not apply to submarine elevations that are natural components of the continental margin. The use of these three different terms in articles 76(3) and 76(6) indicates that these have separate meaning[s]. Any submarine feature can be subsumed under one of these terms.
>
> The definition of the outer edge of the continental margin for the purposes of article 76 is contained in articles 76(4) to 76(6) ... Application of these provisions may lead to the inclusion of (parts of) ridges of oceanic origin in the continental shelf. The inclusion of the reference to oceanic ridges in article 76(3) establishes that such a result does not imply that as a consequence of all the feature concerned can be treated as part of the continental margin for the purpose of article 76. The term "oceanic ridge" does not change the content of the terms "natural prolongation" and "continental margin."
>
> The term "submarine ridges" in article 76(6) ... is applicable to ridges that are (predominantly) of oceanic origin and are the natural prolongation of the land territory of a coastal State.

---

782 *See* Parts III.B-III.D and § 132, defining "other rules of international law."

783 *Accord,* 2 Commentary ¶ 76.18(d).

> The term "submarine elevations that are natural components of the continental margin" is applicable to features which, although at some point in time were not a part of the continental margin or have become detached from the continental margin, through geological processes are or have become so closely linked to the continental margin as to become a part of it.[784]

See also the *Comment* to § 16, "basepoint or point."

Section 28 defines "coast;" § 31, "coastal State;" § 37, "continental rise;" § 38, "continental slope;" § 47, "deep ocean floor;" § 67, "foot of the continental slope;" § 126, "ocean space" or "sea;" § 182, "submarine ridge;" § 184, "subsoil."[785]

§ 129. *Offshore installation*

See Artificial island, § 10.

§ 130. *Opposite coasts*

As used in UNCLOS Articles 15, 74, 76, 83 and 134 and in Annex II, Article 9, "opposite coasts" means the geographical relationship of the coasts of two States facing each other.

Comment

In LOAC-governed situations under the "other rules of international law" clauses in UNCLOS, a different definition may apply. The same may be the situation if the UN Charter supersedes UNCLOS or if jus cogens norms apply.[786]

Consolidated Glossary ¶ 69, echoing Former Glossary ¶ 61, defines "opposite coasts" as "[t]he geographical relationship of the coasts of two States facing each other."

UNCLOS Articles 15, 74(1), 76(1), 83(1) and 134(4), and UNCLOS Annex II, Article 9 declare rules for delimiting sea boundaries for States with opposite and adjacent coasts. Territorial Sea Convention Article 12 and Shelf Convention Article 6 also declare rules for delimiting sea boundaries for States with opposite and adjacent coasts.

---

784 COCS *Second Report*, Conclusion 3, p. 219.

785 *See also* Churchill & Lowe 148–50; ¶¶ 76.1–76.18(a), 76.18(d) & Fig. 2; NWP 1-14M Annotated ¶ 1.6 & Fig. A1-2; 2 O'Connell ch. 18A; Restatement (Third) §§ 511–12, 515, 523; Noyes, *Definitions* 322–23 & Part III.D.3; Walker, *Consolidated Glossary* 278–79.

786 *See* Parts III.B-III.D and § 132, defining "other rules of international law."

Section 2 defines "adjacent coasts;" § 28, "coast;" § 31, "coastal State."[787]

§ 131. *Optimum utilization*

"Optimum utilization," as used in UNCLOS Article 62(1), means use of the living resources of the EEZ at a level of utilization that may be less than full or maximum utilization. Whether measured according to biological or economic terms, optimum utilization may be a lower level of use of the living resources of the EEZ. The Article 62(1) optimum utilization standard is subject to the UNCLOS Article 61 rules concerning conservation of the living resources of the EEZ.

Comment

In LOAC-governed situations under the "other rules of international law" clauses in UNCLOS, a different definition may apply. The same may be the situation if the UN Charter supersedes UNCLOS or if *jus cogens* norms apply.[788]

"Optimum utilization" appears in UNCLOS Article 62(1): "The coastal State shall promote the objective of optimum utilization of the living resources in the exclusive economic zone without prejudice to article 61." Article 61 establishes standards for conserving EEZ living resources.[789] "Optimum utilization" applies only to a coastal State's EEZ under UNCLOS Article 62(1). By contrast, "maximum sustainable yield," defined in § 100, applies to a coastal State's EEZ and the high seas under UNCLOS Articles 61 and 119.

UNCLOS Article 62(1) commentary discusses the origins of "optimum utilization":

> ... The only specific references to utilization in fishery proposals had called for the coastal State to "ensure the full utilization" ... or "assure the maximum utilization" ... Those references differed from the obligation to "promote the objective" of optimum utilization, which contrasts considerably with "ensuring" that objective or "seeking" that objective on all

---

787 *See generally* Churchill & Lowe 148–50, 183, 191–97; 2 Commentary ¶¶ 15.1–15.12(c), 47.1–47.9(m), 83.1–83.19(f); NWP 1–14M Annotated ¶¶ 1.4.3, particularly n.42; 1.6, particularly n.57 & Fig. A1–2; 2 O'Connell 681, 684–90, 699–732; Restatement (Third) §§ 511–12, 516-17; Noyes, *Definitions* 322–23 & Part III.D.3; Walker, *Consolidated Glossary* 279–80.

788 *See* Parts III.B-III.D and § 132, defining "other rules of international law."

789 *See* Parts IV.B §§ 31, 102.

> occasions. ... "[O]ptimum" also differs from "full" and "maximum," and in biological and economic terms may suggest a lower level of utilization.[790]

Fishing Convention Article 2 provides:

> ... [T]he expression "conservation of the living resources of the high seas" means the aggregate of the measures rendering possible the optimum sustainable yield from those resources ... to secure a maximum supply of food and other marine products. Conservation programmes should be formulated with a view to securing in the first place a supply of food for human consumption.

Section 28 defines "coast;" § 31, "coastal State;" § 81, "high seas;" § 102, "maximum sustainable yield."[791]

§ 132. *Other rules of international law*

The traditional understanding is that "other rules of international law" and similar phrases in UNCLOS restate a customary rule, *i.e.*, that the phrase means the law of armed conflict (LOAC), including its components of the law of naval warfare and the law of maritime neutrality. In some instances, however, *e.g.*, UNCLOS Articles 293(1) and 303, the phrase may include international law other than the LOAC in situations where the LOAC does not apply.

Comment

Although the law of naval warfare and the law of neutrality are usually the only branches of the LOAC considered applicable to war at sea, other LOAC components may apply in some situations, *e.g.*, land-based aircraft engaged in combat or attacks over the sea, after which the aircraft return to bases on land. If the UN Charter supersedes UNCLOS or if jus cogens norms apply, a different definition may apply.[792]

This phrase, sometimes stated slightly differently, appears throughout UNCLOS, *i.e.*, in the Preamble and in Articles 2(3) (territorial sea); 19, 21, 31 (territorial sea innocent passage); 34(2) (straits transit passage); 52(1) (archipelagic sea lanes passage; incorporation by reference

---

[790] 2 Commentary ¶ 62.16(b), referring to documentation reprinted in *id.* ¶¶ 62.2, p. 619; 62.4; *see also id.* 62.16(c); Jennings & Watts § 335.

[791] *See also* 2007–08 ABILA Proc. 299–300; Churchill & Lowe 289–91; Walker, *Last Round* 179–80.

[792] *See* Parts III.B-III.C.

of Articles 19, 21, 31); 58(1), 58(3) (EEZ); 78 (continental shelf; coastal State rights do not affect superjacent waters, *i.e.*, territorial or high seas; coastal State cannot infringe or unjustifiably interfere with "navigation and other rights and freedoms of other States as provided in this Convention"); 87(1) (high seas); 138 (the Area); 293 (court or tribunal having jurisdiction for settling disputes must apply UNCLOS and "other rules of international law" not incompatible with UNCLOS); 303(4) (archeological, historical objects found at sea, "other international agreements and rules of international law regarding the protection of objects of an archeological and historical nature"); Annex III, Article 21(1).

The phrase is also in High Seas Convention Article 2 and Territorial Sea Convention Article 1. Although it does not appear in other 1958 LOS Conventions, Shelf Convention Articles 1 and 3 say that treaty does not affect status of waters above as high seas. Fishing Convention Articles 1–8 declare that treaty does not affect other high seas rights. The implication from these two treaties is that except as the Shelf or Fishery Conventions derogate from High Seas or Territorial Sea Convention rules, the latter treaties' terms must be read into the Shelf and Fishing Conventions.

The High Seas Convention[793] and UNCLOS' navigational articles,[794] *i.e.*, those dealing with navigation through the territorial sea, high seas, etc., restate customary law. The increasing number of UNCLOS ratifications strengthens a view that its navigational articles restate custom.[795] The result is that these provisions bind States as custom, even if they are not parties to the 1958 LOS Conventions or UNCLOS. For those countries that are parties to either,[796] they are bound by treaty and customary norms.[797]

---

[793] *See, e.g.*, High Seas Convention, pmbl., declaring it restates custom; United States Department of the Navy, Annotated Supplement to the Commander's Handbook on the Law of Naval Operations: NWP 9 (Rev. A)/FMFM 1–10 ¶ 1.1 at 1–2 n.4 (1989); *cf.* Churchill & Lowe 15; 1 O'Connell 385, 474–76.

[794] Restatement (Third) Part V, *Introductory Note*, 3–5; NWP 1–14M Annotated ¶ 1.1; *cf.* Moore, *Introduction*, note 101; Oxman, *International Law*, note 60, p. 29.

[795] Multilateral Treaties ch. 21 pt. 6 lists 157 States as UNCLOS parties as of April 1, 2009; by then 135 were parties to the 1994 Agreement. *Id.* ch. 21, pt. 6.a.

[796] *See id.* ch. 21, pts. 1–4; TIF 364, 395–96 (38 parties to Fishing Convention, 63 to High Seas Convention, 58 to Shelf Convention, 52 to Territorial Sea Convention); note 791 and accompanying text (157 parties to UNCLOS, 135 parties to 1994 Agreement). Treaty succession principles suggest that even more States have been or were 1958 Convention parties before they ratified UNCLOS. *See generally* Brownlie 661–66; *Final Report*, note 576; Jennings & Watts § 62, pp. 211–13; Symposium, note 576; Walker, *Integration*, note 576.

[797] ICJ Statute art. 38(1); Restatement (Third) §§ 102–03.

Most authorities agree that the phrase, "other rules of international law," refers to the LOAC.[798] This being the case, the phrase means that the LOS is subject to the LOAC in situations where the latter applies. At the same time, as between, *e.g.*, neutrals engaged in merchant ship navigation far from an area of armed conflict on, over or under the sea, the LOS continues in effect. UNCLOS Article 88, declaring that the high seas are reserved for peaceful purposes, is not to the contrary. Like the 1958 LOS Conventions,

> That provision does not preclude ... use of the high seas by naval forces. Their use for aggressive purposes, which would ... violat[e] ... Article 2(4) of the [UN] Charter ..., is forbidden as well by Article 88. See also [UNCLOS] Article 301, requiring parties, in exercising their rights and p[er]forming their duties under the Convention, to refrain from any threat or use of force in violation of the Charter.[799]

---

[798] 1966 ILC Rep., note 38, p. 267–68; 2 Georg Schwarzenberger, A Manual of International Law 376–77 (5th ed. 1967); Walker, The Tanker 191–92; Boczek, *Peaceful*, note 74; Herbert W. Briggs, *Unilateral Denunciation of Treaties: The Vienna Convention and the International Court of Justice*, 68 AJIL 51 (1974); Carl Q. Christol & C.R. Davis, *Maritime Quarantine: The Naval Interdiction of Offensive Weapons and Associated Material to Cuba, 1962*, 56 AJIL 525, 539–40 (1963); Scott Davidson, *United States Protection of Reflagged Kuwaiti Vessels in the Gulf War: The Legal Implications*, 4 Int'l J. Estuarine & Coastal L. 173, 178 (1989); W.J. Fenrick, *Legal Aspects of Targeting in the Law of Naval Warfare*, 1991 Can. Y.B. Int'l L. 238, 245; Lowe, *The Commander's*, note 43, p. 132; Oxman, *The Regime*, note 74, p. 811; Natalino Ronzitti, *The Crisis of the Traditional Law Regulating International Armed Conflicts at Sea and the Need for Its Revision*, in The Law of Naval Warfare: A Collection of Agreements and Documents with Commentaries 1, 15 (N. Ronzitti ed. 1988); Russo, note 74, p. 384; A.G.Y. Thorpe, *Mine Warfare at Sea — Some Legal Aspects of the Future*, 18 Ocean Devel. & Int'l L. 255, 257 (1987); Rudiger Wolfrum, *Reflagging and Escort Operations in the Persian Gulf: An International Law Perspective*, 30 Va. J. Int'l L. 387, 391–92 (1989). Apparent dissenters include 2 O'Connell 1112–13, referring to 1 *id.* 747–69 in the context of merchant ships; Luan Low & David Hodgkinson, *Compensation for Wartime Environmental Damage: Challenges to International Law After the Gulf War*, 35 Va. J. Int'l L. 405, 421 (1995), discussing environmental protections in the LOS context but saying nothing about the clauses, although they elliptically seem to recognize the principle; Margaret T. Okorodudu-Fubara, *Oil in the Persian Gulf War: Legal Appraisal of an Environmental Disaster*, 23 St. Mary's L.J. 123 195–97 (1991). Churchill & Lowe 421 recognize the separate "well-defined body of Laws of War at Sea" but also say that "[T]he extent to which rights and duties under the [LOS] conventions are modified or suspended in time of war is a controversial matter, compounded by the uncertainty of the Law of Treaties on this point."

[799] Restatement (Third) § 521, cmt. b, citing UN Charter art. 2(4); UNCLOS, arts. 88, 301 and referring to Restatement (Third) § 905, cmt. g; *accord*, Legality of Threat of Nuclear Weapons, 1996(1) ICJ 226, 244 (adv. op.); 3 Commentary ¶¶ 87.9(i), 88.1–88.7(d); Russo, *Targeting*, note 74, p. 8; *see also Helsinki Principles*, note 15, Principle 1.2; Boczek, note 74; Oxman, *The Regime*, note 74, p. 814; Parkerson, note 74, pp. 79–85. UNCLOS arts. 19(2)(a), 39(1)(b) forbid activity during a foreign ship's innocent passage or straits transit passage that is a threat or use of force against coastal State sovereignty, territorial integrity or political independence.

(UN Charter Article 103 applies to UNCLOS, like any treaty; UN Security Council decisions[800] or States' individual or collective self-defense responses[801] can supersede inconsistent LOS treaty provisions. The same analysis applies to jus cogens norms, although there is a debate on what principles, if any, have ascended to jus cogens status.[802])

It might be argued that UNCLOS Article 293(1) and Annex III Article 21(1) subordinate other rules of international law to UNCLOS. Those provisions read:

Article 293
Applicable Law

1. A court or tribunal having jurisdiction under this section [UNCLOS Articles 286–96] shall apply this Convention and other rules of international law not incompatible with this Convention.

Article 21
Applicable Law

1. The contract shall be governed by the terms of the contract, the rules, regulations and procedures of the Authority, Part XI [UNCLOS Articles 191–233] and other rules of international law not incompatible with this Convention. …

The negotiating history is sparse on the point.[803] However, part of UNCLOS to which these provisions refer are the other rules clauses. It seems, therefore, that the ultimate result is that a court, tribunal or other decision maker must apply the LOAC as part of the law of UNCLOS incorporated by reference in appropriate situations through the other rules clauses.

The general law of treaties would seem to say that the LOS Conventions may be suspended during armed conflict, at least insofar as LOAC rules apply to a situation.[804]

---

[800] UN Charter arts. 25, 48, 94(2), 103; *see also* Goodrich 614–17; 2 Simma 1292–1302; George K. Walker, *Information Warfare and Neutrality*, 33 Vand. J. Transnat'l L. 1079, 1128–29 (2000) (collecting sources).

[801] UN Charter arts. 51, 103; *see also* sources cited in George K. Walker, *Anticipatory Collective Self-Defense in the Charter Era: What the Treaties Have Said*, 31 Cornell Int'l L.J. 321 (1998), also in Michael J. Schmitt, ed., The Law of Military Operations: Liber Amicorum Professor Jack Grunawalt ch. 15 (Nav. War C. Int'l L. Stud., v. 72, 1998).

[802] *See generally* Vienna Convention, pmbl., arts. 53, 64; Brownlie 510–12 (jus cogens' content uncertain); Elias, note 65, pp. 177–87; Jennings & Watts § 2; Restatement (Third) §§ 102-03, 331, 338(2); Sinclair 17–18, 218–26 (Vienna Convention principles progressive development); Jimenez de Arechaga, note 38, pp. 64–67; Weisburd, note 65.

[803] 5 Commentary ¶¶ 293.1–293.5.

[804] International law is in disarray on whether war terminates or suspends treaties; modern sources, citing *pacta sunt servanda*, emphasize suspension. Vienna Convention

An illustration of the difference between LOAC and LOS standards is the LOAC rule that the flag flown determines whether a merchant ship operates as a neutral or enemy vessel.[805] UNCLOS Articles 91, 94 recite principles for determining a merchantman's nationality, following High Seas Convention Article 5(1), today a customary[806] LOS rule.[807] Another might be "due regard" under the LOS and "due regard" under the LOAC.[808] A third might be the difference between rules for "roadsteads" under UNCLOS and rules for "roadsteads" under the LOAC.[809] A fourth might be the difference between "seaworthiness" under UNCLOS and "seaworthiness" under the LOAC.[810] A fifth is the difference between LOS and LOAC rules for submarine cables,[811] and a sixth is the difference in rules between the LOS and the LOAC for submarine pipelines.[812] There may be different rules for lawful fishing under the LOAC in a given situation.[813] Warnings during armed conflict, although perhaps seemingly similar in scenario (*e.g.*, those

---

art. 60(5) recites the rule that breach of a treaty governing humanitarian law protecting the human person is not subject to the usual treaty breach rules. The Convention does not address the core question of general treaty application, nonapplication, or suspension during armed conflict, however. *See generally* 1966 ILC Rep., note 38, p. 267; Aust 308; Brownlie 620–21; Treaties, 5 Hackworth, Digest § 513, at 390; *compare* Institut de Droit International, *The Effects of Armed Conflicts on Treaties*, Aug. 28, 1985, 61(2) Annuaire 278 (1980) *with id., Regulations Regarding the Effect of War on Treaties*, 1912, 7 AJIL 153 (1913); Harvard Draft Convention art. 35, note 91, pp. 663, 664; Jennings & Watts § 655; McNair ch. 43; 2 Oppenheim, note 69, § 99; Sinclair 6, 163, 165; Walker, The Tanker 190–91; Herbert W. Briggs, *Unilateral Denunciation of Treaties: The Vienna Convention and the International Court of Justice*, 68 AJIL 51 (1974); Louise Doswald-Beck & Sylvain Vite, *International Humanitarian Law and Human Rights Law,* 1993 Int'l Rev. Red Cross 94; G.G. Fitzmaurice, *The Judicial Clauses of the Peace Treaties,* 73 R.C.A.D.I. 255, 312 (1948); Cecil J.B. Hurst, *The Effect of War on Treaties*, 2 Brit. Y.B. Int'l L. 37 (1921); Kearney & Dalton, note 38, p. 557; Walker, *Integration*, note 576, p. 70; David Weissbrodt & Peggy L. Hicks, *Implementation of Human Rights and Humanitarian Law in Situations of Armed Conflict,* 1993 Int'l Rev. Red Cross 120. Some treaties say whether they are or are not in force during war, *e.g.,* Convention on International Civil Aviation, note 484, art. 89 (in force during war); North American Free Trade Agreement, Dec. 8–17, 1992, arts. 2102, 2204, TIAS —, 32 ILM 289, 605, 702 (1993) (may be suspended). The International Law Commission has begun analyzing the issue. *See* 2005 ILC Rep., note 65, pp. 44–72; Matheson, *The Fifty-Seventh,* note 65, pp. 422–24.

805 San Remo Manual ¶¶ 112–13; NWP 1-14M Annotated ¶ 7.5; *see also* the analysis in § 65, "flag State."

806 *See* note 795 and accompanying text.

807 *See* the § 72 *Comment* for "genuine link."

808 *See* the § 56 *Comment* for "due regard."

809 *See* the § 146 *Comment* for "roadstead" or "roads."

810 *See* the § 159 *Comment* for "seaworthy" or "seaworthiness."

811 *See* the § 179 *Comment* for "submarine cable."

812 *See* the § 181 *Comment* for "submarine pipeline."

813 *See* the § 65 *Comment* for "fishing."

incident to approach and visit under the LOS and visit and search under the LOAC), may be different.[814] Erection of coastal defenses in, *e.g.*, a state's territorial sea during an armed conflict situation involving it might involve different rules than those for artificial islands and the like.[815] The customary LOAC applied in a given situation may supply other distinctions.[816] For an example of a possibly different definition in a potential self-defense situation, see the analysis for the definition of "sea-bed," "seabed" or "bed."[817]

Professor Noyes has advocated a broader potential definition of the phrase, particularly with reference to UNCLOS Articles 293, part of the dispute settlement provisions governing the International Tribunal for the Law of the Sea, and 303, protection of the underwater cultural heritage. He concludes that a broader definition does not preclude application of non-LOAC "other rules" if they do not conflict with an applicable LOAC rule; the LOAC may apply in a situation but not necessarily occupy the field to the exclusion of non-LOAC rules.[818] The original definition has been amended to accommodate this view.[819]

Section 28 defines "coast;" § 31, "coastal State;" § 79, "high seas."

§ 133. *Outer limit*

(a) Under UNCLOS, "outer limit" means the extent to which a coastal State claims or may claim a specific jurisdiction in accordance with UNCLOS Articles 4, 75, 76, 84 and Annex II. In particular, "outer limits" in Article 76(9) means the outer limit of a continental shelf beyond 200 nautical miles and may mean the outer limit of a continental shelf at 200 nautical miles.

---

[814] *See* the § 199 *Comment* for "warning."

[815] *See* the § 10 *Comment* for "artificial island, offshore installation, installation (offshore).

[816] *E.g.*, LOAC warnings, many of which have roots in custom. *See* § 199 *Comment*.

[817] *See* the § 157 *Comment* for "sea-bed," "seabed," or "bed." Erecting offshore coastal defenses in a State's territorial sea for self-defense purposes might involve different rules from those for the LOAC or the LOS. *See* Parts III.B-III.D; § 10 *Comment* for "artificial island," "offshore installation," "installation (offshore)."

[818] *See* Part III.D.2.d; Noyes, *Treaty* 374–79, 2001–02 ABILA Proc. 182–89; *see also* 3 Commentary ¶ 87.9(b); Noyes, *Definitions* 311–14; Part III.D.3. Some commentators would agree with Professor Noyes while citing less authority. *See* note 798 and accompanying text.

[819] *Compare* Walker, *Definitions* 360–63 (original text and analysis) *with* Walker, *Defining* 211–14, *and* Walker, *ECDIS Glossary* 232–36, 2003–04 ABILA Proc. 202–06; *see also* 2007–08 ABILA Proc. 300–07; DOD Dictionary 115 (defining "conflict").

(b) "Outer limit" also means the outer boundary of a contiguous zone that States may claim and do claim under UNCLOS Article 33.

Comment

In LOAC-governed situations under the "other rules of international law" clauses in UNCLOS, a different definition may apply. The same may be the situation if the UN Charter supersedes UNCLOS, or if jus cogens norms apply.[820]

The definition for "outer limit" in UNCLOS focuses on UNCLOS provisions using the term and adds a definition for the contiguous zone "outer limit" where UNCLOS Article 33 does not use the phrase.

Consolidated Glossary ¶ 70, echoing Former Glossary ¶ 62, defines "outer limit" as "[t]he extent to which a coastal State claims or may claim a specific jurisdiction in accordance with the provisions of the Convention."

UNCLOS Article 4 provides that the territorial sea outer limit is the line every point of which is at a distance from the nearest point of the baseline equal to the territorial sea's breadth. Territorial Sea Convention Article 6 recites the same formula.

UNCLOS Article 33(2) says the contiguous zone may not extend beyond 24 nautical miles from baselines from which the territorial sea's breadth is measured but does not use the phrase "outer limit." Territorial Sea Convention Article 24(2) uses the same language but limits the contiguous zone to 12 miles.

UNCLOS Article 75(1) says that, subject to Articles 55–75, "the outer limit lines" of the EEZ and the lines of delimitation drawn in accordance with Article 74, stating rules for delimiting EEZs between States with opposite or adjacent coasts, must be shown on charts of a scale or scales adequate for ascertaining their position. Article 57 says the EEZ may not extend beyond 200 nautical miles from baselines from which the territorial sea's breadth is measured.

UNCLOS Article 76(5) says fixed points comprising the continental shelf's "outer limits," drawn in accordance with Articles 76(4)(a)(i) and 76(4)(a)(ii), may not exceed 350 nautical miles from baselines from which the territorial sea's breadth is measured, or may not exceed 100 nautical miles from the 2500-meter isobath, a line connecting the

820 *See* Parts III.B-III.D and § 132, defining "other rules of international law."

depth of 2500 meters. Article 76(8) provides that a coastal State must submit information on shelf "limits" beyond 200 nautical miles from baselines from which the territorial sea's breadth is measured to the Commission on the Limits of the Continental Shelf UNCLOS, Annex II establishes. The Commission must make final and binding recommendations, on matters related to establishing "outer limits" of the shelf. Article 76(9) requires a coastal State to deposit with the UN Secretary-General charts and relevant information, including geodetic data, permanently describing its shelf's "outer limits."

Subject to other provisions in Articles 76–85, Article 84(1) requires that shelf "outer limit lines" must be shown on charts of a scale or scales adequate for ascertaining their position. Where appropriate, lists of geographical coordinates of points, specifying the geodetic datum, may be substituted for these outer limit lines. Article 84(2) inter alia requires a coastal State, in the case of charts or lists showing "outer limit lines," to deposit these with the Secretary-General of the Authority. Article 134(4) declares that nothing in Article 134 affects establishing shelf "outer limits" in accordance with Articles 76–85. Annex II Article 3(1)(a) includes considering UNCLOS Article 76(8) material among the functions of the Commission on the Limits of the Continental Shelf. Annex II Article 4 recites rules for coastal State submission of this material. Annex II Article 7 requires establishing shelf "outer limits" in accordance with UNCLOS Article 76(8) and appropriate national procedures. Shelf Convention Article 1(a) defines the continental shelf as referring to the seabed and subsoil of submarine areas adjacent to the coast but outside the territorial sea, to a depth of 200 meters or, "beyond that limit," where the superjacent waters' depth allows exploitation of the area's natural resources.

The ILA Committee on Legal Issues of the Outer Continental Shelf defines the Article 76(9) "outer limits" as referring "to the outer limits of the continental shelf beyond 200 nautical miles." Several Committee members advanced a view that Article 76(9) also applies to the outer limit of the continental shelf at 200 nautical miles.[821] Section 133(a) adds this as a proviso to the general definition.

In discussing baselines, § 16 defines "basepoint" and "point." Section 23 defines "chart" or "nautical chart;" § 28, "coast;" § 31, "coastal State;" § 75, "geodetic datum;" § 87, "isobath;" § 93, "line;" § 157, "sea-bed,"

---

[821] COCS *Second Report*, Conclusion 12, p. 234.

"seabed" or "bed;" § 176, "straight line; straight baseline; straight archipelagic baseline."[822]

§ 134. *Outermost fixed points*

In UNCLOS Article 76(4)(a)(I), "outermost fixed points" means the outermost fixed points at each of which the thickness of sedimentary rocks is at least 1 percent of the shortest distance from such point to the foot of the continental slope. A point also meets the Article 76(4)(a)(I) requirements if there is a continuity of sedimentary rock between the foot of the continental slope and that point but not along the straight line of shortest distance.

Comment

In LOAC-governed situations under the "other rules of international law" clauses in UNCLOS, a different definition may apply. The same may be the situation if the UN Charter supersedes UNCLOS, or if jus cogens norms apply.[823]

UNCLOS Article 76(4)(a) provides that for the purposes of UNCLOS,

> 4(a) ... the coastal State shall establish the outer edge of the continental margin wherever the margin extends beyond 200 nautical miles from the baselines from which the breadth of the territorial sea is measured, by either:
> (i) a line delineated in accordance with [Article] 76(7) by reference to the outermost fixed points at each of which the thickness of sedimentary rocks is at least 1 percent of the shortest distance from such point to the foot of the continental slope; or
> (ii) a line delineated in accordance with [Article] 76(7) by reference to fixed points not more than 60 nautical miles from the foot of the continental slope.

Article 76(3) defines the continental margin; Article 3 establishes the maximum breadth of the territorial sea. Article 4 defines the outer limit of the territorial sea; *see also* § 131, "outer limit." There are no

---

[822] *See also* 2007–08 ABILA Proc. 307–09; Churchill & Lowe 32, 135–37, 148–50; 2 Commentary ¶¶ 4.1–4.5(b), 33.1–33.8(i), 75.1–75.5(b), 76.1–76.18(a), 76.18(h), 84.1–84.9(a); NWP 1–14M Annotated ¶¶ 1.4.2, 1.5.1–1.5.2, 1.6; 1 O'Connell chs. 4–5, 13, 15; 2 *id.* chs.16–18; Restatement (Third) §§ 511-12, 515; Noyes, *Definitions* 322–23 & Part III.D.3; Walker, *Consolidated Glossary* 280–81.

[823] *See* Parts III.B-III.D and § 132, defining "other rules of international law."

Shelf Convention counterparts; Territorial Sea Convention Article 6 is identical with UNCLOS Article 4.[824]

The ILA Committee on the Outer Limits of the Continental Shelf elaborates on Article 76(4)(a)(i):

> Article 76(4)(a)(i) … refers to the outermost fixed points at each of which the thickness of sedimentary rocks is at least 1 percent of the shortest distance from such point to the foot of the continental slope. A point also meets the requirements of article 76(4)(a)(i) if there is a continuity of sedimentary rock between the foot of the slope and the point, but not along the straight line of shortest distance.[825]

The ILA LOS Committee accepts this definition but adds "continental" before "slope" and substitutes "that" for "the" in the second sentence for clarity.

Section 16 defines "basepoint" and "point" and discusses baselines; § 28, "coast;" § 31, "coastal State;" § 38, "continental slope;" § 93, "line;" § 147, "rock;" § 160, "sedimentary rock;" § 176, "straight line, straight baseline, straight archipelagic baseline."

§ 135. *Parallels of latitude or parallels*

See Latitude, § 90.

§ 136. *Point*

See Basepoint, § 16.

§ 137. *Port*

Under UNCLOS, "port" means a place provided with various installations, terminals and facilities for loading and discharging cargo or passengers.

Comment

In LOAC-governed situations under the "other rules of international law" clauses in UNCLOS, a different definition may apply. The same

[824] *See also* Brownlie 205–20; 2 Commentary ¶¶ 3.8(a)–3.8(e), 76.18(d)–76.18(g); Churchill & Lowe ch. 4, pp. 148–50; Jennings & Watts §§ 196, 314-26; NWP 1-14M Annotated ¶ 2.3.2; 1 O'Connell chs. 4–5; 2 *id.* ch. 18A; Restatement (Third) §§ 511(a), 512, 517; Roach & Smith ¶ 2.4, ch. 8; Part IV.B § 131.

[825] COCS *Second Report*, Conclusion 6, p. 225.

may be the situation if the UN Charter supersedes UNCLOS or if jus cogens norms apply.[826]

Consolidated Glossary ¶ 73, echoing Former Glossary ¶ 65, defines "port" as "[a] place provided with various installations, terminals and facilities for loading and discharging cargo or passengers." An often-cited British admiralty case defines "port" as "a place where ships are in the habit of loading or unloading, embarking or disembarking."[827]

UNCLOS Article 18(1), defining innocent passage, says that passage means "traversing [the territorial] sea without entering internal waters or calling at a roadstead or port facility outside internal waters; or ... proceeding to or from internal waters or a call at such roadstead or port facility." Territorial Sea Convention Article 14(2) uses similar but not identical language. UNCLOS Article 25(2) says that in the case of ships proceeding to internal waters "or a call at a port facility outside internal waters," a coastal State also has a right to take necessary steps to prevent a breach of conditions to which admitting these ships to internal waters "or such a call" is subject. Territorial Sea Convention Article 16(2) uses similar but not identical language.

UNCLOS Article 211(3) requires States establishing particular requirements for preventing, reducing and controlling marine environmental pollution as a condition for foreign vessel entry into their ports or internal waters or for a call at their offshore terminals must give due publicity to these requirements and must communicate them to the competent international organization. Subject to Articles 223–33, Article 219 requires a State ascertaining that a vessel within its port or at its offshore terminal is violating international rules and standards relating to seaworthiness and therefore is threatening damage to the marine environment must, as far as practicable, take administrative measures to prevent the vessel from sailing. Article 220(1) provides

---

[826] *See* Parts III.B-III.D and § 132, defining "other rules of international law." *E.g.*, with respect to the LOAC, Hague Convention XIII Concerning Rights & Duties of Neutral Powers in Naval War, note 590; Convention on Maritime Neutrality, Feb. 28, 1928, 47 Stat.1989, 135 LNTS 187, establish rules for neutral ports and roadsteads during international armed conflict. *See also*, *e.g.*, NWP 1-14M Annotated ¶¶ 7.3.2–7.3.2.3; 2 O'Connell 1126–30; San Remo Manual ¶¶ 17, 21 & cmts.; *Helsinki Principles*, note 15, ¶¶ 1.4, 2.2, 5.1.1.

[827] The Mowe, [1915] P. 1, 15, 2 Lloyds Prize Cas. 70. DOD Dictionary 425 defines "port complex" as "... one or more port areas of varying importance whose activities are geographically linked either because these areas are dependent on a common inland transport system or because they constitute a common initial destination for convoys."

that when a vessel is voluntarily within a State's port or at its offshore terminal, that State may, subject to Articles 223–33, institute proceedings for violation of its laws and regulations adopted in accordance with UNCLOS or international rules and standards for preventing, reducing and controlling pollution from vessels when the violation has occurred within that State's territorial sea or EEZ. Article 220(3) provides that when there are clear grounds for believing a vessel navigating in a State's EEZ or territorial sea has committed, in the EEZ, a violation of international rules and standards, or that State's laws and regulations giving effect to these rules and standards, for preventing, reducing and controlling pollution from vessels, that State may require the vessel to give information regarding its identity and port of registry, its last and next ports of call, and other relevant information required to establish whether a violation has occurred. Article 225 requires that States not endanger the safety of navigation or otherwise create a hazard to a vessel, or bring it to an unsafe port or anchorage, or expose the marine environment to an unreasonable risk, in exercising environmentally-related enforcement measures against a foreign vessel.

UNCLOS Article 92(1) requires that ships sail the high seas under one State's flag, and save in exceptional cases for which international treaties or UNCLOS provide, must be subject to flag State exclusive jurisdiction on the high seas. A ship may not change its flag during a voyage or while in a port of call, except in the case of real transfer of ownership or change of registry. High Seas Convention Article 6(1) is the same. UNCLOS Article 98(1)(c) says that a State must require masters of ships flying its flag, insofar as the master can do so without serious danger to the master's ship, its crew or passengers, to render assistance after a collision to the other ship, its crew and passengers, and where possible, to inform the other ship of the master's ship, its port of registry, and the nearest port at which it will call. High Seas Convention Article 12(1)(c) is the same.

Section 10 defines "artificial island," "offshore installation," and "installation (offshore);" § 28, "coast;" § 31, "coastal State;" § 81, high seas;" § 146, "roadstead" or "roads."[828]

---

[828] *See also* Ship Registration Convention art. 4(5); Churchill & Lowe 61–69, 344–51, 435; 2 Commentary ¶¶ 18.1–18.6(b), 25.1–25.8(c); 3 *id.* ¶¶ 92.1–92.6(d), 92.6(f), 98.1–98.11(a), 98.11(c); 4 *id.* ¶¶ 211.1–211.15(b), 211.15(g), 219.1–219.8(d), 220.1–220.11(c), 220.11(f), 220.11(*l*)-220.11(n), 225.1–225.9; NWP 1-14M Annotated ¶ 1.3.6; 1 O'Connell 218–21, 275, 385; 2 *id.* 738, 837, 842–58, 953–63; Restatement (Third) §§ 511-12, 522; Walker, *Consolidated Glossary* 282–84.

§ 138. *Precision*

In UNCLOS analysis, "precision" means the degree of refinement of a value; precision is not to be confused with accuracy.

Comment

In LOAC-governed situations under the "other rules of international law" clauses in UNCLOS, a different definition may apply. The same may be the situation if the UN Charter supersedes UNCLOS or if jus cogens norms apply.[829]

Former ECDIS Glossary, page 18, defined "precision" as "[t]he degree of refinement of a value. Not to be confused with *accuracy*." The newer ECDIS Glossary does not define "precision."

Section 1 defines "accuracy."[830]

§ 139. *Presentation*

In UNCLOS analysis, "presentation" means cartographic design including drawing; use of symbols, colors and conventional practices; etc.

Comment

In LOAC-governed situations under the "other rules of international law" clauses in UNCLOS, a different definition may apply. The same may be the situation if the UN Charter supersedes UNCLOS or if jus cogens norms apply.[831]

Former ECDIS Glossary, page 18, defined "presentation" as "[c]artographic design including drawing, use of symbols, use of colors, use of conventional practices, etc." The newer ECDIS Glossary does not define "precision."

Section 23 defines "chart" or "nautical chart."[832]

§ 140. *Reef*

As used in UNCLOS Articles 6, 47(1) and 47(7), "reef" means a mass of rock or coral that reaches close to the sea surface or is exposed at low tide.

---

829 *See* Parts III.B-III.D and § 132, defining "other rules of international law."

830 *See also* Walker, *ECDIS Glossary* 256–57, 2003–04 ABILA Proc. 229–30.

831 *See* Parts III.B-III.D and § 132, defining "other rules of international law."

832 *See also* Walker, *ECDIS Glossary* 257, 2003–04 ABILA Proc. 230.

Comment

In LOAC-governed situations under the "other rules of international law" clauses in UNCLOS, a different definition may apply. The same may be the situation if the UN Charter supersedes UNCLOS or if jus cogens norms apply.[833]

Consolidated Glossary ¶ 66 defines "reef" as "[a] mass of rock or coral which either reaches close to the sea surface or is exposed at low tide."[834]

UNCLOS Article 6 says that in the cases of islands on atolls or islands having fringing reefs, the baseline for measuring the territorial sea's breadth is the seaward low-water line of the "reef," as shown by the appropriate signal on charts the coastal State officially recognizes. Articles 47(1) and 47(7) refer to "fringing" and "drying" reefs.

Section 12 defines "atoll;" § 23, "chart" or "nautical chart;" § 28, "coast;" § 31, "coastal State;" § 53, "drying reef;" § 69, "fringing reef;" § 98, "low water line" or "low water mark;" § 126, "ocean space" or "sea;" § 127, "oceanic plateau;" § 147, "rock;" § 160, "sedimentary rock;" § 176, "straight line, straight baseline, straight archipelagic baseline." In defining "basepoint" or "point," § 16 discusses baselines.[835]

§ 141. *Regional organization or subregional organization*

(a) "Regional" or "subregional" organization(s) as used in UNCLOS Article 63 means the organization(s) below the global level typically associated by principles, purposes, and functions with action required by particular UNCLOS articles or its Annexes related to the EEZ, and may be the intergovernmental organization(s) (IGO[s]) set up pursuant to the UN Charter, independent IGO(s) or nongovernmental organization(s) (NGO[s]).

(b) "Regional" organization(s) as used in UNCLOS Article 66 means the organization(s) below the global level typically associated by principles, purposes and functions with action required by particular UNCLOS articles or its Annexes related to the EEZ, and may be the intergovernmental organization(s) (IGO[s]) organized

[833] *See* Parts III.B-III.D and § 132, defining "other rules of international law."

[834] *Accord,* 2 Commentary ¶ 6.7(a).

[835] *See also* Churchill & Lowe ch. 2 & pp. 120–26; 2 Commentary ¶¶ 6.1–6.7(e), 47.1–47.9(c), 47.9(*l*); NWP 1-14M Annotated ¶¶ 1.3.5, 1.4.3; 1 O'Connell 183–96, ch. 6; Restatement (Third) §§ 511–12, 514; Walker, *Consolidated Glossary* 284–85.

pursuant to the UN Charter, independent IGO(s), or nongovernmental organization(s) (NGOs).

(c) "Regional" or "subregional" fishing organizations as used in UNCLOS Article 118 means the organization(s) below the global level, typically associated by principles, purposes and functions with action required by particular UNCLOS articles or its Annexes related to fishing on the high seas, and may be the intergovernmental organizations (IGOs) organized pursuant to the UN Charter, independent IGO(s), or nongovernmental organization(s) (NGOs).

Comment

In LOAC-governed situations under the "other rules of international law" clauses in UNCLOS, a different definition may apply. The same may be the situation if the UN Charter supersedes UNCLOS, or if jus cogens norms apply.[836]

The phrase, "regional or subregional organizations," appears in UNCLOS Part V, Article 63, governing the EEZ:

> 1. Where the same stock or stocks of associated species occur within the exclusive economic zones of two or more coastal States, these states shall seek, either directly or through appropriate subregional or regional organizations, to agree upon the measures necessary to coordinate and ensure the conservation and development of such stocks without prejudice to the other provisions of this Part [V, provisions for the EEZ].
> 2. Where the same stock or stocks of associated species occur both within the exclusive economic zone and in an area beyond and adjacent to the zone, the coastal State and the States fishing for such stocks in the adjacent area shall seek, either directly or through appropriate subregional or regional organizations, to agree upon the measures necessary for the conservation of these stocks in the adjacent area.

Article 63 commentaries do not define "subregional" or "regional" organizations, but they underscore the importance of Article 63's obligations to seek agreement, and list agreements, on these stocks.[837]

The phrase, "regional organizations," appears in UNCLOS Article 66(5): " ... The State of origin of anadromous stocks and other States fishing these stocks shall make arrangements for the implementation

---

[836] *See* Parts III.B-III.D and § 132, defining "other rules of international law."

[837] Churchill & Lowe 207–08, 293–96; 2 Commentary ¶¶ 63.12(a), 63.12(c).

of the provisions of this article, where appropriate, through regional organizations." Article 66 commentaries do not define "subregional" or "regional" organizations, but they underscore the importance of Article 66's obligations to seek agreement, and list agreements, on this stock.[838]

The phrase, "subregional or regional fisheries organizations," appears in UNCLOS, Part VII, Article 118, governing the high seas:

> States shall cooperate … in the conservation and management of living resources in … the high seas. States whose nationals exploit identical living resources, or different living resources in the same area, shall enter into negotiations with a view to taking the measures necessary for the conservation of the living resources concerned. They shall, as appropriate, cooperate to establish subregional or regional fisheries organizations to this end.

Although Article 118 commentary does not define "subregional" or "regional" fishing organizations, they illustrate their number and variety, and bilateral or multilateral agreements to manage species or fish stock in a given region of the high seas.[839]

Fishing Convention Articles 4(1) and 6(3) command negotiations for agreements related to conserving high seas resources.

Section 7 defines "appropriate international organization," "appropriate international organizations;" § 11, "associated species or dependent species;" § 28, "coastal State;" § 35, "competent international organization" or "competent international organizations;" § 65, "fishing;" § 81, "high seas."[840]

§ 142. *Rise*

See Continental rise, § 37.

§ 143. *River*

As used in UNCLOS Articles 9 and 66, "river" means a relatively large natural stream of water flowing on, under, or through land territory.

---

[838] Churchill & Lowe 207–08, 293–96; 2 Commentary ¶ 66.9(f).

[839] Churchill & Lowe 296–305; 3 Commentary ¶¶ 118.7(c)-118.7(d).

[840] *See also* 2007–08 ABILA Proc. 314–16; Walker, *Last Round* 180–82, 2005–06 ABILA Proc. 69–71; *Competent*, note 321, p. 79.

Comment

In LOAC-governed situations under the "other rules of international law" clauses in UNCLOS, a different definition may apply. The same may be the situation if the UN Charter supersedes UNCLOS or if jus cogens norms apply.[841]

Consolidated Glossary ¶ 77, echoing Former Glossary ¶ 68, defines "river" as "[a] relatively large natural stream of water."

UNCLOS Article 9 provides that if a river flows directly into the sea, the territorial sea baseline must be a straight line across the river mouth between points on the low-water line of its banks. Territorial Sea Convention Article 13 declares the same rule, substituting "low-tide" for "low-water."

UNCLOS Article 66(1) says that States in whose rivers anadromous stocks of living resources originate have the primary interest in and responsibility for such stocks. Article 66(2) says the State of origin of these stocks must ensure their conservation by establishing appropriate regulatory measures for fishing in all waters landward of its EEZ outer limits and for fishing for which Article 66(3)(b) provides. The State of origin may, after consultations with other States referred to in Articles 3 and 4 that fish these stocks, establish total allowable catches for stocks originating in its rivers. Article 66(3)(c) provides that States to which Article 66(3)(b) refers, participating by agreement with the State of origin in measures to renew anadromous stocks, particularly by expenditures for that purpose, must be given special consideration by the State of origin in harvesting stocks originating in its rivers.

Qualifying words ("flowing on, under or through land territory") following the basic definition eliminate natural streams, *e.g.*, the Gulf Stream in the Atlantic Ocean, which technically flows between land masses (North America, Europe). The definition includes streams that are underground through part or all of their courses, *e.g.*, underground rivers flowing into the Atlantic Ocean from African sources. A "river" can be a part of coastal waters defined as estuaries, *e.g.*, the East River between Manhattan and eastern New York State in the United States.

In defining "basepoint" and "point," § 16 discusses baselines. Section 15 defines "bank, bank(s);" § 61, "estuary;" § 89, "land territory" or "land domain;" § 98, "low water line" or "low water mark;" § 108, "mouth" (of a river); § 176, "straight line, straight baseline, straight archipelagic baseline."

---

841 *See* Parts III.B-III.D and § 132, defining "other rules of international law."

The definition does not include estuaries, defined in § 60, *i.e.*, a tidal area of water denominated "river" where ocean tides meet fresh water, *e.g.*, the River Plate between Argentina and Uruguay.[842]

§ 144. *Road*

See Rules of the Road, § 152.

§ 145. *Roads*

See Roadstead, § 146.

§ 146. *Roadstead or roads*

(a) As used in UNCLOS Article 12, "roadstead" means an area near the shore where vessels are intended to anchor in a position of safety; a roadstead is often situated in a shallow indentation of the coast.
(b) Charts or nautical publications may substitute the word "roads" for "roadstead."

Comment

In LOAC-governed situations under the "other rules of international law" clauses in UNCLOS, a different definition may apply. The same may be the situation if the UN Charter supersedes UNCLOS or if jus cogens norms apply.[843]

Consolidated Glossary ¶ 78, echoing Former Glossary ¶ 69, defines "roadstead" as "[a]n area near the shore where vessels are intended to anchor in a position of safety; often situated in a shallow indentation of

---

842 *See also* Churchill & Lowe 46–47 and *id.* ch. 2 generally; 2 Commentary ¶¶ 9.1–9.5(e), 66.1–66.9(a), 66.9(c), 66.9(g); NWP 1-14M Annotated ¶ 1.3.4; 1 O'Connell 221–30; Restatement (Third) §§ 511–12, 514; Walker, *Consolidated Glossary* 285–86. DOD Dictionary 476 defines "riverine area" as "An inland or coastal area comprising both land and water, characterized by limited land lines of communication, with extensive water surface and/or inland waterways that provide natural routes for surface transportation and communication."

843 *See* Parts III.B-III.D and § 132, defining "other rules of international law." *E.g.*, Hague Convention XIII Concerning Rights & Duties of Neutral Powers in Naval War, note 590 and Convention on Maritime Neutrality, note 826, recite rules for neutral ports and roadsteads during international armed conflict. *See also, e.g.*, NWP 1-14M Annotated ¶¶ 7.3.2-7.3.2.3; 2 O'Connell 1126–30; San Remo Manual ¶¶ 17, 21 & cmts; *Helsinki Principles*, note 15, ¶¶ 1.4, 2.2, 5.1.1.

the coast." The Glossary and Former Glossary add: "In most cases roadsteads are not clearly delimited by natural geographical limits, and the general location is indicated by the position of its geographical name on charts."

UNCLOS Article 12 provides that roadsteads normally used for loading, unloading, and anchoring ships, and which would otherwise be situated wholly or partly outside the territorial sea's outer limit, are included in the territorial sea. Territorial Sea Convention Article 9 applies the same rule, adding that "the coastal State must clearly demarcate such roadsteads and indicate them on charts together with their boundaries, to which due publicity must be given." There is no equivalent for the latter requirement in UNCLOS Article 12. However, as Glossary ¶ 69 notes, "In most cases roadsteads are not delimited by natural geographical limits, and the general location is indicated by ... its geographical name on charts. If [A]rt[.] 12 applies, ... the limits must be shown on charts or must be described by ... geographical coordinates." *See* UNCLOS, Article 16.

Sometimes anchorage areas known in UNCLOS as a "roadstead" are shortened in nautical publications or charts to "roads," *e.g.*, Roosevelt Roads in Puerto Rico. Occasionally a general geographic area may be meant, *e.g.*, Hampton Roads, but this should not be included within the definition, any more than "road" as a synonym for highway or street. "Road" in the sense of "rules of the road" refers to rules for seagoing traffic found in the Collision Regulations (COLREGS).[844]

Section 9 defines "Area" and "area;" § 23, "chart" or "nautical chart;" § 28, "coast;" § 31, "coastal State;" § 152, "Rules of the Road;" § 163, "ship" or "vessel."[845]

[844] Convention on International Regulations for Preventing Collisions at Sea, note 282, replacing International Regulations for Preventing Collisions at Sea, note 282, for most States. *See* TIF 379–80. Many mariners know these treaties as the Collision Regulations or COLREGS. UNCLOS arts. 21(1)(a), 22(1), 39(2)(a), 41, 42(1)(a), 60(3), 94(3), 98(2), 147(2)(c), 194(3)(b), 194(3)(c), 194(3)(d), 225, 242(2), 262 authorize promulgation of safety at sea rules, sometimes by international agreement and sometimes by coastal States, an example of the latter being innocent passage rules. *See also* Roach & Smith 382–86. Agreements like COLREGS cannot be inconsistent with UNCLOS. UNCLOS art. 311; *see also* Part III.C.

[845] *See also* Churchill & Lowe 47–48; 2 Commentary ¶¶ 12.1-12.4(c); NWP 1-14M Annotated ¶ 1.4.2.3; 1 O'Connell 218–21, 385; Restatement (Third) §§ 511–12; Roach & Smith ¶ 4.5.6; Walker, *Consolidated Glossary* 286–87.

§ 147. *Rock*

As used in UNCLOS Articles 76 and 121, "rock" means a consolidated lithology, *i.e.*, a solid natural mass, of limited extent, including sand, sandstone, otherwise solidified sand, or igneous matter.

Comment

In LOAC-governed situations under the "other rules of international law" clauses in UNCLOS, a different definition may apply. The same may be the situation if the UN Charter supersedes UNCLOS or if jus cogens norms apply.[846]

Consolidated Glossary ¶ 79 defines "rock" as "[c]onsolidated lithology of limited extent." Former Glossary ¶ 70 defined "rock" as "[a] solid mass of limited extent." Section 147 combines the definitions and adds language to include sand, sandstone, solidified sand or igneous rock.[847]

UNCLOS Article 76(4)(a)(i) says that for UNCLOS purposes, a coastal State must establish the continental margin's outer edge wherever the margin extends beyond 200 nautical miles from baselines from which the territorial sea's breadth is measured, by a line delineated in accordance with Article 76(7) "by reference to the outermost fixed points at each of which the thickness of sedimentary rocks is at least 1 percent of the shortest distance from such point to the foot of the continental slope;" or by another method not relevant to § 145. Article 121(3) declares: "Rocks which cannot sustain human habitation or economic life of their own have no exclusive economic zone or continental shelf." Territorial Sea Convention Article 10 has no equivalent.

Adding the word "natural" before "mass" excludes human-made materials like concrete, which UNCLOS does not appear to contemplate. "Rock" can also refer to land masses, *e.g.*, the Rock of Gibraltar or Plymouth Rock on the Massachusetts shore of the United States. UNCLOS Articles 76 and 121 refer to rocks in ocean space.

Section 28 defines "coast;" § 31, "coastal State;" § 160, "sedimentary rock."[848]

---

[846] *See* Parts III.B-III.D and § 132, defining "other rules of international law."

[847] Alex Oude Elferink commented that "it is almost universally considered that a 'rock' under Article 121(3) can consist of sand." This addition should cure the problem.

[848] *See also* 2007–08 ABILA Proc. 320–21; Churchill & Lowe 49–50, 163–64; 2 Commentary ¶¶ 76.1–76.18(a), 76.18(e)–76.18(g), 76.18(j); 3 *id.* ¶¶ 121.1–121.11,

§ 148. *Route*

In UNCLOS analysis, "route" means a sequence of waypoints and legs.

Comment

In LOAC-governed situations under the "other rules of international law" clauses in UNCLOS, a different definition may apply. The same may be the situation if the UN Charter supersedes UNCLOS or if jus cogens norms apply.[849]

Former ECDIS Glossary, page 18, defined "route" as "[a] sequence of *waypoints* and *legs*." The ECDIS Glossary, page 9 definition is the same.

Section 91 defines "leg;" § 149, "route planning;" § 150, "routing system" or "routeing system;" § 201, "waypoint."[850] In discussing baselines, § 16 defines "basepoint" or "point."

§ 149. *Route planning*

In UNCLOS analysis, "route planning" means the predetermination of course, speed, waypoints, and radius in relation to the waters to be navigated, and in relation to other relevant information and conditions.

Comment

In LOAC-governed situations under the "other rules of international law" clauses in UNCLOS, a different definition may apply. The same may be the situation if the UN Charter supersedes UNCLOS or if jus cogens norms apply.[851]

Former ECDIS Glossary, page 19, defined "route planning" as "[t]he pre-determination of *course*, speed, *waypoints* and radius in relation to the waters to be navigated, and in relation to other relevant information and conditions." The newer ECDIS Glossary, page 9 definition is the same.

121.12(c); 2 O'Connell 731–32; Restatement (Third) §§ 511-12, 515; Noyes, *Definitions* 322–23 & Part III.D.3; Walker, *Consolidated Glossary* 287–88.

849 *See* Parts III.B-III.D and § 132, defining "other rules of international law."

850 *See also* Walker, *ECDIS Glossary* 257, 2003–04 ABILA Proc. 230–31. DOD Dictionary 478 defines "route" as "The prescribed course to be traveled from a specific point of origin to a specific destination."

851 *See* Parts III.B-III.D and § 132, defining "other rules of international law."

Section 41 defines "course;" § 42, "course made good;" § 43, "course over ground;" § 148, "route;" § 150, "routing system" or "routeing system;" § 201, "waypoint."[852] In discussing baselines, § 16 defines "base-point" or "point".

§ 150. *Routing system, also spelled routeing system*

As used in UNCLOS Article 211(1), "routing system" or "routeing system" means any system of one or more routes and/or routing measures aimed at reducing risk of casualties; it includes traffic separation schemes, two-way routes, recommended tracks, areas to be avoided, inshore traffic zones, roundabouts, precautionary areas, and deep-water routes.

Comment

In LOAC-governed situations under the "other rules of international law" clauses in UNCLOS, a different definition may apply. The same may be the situation if the UN Charter supersedes UNCLOS or if jus cogens norms apply.[853]

Consolidated Glossary ¶ 80, echoing Former Glossary ¶ 71, defines "routing system" as "[a]ny system of one or more routes and/or routing measures aimed at reducing the risk of casualties; it includes traffic separation schemes, two-way routes, recommended tracks, areas to be avoided, inshore traffic zones, roundabouts, precautionary areas and deep-water routes."[854]

UNCLOS Article 211(1) provides that States, acting through the competent international organization or general diplomatic conference, must establish international rules and standards to prevent, reduce, and control pollution of the marine environment from vessels and promote adoption, in the same manner, wherever appropriate, of "routing systems designed to minimize the threat of accidents which might cause pollution of the marine environment, including the coastline, and pollution damage" to coastal State related interests. Such rules and standards must be reexamined from time to time in the same manner.

Coastal states may establish sea lanes and traffic separation schemes in the territorial sea, UNCLOS Articles 22(1), 22(3), 22(4); for straits

---

[852] *See also* Walker, *ECDIS Glossary* 257–58, 2003–04 ABILA Proc. 231.
[853] *See* Parts III.B-III.D and § 132, defining "other rules of international law."
[854] *Accord* 2 Commentary ¶ 41.9(h).

transit passage, Article 41; for straits innocent passage, Article 45, incorporating by reference Article 22; for archipelagic sea lanes passage, Articles 53(6)–53(12). Reciting traffic separation schemes among several options suggests the Consolidated Glossary gives a more inclusive definition for "routing system." However, no routing system may deny States rights under UNCLOS like freedom of navigation, UNCLOS Article 87; straits passage, Articles 37–45; innocent passage, Articles 17-32; etc.

Section 9 defines "Area" and "area;" § 28, "coast;" § 31, "coastal State;" § 35, "competent international organization;" § 148, "route;" § 149, "route planning; § 161, "serious act of pollution;" § 190, "track;" § 192, "traffic separation scheme."[855]

§ 151. *Rules of the Nautical Road*

See Rules of the Road, § 152.

§ 152. *Rules of the Road, or Rules of the Nautical Road*

In UNCLOS analysis, "Rules of the Road" or "Rules of the Nautical Road" are synonymous with those parts of the Collision Regulations (COLREGS), dealing with rules for vessel traffic on the ocean when that traffic is not controlled by other law under UNCLOS, *e.g.*, routing systems, traffic separation schemes and the like. Some Rules of the Road apply even when a routing system or traffic separation scheme is in force, *e.g.*, the in extremis or prudent seamanship rules.

Comment

In LOAC-governed situations under the "other rules of international law" clauses in UNCLOS, a different definition may apply. The same

---

[855] *See also* Joint Statement, note 484, ¶¶ 5–6; Churchill & Lowe 267–69; 2 Commentary ¶¶ 22.1-22.9, 41.1–41.9(h), 45.1–45.8(c), 53.1–53.9(a), 53.9(I)–53.9(n); 4 *id.* ¶ 211.1–211.15(e) ; NWP 1-14M Annotated ¶¶ 2.3.2.2, 2.3.3.1; 1 O'Connell ch.6; 2 *id.* 833–36; Restatement (Third) § 513; Walker, *Consolidated Glossary* 288–89. DOD Dictionary 425 defines "port of debarkation," abbreviated as POD, as "The geographic point at which cargo or personnel are discharged. This may be a seaport or aerial port of debarkation; for unit requirements, it may not coincide with the destination." *Id.* defines "port of embarkation," abbreviated as POE, as "The geographic point in a routing scheme that from which cargo or personnel depart. This may be a seaport or a aerial port from which personnel and equipment flow to a port of debarkation; for unit and non-unit requirements, it may or may not coincide with the origin."

may be the situation if the UN Charter supersedes UNCLOS or if jus cogens norms apply.[856]

Nearly all States are party to the Collision Regulations (COLREGS), published in two multilateral conventions.[857] "Rules of the Road" or "Rules of the Nautical Road" are synonymous terms for those parts of COLREGS when ocean vessel traffic is not controlled by other law under UNCLOS, *e.g.*, routing systems or traffic separation schemes and the like. Some Rules of the Road apply even when a routing system or traffic separation scheme is in force, *e.g.*, the in extremis or prudent seamanship rules.

Section 146 defines "roadstead" or "roads;" § 148, "route;" § 149, "routing system" or "routeing system;" § 163, "ship" or "vessel;" § 192, "traffic separation scheme."

§ 153. *Sailing directions, Coast Pilot or Coastal Pilot*

In UNCLOS analysis, "sailing directions," sometimes referred to as "Coast Pilot" or "Coastal Pilot," means a publication, issued under the authority of a marine administration, providing general coastal navigation information such as aids to navigation, harbor approaches and facilities and other necessary details for which it may not be feasible to show on corresponding nautical charts.

Comment

In LOAC-governed situations under the "other rules of international law" clauses in UNCLOS, a different definition may apply. The same may be the situation if the UN Charter supersedes UNCLOS or if jus cogens norms apply.[858]

Former ECDIS Glossary, page 19, defined "sailing directions" as "[a] publication issued under the authority of a marine administration

---

[856] *See* Parts III.B-III.D and § 132, defining "other rules of international law."

[857] Convention on International Regulations for Preventing Collisions at Sea, note 282, replacing International Regulations for Preventing Collisions at Sea, note 282, for most States. *See* TIF 379–80. Many mariners know these treaties as the Collision Regulations or COLREGS. UNCLOS arts. 21(1)(a), 22(1), 39(2)(a), 41, 42(1)(a), 60(3), 94(3), 98(2), 147(2)(c), 194(3)(b), 194(3)(c), 194(3)(d), 225, 242(2), 262 authorize promulgation of safety at sea rules, sometimes by international agreement and sometimes by coastal States, an example of the latter being innocent passage rules. *See also* Roach & Smith 382–86. Agreements like COLREGS cannot be inconsistent with the Convention. UNCLOS art. 311; *see also* Part III.C.

[858] *See* Parts III.B-III.D and § 132, defining "other rules of international law."

providing general coastal navigation information such as *aids to navigation*, harbor approaches and facilities, and other details necessary which it may not be feasible to show on the corresponding nautical *charts*," noting that this publication sometimes is referred to as Coastal Pilots or Coast Pilot. The newer ECDIS Glossary does not define "sailing directions."

Section 3 defines "aid(s) to navigation" or "navigational aid(s);" § 23, "chart" or "nautical chart;" § 44, "danger to navigation;" § 45, "danger to overflight;" § 53, "drying reef;" § 60, "estuary;" § 69, "fringing reef;" § 79, "harbor works;" § 107, "mouth" (of a bay); § 108, "mouth" (of a river); § 121, "notice to airmen;" § 122, "notice to mariners;" § 137, "port;" § 143, "river;" § 146, "roadstead" or "roads;" § 147, "rock;" § 177, "strait" or "straits;" § 192, "traffic separation scheme."[859]

§ 154. *Scale*

In UNCLOS Articles 5, 12, 16, 47, 75, and 84, "scale" means the ratio between a distance on a chart or map and a distance between the same two points measured on the Earth's surface.

Comment

In LOAC-governed situations under the "other rules of international law" clauses in UNCLOS, a different definition may apply. The same may be the situation if the UN Charter supersedes UNCLOS or if jus cogens norms apply.[860]

Consolidated Glossary ¶ 83, echoing Former Glossary ¶ 74, defines "scale" as "[t]he ratio between a distance on a chart or map and a distance between the same two points measured on the surface of the Earth (or other body of the universe)." The Glossary definition parenthetical ("or ... universe") has been deleted as irrelevant.

Glossary ¶ 83 and Former Glossary ¶ 74 add: "Scale may be expressed as a fraction or ... ratio. If on a chart a true distance of 50,000 meters is represented by a length of 1 meter[,] the scale may be expressed as 1:50,000 or as 1/50,000. The larger the divisor the smaller is the scale of the chart."

UNCLOS Articles 16(1), 47(8), 75(1) and 84(1) require that territorial sea baselines and delimitation lines, archipelagic baselines, EEZ

---

[859] *See also* Walker, *ECDIS Glossary* 258–59, 2003–04 ABILA Proc. 231–32.

[860] *See* Parts III.B-III.D and § 132, defining "other rules of international law."

outer limit and delimitation lines and continental shelf outer limit and delimitation lines be shown on charts "of a scale or scales adequate for ascertaining their position." Article 5 says that except where UNCLOS otherwise provides, the normal territorial sea baseline is the low-water line along the coast "as marked on large-scale charts" the coastal State officially recognizes, repeating the Territorial Sea Convention Article 3 formula. UNCLOS Article 12(2) provides that to demarcate opposite or adjacent States' territorial seas, the line of delimitation must be "marked on large-scale charts" the coastal States recognize. Article 234 incorporates Article 134(3) by reference for Area standards.

Section 2 defines "adjacent coasts;" § 16, "basepoint" and "point" in discussing baselines; § 23, "chart" or "nautical chart;" § 31, "coastal State;" § 93, "line;" § 98, "low water line" or "low water mark;" § 130, "opposite coasts;" § 133, "outer limit;" § 176, "straight line; straight baseline; straight archipelagic baseline."[861]

§ 155. *Scale bar*

In UNCLOS analysis, "scale bar" means a graduated line on a chart, map, plan or photograph by which actual ground distances can be determined; sometimes a bar scale depicts one nautical mile divided into tenths, intended to convey an immediate sense of distance. It is replaced at display scales smaller than 1/80,000 by a five-mile latitude scale.

Comment

In LOAC-governed situations under the "other rules of international law" clauses in UNCLOS, a different definition may apply. The same may be the situation if the UN Charter supersedes UNCLOS or if jus cogens norms apply.[862]

Former ECDIS Glossary, page 19, defined "scale bar" as "[a] vertical bar scale of 1 nautical mile divided into 1/10 ths, intended to convey an immediate sense of distance. Replaced at display scales smaller than 1/80,000 by a 5-mile latitude scale." The newer ECDIS Glossary,

---

[861] *See also* Churchill & Lowe 53; 2 Commentary ¶¶ 5.1–5.4(d), 12.1–12.4(c), 16.1–16.8(b), 16.8(e), 47.1–47.8, 47.9(m), 75.1–75.5(b), 84.1–84.9(a); 2 O'Connell 645–47; Restatement (Third) §§ 511–12, 516–17; Walker, *Consolidated Glossary* 290. DOD Dictionary 484 defines "scale" as "The ratio or fraction between the distance on a map, chart, or photograph and the corresponding distance on the surface of the Earth."

[862] *See* Parts III.B-III.D and § 132, defining "other rules of international law."

page 9, defines "scale bar" as "a graduated line on a MAP, PLAN, PHOTOGRAPH, or MOSAIC, by means of which actual ground distances may be determined. [It is a]lso called GRAPHIC SCALE or LINEAR SCALE. ... [I]t is a vertical bar scale of 1 nautical mile divided into 1/10ths, intended to convey an immediate sense of distance." The Committee definition is derived from the newer ECDIS Glossary definition.

Section 23 defines "chart;" § 90 defines "latitude;" § 105, "mile" or "nautical mile;" § 154, "scale."[863]

§ 156. *Sea*

See Ocean space, § 126.

§ 157. *Sea-bed, seabed or bed*

As used in the UNCLOS Preamble and Articles 1, 56, 76, 77, 133 and 194, "sea-bed," sometimes spelled "seabed," means the top of the surface layer of sand, rock, mud or other material lying at the bottom of the sea and immediately above the subsoil. "Bed," as used in UNCLOS Articles 2, 49 and 112, is synonymous with "sea-bed."

Comment

In LOAC-governed situations under the "other rules of international law" clauses in UNCLOS, a different definition may apply. The same may be the situation if the UN Charter supersedes UNCLOS or if jus cogens norms apply.[864]

Consolidated Glossary ¶ 84, echoing Former Glossary ¶ 75, defines "sea-bed," sometimes referred to in this analysis as "seabed," as "[t]he top of the surface layer of sand, rock, mud or other material lying at the bottom of the sea and immediately above the subsoil." The Glossary does not define "bed."

The term appears in UNCLOS Articles 1(1)(1), 56(3), 76(1), 76(3), 77(4), 133(a) and 194(3)(c), usually in conjunction with "subsoil,"

---

[863] *See also* Walker, *ECDIS Glossary* 259, 2003–04 ABILA Proc. 232–33.

[864] *See* Parts III.B-III.D and § 132, defining "other rules of international law;" *see also, e.g.*, Treaty on Prohibition of Emplacement of Nuclear Weapons & Other Weapons of Mass Destruction on the Seabed & the Ocean Floor & in the Subsoil Thereof, Feb. 11, 1971, 23 UST 701, 955 UNTS 155; NWP 1-14M Annotated ¶ 10.2.2.1; 2 O'Connell 824–30.

defined in § 184. The Preamble refers to sea-bed in connection with what became the Area under UNCLOS. Shelf Convention Article 1 has a similar formula in defining the continental shelf.

UNCLOS Article 2(2) refers to "its bed and subsoil" in defining the territorial sea's status. Territorial Sea Convention Article 2 has the same provision as UNCLOS Article 2(2).

UNCLOS Article 49(2) includes within an archipelagic State's sovereignty over archipelagic waters to include "their bed and subsoil, and the resources contained therein." Article 49(4) declares the regime of archipelagic sea lanes passage that Articles 46-54 establish does not otherwise affect archipelagic waters' status, including archipelagic State sovereignty over its archipelagic waters and their "bed and subsoil."

UNCLOS Article 112(1) allows all States to lay submarine cables and pipelines "on the bed of the high seas beyond the continental shelf." High Seas Convention Article 26(1) entitles all States to lay cables and pipelines on "the bed of the high seas."

Section 9 defines "area" and "Area;" § 81, "high seas;" § 126, "ocean space" or "sea;" § 147, "rock;" § 179, "submarine cable;" § 181, "submarine pipeline;" § 184, "subsoil."[865]

§ 158. *Seabed*

See Sea-bed, seabed or bed, § 157.

§ 159. *Seaworthy; seaworthiness*

(a) "Seaworthy" under UNCLOS Articles 94(3)(a), 219 and 226(1)(c) refers to a ship in fit condition to undertake voyages, including perils of the sea that it might reasonably encounter on those voyages.

[865] *See also* 2007–08 ABILA Proc. 327–28; Churchill & Lowe 148–53, 238–39; 2 Commentary ¶¶ 1.1–1.19, 2.1–2.8(d), 49.1–49.8, 49.9(b), 49.9(d), 56.1–56.10, 56.11(g), 76.1–76.18(b), 76.18(d), 77.1–77.6, 77.7(c); 3 *id.* ¶¶ 112.1–112.8(d); NWP 1-14M Annotated ¶¶ 1.5.2, 1.6; 1 O'Connell chs. 12–13; Restatement (Third) §§ 511–12, 515–17; Noyes, *Definitions* 322–23 & Part III.D.3; Walker, *Consolidated Glossary* 291–92. Some commentators suggest that the seabed should be defined in opposition to the water column above and that some features associated with the subsoil, *e.g.*, high-salinity brine pools or water emitted from a hydrothermal vent or mud volcano, could be regarded as part of the Area. *See* Alex Oude Elferink, *The Regime of the Area: Delimiting the Scope of Application of the Common Heritage Principles and the Freedom of the High Seas*, 22 Int'l J. Marine & Coastal L. 143 (2007). DOD Dictionary 486 defines "sea areas" as "Areas in the amphibious objective area designated for the

(b) "Seaworthiness" refers to the condition of a ship that is in fit condition to undertake voyages, including perils of the sea that it might reasonably encounter on those voyages.

Comment

In LOAC-governed situations under the "other rules of international law" clauses in UNCLOS, a different definition may apply. The same may be the situation if the UN Charter supersedes UNCLOS or if jus cogens norms apply.[866] Seaworthiness is a concept in the law of maritime neutrality; a ship considered seaworthy under the LOS might or might not be considered seaworthy in LOAC situations.[867] A ship considered seaworthy under the LOS or the LOAC might or might not be considered seaworthy with respect to a particular situation also governed by a State's admiralty and maritime law jurisprudence.

"Seaworthiness" appears in UNCLOS Articles 94(3)(a), 219 and 226(1)(c). It is also a term with different meanings in countries' admiralty and maritime law jurisprudence. Even within a particular State's admiralty and maritime law, seaworthiness may be defined differently, depending on the admiralty claim at issue, *e.g.*, in U.S. practice, there are different seaworthiness standards for mariner tort claims and cargo damage claims.[868]

Section 126 defines "ocean space" or "sea;" § 163, "ship" or "vessel;" § 198, "voyage plan."[869]

§ 160. *Sedimentary rock*

As used in UNCLOS Article 76(4)(a)(I), "sedimentary rock" means rock formed by consolidation of sediment that has accumulated in layers.

---

stationing of amphibious task ships. Sea areas include inner transport area, sea echelon area, fire support area, etc."

[866] *See* Parts III.B-III.D and § 132, defining "other rules of international law."

[867] *See, e.g.*, Hague Convention XIII Concerning Rights & Duties of Neutral Powers in Naval War, note 590, arts. 14, 17; *Helsinki Principles*, note 15, Principle 2.2; NWP 1-14M Annotated ¶ 7.3.2.1; San Remo Manual ¶ 20(c).

[868] *See generally* 1 & 2 Thomas J. Schoenbaum, Admiralty and Maritime Law §§ 6-25-6-27, 10-24 (4th ed. 2004).

[869] *See also* Churchill & Lowe 265-69; *Definitions* 216; Part IV.B §§ 52, 68, analyzing "distress" and "force majeure."

Comment

In LOAC-governed situations under the "other rules of international law" clauses in UNCLOS, a different definition may apply. The same may be the situation if the UN Charter supersedes UNCLOS or if jus cogens norms apply.[870]

Consolidated Glossary ¶ 85 defines "sedimentary rock" as "[r]ock formed by the consolidation of sediment that has accumulated in layers." Former Glossary ¶ 76 defined "sedimentary rock" as "[r]ock formed by the consolidation of loose sediments that have accumulated in layers in water or the atmosphere."

The term appears in UNCLOS Article 76(4)(a)(I), which provides that for purposes of the Convention, a coastal State must establish the outer edge of the continental margin wherever the margin extends beyond 200 nautical miles from the baselines from which the territorial sea is measured, by a line delineated in accordance with Article 76(7) "by reference to the outermost fixed points at each of which the thickness of sedimentary rocks is at least 1 percent of the shortest distance from such point to the foot of the continental slope[.]" Alternatively, the outer edge of the continental margin wherever the margin extends beyond 200 nautical miles from the baselines from which the territorial sea is measured may be a line delineated in accordance with Article 76(7) "by reference to fixed points not more than 60 nautical miles from the foot of the continental slope[,]" under Article 76(4)(a)(ii). Article 76(3) defines the continental margin as "the submerged prolongation of the land mass of the coastal State, and consists of the sea-bed and subsoil of the shelf, the slope and the rise. It does not include the deep ocean floor with its oceanic ridges or the subsoil thereof."

Section 16 defines "basepoint" or "point" and discusses baselines. Section 31 defines "coastal State;" § 38, "continental slope;" § 47, "deep ocean floor;" § 89, "land territory" or "land domain;" § 93, "line;" § 105, "mile" or "nautical mile;" § 128, "oceanic ridge;" § 142, "rise;" § 147, "rock;" § 157, "sea-bed, "seabed" or "bed;" § 162, "shelf;" § 176, "straight line, straight baseline, straight archipelagic baseline; § 184, "subsoil."[871]

---

[870] *See* Parts III.B-III.D and § 132, defining "other rules of international law."

[871] *See also* Churchill & Lowe 148–50; 2 Commentary ¶¶ 76.1–76.18(a), 76.18(e)–76.18(g); 1 O'Connell chs. 12–13; Restatement (Third) § 515; Noyes, *Definitions* 322–23 & Part III.D.3; Walker, *Consolidated Glossary* 292–93.

§ 161. *Serious act of pollution*

As used in UNCLOS Articles 19(2)(h) and 230(2), "serious act of pollution" means an act of pollution, under circumstances prevailing at the time, that results in a major harmful effect or major harmful effects, or that may reasonably be expected to have such effect or effects, on the coastal State's marine environment or its territorial sea as defined in UNCLOS.

Comment

In LOAC-governed situations under the "other rules of international law" clauses in UNCLOS, a different definition may apply. The same may be the situation if the UN Charter supersedes UNCLOS or if jus cogens norms apply.[872]

UNCLOS Article 230(2) declares:

> Monetary penalties only may be imposed with respect to violations of national laws and regulations or applicable international rules and standards for the prevention, reduction and control of pollution of the marine environment, committed by foreign vessels in the territorial sea, except in the case of a wilful and serious act of pollution in the territorial sea.

Article 19(2)(h), reciting acts that are not innocent passage, declares that a foreign ship's territorial sea passage shall be considered prejudicial to the peace, good order, or security of the coastal State, if in that State's territorial sea that ship engages in "any act of wilful and serious pollution contrary to this Convention." Article 230(2) commentary does not elucidate the phrase.[873] Article 19(2)(h) commentary inter alia says that "The expression 'wilful and serious pollution' reflects a combination of intent ('wilful') and objective circumstances ('serious'). It introduces factors ... not found explicitly in Part XII[,]" which declares protections for the marine environment.[874] UNCLOS negotiators considered but rejected provisions for "wilful pollution," "reasonably be expected to result in major harmful consequences to the coastal State," "grave and imminent danger of pollution that which may reasonably be expected to result in major harmful consequences to the coastal State," before settling on the "wilful and serious" formula.[875]

---

872 *See* Parts III.B-III.D and § 132, defining "other rules of international law."

873 4 Commentary ¶¶ 230.1–230.8, 230.9(b).

874 2 *id.* ¶ 19.10(h); *see also id.* ¶¶ 19.1–19.10(b).

875 *Id.* ¶¶ 19.5–19.6.

The conference did not adopt later proposals to amend Article 19(2)(h) to read "reasonably be expected to result in major consequences to the coastal State," and "Any act of wilful pollution having harmful effects, contrary to the present Convention."[876] The ILA Committee on Coastal State Jurisdiction Relating to Marine Pollution's 1998 *Second Report* came to no specific conclusion about "serious" acts of pollution in the Article 230(2) context.[877]

Citing Article 230(2), a U.S. District Court held that a wilful 30-gallon oil dump was not a "serious act of pollution …" "… [N]o immediate threat to the environment was posed by the 30-gallon spill."[878] From this authority it might be deduced that "serious" act of pollution means an act that is an immediate threat to the marine environment. On the other hand, the case involved a 30-gallon spill; 30 gallons in one context might be "serious," but not so in another.

To be sure, the § 161 definition borrows language UNCLOS negotiators rejected,[879] but it seems to flesh out what "serious" means in the Article 19(2)(h) and 203(2) context. Both Articles refer to a coastal State's territorial sea; the definition should be clear in focusing on that sea area and not the oceans generally.

There is no definition in the Consolidated Glossary or the ECDIS Glossary for "serious" act of pollution as stated in UNCLOS Articles 19(2)(h) or 230(2).

Section 31 defines "coastal State;" § 106, "monetary penalties only" or "monetary penalties."[880]

§ 162. *Shelf*

As used in UNCLOS Article 76(3), "shelf" means "continental shelf," for which UNCLOS Articles 76-85 supply definitions and rules.

[876] *Id.* ¶ 19.8.

[877] *Second Report*, note 285, pp. 372, 388–400.

[878] United States v. Royal Caribbean Cruises, Ltd., 24 F. Supp. 2d 155, 159–60 (D.P.R. 1997); *see also* David G. Dickman, *Recent Developments in the Criminal Enforcement of Maritime Environmental Laws*, 24 Tulane Marit. L.J. 1, 28–29 (1999); Keith B. Letourneau & Wesley T. Welmaker, *The Oil Pollution Act of 1990: Federal Judicial Interpretation Through the End of the Millenium*, 12 U. San Francisco Marit. L.J. 147, 216–18 (2000); Shaun Gean, Note, United States v. Royal Caribbean Cruises, Inc.*: Use of Federal "False Statements Act" to Extend Jurisdiction Over Polluting Incidents into Territorial Seas of Foreign States*, 7 Ocean & Coastal L.J. 167, 172 (2001).

[879] *See* notes 869–73 and accompanying text.

[880] *See also* 2007–08 ABILA Proc. 330–32; Walker, *ECDIS Glossary* 259–60, 2003–04 ABILA Proc. 233–34.

The geological definition of "shelf," which may differ from the "continental shelf" as defined and used in UNCLOS, means an area adjacent to a continent or around an island and extending from the low-water line to the depth at which there is usually a marked increase of slope to a greater depth.

Comment

In LOAC-governed situations under the "other rules of international law" clauses in UNCLOS, a different definition may apply. The same may be the situation if the UN Charter supersedes UNCLOS or if jus cogens norms apply.[881]

Consolidated Glossary ¶ 87, echoing Former Glossary ¶ 78, defines "shelf" as "[g]eologically an area adjacent to a continent or around an island and extending from the low-water line to the depth at which there is usually a marked increase of slope to greater depth."

"Shelf" as an unmodified word does not appear in UNCLOS, except in Article 76(3), defining the continental margin. Articles 76-85 define and establish rules for the "continental shelf," as does the Shelf Convention. Other rules in UNCLOS, *e.g.*, Article 121(2) regarding islands, also refer to the "continental shelf." It is obvious that "shelf" in Article 76(3) refers to the continental shelf. This analysis occasionally refers to the "shelf" for brevity where "continental shelf" is meant. As Glossary ¶ 87 makes clear, its definition for "shelf" refers to the meaning in marine geology. This is similar to the UNCLOS Articles 46-75 definition and use of "archipelago" and "archipelagic," which include some but not all geographic archipelagos. *E.g.*, although the Hawaiian Islands may be referred to colloquially and defined as a geographic archipelago, under UNCLOS Articles 46(b) and 47 they are not a juridical archipelago. The Islands are subject to the UNCLOS regime for islands in Article 121.[882]

Section 37 defines "continental rise;" § 38, "continental slope;" § 67, "foot of the continental slope;" § 93, "line;" § 98, "low water line" or "low water mark;"§ 176, "straight line, straight baseline, straight archipelagic baseline."[883]

---

[881] *See* Parts III.B-III.D and § 132, defining "other rules of international law."

[882] *See generally* 2 Commentary Part VI; NWP 1-14M Annotated ¶ 1.6; 1 O'Connell chs. 12-13; Restatement (Third) §§ 511-12, 515, 523.

[883] *See also* 2007-08 ABILA Proc. 332-33; Churchill & Lowe 148-50; Noyes, *Definitions* 322-23 & Part III.D.3; Walker, *Consolidated Glossary* 293; Part IV.B § 160.

§ 163. *Ship or vessel*

"Ship" or "vessel" have the same, interchangeable meaning in the UNCLOS English language version. "Ship" is defined as a human-made device, including a submersible vessel, capable of traversing the sea. Where "ship" or "vessel" is modified by other words, prefixes or suffixes in UNCLOS as in its Article 29 definition of "warship," those particular definitions apply. A narrower definition of "ship" or "vessel," otherwise unmodified, should be used if a particular rule's context or purposes indicate a narrower definition is appropriate.

Comment

In LOAC-governed situations under the "other rules of international law" clauses in UNCLOS, a different definition may apply. The same may be the situation if the UN Charter supersedes UNCLOS or if jus cogens norms apply.[884]

The UNCLOS English text uses "ship" or "vessel" interchangeably throughout UNCLOS; the French, Russian and Spanish language versions use one word.[885] "[A]s far as concerns [UNCLOS], there is no difference between the two English words."[886] There is no consensus on the definition of "ship;"[887] three treaties, one of them not in force, offer similar definitions. The 1962 amendments to the 1954 Oil Pollution Convention say a ship is "any sea-going vessel of any type whatsoever, including floating craft, whether self-propelled or towed by another vessel, making a sea voyage."[888] The MARPOL 73/78 definition is similar: "a vessel of any type whatsoever operating in the marine environment ... includ[ing] hydrofoil boats, air-cushion vehicles, submersibles, floating craft and fixed or floating platforms."[889] The Ship Registration

[884] *See* Parts III.B-III.D and § 132, defining "other rules of international law."

[885] 2 Commentary ¶ 1.28, the basis for this analysis. UNCLOS has six equally authentic texts: Arabic, Chinese, English, French, Russian and Spanish. UNCLOS art. 320.

[886] 2 Commentary ¶ 1.28.

[887] 2 O'Connell 747–50.

[888] 1962 Amendments to 1954 Convention for Prevention of Pollution of the Sea by Oil, Apr. 11, 1962, Annex, art. 1(1), 17 UST 1523, 1524, 600 UNTS 332, 334. International Regulations for Preventing Collisions at Sea, note 282, Rule 1(c)(1), still in force for a few States, similarly defines "ship." Most States are party to Convention on International Regulations for Preventing Collisions at Sea, note 282, the newer COLREGS. TIF 379–80, 391.

[889] MARPOL 73/78, note 153. By 1995 countries including the United States, representing 92 percent of world merchant fleets measured in gross registered tons (GRT),

Convention, not in force, defines a ship as "any self-propelled sea-going vessel used in international seaborne trade for the transport of goods, passengers, or both ..."[890] National legislation occasionally supplies varying definitions, most of which are in accordance with the Registration Convention statement.[891] General as they are, the 1962 and MARPOL definitions are more inclusive; most seafaring States have accepted them, although MARPOL's reference to platforms seems inappropriate to include in an UNCLOS definition, given the Convention's separate treatment of them.[892] For this reason § 163 adds the phrase, "capable of traversing the sea," to exclude fixed platforms when in place on and affixed to the ocean floor.

No IHO-published Glossary has defined "ship" or "vessel."

Professor Noyes suggests that a precise definition of "ship" or "vessel" may be impossible but agrees that "ship" and "vessel" have the same meaning.[893] He does not dissent from the view that if UNCLOS includes a specific definition, *e.g.*, for "warship" in UNCLOS Article 29, that definition should apply.[894]

Section 66 defines "flag State;" § 72, "genuine link;" § 126, "ocean space" or "sea."

§ 164. *Slope*

See "Continental slope," § 38.

---

had accepted MARPOL 73/78. M.J. Bowman & D.J. Harris, Multilateral Treaties: Index and Current Status 292–93 (11th Cum. Supp. 1995); TIF 391; Wiktor 1127–28.

[890] Ship Registration Convention art. 2(4), excluding ships under 500 GRT. *See also* Restatement (Third) § 501 r.n.1.

[891] *See, e.g.,* 1 U.S.C. § 3 (2006) ; 16 U.S.C. § 916(e) (2006); 33 U.S.C. §§ 1471(5), 1502(19) (2006); 46 U.S.C. § 23 (2006) (includes seaplanes on the water); Stewart v. Dutra Constr. Co., 543 U.S. 481, 484–98 (2005) (1 U.S.C. § 3 definition codifies general maritime law definition); 2 O'Connell 747–50.

[892] *See generally* UNCLOS, arts. 1(1)(5)(a), 1(1)(5)(b)(I), 11, 56(1)(b)(I), 60, 79(4), 80, 87(1)(d), 208(1), 214, 246(5)(c).

[893] Noyes, *Definitions* 316–22.

[894] *See also* Walker, *Defining* 366, 2000–01 ABILA Proc. 174; *id.*, *ECDIS Glossary* 236–38, 2003–04 ABILA Proc. 207–09; High Seas Convention art. 8(2); Hague Convention VII Relative to Conversion of Merchant-Ships into War-Ships, note 576, arts. 1–6; Churchill & Lowe 421–32; 2 Commentary, ¶¶ 29.1–29.8(b) (UNCLOS Art. 29 definition broader than Hague Convention VII definition, the basis for High Seas Convention definition); NWP 1-14M Annotated ¶ 2.1.1; San Remo Manual ¶ 13(g). DOD Dictionary 340 defines "merchant ship" as "A vessel engaged in mercantile trade except river craft, estuarial craft, or craft which operate solely within harbor limits." *Id.* 592 defines "watercraft" as "Any vessel or craft designed specifically and only for movement on the surface of the water."

§ 165. *SMG*

Abbreviation for "Speed made good," § 170.

§ 166. *SOA*

Abbreviation for "Speed of advance," § 171.

§ 167. *SOG*

Abbreviation for "Speed over ground," § 172.

§ 168. *Spatial object*

In UNCLOS analysis, "spatial object" means an object containing locational information about real world entities, *e.g.*, a buoy's location or a caution area boundary.

Comment

In LOAC-governed situations under the "other rules of international law" clauses in UNCLOS, a different definition may apply. The same may be the situation if the UN Charter supersedes UNCLOS or if jus cogens norms apply.[895]

Former ECDIS Glossary, page 20, defined "spatial object" as "[a]n *object* which contains locational information about real world *entities*," noting examples of a buoy's location or a caution area boundary. The newer ECDIS Glossary, page 10 definition is the same.

Section 9 defines "Area" and "area;" § 57, "entity;" § 125, "object."[896]

§ 169. *Speed*

In UNCLOS analysis, "speed" in general means the rate of motion or distance per time.

Comment

In LOAC-governed situations under the "other rules of international law" clauses in UNCLOS, a different definition may apply. The same

---

895 *See* Parts III.B-III.D and § 132, defining "other rules of international law."
896 *See also* Walker, *ECDIS Glossary* 261, 2003–04 ABILA Proc. 235.

may be the situation if the UN Charter supersedes UNCLOS or if jus cogens norms apply.[897]

Former ECDIS Glossary, page 20, defined "speed" as "[i]n general, the rate of motion or distance per time," noting that speed could be speed made good, speed of advance, or speed over ground. The newer ECDIS Glossary does not define "speed." Customarily speed over the ocean and through the air is measured in knots, *i.e.*, nautical miles per hour.

Section 105 defines "mile" or "nautical mile;" § 170, "speed made good, abbreviated SMG;" § 171, "speed of advance, abbreviated SOA;" § 172, "speed over ground, abbreviated SOG."[898]

§ 170. *Speed made good, abbreviated SMG*

In UNCLOS analysis, "speed made good," abbreviated SMG, means the speed along the course made good, *i.e.*, the actual speed in proceeding through the sea from one point to another along a projected course.

Comment

In LOAC-governed situations under the "other rules of international law" clauses in UNCLOS, a different definition may apply. The same may be the situation if the UN Charter supersedes UNCLOS or if jus cogens norms apply.[899]

The ECDIS Glossary, page 20, defines "speed made good," abbreviated SMG, as "[t]he speed along the *course made good*."

Section 16 defines "basepoint" or "point" and discusses baselines. Section 41 defines "course;" § 42, "course made good, abbreviated CMG;" § 93, "line;" § 126, "ocean space" or "sea;" § 169, "speed;" § 171, "speed of advance, abbreviated SOA;" § 172, "speed over ground, abbreviated SOG;" § 176, "straight line, straight baseline, straight archipelagic baseline."[900]

§ 171. *Speed of advance, abbreviated SOA*

In UNCLOS analysis, "speed of advance," abbreviated SOA, means the speed intended to be made along the track.

---

897 *See* Parts III.B-III.D and § 132, defining "other rules of international law."
898 *See also* Walker, *ECDIS Glossary* 261–62, 2003–04 ABILA Proc. 235.
899 *See* Parts III.B-III.D and § 132, defining "other rules of international law."
900 *See also* Walker, *ECDIS Glossary* 262, 2003–04 ABILA Proc. 236.

Comment

In LOAC-governed situations under the "other rules of international law" clauses in UNCLOS, a different definition may apply. The same may be the situation if the UN Charter supersedes UNCLOS or if jus cogens norms apply.[901]

Former ECDIS Glossary, page 20, defined "speed of advance," abbreviated SOA, as "speed intended to be made along the *track*." The newer ECDIS Glossary does not define "speed of advance."

Section 169 defines "speed;" § 170, "speed made good, abbreviated SMG;" § 171, "speed over ground, abbreviated SOG;" § 190, "track."[902]

§ 172. *Speed over ground, abbreviated SOG*

In UNCLOS analysis, "speed over ground," abbreviated SOG, means the speed along the path actually followed.

Comment

In LOAC-governed situations under the "other rules of international law" clauses in UNCLOS, a different definition may apply. The same may be the situation if the UN Charter supersedes UNCLOS or if jus cogens norms apply.[903]

Former ECDIS Glossary, page 20, defined "speed over ground," abbreviated SOG, as "[t]he speed along the path actually followed." The newer ECDIS Glossary does not define "speed over ground."

Section 169 defines "speed;" § 170, "speed made good, abbreviated as SMG;" § 171, "speed of advance, abbreviated SOA."[904]

---

901 *See* Parts III.B-III.D and § 132, defining "other rules of international law."

902 *See also* Walker, *ECDIS Glossary* 262–63, 2003–04 ABILA Proc. 236. DOD Dictionary 515 publishes an almost identical definition for "speed of advance": "In naval usage, the speed expected to be made good over the ground. Also called SOA." *Id.*, Appendix A, *Abbreviations and Acronyms*, p. A-134, defines SOA variously as "separate operating agency," "special operations aviation," "speed of advance," "status of action," or "sustained operations ashore."

903 *See* Parts III.B-III.D and § 132, defining "other rules of international law."

904 *See also* Walker, *ECDIS Glossary* 263, 2003–04 ABILA Proc. 237. DOD Dictionary, Appendix A, *Abbreviations and Acronyms*, p. A-136, defines SOG as "special operations group."

§ 173. *Spur*

(a) As used in UNCLOS Article 76(6), "spur" means a subordinate elevation, ridge or rise projecting outward from a larger feature, like the continental margin or an undersea mountain.
(b) Although "spur" may also have the same meaning as the word might be used on charts or maps showing features on land, a definition based on similar land formations may not necessarily apply to the law of the sea.

Comment

In LOAC-governed situations under the "other rules of international law" clauses in UNCLOS, a different definition may apply. The same may be the situation if the UN Charter supersedes UNCLOS or if jus cogens norms apply.[905]

Consolidated Glossary ¶ 90 defines "spur" as "[a] subordinate elevation, ridge or rise projecting outward from a larger feature." Former Glossary ¶ 81 defined "spur" as "[a] subordinate elevation, ridge or projection outward from a larger feature."[906]

UNCLOS Article 76(6) says that notwithstanding Article 76(5), on submarine ridges the continental shelf outer limit may not exceed 350 nautical miles from baselines from which the territorial sea's breadth is measured. Article 76(6)'s provisions do not apply "to submarine elevations that are natural components of the continental margin, such as its plateaux, rises, caps, banks and spurs."

Besides being used to describe undersea geography or geology, "spur" can refer to a similar land formation, *i.e.*, a "spur" as meaning a subordinate elevation, ridge or projection outward from a larger feature, *e.g.*, a mountain. "Spur" used in this sense might appear on charts or maps. Railway trackage may be referred to as a spur line.

Section 15 defines "bank, bank(s);" § 16, "basepoint" or "point" while discussing baselines; § 22, "cap;" § 23, "chart" or "nautical chart;" § 37, "continental rise;" § 93, "line;" § 133, "outer limit;" § 176, "straight line, straight baseline, straight archipelagic baseline."[907]

---

905 *See* Parts III.B-III.D and § 132, defining "other rules of international law."

906 *Accord*, 2 Commentary ¶ 76.18(i).

907 *See also* Churchill & Lowe 148–50; 2 Commentary ¶¶ 76.1–76.18(a), 76.18(i); Noyes, *Definitions* 322–23 & Part III.D.3; Walker, *Consolidated Glossary* 294–95.

§ 174. *Straight archipelagic baseline*

See "straight line;" "straight baseline;" "straight archipelagic baseline," § 176.

§ 175. *Straight baseline*

See "straight line;" "straight baseline;" "straight archipelagic baseline," § 176.

§ 176. *Straight line; straight baseline; straight archipelagic baseline*

(a) As used in UNCLOS Article 76(7), "straight line" means a line of the shortest distance between two points.
(b) As used in UNCLOS Articles 7 and 10, "straight baseline" means a baseline of the shortest distance between two points that are derived in accordance with UNCLOS.
(c) As used in UNCLOS Article 47, "straight archipelagic baseline" means a baseline of the shortest distance between two points that are derived in accordance with UNCLOS.

Comment

In LOAC-governed situations under the "other rules of international law" clauses in UNCLOS, a different definition may apply. The same may be the situation if the UN Charter supersedes UNCLOS or if jus cogens norms apply.[908]

Consolidated Glossary ¶ 93, echoing Former Glossary ¶ 83, defines "straight line" as "[m]athematically[,] the line of shortest distance between two points." *Annex I* has the same definition.

UNCLOS uses "straight line" in Article 76(7), requiring a coastal State to delineate the outer limits of its continental shelf, where that shelf extends beyond 200 nautical miles from the baselines from which the territorial sea's breadth is measured, "by straight lines not exceeding 60 nautical miles in length, connecting fixed points, defined by coordinates of latitude and longitude." UNCLOS Articles 76(1), 76(4)(a), 76(5)–76(8), 82(1) and 246(6) refer to "baselines."

[908] *See* Parts III.B-III.D and § 132, defining "other rules of international law."

UNCLOS Article 7(1) says that where the coastline is deeply indented and cut into, or if there is a fringe of islands along the coast in its immediate vicinity, "the method of straight baselines joining appropriate points" may be used to draw the baseline from which the territorial sea's breadth is measured. Article 7(2) allows straight baselines where there is a delta or an otherwise highly unstable coastline. However, in drawing these baselines, Article 7(3) requires the coastal State not to depart to any appreciable extent from the general direction of the coast; sea areas within the lines must be sufficiently closely linked to the land to be subject to the territorial waters regime. Article 7(4) says that straight baselines may not be drawn to and from low-tide elevations unless lighthouses or similar installations that are permanently above sea level have been built on them or except where drawing baselines to and from such elevations has received general international recognition. Where Article 7(1) baselines are used, account may be taken of economic interests peculiar to the region concerned, "the reality and the importance of which are clearly evidenced by long usage." Article 7(6) says a State may not apply a straight baseline system as to cut off another State's territorial sea from the high seas or an EEZ. Territorial Sea Convention Articles 4(1)–4(5) have provisions similar to UNCLOS Articles 7(1)–7(2), 7(4)–7(6).

UNCLOS Article 10(5) provides that where the distance between low water marks of a bay's natural entrance points exceeds 24 nautical miles, "a straight baseline of 24 nautical miles shall be drawn within the bay ... to enclose the maximum area of water ... possible with a line of that length." Article 10(6) excludes from its terms cases where the Article 7(1) "system of straight baselines" applies. Territorial Sea Convention Articles 7(5)–7(6), have similar provisions.

UNCLOS Article 47(1) allows an archipelagic State to draw "straight archipelagic baselines joining the outermost points of the outermost islands and drying reefs of the archipelago[,] provided that within such baselines" the main islands are included and an area in which the ratio of the water area to the land area, including atolls, is between 1 to 1 and 9 to 1.

Section 16, in discussing baselines, defines "basepoint" or "point;" § 9, "Area" and "area;" § 12, "atoll;" § 31, "coastal State;" § 76, "geographic coordinates," geographical coordinates" or "coordinates;" § 81, "high seas;" § 82, "historic bay;" § 90, "latitude;" § 93, "line;" § 97, "longitude;" § 98, "low water line" or "low water mark;" § 105, "mile or nautical mile;" § 140, "reef."[909]

§ 177. *Strait; straits*

(a) The geographic definition of a strait is a narrow passage of water between two land masses, between a land mass and an island or a group of islands, or between islands or groups of islands connecting two sea areas.
(b) UNCLOS Articles 34–45 and 233 define and establish rules for straits where ocean waters ranging from the territorial sea to the high seas are involved, *i.e.*, straits used for international navigation. For all but Article 45-defined straits the right of transit passage may not be suspended. The right of innocent passage for Article 45-defined straits may not be suspended. Under Article 35(c), Articles 34–45 and 233 rules do not apply to the legal regime in straits in which passage is regulated in whole or in part by long-standing international conventions in force specifically relating to such straits.
(c) The geographic definition of a strait may not necessarily be the same as those in UNCLOS; *e.g.*, narrow water passages between two lakes in inland waters may be straits in a geographic sense, but UNCLOS's terms do not apply to them.
(d) The geographic definition of a strait may include those oceanic passages between land masses that are not governed by UNCLOS Articles 34–45 and 233, *e.g.*, a high seas passage between land masses separated by waters through which rights of high seas freedoms may be exercised but which are commonly known as a strait.
(e) In the case of UNCLOS-governed and geographically-defined straits, "strait" includes the singular and plural versions of the word.

Comment

In LOAC-governed situations under the "other rules of international law" clauses in UNCLOS, a different definition may apply. The same

[909] *See also* Churchill & Lowe ch. 2; 2 Commentary ¶¶ 7.1–7.9(d), 10.1–10.6, 47.1–47.9(c), 76.1–76.18(a), 76.18(i); NWP 1-14M Annotated ¶¶ 1.3.2, 1.3.3–1.3.5, 1.4.3, 1.4.3.1; 1 O'Connell chs. 6, 9A, 10, 15; Restatement (Third) §§ 511-12; Walker, *Consolidated Glossary* 295–97.

may be the situation if the UN Charter supersedes UNCLOS or if jus cogens norms apply.[910]

Consolidated Glossary ¶ 94, echoing Former Glossary ¶ 84, defines "strait" as "[g]eographically, a narrow passage between two land masses or islands or groups of islands connecting two sea areas."

UNCLOS Articles 34–45 and 233 establish rules for "straits used for international navigation," through which the right of transit passage for all but Article 45-defined straits may not be suspended, and through which the right of innocent passage for Article 45-defined straits may not be suspended. Article 35(c) says these rules do not apply to straits in which passage is regulated in whole or in part by longstanding international conventions in force specifically relating to such straits, and Article 35(b) says these rules do not apply for the legal status of waters beyond the territorial seas of States bordering straits as EEZs or high seas. Article 54 incorporates Articles 39–40, 42 and 44 *mutatis mutandis* by reference for archipelagic sea lanes passage.

Territorial Sea Convention Article 16(4) declares that there shall be no suspension of the right of innocent passage of foreign ships through straits used for international navigation between one part of the high seas and another part of the high seas or the territorial sea of a foreign state.

As in the case of archipelagoes and the continental shelf, where not all archipelagoes or every continental shelf is within the UNCLOS definition, not every body of water geographically defined as a strait is a "strait" within the meaning of UNCLOS, although UNCLOS Articles 34–45 and 233 define, and establish rules for, where ocean waters ranging from the territorial sea to the high seas are involved. For example, the Straits of Mackinac connect Lakes Huron and Michigan among the Great Lakes that Canada and the United States border. Some straits connecting high seas areas may be wider than 24 nautical miles, through which States may safely exercise high seas freedoms, *e.g.*, freedom of navigation and overflight, in waters not part of the territorial seas of States bordering the strait.

Some geographic straits and straits used for international navigation as regulated by UNCLOS are commonly known in the plural, *e.g.*, Mackinac or the Straits of Gibraltar. Others commonly use the singular form of the word, *e.g.*, the Strait of Hormuz. Some commonly use both the singular and the plural.

---

910 *See* Parts III.B-III.D and § 132, defining "other rules of international law."

Section 81 defines "high seas;" § 126, "ocean space" or "sea."[911]

§ 178. *Straits*

See Strait, § 177.

§ 179. *Submarine cable*

As used in UNCLOS Articles 51, 58, 79, 87, 112–15, and 297, "submarine cable" means an insulated, waterproof wire or bundle of wires or fiber optics for carrying an electric current or a message under water.

Comment

In LOAC-governed situations under the "other rules of international law" clauses in UNCLOS, a different definition may apply. The same may be the situation if the UN Charter supersedes UNCLOS or if jus cogens norms apply.[912]

Consolidated Glossary ¶ 96, echoing Former Glossary ¶ 86, defines "submarine cable" as "[a]n insulated, waterproof wire or bundle of wires or fiber optics for carrying an electric current or a message under water." The Glossary adds that these cables are laid on or in the seabed; the most common are telephone or telegraph cables, but they may also carry high-voltage electric current for national power distribution or to offshore islands or structures.

UNCLOS Article 87(1)(c) lists laying submarine cables and pipelines, subject to UNCLOS Articles 76–85, which define and recite rules for the continental shelf, as among the freedoms of the high seas, which must be exercised with due regard for others' high seas freedoms under Article 87(2). Article 112(1) says all States may lay these cables and pipelines on the bed of the high seas beyond the continental shelf. Article 112(2) says Article 79(5) applies to such cables and pipelines. Articles 113–15 recite rules for breakage of or injury to a submarine cable or pipeline, including indemnity principles. Article 79 allows all States to lay submarine cables and pipelines on a continental shelf, subject to Article 79 rules. Article 58(1) declares that all States have the

[911] *See also* 2007–08 ABILA Proc. 341–42; Churchill & Lowe ch. 5; 2 Commentary Part III; 4 *id.* ¶¶ 233.1–233.9(f); NWP 1-14M Annotated ¶¶ 2.3.3–2.3.3.2; 1 O'Connell ch. 8; Restatement (Third) § 513; Roach & Smith ch. 11; Walker, The Tanker 278–85; *id.*, *Consolidated Glossary* 297–98.

[912] *See* Parts III.B-III.D and § 132, defining "other rules of international law."

right to lay submarine cables and pipelines, subject to other UNCLOS provisions, in the EEZ and must have due regard for coastal State rights and duties. Article 51(2) requires an archipelagic State to respect other States' existing submarine cables, and their maintenance or replacement, passing through its waters without making landfall. Article 297(1)(a) establishes a dispute resolution mechanism for cable and pipeline issues.

High Seas Convention Article 2(1) lists laying submarine cables and pipelines as a high seas freedom which must be exercised with reasonable regard for others' high seas freedoms. Article 26(1) is similar to UNCLOS Article 112(1); High Seas Convention Article 26(2) says that subject to a coastal State's right to take reasonable measures for exploiting its continental shelf, it may not impede laying or maintenance of such cables or pipelines. Article 26(3) requires a State laying such cables or pipelines to have due regard to those already in position on the seabed. The possibility of repairing existing cables or pipelines may not be prejudiced. Articles 27–29 have provisions similar to UNCLOS Articles 113–15 for cable or pipeline breakage, repair and indemnity. Shelf Convention Article 4 says that subject to a coastal State's right to explore or exploit its continental shelf and natural resources, it may not impede the laying of submarine cables or pipelines on the shelf.

Earlier treaties also govern submarine cable rights and may be in force as to their terms that UNCLOS or the 1958 LOS Conventions do not cover.[913] Different rules apply during armed conflict to submarine cables and related facilities.[914]

Section 9 defines "Area" and "area;" § 23, "chart" and "nautical chart;" § 28, "coast;" § 31, "coastal State;" § 56, "due regard;" § 81, "high seas;" § 157, "sea-bed," "seabed" or "bed;" § 181, "submarine pipeline."[915]

---

[913] *E.g.*, Convention for Protection of Submarine Cables, Mar. 14, 1884, 24 Stat. 989; Declaration Respecting Interpretation of Articles II and IV, Dec. 1, 1886, 25 *id.* 1424; Final Protocol of Agreement Fixing May 1, 1888 as the Date of Effect of the Convention, July 7, 1887, 1 Bevans 114. *See also* TIF 448; Wiktor 78, 84. Treaty succession principles may bind other States. *See* Brownlie 661–66; *Final Report*, note 576; Jennings & Watts § 62, pp. 211–13; Symposium, note 576; Walker, *Integration*, note 576.

[914] Hague Convention V Respecting Rights & Duties of Neutral Powers & Persons in Case of War on Land, Oct. 18, 1907, arts. 3, 8–9, 36 Stat. 2310; Hague Convention IV Respecting Laws & Customs of War on Land, Regulations, Art. 54, *id.* 2227; Institute of International Law, The Laws of Naval War Governing the Relations Between Belligerents (Oxford Manual of Naval War), Aug. 9, 1913, *reprinted in* Schindler & Toman 1123, 1131; San Remo Manual § 37.

[915] *See also* Churchill & Lowe 94, 126–27, 156, 174, 205–09; 2 Commentary ¶¶ 51.1-51.6, 51.7(g)–51.7(i), 58.1–58.10(f), 79.1–79.8(f); 3 ¶¶ 87.1–87.9(i),

§ 180. *Submarine elevation*

As used in UNCLOS Article 76(6), "submarine elevation" means a seabed elevation that is below the surface of the sea at all times that could be part of the continental margin as defined in UNCLOS Article 76(3). Submarine elevations include plateaus, continental rises, caps, banks and spurs.

Comment

In LOAC-governed situations under the "other rules of international law" clauses in UNCLOS, a different definition may apply. The same may be the situation if the UN Charter supersedes UNCLOS or if jus cogens norms apply.[916]

UNCLOS Article 76(6) mentions "submarine elevation" in providing:

> ... Notwithstanding ... [UNCLOS Article 76(5), providing for fixed points not to exceed 350 nautical miles from baselines or 100 nautical miles beyond the 2500-meter isobath], on submarine ridges, the outer limit of the continental shelf shall not exceed 350 nautical miles from the baselines from which the breadth of the territorial sea is measured. [Article 76(6)] does not apply to submarine elevations that are natural components of the continental margin, such as its plateaux, rises, caps, banks and spurs.

Annex 1 defines "submarine elevation" as "The seabed elevations that are below the surface at all times. They could be part of the continental margin or oceanic. They include plateaux, rises, caps, banks, and spurs." UNCLOS Article 76(3) defines "continental margin" as "the submerged prolongation of the land mass of the coastal State, and consists of the seabed and subsoil of the [continental] shelf, the [continental] slope and the [continental] rise. It does not include the deep ocean floor with its oceanic ridges or the subsoil thereof." The ILA Committee on Legal Issues of the Outer Continental Shelf comments on "oceanic ridges":

> Article 76(3) ... provides that the continental margin does not include the deep ocean floor with its oceanic ridges or the subsoil thereof. Article 76(6) ... provides that on submarine ridges the outer limit of the

112.1–115.7(d); NWP 1-14M Annotated ¶¶ 1.6, 2.4.3; 1 O'Connell 508–09; 2 *id.* 796–99, 819–24; Restatement (Third) §§ 515, 521; Walker, *Consolidated Glossary* 298–99.

916 *See* Parts III.B-III.D and § 132, defining "other rules of international law;" *see also* San Remo Manual ¶ 37.

> continental shelf shall not exceed 350 nautical miles from the baselines. Article 76(6) does not apply to submarine elevations that are natural components of the continental margin. The use of these three different terms in articles 76(3) and 76(6) indicates that these have separate meaning[s]. Any submarine feature can be subsumed under one of these terms.
>
> The definition of the outer edge of the continental margin for the purposes of article 76 is contained in articles 76(4) to 76(6) … Application of these provisions may lead to the inclusion of (parts of) ridges of oceanic origin in the continental shelf. The inclusion of the reference to oceanic ridges in article 76(3) establishes that such a result does not imply that as a consequence of all the feature concerned can be treated as part of the continental margin for the purpose of article 76. The term "oceanic ridge" does not change the content of the terms "natural prolongation" and "continental margin."
>
> The term "submarine ridges" in article 76(6) … is applicable to ridges that are (predominantly) of oceanic origin and are the natural prolongation of the land territory of a coastal State.
>
> The term "submarine elevations that are natural components of the continental margin" is applicable to features which, although at some point in time were not a part of the continental margin or have become detached from the continental margin, through geological processes are or have become so closely linked to the continental margin as to become a part of it.[917]

See also the *Comment* to § 16, "basepoint or point."

Section 15 defines "bank, bank(s);" § 16, "basepoint" and "point" in discussing baselines; § 22, "cap;" § 37, "continental rise;" § 38, "continental slope;" § 47, "deep ocean floor;" § 93, "line;" § 105, "mile" or "nautical mile;" § 126, "ocean space" or "sea;" § 127, "oceanic plateau;" § 128, "oceanic ridge;" § 133, "outer limit;" § 157, "sea-bed," "seabed" or "bed;" § 173, "spur;" § 176, "straight line, straight baseline, straight archipelagic baseline;" § 182, "submarine ridge;"[918]

§ 181. *Submarine pipeline*

As used in UNCLOS Articles 58, 79, 87, 112–15, and 297, "submarine pipeline" means a line of pipes for conveying water, gas, oil, etc. under water.

---

917 COCS *Second Report*, Conclusion 3, p. 219.

918 *See also* Churchill & Lowe 148–50; 2 Commentary ¶ 76.1–78.18(a), 76.18(I); NWP 1-14M Annotated ¶ 1.6; 1 O'Connell chs. 12–13; Restatement (Third) § 515; Noyes, *Definitions* 322–23 & Part III.D; Walker, *Consolidated Glossary* 301–02.

Comment

In LOAC-governed situations under the "other rules of international law" clauses in UNCLOS, a different definition may apply. The same may be the situation if the UN Charter supersedes UNCLOS or if jus cogens norms apply.[919]

Consolidated Glossary ¶ 97, echoing Former Glossary ¶ 87, defines "submarine pipeline" as "[a] line of pipes for conveying water, gas, oil, etc. under water." The Glossary says these cables are laid on or trenched into the seabed; they can stand at some height above the seabed. In areas of strong tidal streams and soft seabed material the seabed may be scoured from beneath sections of pipe, leaving them partially suspended. Pipelines are usually shown on charts if they lie in areas where trawling or anchoring ships may damage them.

UNCLOS Article 87(1)(c) lists laying submarine cables and pipelines, subject to UNCLOS Articles 76–85, which define and recite rules for the continental shelf, as among the freedoms of the high seas, which must be exercised with due regard for others' high seas freedoms under Article 87(2). Article 112(1) says all States may lay these cables and pipelines on the bed of the high seas beyond the continental shelf. Article 112(2) says Article 79(5) applies to such cables and pipelines. Articles 113–15 recite rules for breakage of or injury to a submarine cable or pipeline, including indemnity principles. Article 79 allows all States to lay submarine cables and pipelines on a continental shelf, subject to Article 79 rules. Article 58(1) declares that all States have the right to lay submarine cables and pipelines, subject to other UNCLOS provisions, in the EEZ and must have due regard for coastal State rights and duties. Article 297(1)(a) establishes a dispute resolution mechanism for cable and pipeline issues.

High Seas Convention Article 2(1) lists laying submarine cables and pipelines as a high seas freedom which must be exercised with reasonable regard for others' high seas freedoms. Article 26(1) is similar to UNCLOS Article 112(1); High Seas Convention Article 26(2) says that subject to a coastal State's right to take reasonable measures for exploiting its continental shelf, it may not impede laying or maintenance of such cables or pipelines. Article 26(3) requires a State laying such cables or pipelines to have due regard to those already in position on

[919] *See* Parts III.B-III.D and § 132, defining "other rules of international law;" *see also* San Remo Manual ¶ 37.

the seabed. The possibility of repairing existing cables or pipelines may not be prejudiced. Articles 27–29 have provisions similar to UNCLOS Articles 113–15 for cable or pipeline breakage, repair and indemnity. Shelf Convention Article 4 says that subject to a coastal State's right to explore or exploit its continental shelf and natural resources, it may not impede the laying of submarine cables or pipelines on the shelf.

Section 9 defines "Area" or "area;" § 23, "chart" or "nautical chart;" § 28, "coast;" § 31, "coastal State;" § 56, "due regard;" § 81, "high seas;" § 157, "sea-bed," "seabed" or "bed;" § 179, "submarine cable."[920]

§ 182. *Submarine ridge*

Under UNCLOS Article 76(6), "submarine ridge" means an elongated elevation of the sea floor with irregular or relatively smooth topography and steep sides. "Submarine ridge" is not synonymous with "oceanic ridge," defined in § 128.

Comment

In LOAC-governed situations under the "other rules of international law" clauses in UNCLOS, a different definition may apply. The same may be the situation if the UN Charter supersedes UNCLOS or if jus cogens norms apply.[921]

Consolidated Glossary ¶ 98 defines "submarine ridge" as "[a]n elongated elevation of the sea floor, with either irregular or relatively smooth topography and steep sides." Former Glossary ¶ 88 defined "submarine ridge" as "[a]n elongated elevation of the sea floor, with either irregular or relatively smooth topography and steep sides, which constitutes a natural prolongation of land territory."

UNCLOS Article 76(6) says that notwithstanding Article 76(5), "on submarine ridges," the continental shelf outer limit may not exceed 350 nautical miles from baselines from which the territorial sea's breadth is measured. Article 76(6)'s provisions do not apply to

---

[920] *See also* Churchill & Lowe 94, 126–27, 156, 174, 205–09; 2 Commentary ¶¶ 51.1–51.6, 51.7(g)–51.7(I), 58.1–58.10(f), 79.1–79.8(f); 3 *id.* ¶¶ 87.1–87.9(I), 112.1–115.7(d); NWP 1-14M Annotated ¶¶ 1.6, 2.4.3; 1 O'Connell 508–09; 2 *id.* 796–99, 819–24; Restatement (Third) §§ 515, 521; Walker, *Consolidated Glossary* 300–01. DOD Dictionary 421 has a different definition for "pipeline": "In logistics, the channel of support or a specific portion thereof by means of which materiel or personnel flow from sources of procurement to their point of use."

[921] *See* Parts III.B-III.D and § 132, defining "other rules of international law."

submarine elevations that are the continental margin's natural components, *e.g.*, its plateaus, rises, caps, banks and spurs. The ILA Committee on Legal Issues of the Outer Continental Shelf comments on "oceanic ridges":

> Article 76(3) … provides that the continental margin does not include the deep ocean floor with its oceanic ridges or the subsoil thereof. Article 76(6) … provides that on submarine ridges the outer limit of the continental shelf shall not exceed 350 nautical miles from the baselines. Article 76(6) does not apply to submarine elevations that are natural components of the continental margin. The use of these three different terms in articles 76(3) and 76(6) indicates that these have separate meaning[s]. Any submarine feature can be subsumed under one of these terms.
>
> The definition of the outer edge of the continental margin for the purposes of article 76 is contained in articles 76(4) to 76(6) … Application of these provisions may lead to the inclusion of (parts of) ridges of oceanic origin in the continental shelf. The inclusion of the reference to oceanic ridges in article 76(3) establishes that such a result does not imply that as a consequence of all the feature concerned can be treated as part of the continental margin for the purpose of article 76. The term "oceanic ridge" does not change the content of the terms "natural prolongation" and "continental margin."
>
> The term "submarine ridges" in article 76(6) … is applicable to ridges that are (predominantly) of oceanic origin and are the natural prolongation of the land territory of a coastal State.
>
> The term "submarine elevations that are natural components of the continental margin" is applicable to features which, although at some point in time were not a part of the continental margin or have become detached from the continental margin, through geological processes are or have become so closely linked to the continental margin as to become a part of it.[922]

See also the *Comment* to § 16, "basepoint or point."

Section 15 defines "bank, bank(s);" § 16, "basepoint" and "point" in discussing baselines; § 22, "cap;" § 37, "continental rise;" § 38, "continental slope;" § 47, "deep ocean floor;" § 93, "line;" § 105, "mile" or "nautical mile;" § 126, "ocean space" or "sea;" § 127, "oceanic plateau;" § 128, "oceanic ridge;" § 133, "outer limit;" § 157, "sea-bed," "seabed" or "bed;" § 173, "spur;" § 176, "straight line, straight baseline, straight archipelagic baseline;" § 179, "submarine elevation."[923]

---

[922] COCS *Second Report*, Conclusion 3, p. 219.

[923] *See also* Churchill & Lowe 148–50; 2 Commentary ¶ 76.1–78.18(a), 76.18(I); NWP 1-14M Annotated ¶ 1.6; 1 O'Connell chs. 12–13; Restatement (Third) § 515; Noyes, *Definitions* 322–23 & Part III.D.3; Walker, *Consolidated Glossary* 301–02.

§ 183. *Subregional organization*

See Regional organization, § 141.

§ 184. *Subsoil*

As used in UNCLOS Articles 1, 2, 49, 56, 76, 77, 85 and 194, "subsoil" means all naturally occurring matter lying beneath the seabed or deep ocean floor. The subsoil includes residual deposits and minerals as well as the bedrock below.

Comment

In LOAC-governed situations under the "other rules of international law" clauses in UNCLOS, a different definition may apply. The same may be the situation if the UN Charter supersedes UNCLOS or if jus cogens norms apply.[924]

Consolidated Glossary ¶ 99, echoing Former Glossary ¶ 89, defines "subsoil" as "[a]ll naturally occurring matter lying beneath the seabed or deep ocean floor. The subsoil includes residual deposits and minerals as well as the bedrock below."[925]

UNCLOS Article 2(2) declares that coastal State sovereignty extends to the territorial sea "bed and subsoil." Territorial Sea Convention Article 2 is similar.

UNCLOS Article 56(1)(a) provides that a coastal State has sovereign rights in its EEZ to explore and exploit, conserve and manage living or non-living natural resources of the waters superjacent to the seabed and of the seabed "and its subsoil," and with regard to other EEZ economic exploitation and exploration activities. Article 68 says UNCLOS EEZ provisions do not apply to sedentary species defined in Article 77(4), discussed below in connection with the continental shelf.

UNCLOS Article 76(1) defines a continental shelf of a coastal State as "the seabed and subsoil of the submarine areas that extend beyond its territorial sea throughout the natural prolongation of its land territory to the outer edge of the continental margin, or to a distance of 200 nautical miles from the baselines from which the territorial sea's breadth is measured where the continental margin's outer edge does not extend up to that distance. Article 76(3) defines the continental

[924] *See* Parts III.B-III.D and § 132, defining "other rules of international law."
[925] *Accord*, 2 Commentary ¶ 2.8(e).

margin as the submerged portion of a coastal State's land mass, consisting of the seabed and "the subsoil of the shelf, the slope and the rise. It does not include the deep ocean floor with its oceanic ridges or the subsoil thereof." Article 77(4) says shelf resources to which Articles 76–85 refer consist of the mineral and other non-living resources of the seabed "and subsoil together with living organisms belonging to sedentary species," *i.e.*, organisms which at the harvestable stage are immobile on or under the seabed or are unable to move except in constant physical contact with the seabed "or the subsoil." Article 246(7) cites Article 77 with respect to MSR. Article 85 says Articles 76-85 do not prejudice coastal States' rights "to exploit the subsoil" by tunnelling, irrespective of the water depth "above the subsoil."

Shelf Convention Article 1 defines the continental shelf as referring to "(a) to the seabed and subsoil of the submarine areas" adjacent to the coast but outside the territorial sea to a depth of 200 meters or to where the superjacent waters admits of exploitation of the area's natural resources, or "(b) to the seabed and subsoil of similar submarine areas adjacent to the coasts of islands." Article 2(4) defines natural resources as mineral and other non-living resources of the seabed "and subsoil" together with living organisms which at the harvestable stage are immobile on or under the seabed or are unable to move except in constant physical contact with the seabed "or the subsoil," the same language as in UNCLOS Article 77(4). Like UNCLOS Article 85, Shelf Convention Article 7 says its provisions do not prejudice coastal State rights "to exploit the subsoil" by tunnelling irrespective of the water depth "above the subsoil."

UNCLOS Article 49(2) declares that archipelagic State sovereignty extends to archipelagic waters' "bed and subsoil, and the resources contained therein."

UNCLOS Article 1(1)(1) defines the Area as the seabed "and ocean floor and subsoil thereof, beyond the limits of national jurisdiction." Article 133(a) says Area "resources" are all solid, liquid or gaseous mineral resources *in situ* in the Area at or beneath the seabed, including polymetallic nodules.

UNCLOS Article 194(3)(c) defines measures taken pursuant to UNCLOS' rules for protecting and preserving the marine environment, Articles 192–237, including those designed to minimize, to the fullest possible extent, pollution from installations and devices used in exploring or exploiting natural resources of the seabed "and subsoil," in particular measures to prevent accidents, deal with emergencies, ensure safety of operations at sea, or regulate design, construction, equipment, operation and manning of such installations or devices.

Section 9 defines "Area" or "area;" § 10, "artificial island," "offshore installation" and "installation (offshore);" § 16, "basepoint" or "point" while discussing baselines; § 31, "coastal State;" § 47, "deep ocean floor;" § 93, "line;" § 126, "ocean space" or "sea;" § 146, "rock;" § 157, "sea-bed," "seabed" and "bed;" § 176, "straight line, straight baseline, straight archipelagic baseline;" § 185, "superjacent waters, or water column."[926]

§ 185. *Superjacent waters, or water column*

(a) Under UNCLOS Articles 56, 78 and 135, "superjacent waters" means waters lying immediately above the seabed or deep ocean floor.
(b) "Superjacent waters" is synonymous with "water column" in UNCLOS Article 257.

Comment

In LOAC-governed situations under the "other rules of international law" clauses in UNCLOS, a different definition may apply. The same may be the situation if the UN Charter supersedes UNCLOS or if jus cogens norms apply.[927]

Consolidated Glossary ¶ 100 defines "superjacent waters" as the "waters overlying the sea-bed or deep ocean floor. Former Glossary ¶ 90 defined "superjacent waters" as the "waters lying immediately above the seabed or deep ocean floor up to the surface."[928] Consolidated Glossary ¶ 105, echoing Former Glossary ¶ 94, defines "water column" as "[a] vertical continuum of water from sea surface to seabed."[929]

UNCLOS Article 56(1)(a) declares that a coastal State has sovereign rights in its EEZ to explore and exploit, conserve and manage living or non-living natural resources of the waters "superjacent to" the seabed

[926] *See also* Churchill & Lowe 75–77, 125–29, 145, 148–53, 156–57, 165–69, 374; 2 Commentary ¶¶ 1.1–1.19, 2.1–2.7, 2.8(d)–2.8(e), 49.1–49.8, 49.9(b), 56.1–56.11(c), 68.1–68.5(b), 74.1–74.11(f), 76.1–76.18(a), 76.18(d), 77.1–77.6, 77.7(d), 85.1–85.6, 4 *id.* ¶¶ 194.1–194.10(d), 194.10(h)–194.10(m), 246.1–246.7(f); NWP 1-14M Annotated ¶¶ 1.4.2, 1.4.3, 1.5.2, 1.6; 1 O'Connell chs. 3–4, 6, 12–13, 15; 2 *id.* chs. 17–18; Restatement (Third) §§ 511-12, 515, 523; Noyes, *Definitions* 322–23 & Part III.D.3; Walker, *Consolidated Glossary* 302–04.

[927] *See* Parts III.B-III.D and § 132, defining "other rules of international law."

[928] *Accord,* 4 Commentary ¶ 257.6(c).

[929] *Accord, id.*

and of the seabed and its subsoil, and with regard to other EEZ economic exploitation and exploration activities. Article 78(1) says a coastal State's rights over the continental shelf "do not affect the legal status of the superjacent waters or of the air space above those waters." Article 58 also preserves high seas freedoms in the EEZ, insofar as they are not incompatible with Article 55-85, which state EEZ rules and standards. Article 121(2) incorporates UNCLOS EEZ and shelf principles, including Articles 56 and 78, for the regime of islands. Article 135 declares that Articles 133–91, stating UNCLOS terms for the Area, nor any rights granted or exercised pursuant thereto, affect "the legal status of the waters superjacent to the Area or that of the air space above those waters." Article 135(2) says the Review Conference for the Area must, inter alia, ensure maintaining principles in Article 133–91 with regard to "the legal status of the waters superjacent to the Area and that of the air space above those waters …"

UNCLOS Article 257, in according all States and competent international organizations the right in conformity with UNCLOS to conduct MSR "in the water column" beyond EEZ limits, is the sole reference to the term. UNCLOS Articles 56(1)(a), 78, 135 and 155(2) refer to "superjacent waters," as does Shelf Convention Article 3. "Water column" corresponds to "superjacent waters" in those articles.[930]

Shelf Convention Article 3, like UNCLOS Article 78(1), says coastal State rights "do not affect the legal status of the superjacent waters as high seas, or that of the air space above those waters."

Section 9 defines "Area" and "area;" § 31, "coastal State;" § 47, "deep ocean floor;" § 81, "high seas;" § 126, "ocean space" or "sea;" § 157, "sea-bed," "seabed" or "bed;" § 184, "subsoil."[931]

§ 186. *Supplementary information*

In UNCLOS analysis, "supplementary information" means hydrographic information that is not on charts, *e.g.*, sailing directions, tide tables, or list of lights.

---

[930] *Id.*; *see also id.* ¶ I.11.

[931] *See also* Churchill & Lowe 151–57, 165–69, 289–90, 404–05; 2 Commentary ¶¶ 56.1–56.11(c), 58.1–58.10(f), 78.1–78.8(b); 4 *id.* ¶¶ 247.1–257.6(c); NWP 1-14M Annotated ¶¶ 1.5.2, 1.6; 1 O'Connell chs. 12–13, 15; 2 *id.* ch. 18; Restatement (Third) §§ 514-15, 523; Walker, *Consolidated Glossary* 304–05, 308–09.

Comment

In LOAC-governed situations under the "other rules of international law" clauses in UNCLOS, a different definition may apply. The same may be the situation if the UN Charter supersedes UNCLOS or if jus cogens norms apply.[932]

Former ECDIS Glossary, page 20, defined "supplementary information" as "[n]on-chart HO [hydrographic office] information, such as *sailing directions*, tide tables, *light list*." The newer ECDIS Glossary, page 10, definition is the same. Former ECDIS Glossary, page 11, defined "HO - information" as "[i]nformation content of the *SENC* originated by hydrographic offices. It consists of the *ENC* content and *updates* to it." That Glossary, page 20, defined "SENC" as "[a] data base resulting from transformation of the *ENC* by ECDIS for appropriate use, updates to the *ENC* by appropriate means and other data added by the mariner." That Glossary, pages 8–9, defined "ENC," or electronic navigational chart, as a "very broad term to describe the data, the software, and the electronic system, capable of displaying *chart information*. An electronic chart may or may not be equivalent to the paper chart required by *SOLAS*." Former ECDIS Glossary, page 20, defined "SOLAS" as the "International Convention for the Safety of Life at Sea developed by IMO," the International Maritime Organization.[933] ECDIS is the acronym for electronic chart display and information system.

The newer ECDIS Glossary, page 5, definition for HO information, is the same. Its definition for ENC, or electronic navigational chart, page 4, is different:

> The data base, standardized as to content, structure and format, issued for use with ECDIS on the authority of government authorized

---

[932] *See* Parts III.B-III.D and § 132, defining "other rules of international law."

[933] Because some States have not ratified the 1974 SOLAS, two SOLAS standards are in force: Convention for Safety of Life at Sea, June 17, 1960, 16 UST 185, 536 UNTS 27, modified by Proces-Verbal of Rectification, Feb. 15, 1966, 18 UST 1289; International Convention for Safety of Life at Sea, note 505, modified by Protocol of 1978 Relating to International Convention for Safety of Life at Sea, Feb. 17, 1978, 32 UST 5577, 1226 UNTS 237; Proces-Verbal of Rectification, Dec. 22, 1982, 34 UST 4644, 1300 UNTS 391; Protocol of 1988 Relating to International Convention for Safety of Life at Sea, 1974, Nov. 11, 1988, TIAS —, U.S. Treaty Doc. 102–2, abrogating Protocol of 1978 for States parties to the 1988 Protocol. *See* TIF 396–97, 399–401, 405; Wiktor 708, 1041–42, 1128, 1188; *see also* Churchill & Lowe 265–73; 2 O'Connell 770–74; Roach & Smith 386, 496–98. Treaty succession rules may apply. *See generally* Brownlie 661–66; *Final Report*, note 576; Jennings & Watts § 62, pp. 211–13; Symposium, note 576; Walker, *Integration*, note 576.

> hydrographic offices. The ENC contains all the chart information necessary for safe navigation and may contain supplementary information in addition to that contained in the paper chart (*e.g.*, sailing directions) which may be considered necessary for safe navigation.

Its definition for SENC, or system electronic navigational chart, page 10, is also different:

> a database, in the manufacturer's international ECDIS format, resulting from the lossless transformation of the entire ENC contents and its updates. It is this database that is accessed by ECDIS for the display generation and other navigational functions, and is equivalent to an up-to-date paper chart. The SENC may also contain information added by the mariner and information from other sources.

The newer ECDIS Glossary does not define "SOLAS." That definition, a commonplace acronym in LOS and municipal law admiralty practice, remains the same.[934]

Section 23 defines "chart" or "nautical chart;" § 95, "List of lights" or "light list;" § 153, "sailing directions," "Coastal Pilots" or "Coast Pilot;" § 189, "tide."[935]

§ 187. *Textual HO [hydrographic office] information*

In UNCLOS analysis, "textual HO information" means hydrographic office information, presently contained in separate publications (*e.g.*, sailing directions) that may be incorporated in electronic navigational charts, and textual information in explanatory attributes of specific objects.

Comment

In LOAC-governed situations under the "other rules of international law" clauses in UNCLOS, a different definition may apply. The same may be the situation if the UN Charter supersedes UNCLOS or if jus cogens norms apply.[936]

Former ECDIS Glossary, page 21, defined "textual HO information" as "[i]nformation presently contained in separate publications (e.g. *Sailing Directions*) which may be incorporated in the *ENC*, and

[934] *See* note 933 and accompanying text.
[935] *See also* Walker, *ECDIS Glossary* 263–64, 2003–04 ABILA Proc. 237–38.
[936] *See* Parts III.B-III.D and § 132, defining "other rules of international law."

also textual information contained in explanatory attributes of specific objects." The newer ECDIS Glossary, page 10 definition is the same. The Glossary, page 11, defines "HO-information" as "[i]nformation content of the *SENC* originated by hydrographic offices. It consists of the *ENC* content and *updates* to it." The Glossary, page 20, defines "SENC" as "[a] data base resulting from transformation of the *ENC* by ECDIS for appropriate use, updates to the *ENC* by appropriate means and other data added by the mariner." The Glossary, pages 8–9, defines "ENC," or electronic navigational chart, as a "very broad term to describe the data, the software, and the electronic system, capable of displaying *chart information*. An electronic chart may or may not be equivalent to the paper chart required by *SOLAS*."[937] The newer ECDIS Glossary offers different definitions for ENC and SENC, but the same for HO-information. It drops the definition for SOLAS.[938]

Section 23 defines "chart" or "nautical chart;" § 125, "object;" § 153, "sailing directions," "Coast Pilot" or "Coastal Pilot.[939]

§ 188. *Thalweg*

In UNCLOS analysis, "thalweg" means the line of maximum depth along a river channel. It may also refer to the line of maximum depth along a river valley or in a lake.

Comment

In LOAC-governed situations under the "other rules of international law" clauses in UNCLOS, a different definition may apply. The same may be the situation if the UN Charter supersedes UNCLOS, or if jus cogens norms apply.[940]

Consolidated Glossary § 102 defines "thalweg" as "the line of maximum depth along a river channel. It may also refer to the line of maximum depth along a river valley or in a lake." The term does not appear in UNCLOS but might be involved in determining coastal borders.

Section 93 defines "line;" § 143, "river;" § 176, "straight line; straight baseline; straight archipelagic baseline."

---

[937] *See also* the *Comment* to § 186, "Supplementary information."
[938] *See id.*
[939] *See also* Walker, *ECDIS Glossary* 264–65, 2003–04 ABILA Proc. 238–39.
[940] *See* Parts III.B-III.D and § 132, defining "other rules of international law."

§ 189. *Tide*

In UNCLOS analysis, "tide" means the periodic rise and fall of the surface of the oceans and other large bodies of water, due principally to the gravitational attraction of the Moon and Sun on the rotating Earth.

Comment

No specific UNCLOS Articles are cited; this definition generally covers "tide" as used in UNCLOS and this Report.

In LOAC-governed situations under the "other rules of international law" clauses in UNCLOS, a different definition may apply. The same may be the situation if the UN Charter supersedes UNCLOS, or if jus cogens norms apply.[941]

Consolidated Glossary ¶ 103, echoing Former Glossary ¶ 92, defines "tide" as "[t]he periodic rise and fall of the surface of the oceans and other large bodies of water due principally to the gravitational attraction of the Moon and Sun on a rotating Earth."

UNCLOS does not refer to "tide" without modifying adjectives. Articles 7(4), 13 and 47(4) refer to "low-tide elevations." Article 13 defines "low-tide elevation" as land "above water at low-tide but submerged at high tide." Articles 5, 6, 7(2), 9 and 13(1) refer to "low-water line;" Articles 10(3)-10(5) refer to "low-water mark."

Territorial Sea Convention Articles 7(3), 11(1) and 13 refer to "low-tide elevations." Article 11(1) defines "low-tide elevation" as "above water at low-tide but submerged at high tide." Article 3 refers to the "low-water line." Articles 7(3)-7(4) refer to "low-water marks."

Sections 53, 89 and 140 define "drying reef," "land territory" or "land domain," and "reef" by citing low and high tide as reference points; *see also* § 16, defining "basepoint" or "point" and discussing baselines; § 23, defining "chart" or "nautical chart;" § 24, "chart datum;" § 93, "line;" § 98, "low water line" or "low water mark;" § 126, "ocean space" or "sea."[942]

---

941 *See* Parts III.B-III.D and § 132, defining "other rules of international law."

942 *See also* Churchill & Lowe 32–33, 37, 39, 47–50, 52–53, 55; 2 Commentary ¶¶ 5.1–5.4(d), 6.1–6.7(e), 7.1–7.9(d), 7.9(f), 10.1–10.6, 13.1–13.5(b), 47.1–47.8, 47.9(f); NWP 1-14M Annotated ¶¶ 1.4.2, 1.4.3; 1 O'Connell chs. 3–6; 2 *id.* ch. 17; Restatement (Third) §§ 511–12; Walker, *Consolidated Glossary* 305–06.

§ 190. *Track*

In UNCLOS analysis, "track" means the intended path and past path of a ship.

Comment

In LOAC-governed situations under the "other rules of international law" clauses in UNCLOS, a different definition may apply. The same may be the situation if the UN Charter supersedes UNCLOS or if jus cogens norms apply.[943]

Former ECDIS Glossary, page 21, defined "track" as "[t]he intended path and past path of a ship," adding that when used in connection with ECDIS, additional terminology related to "track" can include "planned route" or "planned track," the intended path of a ship; "past track," the past path of a ship; "cross-track distance," the distance right or left of an intended path. The newer ECDIS Glossary does not define "track."

Section 148 defines "route;" § 163, "ship" or "vessel;" § 191, "track keeping."[944]

§ 191. *Track keeping*

In UNCLOS analysis, "track keeping" means sailing a ship in accordance with a predetermined route, in relation to the seas.

Comment

In LOAC-governed situations under the "other rules of international law" clauses in UNCLOS, a different definition may apply. The same may be the situation if the UN Charter supersedes UNCLOS or if jus cogens norms apply.[945]

Former ECDIS Glossary, page 21, defined "track keeping" as "[s]ailing a ship in accordance with a pre-determined route, and in relation

[943] *See* Parts III.B-III.D and § 132, defining "other rules of international law."

[944] *See also* Walker, *ECDIS Glossary* 265, 2003–04 ABILA Proc. 239. Among seven definitions for "track," DOD Dictionary 562 defines "track" as "The actual path of an aircraft or a ship on the face of the Earth," among seven definitions.

[945] *See* Parts III.B-III.D and § 132, defining "other rules of international law."

to the waters." "[T]he waters" appears ambiguous; "the seas" has been substituted in the Committee definition. The newer ECDIS Glossary does not define "track keeping."

Section 126 defines "ocean space" or "sea;" § 148, "route;" § 163, "ship" or "vessel;" § 190, "track."[946]

§ 192. *Traffic separation scheme*

Under UNCLOS Articles 22, 41 and 53, "traffic separation scheme" means a routing measure aimed at separating opposing streams of waterborne traffic by appropriate means and by establishing traffic lanes.

Comment

In LOAC-governed situations under the "other rules of international law" clauses in UNCLOS, a different definition may apply. The same may be the situation if the U.N. Charter supersedes UNCLOS or if jus cogens norms apply.[947]

Consolidated Glossary ¶ 104, echoing Former Glossary ¶ 93, defines "traffic separation scheme" as "[a] routing measure aimed at the separation of opposing streams of traffic by appropriate means and by the establishment of traffic lanes."[948] The Glossary definition was modified by adding "waterborne." This excludes air traffic lawfully flying over the territorial sea, straits and archipelagic waters.

UNCLOS Article 22(1) allows a coastal State to require foreign ships exercising innocent passage to use "traffic separation schemes as it may designate or prescribe for the regulation of the passage of ships." Article 22(3) requires a coastal State, in prescribing these schemes, to take into account competent international organizations' recommendations, channels customarily used for international navigation, particular ships' and channels' special characteristics and traffic density. Article 22(4) requires coastal States to clearly indicate schemes on charts and give them "due publicity." Article 121(2) incorporates Article 22 standards for islands.

Article 41 establishes a similar regime for international straits and States bordering them; these schemes may be described to promote

---

[946] *See also* Walker, *ECDIS Glossary* 265–66, 2003–04 ABILA Proc. 239–40.

[947] *See* Parts III.B-III.D and § 132, defining "other rules of international law."

[948] These repeat a definition in *IMO and the Safety of Navigation*, Focus on IMO 9 (Jan. 1998).

safe ship passage. States may, when circumstances require and after due publicity, substitute other schemes for previously prescribed schemes. These schemes must conform to generally accepted international regulations. Before designating or substituting schemes, States bordering these straits must refer proposals to competent international organizations with a view to their adoption. The organization may adopt only such schemes as may be agreed with States bordering a strait, after which States may designate, prescribe or substitute them. If there is a strait where schemes are proposed through two or more States' waters, States concerned must cooperate in proposals in consultation with the organization. States must clearly indicate prescribed schemes on charts to which due publicity must be given. Ships in transit passage must respect schemes established in accordance with Article 41. Article 44 declares that "States bordering straits shall not hamper transit passage ... There shall be no suspension of transit passage."

Article 45, incorporating Article 22 traffic separation scheme standards for certain straits, declares that "[t]here shall be no suspension of innocent passage through such straits."

Articles 53(6)-53(11) allow archipelagic States to prescribe similar traffic separation schemes for narrow channels in sea lanes through their archipelagic waters and territorial seas.

UNCLOS Annex VIII, Article 2(2) designates IMO as the competent international organization in matters of navigational safety, safety of shipping traffic and marine environmental protection. Regulation 10[949] of Chapter V of the 1974 Convention for the Safety of Life at Sea,[950] as amended, gives IMO authority for adopting ships' routing systems. They can be made mandatory for all ships, certain categories of ships, or ships with certain cargoes.[951]

---

[949] IMO, SOLAS Reg. V/10 (2000), being renumbered as Reg. V/33, IMO, Information Resources on Stowaways / Illegal Migrants / Treatment of Persons Rescued at Sea, IMO Information Sheet No. 33, p. 3 (Mar. 22, 2007), *available at* www.imo.org/includes/blastDataOnly.asp/data_id%3D18129/Stowaways-IllegalMigrants-Treatmentofpersonsrescuedatsea%2822March2007%29.doc (visited May 25, 2007); *see also* Anna Mihneva-Natova, The Relationship Between United Nations Convention on the Law of the Sea and the IMO Conventions 11–12 (2005), *available at* www.un.org/Depts/los/nippon/unnff_programme_home/fellows_pages/fellows_papers/natova_0506_bulgaria.pdf (visited May 25, 2007).

[950] International Convention for the Safety of Life at Sea, note 505.

[951] IMO, Guidance Note on the Preparation of Proposals on Ships' Routeing Systems and Ship Reporting Systems for Submission to the Sub-Committee on Safety of Navigation, Annex, IMO Doc. MSC/Circ. 1060 ¶ 2.2 (Jan. 6, 2003).

The 1958 LOS Conventions have no comparable provisions. Territorial Sea Convention Article 17 requires foreign ships exercising innocent passage to comply with coastal State laws and regulations conforming to UNCLOS and other 132, defining "other rules of international law, particularly those relating to transport and navigation. Territorial Sea Convention Article 16(4) declares that there shall be no suspension of foreign ship innocent passage through straits used for international navigation between one part of the high seas and another part of the high seas or the territorial sea of a foreign State.

Section 23 defines "chart" or "nautical chart;" § 28, "coast;" § 31, "coastal State;" § 54, "due notice," "appropriate publicity" and "due publicity;" § 66, "flag State;" § 72, "genuine link;" § 81, "high seas;" § 150, "routing system" or "routeing system;" § 163, "ship" or "vessel;" § 177, geographic "strait," or "straits," distinguishing juridical straits, for which UNCLOS lays down definitions and rules.[952]

§ 193. *True distance*

In UNCLOS analysis, "true distance" means distance on the Earth's surface, based on ellipsoid calculations.

Comment

In LOAC-governed situations under the "other rules of international law" clauses in UNCLOS, a different definition may apply. The same may be the situation if the UN Charter supersedes UNCLOS or if jus cogens norms apply.[953]

Former ECDIS Glossary, page 21, defined "true distance" as "[d]istance on the earth's surface, based on ellipsoid calculations." The newer ECDIS Glossary does not define "true distance."

Section 105 defines "mile" or "nautical mile."[954]

[952] *See also* Joint Statement, note 484, ¶¶ 5–6; Churchill & Lowe 91–92, 94–95, 108, 127–28, 267–69; 2 Commentary ¶¶ 22.1–22.9, 41.1–41.9(h), 45.1–45.8(c), 53.1–53.9(a), 53.9(i)-53.9(n); NWP 1-14M Annotated ¶¶ 2.3.2.2, 2.3.3.1; 1 O'Connell ch. 6; 2 *id*. 833–36; Restatement (Third) § 513; Walker, *Consolidated Glossary* 307–08. DOD Dictionary 563 defines "track management" as a "Defined set of procedures whereby the commander ensures accurate friendly and enemy unit and/or platform locations, and a dissemination procedure for filtering, combining, and passing that information to higher, adjacent and subordinate commanders."

[953] *See* Parts III.B-III.D and § 132, defining "other rules of international law."

[954] *See also* Walker, *ECDIS Glossary* 266, 2003–04 ABILA Proc. 240.

§ 194. *Vector*

In UNCLOS analysis, "vector" means direct connection between two points, either given as two sets of coordinates (points), or by direction and distance from one set of coordinates, or a point in a vector space defined by one set of coordinates relative to the origin of a coordinate system.

Comment

In LOAC-governed situations under the "other rules of international law" clauses in UNCLOS, a different definition may apply. The same may be the situation if the UN Charter supersedes UNCLOS or if jus cogens norms apply.[955]

Former ECDIS Glossary, page 22, defined "vector" as "[d]irect connection between two *points*, either given as two sets of coordinates (points), or by direction and distance from one set of coordinates, or a point in a vector space defined by one set of coordinates relative to the origin of a coordinate system." The newer ECDIS Glossary does not define "vector."

Section 16 defines "basepoint" or "point;" § 76, "geographic coordinates," "geographical coordinates" or "coordinates."[956]

§ 195. *Vertical datum*

See Datum (vertical), § 46.

§ 196. *Vessel*

See Ship or vessel, § 163.

§ 197. *Voyage data recorder, sometimes referred to as a "black box"*

In UNCLOS analysis, "voyage data recorder," sometimes referred to as a "black box," means a system that may be in the form of several separate but interconnected units that are intended to maintain, in a secure and retrievable form, information concerning a vessel's position, movement, physical status, command and control over a period leading up to and following an incident.

[955] *See* Parts III.B-III.D and § 132, defining "other rules of international law."
[956] *See also* Walker, *ECDIS Glossary* 266–67, 2003–04 ABILA Proc. 240–41.

Comment

In LOAC-governed situations under the "other rules of international law" clauses in UNCLOS, a different definition may apply. The same may be the situation if the UN Charter supersedes UNCLOS or if jus cogens norms apply.[957]

Former ECDIS Glossary, page 22, defined "voyage data recorder" as "[a] system that may be in the form of several separated but interconnected units, intended to maintain, in a secure and retrievable form, information concerning the position, movement, physical status, command and control of a vessel over a period leading up to, and following an incident," noting that it is sometimes referred to as a "Black Box." The analogous device for aircraft is the flight data recorder, also known as a "black box." The newer ECDIS Glossary does not define "voyage data recorder."

Section 163 defines "ship" or "vessel;" § 198, "voyage plan."[958]

§ 198. *Voyage plan*

In UNCLOS analysis, "voyage plan" means a defined series of waypoints, legs, and routes.

Comment

In LOAC-governed situations under the "other rules of international law" clauses in UNCLOS, a different definition may apply. The same may be the situation if the UN Charter supersedes UNCLOS or if jus cogens norms apply.[959]

Former ECDIS Glossary, page 22, defined "voyage plan" as "[a] defined series of *waypoints, legs* and *routes*." The newer ECDIS Glossary does not define "voyage plan."

Section 90 defines "leg;" § 148, "route;" § 149, "route planning;" § 150, "routing system" or "routeing system;" § 197, "voyage data recorder" or "black box;" § 201, "waypoint."[960]

---

[957] *See* Parts III.B-III.D and § 132, defining "other rules of international law."

[958] *See also* Walker, *ECDIS Glossary* 267, 2003–04 ABILA Proc. 241–42.

[959] *See* Parts III.B-III.D and § 132, defining "other rules of international law."

[960] *See also* Walker, *ECDIS Glossary* 267–68, 2003–04 ABILA Proc. 242.

§ 199. *Warning*

(a) In general UNCLOS analysis, "warning" may mean an alarm or indicator.
(b) In other contexts, *e.g.*, UNCLOS Articles 60(3), 147(2)(a) and 262, "warning" has other and more specific meanings.
(c) In other contexts that UNCLOS does not mention, "warning" may have other specific meanings in usage and analysis under UNCLOS, *e.g.*, for notices to airmen or notices to mariners, alerting to presence or danger.

Comment

In LOAC-governed situations under the "other rules of international law" clauses in UNCLOS, a different definition may apply. The same may be the situation if the UN Charter supersedes UNCLOS or if jus cogens norms apply.[961]

Former ECDIS Glossary, page 23, defined "warning" as "[a]n *alarm* or *indicator*." The newer ECDIS Glossary, page 11, definition is the same.

UNCLOS Article 60(3) requires due notice of construction of artificial islands, installations or structures in the EEZ; "permanent means for giving warning of their presence must be maintained." Article 147(2)(a) has a similar requirement for Area installations. Article 262 requires internationally agreed warning signals for MSR installations or equipment to ensure safety at sea and safety of aerial navigation.[962] Safety of aerial navigation comes under the International Civil Aviation Organization; the IMO's purview is safety at sea, and the International Telecommunication Union largely determines internationally agreed warning signals.[963]

"Warning" may have other meanings, *e.g.*, in the context of notices to airmen (NOTAMs) or notices to mariners (NOTMARs), defined in §§ 121–22, used in UNCLOS analysis, but which UNCLOS does not

---

[961] *See* Parts III.B-III.D and § 132, defining "other rules of international law."

[962] *See also* 2 Commentary ¶¶ 60.1–60.15(c), 60.15(d)–60.15(e), 60. 15(*l*)-60 .15(m); 4 *id.* ¶¶ 262.1–262.5.

[963] *See generally* 4 *id.* ¶ 262.5; Part IV.B § 7, "appropriate international organization" and "appropriate international organizations."

cite or discuss.[964] Another example is a warning shot incident to high seas approach and visit.[965]

Section 4 defines "alarm;" § 9, "Area" and area;" § 10, "artificial island," "offshore installation" and installation (offshore);" § 54, "due notice, "appropriate publicity" and "due publicity;" § 81, "high seas;" § 84, "indicator;" § 126, "ocean space" or "sea."[966]

§ 200. *Water column*

See § 185, "superjacent waters."

§ 201. *Waypoint*

In UNCLOS analysis, "waypoint" means, in conjunction with route planning, a geographical location (*e.g.*, latitude and longitude) indicating a significant event on a vessel's planned route (*e.g.*, course alteration point, calling in point, etc.).

Comment

In LOAC-governed situations under the "other rules of international law" clauses in UNCLOS, a different definition may apply. The same may be the situation if the UN Charter supersedes UNCLOS or if jus cogens norms apply.[967]

Former ECDIS Glossary, page 23, defined "waypoint" as "[i]n conjunction with *route planning*, a geographical location (e.g. latitude and longitude) indicating a significant event on a vessel's planned route

---

964 Different NOTAM warnings may apply during armed conflict. *See* § 132, "other rules of international law."

965 *See* NWP 1-14M Annotated ¶¶ 3.4, 3.11.5.2; this procedure might be compared with LOAC-governed visit and search. *See id.* ¶¶ 7.6–7.6.2; San Remo Manual ¶¶ 118–34; Part IV.B § 132.

966 *See also* 2007–08 ABILA Proc. 363–64; Churchill & Lowe 155, 168, 414; Walker, *ECDIS Glossary* 268–69, 2003–04 ABILA Proc. 242–43. DOD Dictionary 590 has two definitions for "warning": "1. A communication and acknowledgment of dangers implicit in a wide spectrum of activities by potential opponents ranging from routine defense measures to substantial increases in readiness and force preparedness and to acts of terrorism or political, economic, or military provocation. 2. Operating procedures, practices, or conditions that may result in injury or death if not carefully observed or followed."

967 *See* Parts III.B-III.D and § 132, defining "other rules of international law."

(e.g. course alteration point, calling in point, etc.)." The newer ECDIS Glossary, page 11, definition is the same.

Section 16 defines "basepoint" or "point;" § 41, "course;" § 90, "latitude;" § 97, "longitude;" § 148, "route;" § 149, "route planning;" § 150, "routing system" or "routeing system;" § 163, "ship" or "vessel."[968]

[968] *See also* Walker, *ECDIS Glossary* 269, 2003–04 ABILA Proc. 243–44.

CHAPTER V

CONCLUSIONS

As stated in the Introduction, there are several reasons for and uses of the *Report*. It has attempted to provide meanings for words and phrases in UNCLOS for which the Convention does not give definitions, or which will be useful in Convention analysis. It has tried to consolidate and publish definitions for these terms after research in several sources, some of which are on line and some are in print, perhaps in less accessible books. Some sources may be out of date although in print or on line. The Committee has not sought to rewrite UNCLOS by redefining terms for which the Convention supplies meanings. Some glossaries have done so. The result for a less than careful user of the latter sources is that they can lead a researcher to apply UNCLOS-defined words or phrases in a way that is incompatible with the Convention. For all definitions in this *Report*, except those for "shelf" and "strait,"[965] the Committee has endeavored to publish a definition oriented toward UNCLOS and not a geographic, geological, or geomorphological definition; these may be similar but not identical.

The *Report* is at best a secondary source, or perhaps a source that aids in determining and giving content to primary sources like custom, treaties (including interpretive statements appended to UNCLOS), and general principles of law. The definitions can be a counterweight or support to the research from other, similar secondary sources. Where there is no other source, the *Report* may be the only source. It is hoped that wide distribution of the work of the Committee, through publication in the ABILA *Proceedings* and the *California Western International Law Journal*, citation in other journals, offprint distribution, discussion, and correspondence, has broadened the Committee's resources beyond its membership.

The published discussion of the context of the project cautions UNCLOS researchers; this *Report* is not the end of the story. For example, the UNCLOS Commission on the Limits of the Continental Shelf and the ILA Committee on Legal Issues of the Outer Limits of the

---

[965] *See* Part IV.B §§ 162, 177.

Continental Shelf and other ILA committees have supplied and will supply context in the future for UNCLOS terms.

The *Report* has served, and hopefully will continue to serve, as a platform for discussion among those who research UNCLOS and those, including governments, who as oceans users are governed or guided by UNCLOS.

The *Report* has also attempted the placement of definitions for UNCLOS in broader contexts of international law.

First, it is axiomatic that Security Council decisions (a term of art distinguishing them from Council recommendations and the like) trump treaties through a combination of UN Charter Articles 25, 48, 94, and 103. To be sure, thus far the Council has usually spoken in general terms in its resolutions, but applying Charter-based law might come in implementing actions, *e.g.*, peacemaking or peacekeeping operations or agreements under a general Council mandate.[966]

Second, applying the LOAC may result in a different definition where the LOAC applies. The *Report*'s analysis of "other rules of international law" and similar clauses appearing throughout UNCLOS and the 1958 LOS Conventions is important in this regard.[967] Its analysis of the "due regard" phrase,[968] primarily in the UNCLOS context, notes a trend toward requiring belligerents to have regard for certain UNCLOS principles during armed conflict, and should also be consulted. Law of treaties rules for armed conflict situations may also influence application of UNCLOS and the 1958 Conventions, as these principles can for any international agreement.

Third, it is also axiomatic in today's international law that jus cogens-girded rules trump traditional sources like treaties and custom; there is, of course, the problem of finding and defining jus cogens for a particular situation.[969]

A fourth factor is the impact of UNCLOS parties' interpretive statements on the treaty, the law to be applied to these statements and how these statements interact with definitions the Committee has developed.[970]

---

[966] *See* Part III.B.
[967] *See* Parts III.B-III.D and Part IV.B § 132.
[968] *See* Part IV.B § 56.
[969] *See* Part III.B.
[970] *See* Parts III.C-III.D.

A fifth factor is the impact of developing custom under UNCLOS. Is it a factor for interpreting UNCLOS, as the Vienna Convention would say, or is later custom a balancing factor for UNCLOS as a treaty?[971]

The result is that researchers seeking a definition for an UNCLOS term are on notice that they must consider the factors of Charter-based law, the LOAC for situations involving armed conflict, jus cogens, interpretive statements appended to UNCLOS, and the status of custom developing subsequent to UNCLOS, in their analysis.

The *Report*'s citations under the definitions are not a research mine of every journal on the subject. Researchers should continue beyond these general, frequently-cited sources, *e.g.*, the Restatement (Third), into secondary and newer primary sources, *e.g.*, LOS treaties subordinate to UNCLOS. The *Report* also discusses the UNCLOS primacy principles for these treaties.

Cross-references to other definitions at the end of every *Comment* to the definitions should help with terms related to defined terms and words within each definition for a more complete understanding of what a word or phrase means.

This aspect of the Committee's work is at an end, at least for now. Will there be a second edition or supplement to the *Report*? The IHO Consolidated Glossary appeared in its fourth edition in early 2006. This suggests that meanings, like United States Supreme Court Justice Oliver Wendell Holmes's definition of a word as the skin of a living thought,[972] have evolved and will evolve through time. State practice under UNCLOS, new international agreements, judicial and other tribunal decisions, researchers' conclusions, intergovernmental and non-governmental organizations' work, all assure that the process of definition, like the process of decision for use of UNCLOS terms, will not be static. What role the Committee, the ABILA, or the ILA will play is for the future to determine.

---

[971] *See* Part III.B.

[972] Tower v. Eisner, 245 U.S. 418, 425 (1918).